A U-Turn to the Future

## Explorations in Mobility

*Series Editors:*
Gijs Mom, Eindhoven University of Technology
Mimi Sheller, Drexel University
Georgine Clarsen, University of Wollongong

The study of mobility opens up new transnational and interdisciplinary approaches to fields including transport, tourism, migration, communication, media, technology, and environmental studies. The works in this series rethink our common assumptions and ideas about the mobility of people, things, ideas, and cultures from a broadly understood humanities perspective. The series welcomes projects of a historical or contemporary nature and encourages postcolonial, non-Western, and critical perspectives.

# A U-Turn to the Future

*Sustainable Urban Mobility since 1850*

Edited by
**Martin Emanuel, Frank Schipper, and Ruth Oldenziel**

berghahn
NEW YORK · OXFORD
www.berghahnbooks.com

First published in 2020 by

Berghahn Books

www.berghahnbooks.com

**Library of Congress Cataloging-in-Publication Data**

Names: Emanuel, Martin, 1977- editor. | Schipper, Frank, 1976- editor. |
Oldenziel, Ruth, 1958- editor.
Title: A U-Turn to the Future: Sustainable Urban Mobility since 1850 / edited
by Martin Emanuel, Frank Schipper, and Ruth Oldenziel.
Description: New York, NY: Berghahn Books, 2020. | Series: Explorations in
Mobility; volume 4 | Includes bibliographical references and index.
Identifiers: LCCN 2019042410 (print) | LCCN 2019042411 (ebook) |
ISBN 9781789205596 (hardback) | ISBN 9781789205602 (ebook)
Subjects: LCSH: Urban transportation—History. | Sustainable urban
development—History.
Classification: LCC HE305 .A79 2020 (print) | LCC HE305 (ebook) |
DDC 388.4—dc23
LC record available at https://lccn.loc.gov/2019042410
LC ebook record available at https://lccn.loc.gov/2019042411

**British Library Cataloguing in Publication Data**

A catalogue record for this book is available from the British Library

ISBN 978-1-78920-559-6 hardback
ISBN 978-1-80073-650-4 paperback
ISBN 978-1-78920-560-2 ebook

# Contents

# Illustrations

### Figures

## Maps

## Tables

# Acknowledgments

It takes an entire community to compile an anthology. This book is indeed the culmination of joint intellectual efforts through an extensive series, over several years, of dedicated workshops and sessions at Tensions of Europe network (ToE) and International Association for the History of Traffic, Transport and Mobility (T2M) annual conferences, all organized by the international research network Cultural Politics of Sustainable Urban Mobility since 1890. We thank everyone who organized local workshops, in Eindhoven (Sonja Beekers, Martin Emanuel, Jan Korsten, Ruth Oldenziel, and Frank Schipper), Caserta (Massimo Moraglio and Federico Paolini), Munich (Bettina Gundler and Frank Steinbeck), Paris (Mathieu Flonneau and Arnaud Passalacqua), Shanghai (Xu Tao), and Gothenburg (Per Lundin and Tiina Männistö-Funk).

The workshops were made possible thanks to core network funding from the Netherlands Organization for Scientific Research NWO and generous support from Chalmers University of Technology's Area of Advance Building Futures; Deutsches Museum, Munich; Eindhoven University of Technology; Formas, the Swedish government research council for sustainable development; Eindhoven University of Technology, TIS group; Foundation for the History of Technology, Eindhoven; Labex EHNE (Laboratoire d'excellence Écrire une Histoire Nouvelle de l'Europe), Paris; the Municipality of The Hague; the P2M (Passé-Présent-Mobilité) Association, Paris; the Royal Dutch Academy of Sciences KNAW; the Shanghai Academy of Social Sciences; the Society for the History of Technology; and the Wenner-Gren Foundation. We thank them all for their support.

Above all, we are grateful to those who have nurtured our thinking and substantially enriched our work over the years. We would like to thank all the workshop participants in the international research network Cultural Politics of Sustainable Urban Mobility since 1890, as well as colleagues in the NWO-SURF community of Smart Cycling Futures, in particular: Julian Alexandrakis, Floor Alkemade, Malin Andersson, Louis Baldasseroni, Frauke Behrendt, Patrick Bek, Bas Braakman, Marco te Brömmelstroet, Matthew Bruno, Veronica Saud Casanova, Mila Davids,

Samuel Nello-Deakin, Henk-Jan Dekker, Marc Dijk, Pelle Envall, Jacco Farla, Bipashyee Ghosh, Bettina Gundler, Mikael Hård, Lucas Harms, Maxime Huré, Sven Kesselring, Georg-Friedrich Koppen, Michael Koucky, Maria Krafft, Fabian Kröger, Alan Latham, Laetiticia Lindeberg Lemos, Rick Lindeman, George Liu, Per Lundin, Yusuf Umar Madugu, Malin Månsson, Massimo Moraglio, Njogu Morgan, Imran Muhammad, Michael Nattras, Anna Nikolaeva, Anna Nilsson-Ehle, Denver Nixon, Daniel Normark, Pan Haixiao, Federico Paolini, Hugo Silveira Pereira, Brett Petzer, Jan Ploeger, Cosmin Popan, Marcus Popkema, Rob Raven, Carlton Reid, Marika Rupeka, Gabriele Schliwa, Lise Sedrez, Frans Sengers, Fariyan Sharmeen, Gustav Sjöblom, Andreas Spahn, Hugo van der Steenhoven, Frank Steinbeck, Sun Qi, Xu Tao, Claes Tingvall, Kátalin Tóth, Geetam Tiwari, Helmuth Trischler, Eleftheria Vasileiadou, Geert Verbong, Matt Watson, Kirsten Wehner, Carlo van de Weijer, and Bernhard Wieser. We thank Iris Houx for her help in preparing the index. We thank Berghahn Books for the very smooth process of book production, in particular Chris Chappell, Mykelin Higham, and Lizzie Martinez.

To the many contributors to these intellectually stimulating events, we would like to express our gratitude, in particular Adri A. Albert de la Bruhèze, Mathieu Flonneau, Carlos Lopez Galviz, Gijs Mom, and Arnaud Passalacqua—without their generous input, this would certainly have been a much lesser book.

# Historicizing Sustainable Urban Mobility

Frank Schipper, Martin Emanuel, and Ruth Oldenziel

## Introduction

In 1979, the local chapter of the First and Only Dutch Cyclists' Union (Eerste Enige Echte Nederlandse Wielrijdersbond, or ENWB) took to the streets of the town Amersfoort, posing as cyclists, pedestrians, car drivers, and bus passengers for a series of eight photographs titled "Use of Space" (see figure 0.1). By juxtaposing the eight street images, shown on our book cover, the activists were making a simple point. From a spatial perspective, designing city streets for cars makes no sense. It is unsustainable. Cycling, walking, and public transit are more efficient ways to use valuable urban space. Such photographic intervention—reenacted many times in other parts of the world since—has become iconic. The 1970s contest for what constitutes sustainable urban mobility was not new, however, as the issue had been debated earlier and elsewhere—also by policymakers.

London's expansion in the 1950s was spectacular. To house the capital's overflow, neighboring county Buckinghamshire appointed Frederick Bernard Pooley as chief planner in 1953. Articulating the emerging dominant view at the time, Pooley was convinced that automobility demanded a new kind of city. He rejected the car-based sprawl of Los Angeles as a model for the so-called North Bucks New City. Instead, he felt a monorail-based mobility system would be a much better way to inhibit the negative impacts of cars on the urban landscape.[1] In the end, neither North Bucks New City nor its monorail ever got off the ground.

We tend to think of the 1950s as the era of inevitable development of car-centered cities, which corporations like General Motors projected at the highly popular 1939 Futurama exhibition and planners like Robert Moses achieved. We also often position the 1970s countermovement as a singular and clear-cut moment of resistance. The examples of Pooley and the ENWB remind us how social actors in the past considered the full range of urban mobility beyond automobility. By offering stories that

**Figure 0.1.** Poster, "Ruimtegebruik," made by the Eerste Enige Echte Neder-landse Wielrijdersbond, 1979.
Source: In collection IISG Amsterdam. Permission by Fietsersbond.

narrate the roads-not-taken, we avoid a Whig view of history limited to the plans that were realized. To understand the historical process, we also need to consider the countertradition of the incisive critiques from Lewis Mumford and Jane Jacobs embracing the walkable city, or the many social movements they inspired.[2]

Contestations and alternative visions have always been part of the way our cities developed. Indeed, the search for alternative narratives points to the longer trajectory of current debates on how best to shape our cities. This collection of essays offers historical discussions and concepts to deal with today's grand challenge of sustainable urban mobility.

In current visions of future cities, mobility looms large. In the twenty-first century, more people will live in cities. The United Nations Sustainable Development Goals include the ambition to realize sustainable cities and communities by 2030.[3] To achieve truly sustainable urban mobility, we will have to disengage from motorized mobility.[4] This might be even more challenging for cities in the Global South. There, motorbikes fill mobility gaps whenever authorities fail to provide transit systems for the working poor, and cars are still welcomed as middle-class status symbols or as a convenient and safe mode of mobility to move through more dangerous parts of the city unhindered.[5] Still, the days of petroleum-and-steel motorized mobility are numbered. Cars everywhere put pressure on public spaces—the urban Global North treats cars in the city increasingly as merely guests or bans them altogether.[6] The current destabilization of the automobility regime may open up the possibility of post-car futures.[7] To some, electrification of automobility suffices to make the transition; for others, a more radical break is necessary to achieve mobility deserving the qualification "sustainable." Nevertheless, the challenge is how to provide urban citizens with accessible, affordable, and safe mobility that is at the same time sustainable.

In *A U-Turn to the Future*, we posit that historians have a role to play in this discussion. Exploring the sustainability challenge from a long-term perspective is vital for at least three reasons. First, Article 2 of the United Nations Framework Convention on Climate Change (UNFCCC) has set the long-term basis for our current global challenge. It stipulates that global average temperatures should not reach 2°C higher than pre–Industrial Revolution levels. In order to achieve such a goal, we need to know precisely how much our ecological world has changed in the past 150 years. The Intergovernmental Panel on Climate Change estimates that the transport sector produced 14 percent of global greenhouse gas emissions in 2010, and this level is projected to rise in the coming decades. In the European Union, urban mobility is responsible for some 40 percent of transport-related carbon dioxide emissions, and a staggering 70 percent of other transport-derived pollutants.[8] This long-term perspective of the climate challenge emphasizes a historical framework in the current discussions.[9]

Second, urban mobility systems have a long lifespan. Consequently, the systems we have today do not reflect current ideals, but rather those of the past. It takes decades to build—and by the same token to unbuild—systems that include infrastructures (from bridges to airports) and vehicles (from trams to planes), as well as the institutions (from semi-governmental transport agencies to powerful lobbies) sustaining them. Making cities less car-centered means changing the supporting coalitions of vested interests built around them over decades. Transforming these systems requires the kind of long-term thinking that comes naturally to historians. Understanding the past is key to envisioning the future and changing the present.[10]

Third, the past is an inspiring place, demonstrating how things could be different and revealing the roads-not-taken. Such alternative roads can be an inspiration. Moreover, the past harbors persistent but neglected paths—usually ignored—offering future possibilities for innovation, rediscovery, and re-use. The history of urban cycling is a case in point: once modern before becoming old-fashioned, even obsolete, cycling as an ecologically sustainable practice has been resurrected as the most promising urban mobility mode for the future. Historians are well positioned to identify such pockets of persistence over time and show how these can be mobilized to facilitate transitions to sustainability today.[11] Historical analysis helps us understand the divergent development paths of innovation and issues of continuity and change. Such historical perspectives offer insights into how to break from undesirable development paths and shift course toward a more sustainable future.

For these reasons, the contributing authors believe that the past holds valuable insights for the present as well as for the future. Historical insights suggest a "usable past," in the famous phrase coined by American historian Van Wyck Brooks in 1918. In the aftermath of his country's tradition of nationalist storytelling about winners, he called for a history that would incorporate a more complete story: covering both the achievements and regrets that highlight the struggles of a more communal aspiration.[12] This volume contributes to our contemporary aspiration for sustainable urban mobility by providing historical analyses and concepts. A better understanding of the long trajectories of urban mobility systems serves as a stepping-stone to what is needed and feasible for future sustainable urban mobility. All the authors of this volume seek to solve three simple sets of questions, corresponding with the first three sections of this book. First, why did the mobilities we presently deem environmentally and socially unsustainable come to dominate many cities? Who shaped these mobilities in our cities and why? What were the mechanisms for selling unsustainable urban mobility? Second, how can historians accurately account for and recover the city's sustainable mobilities, above all walking and cycling? Third, what use can we make of persistent patterns of the past in a transition to more sustainable urban mobility? How do material and nonmaterial mobility legacies impact us today? Before introducing the contributions in this volume, we discuss our working terms and identify historians' critical contribution to the thinking about making our urban mobilities more sustainable.

## Sustainable Urban Mobility: Definitions

*A U-Turn to the Future* focuses on mobility in the city. The prospects for sustainable mobility are looking relatively bright in urban environments. The compactness of cities makes active modes like walking and cycling combined with public transit viable—despite the dominance of urban automobility in many highly mobile cities. Hong Kong, for example, is already well below the energy threshold (energy consumption per passenger kilometer) that sustainable passenger transport requires.[13] Furthermore, cities more often than nation-states are showing the political will to curb automobility. Some urban policymakers have embarked on ambitious agendas to mitigate climate change in their cities. Until recently, proposing such measures equaled political suicide. That is changing quickly.[14] The late political scientist Benjamin Barber asserted that for cities—and their mayors—global issues ranging from terrorism to sustainability are their best governance opportunities. Cities are key sites of change: they are part of the global economy, home to over half the world's population, and the primary incubators of innovations. Many mayors have become the agents of change, Barber argued, because they interact with their electorates more directly and effectively than national politicians.[15] These observations highlight sustainable urban mobility as a critical issue of our age.

The timeframe of this volume begins with the industrial and urban revolutions in the 1850s and covers the century when the unsustainable consumption of fossil fuels skyrocketed, particularly since the 1950s.[16] We see urban mobility primarily as the movement of people within the perimeter of the city. While the city is our unit of analysis, we are aware of—and equally interested in—the position of cities in urban regions, as well as in provincial, national, and global frameworks.[17] Cities typically do not operate in isolation; they interact. Large cities have often been at the forefront of the transnational circulation of urban planning ideals and sustainable mobility.[18]

Urban policymakers, active members of international networks when they first met at World Fairs since 1851, shared best practices globally and implemented them locally.[19] The transnational circulation of urban planning and sustainable urban mobility ideas produced similar developments with many local variations.[20] For example, state projects to re-engineer traffic patterns or transform cities according to high-modernist visions had a worldwide impact.[21] Planners sought to impose order on what they considered the "chaos" of organically grown historic cities, built grids as an antidote to urban disorder, and created cities like Brasília and Chandigarh from scratch.[22] The protest against and demise of modern large-scale urban planning share the same story.[23] The worldwide circulation of ideas and protests suggests the need to examine sustainable urban mobility in a wider global governance context.

In social geographical terms, we see cities as large and relatively dense human settlements, serving functions distinctive from those of rural areas. Administrative borders define the city's perimeter, including what counts as "urban mobility." In absolute terms, cities have large ecological footprints: they depend on large swaths of territory outside their administrative borders. For example, historian William Cronon showed—a year before William Rees published his landmark article on the "ecological footprint"—how Chicago was intimately linked to, and appropriated the carrying capacity of, its hinterland, drawing natural resources from it and returning waste to it.[24] At the same time, thanks to their compact land use, cities can also support more sustainable mobility practices. In economic sustainability terms, compactness enables urban transit operators to run profitable enterprises. In ecological sustainability terms, compact cities allow more people to walk and to cycle. Sustainable urban mobility, however, does suffer from rebound effects. Cycling urbanites may jump on a plane for a weekend trip elsewhere. We must somehow examine urban sustainability practices taking place "here" and "elsewhere" in one analytical frame.[25]

The sustainability question also goes beyond the concerns of our own times. We use sustainability in this volume as defined by the UN Brundtland Commission: "the development that meets the needs of the present without compromising the ability of future generations to meet their own need." Its criterion of intra- and intergenerational equity takes a long-term perspective: one person's mobility should not come at the expense of another's mobility in present or future generations. In this vein, today's concern for sustainability involves, as Smits and Veraart argue in this volume, the tradeoff between "now" and "later."[26] In his seminal article on the "sustainable mobility paradigm," David Banister focused on ways to achieve environmentally sustainable mobility: through modal shifts, land-use planning, ICT technologies to reduce people's need to travel, and increased transport and fuel efficiency.[27] Such strategies aim to improve efficiency, shift from less to more sustainable modes, and reduce mobility overall. The Brundtland definition, however, not only covers ecological, but also social and economic aspects of sustainability. It means we also need to focus on social justice and accessibility—key to transport justice.[28] Sustainable mobility within development theory often seeks to satisfy current consumption levels while not compromising future consumption.[29] Yet, future scenarios are often based on the premise that mobility will continue to grow, and they ignore low mobility.[30] Throughout the world, significant numbers of people—including in highly mobile societies—are not, cannot, or do not want to be mobile. Sustainable mobility then involves social sustainability (mobility justice) as well as ecological sustainability (cleaner air, livability).

We are fully aware that the use of the term "sustainability" is not neutral—and even may be considered anachronistic. In the German-speaking world, sustainability was already coined in the eighteenth century. In 1713, Hans Carl von Carlowitz, responsible for managing mines on behalf of the Saxon court in Freiberg for decades, observed the dire impact of timber shortages on the metallurgy industries and introduced the term sustainability (*Nachhaltigkeit*).[31] "Sustainable use" of a forest could only be achieved by not extracting more wood than could be regrown through reforestation management. His work was an early response to the limits to growth.[32] From a historical perspective, we observe that citizens have worried for centuries about urban mobility issues because of what we would nowadays call ecological and social sustainability concerns. Although Google Analytics books (Ngram viewer), for example, show that the terms "sustainability" and "durabilité" were not in the actor category in the English and French-speaking world until the 1990s—we also note that contemporaries used terms like "waste" (constant since 1800), "unhealthy cities" (since the 1830s), "traffic jams" and "traffic accidents" (since the 1920s), and air pollution (since the 1970s), while several urban planning movements (City Beautiful, 1880s–1914; Garden City, 1900–1950; regional planning, 1920s–1970s) sought to offer solutions for the grand challenge. As a category of analysis, the term "sustainability" allows us to build bridges between present-day concerns and past challenges that people faced.

Indeed, the concern for sustainable urban mobility is not new. Piles of horse manure on streets were identified as a disease hazard by the late nineteenth century.[33] Roadbuilders asphalted American streets because it was then easier to remove horse manure.[34] The pounding of hooves on the street produced noise and stone-powder, further nuisances for urbanites. Mobility could come to a complete standstill when large numbers of horses fell ill or died.[35] For many contemporaries, the horse-based economy was unsustainable, and they welcomed the fossil fuel alternative. Today, we realize that the fossil fuel–based urban mobility systems that replaced horse-drawn traffic have generated pollution and other problems of their own as unintended consequences.[36]

Neither is the concern for social (in)justice in urban mobility systems new. Rapid growth rates in cities created—and continue to create—divisions between rich and poor. Cities generate an unequal distribution of wealth and persistent socio-spatial segregation. Mobility has a major effect on this inequality and the related competition over land, labor, and capital. Poor transport planning resulted in segregation by cutting off neighborhoods where the less well-off happen to live, from Chicago's South Side to Amsterdam's Bijlmer.[37] Transport poverty limits some social groups' access to urban mobility. Racial hierarchies were a feature of urban mobility systems in segregated societies like South Africa and the American South in the nineteenth and most of the twentieth century. Even in Philadelphia, policymakers preserved racial order at the cost of delays in its streetcar service.[38] Car-less individuals abound even in so-called "car societies." As car-oriented postwar transport planners focused on commuting, they neglected the mobility needs of children, married women, and the elderly. Moreover, they sought to secure traffic safety not by slowing down motorized traffic, but by removing pedestrians and cyclists through traffic separation schemes.[39] The great social costs for the urban poor and society are the result of decisions made over many decades, as UN-Habitat also acknowledged in 2008.[40]

By analyzing the trajectory of urban mobility from a long-term perspective, historians lay bare the trade-offs between different aspects of sustainability. As a discipline sensitive to issues of power, history helps us understand the political issues and the cultural definitions involved in shaping urban mobility and analyze how powerful social actors have pushed through their preferred trade-off, while sidelining the wishes and needs of others. The triumph of car-based urban mobility—or motordom as contemporaries called it—is a case in point.

### History and Sustainable Urban Mobility: Toward a Usable Past

In this collection of essays, we offer insights to help analyze sustainable urban mobility in a long-term perspective in the same way that Van Wyck Brooks understood the usable past. Transport and urban planning scholars have been concerned about the environmental unsustainability of urban mobility systems.[41] Changing urban mobility in a sustainable direction demands a broad social change, however. Mobility scholars in the social sciences have analyzed how the "politics of mobility"—ranging from a focus on struggles at street level, to showing how car-oriented developments became the norm—are bound up in a global system of automobility. These scholars are exploring how our current mobilities can best transition to a more sustainable future.[42]

What do historians have to offer? History can be useful when discussing future mobilities, as Colin Divall, Julian Hine, and Colin Pooley have shown elsewhere.[43] Built-in resistance may prevent change: once a society settles on a particular mobility such as trains or cars, it becomes more difficult to shift course. The social and material norms around dominant mobility systems benefit certain future urban mobility scenarios over others.[44] Historical research, though, helps situate today's trendy and technology-oriented visions (e.g., "smart mobility") in the long tradition of how people envisioned the future to deal with the challenges of their time. Such "past futures" enable us to reflect critically on present-day promises that technology can solve sociocultural challenges.[45] Historical inquiry most of all helps counter the exceedingly short time spans, breathlessness, and gullibility typical of current expectations about innovative, smart solutions, which are rampant in urban mobility scenarios for the future.[46]

We distinguish three different manifestations of the usable past in this book. Providing a long-term perspective first of all helps explain the cultural politics of successfully "selling" unsustainable mobility in the city; second, it paints an inclusive picture of the mobile past, reconstructing those urban mobilities that have left few historical traces and are as a result "forgotten" in the histories of urban mobility; third, it enables us to discuss how persistent remnants of the past provide barriers and opportunities to transition toward more sustainable urban mobility. One particular obstacle is that dominant cultural representations play a key role in policymaking.[47] Policymakers have made many—unsuccessful—attempts to change people's mobile behavior. As current transport studies observe, we also need to consider persistent sociocultural factors in mobility that impede a sustainable mobility transition.[48]

The first usable past approach shows how unsustainable urban mobilities have been successfully promoted. Today's omnipresent automobility was never the inevitable outcome of progress. What we now see as sustainable mobility practices, such as walking and cycling, have long been contested or even delegitimized as mobilities of a different age, and as dangerous—tactics that allowed automotive interests to successfully transform the street into thoroughfares for motorists. Initially, streets were shared spaces where all modalities could travel and claim as theirs—and car drivers were held accountable for the victims they made in road traffic. Until automotive interests—worried about their prospects in American cities—employed a broad set of discursive practices (media campaigns, theatrical public safety parades in the street) that ridiculed pedestrians as "jaywalkers" unless they crossed the street at designated spots. These campaigns effectively taught pedestrians not to hinder the flow in the street, which was redefined as a motorized traffic thoroughfare along which cars traveled speedily in an even flow at the expense of all other traffic.[49] Moreover, this transformation of the street into thoroughfares for motors has been translated in ostensibly objective assessments of urban mobility options that masked the extraordinary car-oriented biases in traffic policy.[50]

Selling automobility involved narrating a future with its own past. In the United States, automotive interests promoted "motordom" as the inevitable future—a vision also exported abroad. On their visit to the United States, Swedish experts saw what they thought their country's mobility future could—and should—look like in both technical and cultural terms.[51] Narrating the future often involved suppressing others' stories by relegating them to the dumpsite of history. Realizing one future often dismisses—and marginalizes—other possible futures.[52] Since the 1920s, the boosters of automobility excluded pedestrians and cyclists by choice and political design, to cast them as "slow traffic" and modes of the past.[53] As innovation scholars point out, mobilizing the future is a powerful weapon. When a novelty first comes on the scene, its promoters offer a so-called technological promise: the innovation is the "fix" for all society's problems.[54] Such technological fixes are particularly appealing because they suggest no behavior change is required to reap the full benefits. Today techno-tales dominate again the current debates about car-bound futures of "smart mobility" and "smart cities"—with promises of the driverless-car future being just around the corner for over half a century.[55] The opposite is also true. To break away from single-driver automobility that consumes too much energy also requires an alternative vision. The point is not to go back to a pre-car, nineteenth-century urban world—after all, automobility has shaped contemporary societies too profoundly—but to imagine what a car-less society looked like. Such a historical analysis points out alternative pathways or—from today's perspective—the opportunities we missed.

A second usable past approach helps to reveal such alternatives by drawing a more accurate picture of their continued existence alongside the dominant urban (auto) mobility paradigm. As a result of high technology narratives dominating our view of the past, we have lost our ability to accurately gauge the significance of walking and cycling in cities. Our comparative research in over fifteen European cities showed that from the 1920s until the 1950s, urban cycling had a far larger modal share (40 percent and above) in most European cities and continued far longer, in many places well into the 1960s.[56] While most mobility studies have focused particularly on motorized and rail-based modalities at the expense of histories of cyclists and pedestrians, the modal split analysis considers cycling in relation to—rather than in isolation from—other modalities.[57] Such insights not only uncover "slow" or "active" modes like pedestrianism and cycling, but consider them in the context of sustainability. The second approach foregrounds the methods to reconstruct these mobilities that were relatively invisible in the past.

A third usable past approach analyses how persistent past practices could be employed for a mobility transition toward sustainability. Actions in the past often turn into lock-ins that restrict change, induce inertia against the call for sustainability, and become "monuments of unsustainability."[58] Yet older practices persist. The continued presence of cycling also has theoretical implications. According to Elizabeth Shove, innovation studies should not focus exclusively on novel things at their point of innovation. They should also look at reviving the more durable practices of the past in order to achieve sustainable urban mobility. Based on historical case studies of urban cycling, she argues that older technologies and more sustainable pastimes like walking and cycling in the park may present opportunities for shifting course through rediscovery and re-use.[59]

*A U-Turn to the Future* explores these three manifestations of the usable past: showing how unsustainable urban mobility systems acquired preeminence; making invisible sustainable low-tech alternatives visible in the historical records; and suggesting how path dependencies may facilitate or hinder sustainable urban mobility. A more comprehensive historical account of urban mobility thus includes the contestation between the mobilities that came into being and the mobilities that were considered low-tech (like cycling) or not technological (like walking). Historical analysis uncovers how dominant narratives, masking other (more sustainable) features, came about.[60] Our efforts are first and foremost exploratory.

## Exploring Sustainable Urban Mobility: Our Contributions

Three sections of the book offer approaches on how to recover past sustainable urban mobility. The final section offers pathways for future research and policy applications. The authors aim to build a research agenda for the long-term dynamics of sustainable urban mobility.

Section I, "Selling Unsustainable Urban Mobility," focuses on how automobility became dominant in the twentieth century and created path dependencies at the expense of other mobilities. The three contributions in this section offer explanations for the success of private automobility, showing how powerful actors managed to overcome the diversity of mobility that had characterized cities in the second half of the nineteenth century.

Ruth Oldenziel, Pieter van Wesemael, and Luísa Sousa cast a wide net. They focus on transnational actors to understand how ideals, ideas, and tools spread and shaped urban mobility over two centuries, shifting from a pedestrian to a car-dominated norm. Their purpose: to understand how modes of urban mobility we consider today as sustainable—walking, cycling, and public transit—have been contested, sidelined, and reinvented. They examine three transnational organizations: l'Union Internationale des Villes (UIV), the International Federation of Housing and Planning (IFHP), and the Permanent International Association for Road Congresses (PIARC). Initially part of the "Urban Internationale" movement promoting international socialism and urbanism, both UIV and IFHP lost some ground in the aftermath of World War I when nation-states came to dominate policies pushing automobility at the expense of walking, cycling, and public transit. PIARC successfully promoted cars and roads for cars—even in cities—as vital for national economic growth. Only at the end of the Cold War in the 1990s when nation-states retreated from urban governance, have new city networks re-emerged as alternatives to national agendas—some with major commitments to sustainable urban mobility—by resuscitating old practices for new purposes.

No book on urban mobility covering the twentieth century can ignore the dominant role of automobility and especially the United States in successfully hailing the inevitability of the car. Peter Norton addresses how "motordom" developed the account of the United States as a car-loving nation, effectively downplaying the conflicts surrounding the car's arrival in American cities. He suggests that control over the public's former vision of the relationship between Americans and their automobiles enabled motordom to construct a powerful narrative that nurtured the U.S. car market. Based on case studies of the interwar period, the 1950s, and the 2000s, Norton reconstructs how motordom was able to transform the car's image in America from a necessity to the object of a love affair. The persistence of this powerful narrative about America's love affair with the car effectively hinders the route to more sustainable urban mobility today. The two other contributions in this section show the enormous impact of the narrative beyond U.S. borders.

In the nineteenth century, Britain stands out as key player in the Industrial Revolution, with the railroads as the engines of that transformation. Railroads lost out to the dominance of automobility in the twentieth century. From his case study, Colin Divall draws lessons from the tensions between regional and local politics and policymaking in facilitating or impeding sustainable mobility. Analyzing the debates around railway closures in a British district in the 1960s, he shows how national elites mobilized the term "modernization" to justify axing the area's non-profitable railways, while regional government and advocacy groups tried to frame the same routes as more sustainable and thus valuable parts of the area's transport system. Automobility as symbol of modernity proved hard to beat, however, and helped secure a decisive policy shift toward highway construction. Divall claims that sustainability is a similarly flexible and contestable term today as modernization was in the 1960s. In his reading of present-day mobility policy documents and their implementation in the same area, he finds that in spite of lip service to ecological sustainability, in practice, economic concerns remain at the top of the agenda.

Section II, "Recovering Sustainable Mobilities of the Past," provides a bottom-up counterpoint to section I. The authors take novel methodological approaches to reconstruct pedestrians' everyday mobility using visual sources and diaries. The chapters help us capture mobilities that were not counted in official statistics. The resulting histories on pedestrianism—combined with other studies on cycling—are an important reminder that the most sustainable form of urban mobility is omnipresent, yet rendered invisible. Methods of data collection, such as traffic counts, are never neutral, but framed by those who commission and undertake them. Believing the future belonged to cars, postwar urban and traffic planners stopped counting cyclists (pedestrians were hardly ever counted) to focus almost exclusively on motorized vehicles, particularly cars. Their numbers reinforced the feeling of urgency to provide for motorists: car parking, wider streets, ring roads—far ahead of actual need, or "demand." Concerns about the economic growth of businesses in cities had short-term social effects (e.g., destruction of the urban poor's housing) and long-term environmental effects (e.g., air pollution).

Colin Pooley introduces diaries as key evidence for everyday mobility patterns. He presents the ebbs and flows of a century of urban walking by investigating how, in postwar Britain, walking lost ground as a universal mode of mobility, while "modern" planning models led to car-oriented cities. His analysis focuses on three factors he deems essential for explaining the downward trend: walking's normality declined; its convenience nose-dived; and the risks associated with it increased significantly in car-centered cities. The greater trends notwithstanding, his contribution, like the following two, help capture the continued significance of walking in the urban mobility mix and question its loss of normality as an urban mobility mode.

In their chapters, Tiina Männistö-Funk and Frank Cochoy and his co-authors employ visual analysis, showing how past traffic counts failed to capture social practices in the street. Using street photographs from the Finnish city of Turku in the postwar period, Tiina Männistö-Funk highlights how close reading of individual photographs offers a better understanding of people's mobility experiences. For example, even at data points where cars did not outnumber pedestrians and cyclists, their sheer size and speed would give the feeling of a higher "presence" than the traffic counts conveyed. Moreover, her visual analysis of geographical and gendered distribution shows more women walking and cycling—often near working-class streets and districts—who had to yield when streets were remodeled into car-traffic corridors in the 1960s. While urban and traffic planners found the motorized commuter patterns of mainly (breadwinning) men socially desirable, they ignored women's mobility practices. The traffic plans promoting large-scale motorization thus created not only environmental but also socially unsustainable mobility, she argues.

Franck Cochoy, Roland Canu, and Cédric Calvignac apply a close reading of photographs from Toulouse over a century to show how mundane things like carrying technologies—bags, rucksacks, plastic bags—helped sustain green modes of walking that competed with supposedly more "comfortable" modes of driving. Their chapter looks at the transport of goods, but challenges the notion that only trucks carried stuff. They also imply people neither stopped walking nor passively accepted urban designers' and transport planners' schemes. For example, they shifted to using bags with straps and backpacks that helped them to carry more goods without hindering their freedom of movement. And here is a lesson for policymakers and planners: to achieve sustainable "consumer logistics," as the authors call it, container technologies and the comfort of carrying things while walking are important. Such mobility presents a far simpler way to render city centers commercially and ecologically viable than building external shopping centers.

Section III, "Persistence and Sustainable Urban Mobilities," offers potential pathways toward sustainable futures. In a blend of bottom-up and top-down perspectives, the section spotlights how some urban mobilities have persisted that may either facilitate or hinder sustainability in urban mobility. Issues of path dependency come into play. This section discusses how the communist legacy of public transit and the persistence of sustainable mobility practices in urban green spaces may help nurture sustainable urban mobility today in the face of "monuments of unsustainability."

Alexandra Bekasova, Julia Kulikova, and Martin Emanuel pose the question whether there is a divergent and potentially more sustainable urban mobility development trajectory in the former communist world. Taking St. Petersburg during tsarist and communist Russia as a case study, they investigate whether the communists' seizure of power in 1917 brought a more inclusive approach to providing mobility services. The authors reconstruct the shift from the walkable to a tram-based city during the tsarist regime before it invested in subways during the communist period and car-based planning since the collapse of the Soviet Union. They end on the hopeful note that the broad public transit legacy of earlier times may still be an asset for today's urban mobility challenge.

In his chapter, Martin Emanuel narrates the biography of an emergent livable street in Stockholm. A closer look reveals how its redesign followed a century-long effort to plan and construct a parallel underground route for motorized traffic that continued to encourage car traffic into the heart of the city, but was realized at the cost of demolishing working-class neighborhoods. Further complicating matters, the tunneling solution became an issue by the early twentieth century, when the urban elite's houses were deemed too valuable to allow for street leveling and widening. Only by uncovering such "hidden unsustainabilities" will it be possible to start unbuilding the path dependencies of large infrastructures.

Frank Schipper, in turn, notes the divergent trajectories of mobility in the green parts of cities and the city overall. In proposing a research agenda for the future, he questions whether we should consider parks as "pockets of persistence" that might be mobilized to make urban mobility more sustainable today. He traces the history of urban parks and their mobility since the 1830s, when they changed meaning in urbanizing, industrializing societies, and explores the pockets of persistence hypothesis with Singapore and Washington, D.C., as possible sources of inspiration. Schipper's exercise suggests that in order to substantially support a transition to sustainable urban mobility, we need a networked approach to urban green spaces so that the infrastructures associated with sustainable urban mobility benefit from these pockets of persistence.

Section IV, "Research Agendas for the Future," offers three important elements for scholarship and policymaking when working toward a future-oriented research agenda. First, the mobility justice problems emanating from ecologically sustainable bike programs in North America serve as a reminder that it is crucial to prevent a clash between social and ecological sustainability. Second, we need to provide a quantitative basis to assess the sustainability performance of mobilities in the city. Third, a policy perspective helps us consider the feasibility of a sustainability transition in urban mobility from a governance perspective.

Mimi Sheller compares her concept of mobility as a commons to modal-split analysis. Her chapter shows how social and ecological well-being are intricately related—and sometimes even clash. Cleaner vehicles and fuels, as well as bicycle lanes and bus rapid transit systems, will do little to promote sustainability unless the underlying power relations are also considered. Cycling infrastructures may have been intended to encourage green mobility, but as U.S. scholars and activists point out, today's cycling policies are racialized and framed as "white lanes": they typically run through traditionally white, middle-class, gentrified neighborhoods from which minority groups have recently been displaced. Drawing on present cycling activism in the United States, Sheller elaborates the concept of mobility commons to sensitize us to the profound policies of inclusion and exclusion that are at work. The comprehensive notion of mobility commons should encompass all three aspects of sustainable urban mobility: ecological, social, and economic.

Jan Pieter Smits and Frank Veraart present a measurement framework for sustainable mobility and discuss what sources are available for historians to understand trends in sustainability from a long-term perspective—a most welcome outlook on two centuries of energy-intensive developments in mobility. They highlight how quantitative and qualitative analyses of sustainable urban mobility can inform and strengthen each other. Qualitative historical analysis helps debunk myths and hidden assumptions, for example, by challenging the collection and interpretation of powerful actors' quantitative mobility-related data. Quantitative methods may help create a more stringent analysis of the trade-offs occurring between different kinds of wellbeing in the past. Smits and Veraart's chapter is a call to historians of urban mobility for a truly mixed method approach, pointing to the strengths and limitations of the present volume. At the same time, they find qualitative historical sources like photographs useful to counter omissions in statistical data collection and for their own understanding of sustainable urban mobility.

Finally, Hans Jeekel and Bert Toussaint discuss the value of the historical contributions in this volume for policymakers today. Working in settings where infrastructural projects can take decades to materialize, policymakers appreciate the long-term perspective that historians provide. Historical inquiry, Jeekel and Toussaint argue, raises an awareness of how statistics have been constructed differently over time, underscoring the importance of good numbers. It raises awareness of how "sustainability" has been defined differently over time and of the need to unpack and discuss its specific criteria. It underscores the importance of preserving "pockets of persistence" for present-day purposes and provides insights into the power relations that shape what is possible by supporting or blocking certain types of mobility. Finally, Jeekel and Toussaint point to how historical analysis makes clear that it is essential to take actual practice into consideration as part of any scientific analysis of mobility.

Together these essays may bring insights from a usable past. Our contributions focus on the Atlantic world, Europe in particular, in a context of transnational circulation and globalization. We believe the themes are useful for a more global approach. Most importantly, they help us avoid retelling versions of history that present automobility as the inevitable future for our cities and help us envision an alternative future of more sustainable urban mobility.

**Frank Schipper**, an independent scholar specializing in mobility and infrastructure studies, has researched the history of roads, telegraphy, and tourism. Currently he is working on pedestrians and cyclists in cities and nature. He is author of *Driving Europe: Building Europe on Roads in the Twentieth Century* (Amsterdam University Press, 2008), co-author of *The History of the European Travel Commission* (European Travel Commission, 2018), and *Cycling Cities: The Rotterdam Experience* (SHT, 2019), and has edited special issues on infrastructure-related topics for the journals *Comparativ*, *History and Technology*, and *Métropoles*.

**Martin Emanuel**, historian of technology and researcher at the Departmnt of Urban Planning and Environment, KTH Royal Institute of Technology, Stockholm, works at the intersection of mobility, urban, and environmental history, including tourism history. His research is on wide-ranging historical dimensions of cycling culture, urban planning, and traffic management. He has published several articles on the history of cycling and sustainable mobility, as well as the 2012 monograph *Trafikslag på undantag: Cykeltrafiken i Stockholm 1930–1980* (Excluded through planning: Bicycle traffic in Stockholm 1930–1980). He coedited and authored *Cycling Cities: The European Experience* (Stichting Historie der Techniek [SHT], 2016).

**Ruth Oldenziel**, professor in the history of technology at Eindhoven University of Technology, is editor in chief of *Technology and Culture*.

She has published in American, transatlantic, gender, technology, and mobility studies including *Cycling Cities* (coeditor with Martin Emanuel, Adri Albert de la Bruhèze, and Frank Veraart; SHT, 2016), *Cycling and Recycling* (coeditor with Helmuth Trischler; Berghahn, 2016), *Consumers, Tinkerers, Rebels* (Palgrave, 2015), *Hacking Europe* (coeditor with Gerard Alberts; Springer, 2014), *Cold-War Kitchen* (coeditor with Karin Zachmann; MIT, 2009), *Gender and Technology* (Hopkins, 2003), *Crossing Boundaries, Building Bridges* (with Karin Zachmann and Annie Canel; Routledge 2000), and *Making Technology Masculine* (AUP, 1999).

## Notes

1. Guy Ortolano, "Planning the Urban Future in 1960s Britain," *Historical Journal* 54, no. 2 (2011): 477–507.
2. Cliff Ellis, "Lewis Mumford and Norman Bel Geddes: The Highway, the City and the Future," *Planning Perspectives* 20, no. 1 (2005): 51–68; Scott Larson, *"Building Like Moses with Jacobs in Mind": Contemporary Planning in New York City* (Philadelphia: Temple University Press, 2013). Counterfactual history provides another way to engage with historical alternatives; see Colin G. Pooley, "Landscapes without the Car: A Counterfactual Historical Geography of Twentieth-Century Britain," *Journal of Historical Geography* 36, no. 3 (2010): 266–75.
3. United Nations, "About the Sustainable Development Goals," http://www.un.org/sustainabledevelopment/sustainable-development-goals/ (accessed 25 November 2019).
4. Frank Geels, René Kemp, Geoff Dudley, and Glenn Lyons, *Automobility in Transition: A Socio-Technical Analysis of Sustainable Transport* (New York: Routledge, 2012).
5. Eduardo Alcântara Vasconcellos, *Urban Transport, Environment and Equity: The Case for Developing Countries* (London: Earthscan, 2001); Harry T. Dimitriou and Ralph Albert Gakenheimer, *Urban Transport in the Developing World: A Handbook of Policy and Practice* (Cheltenham: Edward Elgar, 2011).
6. John Urry, "The 'System' of Automobility," *Theory, Culture & Society* 21, nos. 4–5 (2004): 25–39.
7. Dennis Kingsley and John Urry, *After the Car* (Cambridge: Polity Press, 2009).
8. IPCC, *Climate Change 2014: Synthesis Report* (Geneva: IPCC, 2015), fig. 1.07-01; European Commission, "Urban Mobility," https://ec.europa.eu/transport/themes/urban/urban_mobility_en (accessed 25 November 2019).
9. Paul Edwards, *A Vast Machine: Computer Models, Climate Data, and the Politics of Global Warming* (Cambridge, MA: MIT Press, 2010).
10. Gerardo Marletto, "Car and the City: Socio-Technical Transition Pathways to 2030," *Technological Forecasting and Social Change* 87 (2014): 164–78.
11. Elizabeth Shove, "The Shadowy Side of Innovation: Unmaking and Sustainability," *Technology Analysis & Strategic Management* 24, no. 4 (2012): 363–75. On this point, see also the introduction in Ruth Oldenziel and Helmut Trischler, eds., *Cycling and Recycling: Histories of Sustainable Practices* (New York: Berghahn Books, 2015); Schipper, this volume; Oldenziel, Sousa, and Van Wesemael, this volume.
12. Van Wyck Brooks, "On Creating a Usable Past," *Dial*, 11 April 1918, 337–341.

13. Erling Holden, Kristin Linnerud, and David Banister, "Sustainable Passenger Transport: Back to Brundtland," *Transportation Research Part A: Policy and Practice* 54 (2013): 67–77.
14. Frank W. Geels, "A Socio-Technical Analysis of Low-Carbon Transitions: Introducing the Multi-Level Perspective into Transport Studies," *Journal of Transport Geography* 24 (2012): 471–82.
15. Benjamin R. Barber, *If Mayors Ruled the World: Dysfunctional Nations, Rising Cities* (New Haven: Yale University Press, 2013).
16. See Christian Pfister's qualitative analysis, "The '1950s Syndrome' and the Transition from a Slow-Going to a Rapid Loss of Global Sustainability," in *Turning Points in Environmental History*, ed. Frank Uekötter (Pittsburgh: University of Pittsburgh Press, 2010), 90–117; and recently Harry Lintsen, Frank Veraart, Jan-Pieter Smits, and John Grin, *De Kwetsbare Welvaart van Nederland* (Amsterdam: Prometheus, 2018), for statistical evidence of the 1950s take-off.
17. Divall, this volume.
18. Pierre-Yves Saunier, "Taking Up the Bet on Connections: A Municipal Contribution," *Contemporary European History* 11, no. 4 (2002): 507–27. See also Oldenziel et al., this volume.
19. Hans Buiter, "Constructing Dutch Streets: A Melting Pot of European Technologies," in *Urban Machinery: Inside Modern European Cities*, ed. Mikael Hård and Thomas J. Misa (Cambridge, MA: MIT Press, 2008), 141–62.
20. For transnational circulation, see the book series with Palgrave Macmillan *Inventing Europe,* particularly Helmuth Trischler and Martin Kohlrausch, *Building Europe on Expertise: Innovators, Organizers, Networkers* (Houndmills: Palgrave Macmillan, 2014); Wolfram Kaiser and Johan W. Schot, *Writing the Rules for Europe: Experts, Cartels, International Organizations* (Houndmills: Palgrave Macmillan, 2014); Ruth Oldenziel and Mikael Hård, *Consumers, Tinkerers, Rebels: The People Who Shaped Europe* (Houndmills: Palgrave Macmillan, 2013).
21. James C. Scott, *Seeing Like a State: How Certain Schemes to Improve the Human Condition Have Failed* (New Haven: Yale University Press, 1998).
22. Kate Brown, "Gridded Lives: Why Kazakhstan and Montana Are Nearly the Same Place," *American Historical Review* 106, no. 1 (2001): 17–48.
23. Christopher Klemek, *The Transatlantic Collapse of Urban Renewal: Postwar Urbanism from New York to Berlin* (Chicago: University of Chicago Press, 2011).
24. William Cronon, *Nature's Metropolis: Chicago and the Great West* (New York: W.W. Norton, 1991); William E. Rees, "Ecological Footprints and Appropriated Carrying Capacity: What Urban Economics Leaves Out," *Environment and Urbanization* 4, no. 2 (1992): 121–30.
25. Peter H. G. Berkhout et al., "Defining the Rebound Effect," *Energy Policy* 28, nos. 6–7 (2000): 425–432. See also Smits and Veraart, this volume.
26. Smits and Veraart, this volume.
27. David Banister, "The Sustainable Mobility Paradigm," *Transport Policy* 15, no. 2 (2008): 72–80.
28. Karel Martens, *Transport Justice: Designing Fair Transportation Systems* (London: Routledge, 2016). See also Hans Jeekel, *Inclusive Transport: Fighting Involuntary Transport Disadvantages* (London: Elsevier, 2018); Mimi Sheller, *Mobility Justice: The Politics of Movement in an Age of Extremes* (London: Verso, 2018).
29. A. D. Basiago, "Economic, Social, and Environmental Sustainability in Development Theory and Urban Planning Practice," *Environmentalist* 19, no. 2 (1998): 145–61.

30.  Patrick Moriarty and Damon Honnery, "Low-Mobility: The Future of Transport," *Futures* 40, no. 10 (2008): 865–72.

31.  Carl von Carlowitz, *Sylvicultura oeconomica oder Haußwirthliche Nachricht und Naturmäßige Anweisung zur Wilden Baum-Zucht*, ed. Joachim Hamberger (Munich: Oekom Verlag, 2013 [1713]).

32.  Ulrich Grober, "Von Freiberg nach Rio—Carlowitz und die Bildung des Begriffs "Nachhaltigkeit," in *Die Erfindung der Nachhaltigkeit: Leben, Werk und Wirkung des Hans Carl von Carlowitz* (Munich: Sächsische Hans Carl von Carlowitz-Gesellschaft, 2013), 13–30; Franz Josef Radermacher, "Die Ressourcen der Erde setzen uns Grenzen—vom sächsischen Bergmann Hans Carl von Carlowitz 1713 bis zum neuen Report an den Club of Rome 2052," in ibid., 141–56.

33.  Horse manure, however, also represented an asset sold off to farmers to fertilize their fields, reminiscent of the circular economy debate today. Clay McShane and Joel Tarr, *The Horse in the City: Living Machines in the Nineteenth Century* (Baltimore: John Hopkins University Press, 2007).

34.  Clay McShane, "Transforming the Use of Urban Space: A Look at the Revolution in Street Pavements, 1880–1924," *Journal of Urban History* 5, no. 3 (1979): 279–307.

35.  Ralph Turvey, "Horse Traction in Victorian London," *Journal of Transport History* 26, no. 2 (2005): 38–59.

36.  Joel Arthur Tarr, *The Search for the Ultimate Sink: Urban Pollution in Historical Perspective* (Akron: University of Akron Press, 1996). For concerns about "sound" pollution, see Karin Bijsterveld, *Mechanical Sound: Technology, Culture, and Public Problems of Noise in the Twentieth Century* (Cambridge, MA: MIT Press, 2008).

37.  Shane Ewen, *What Is Urban History?* (Cambridge: Polity, 2016), 3–5; Anique Hommels, *Unbuilding Cities: Obduracy in Urban Socio-Technical Change* (Cambridge, MA: MIT Press, 2005).

38.  Geoff D. Zylstra, "Whiteness, Freedom, and Technology: The Racial Struggle over Philadelphia's Streetcars, 1859–1867," *Technology and Culture* 52, no. 4 (2011): 678–702.

39.  Martin Emanuel, "Constructing the Cyclist: Ideology and Representations in Urban Traffic Planning in Stockholm, 1930–70," *Journal of Transport History* 33 (2011): 67–91; Per Lundin, *Bilsamhället: Ideologi, expertis och regelskapande i efterkrigstidens Sverige* (Stockholm: Stockholmia, 2008); Ruth Oldenziel, Martin Emanuel, Adri A. Albert de la Bruhèze, and Frank Veraart, eds., *Cycling Cities: The European Experience* (Eindhoven: Foundation of the History of Technology and LMU Rachel Carson Center, 2016).

40.  UN-HABITAT, *State of the World's Cities 2010/11: Cities for All: Bridging the Urban Divide* (London: Earthscan, 2008), xix.

41.  Some notable examples are Peter Newman and Jeffrey R. Kenworthy, *Sustainability and Cities: Overcoming Automobile Dependence* (Washington, DC: Island Press, 1999); David Banister, *Unsustainable Transport: City Transport in the New Century* (London: Routledge, 2005); Katie Williams, *Spatial Planning, Urban Form and Sustainable Transport* (Aldershot: Ashgate, 2005); Martens, *Transport Justice*; David Banister, *Inequality in Transport* (Marcham: Alexandrine Press, 2018).

42.  On the politics of mobility, see Tim Cresswell, "Towards a Politics of Mobility." On the "system" of automobility, see Urry, "The 'System' of Automobility." A standard work on mobility studies is Peter Adey, David Bissell, Kevin Hannam,

Peter Merriman, and Mimi Sheller, *The Routledge Handbook of Mobilities* (Milton Park: Routledge, 2013). Examples of other social science approaches to sustainable urban mobility are Nicholas Low and Brendan Gleeson, *Making Urban Transport Sustainable* (Basingstoke: Palgrave Macmillan, 2002); Alan Walks, *The Urban Political Economy and Ecology of Automobility: Driving Cities, Driving Inequality, Driving Politics* (London: Routledge, 2015). Specifically on the issue of transitioning away from automobility, see Frank W. Geels et al., *Automobility in Transition?*

43. Colin Divall, Julian Hine, and Colin G. Pooley, *Transport Policy: Learning Lessons from History*; Colin Divall, "Transport History, the Usable Past and the Future of Mobility," in *Mobilities: New Perspectives on Transport and Society*, ed. Margret Grieco and John Urry (Farnham: Routledge, 2011), 305–319.

44. See how path dependencies affect the success of public transit systems in Geraldine Pflieger et al., "How Does Urban Public Transport Change Cities? Correlations between Past and Present Transport and Urban Planning Policies," *Urban Studies* 46, no. 7 (2009): 1421–37.

45. Hans-Liudger Dienel and Helmuth Trischler eds., *Geschichte der Zukunft des Verkehrs: Verkehrskonzepte von der Frühen Neuzeit bis zum 21. Jahrhundert* (Frankfurt am Main: Campus, 1997); Carlos López Galviz, *Cities, Railways, Modernities: London, Paris and the Nineteenth Century* (New York: Routledge, 2019), particularly chapter 1, "Past Futures." Also see Reinhart Koselleck, *Futures Past: On the Semantics of Historical Time* (Cambridge, MA: MIT Press, 1985).

46. Jo Guldi and David Armitage, *The History Manifesto* (Cambridge: Cambridge University Press, 2014).

47. Colin Divall and George Revill, "Cultures of Transport: Representation, Practice and Technology," *Journal of Transport History* 26, no. 1 (2005): 99–111.

48. Colin Divall, "Mobilizing the History of Technology," *Technology and Culture* 51, no. 4 (2010): 938–960.

49. Peter D. Norton, "Street Rivals: Jaywalking and the Invention of the Motor Age Street," *Technology and Culture* 48, no. 2 (2007): 331–59.

50. Oldenziel et al., this volume.

51. Lundin, *Bilsamhället*.

52. Norton, this volume.

53. Ruth Oldenziel, "Accounting Tricks: How Pedestrians & Cyclists Were Thrown under the Bus, 1910s-1940s," Presentation T2M Philadelphia, 25 September 2014; Oldenziel et al., *Cycling Cities*; Norton, "Streets Rivals"; and *Fighting Traffic: The Dawn of the Motor Age in the American City* (Cambridge, MA: MIT Press, 2008).

54. Harro van Lente, *Promising Technology: The Dynamics of Expectations in Technological Developments* (Enschede: Universiteit Twente, 1993), 145–73; Harro van Lente and Arie Rip, "Expectations in Technological Developments: An Example of Prospective Structures to Be Filled In by Agency," in *Getting New Technologies Together*, ed. Cornelis Disco and Bart van der Meulen (Berlin: Walter de Gruyter, 1998), 195–220.

55. Fabian Kröger, "Automated Driving in Its Social, Historical and Cultural Contexts," in *Autonomous Driving*, ed. Markus Maurer et al. (Berlin Heidelberg: Springer, 2016), 41–68; Divall, "Mobilizing."

56. In their pioneering 1999 book, historians Albert de la Bruhèze and Veraart compared cycling practice and policy in nine European cities in relation to public transit and automobility since the 1920s. Adri A. Albert de la Bruhèze and

Frank Veraart, *Fietsverkeer in praktijk en beleid in de twintigste eeuw* (Eindhoven: Stichting Historie der Techniek, 1999). The subsequent book, Oldenziel et al., *Cycling Cities*, expanded and elaborated this work further.

57.  Gijs Mom, "The Crisis of Transport History: A Critique, and a Vista," *Mobility in History: The Yearbook of the International Association for the History of Transport, Traffic and Mobility* 6, no. 1 (2015): 7–19.

58.  Martin Emanuel, "Monuments of Unsustainability: Planning, Path Dependence and Cycling in Stockholm," in *Cycling and Recyling: Histories of Sustainable Practices*, ed. Ruth Oldenziel and Helmuth Trischler (New York: Berghahn Books, 2015), 101–21. There is also a close link with the notion of momentum in Thomas Hughes's work on LTS as introduced in *Networks of Power: Electrification in Western Society, 1880–1930* (Baltimore: Johns Hopkins University Press, 1983). Hommels highlights these factors as reasons for obdurate resistance to urban change, even though these refute commonsense explanations of obduracy (e.g., change would be too expensive) and the idea that urban change alone will be decisive. She also stresses cultural factors. Hommels, *Unbuilding Cities*.

59.  Shove, "The Shadowy Side of Innovation"; James Mahoney, "Path Dependence in Historical Sociology," *Theory and Society* 29, no. 4 (2000): 507–48; Emanuel, this volume.

60.  Männistö-Funk; Pooley; and Emanuel, this volume.

## Bibliography

Adey, Peter, David Bissell, Kevin Hannam, Peter Merriman, and Mimi Sheller. *The Routledge Handbook of Mobilities*. Milton Park: Routledge, 2013.

Albert de la Bruhèze, Adri A., and Frank Veraart. *Fietsverkeer in Praktijk en Beleid in de Twintigste Eeuw*. Eindhoven: Stichting Historie der Techniek, 1999.

Banister, David. *Inequality in Transport*. Marcham: Alexandrine Press, 2018.

———. "The Sustainable Mobility Paradigm." *Transport Policy* 15, no. 2 (2008): 72–80.

———. *Unsustainable Transport: City Transport in the New Century*. London: Routledge, 2005.

Barber, Benjamin R. *If Mayors Ruled the World: Dysfunctional Nations, Rising Cities*. New Haven: Yale University Press, 2013.

Basiago, A. D. "Economic, Social, and Environmental Sustainability in Development Theory and Urban Planning Practice." *Environmentalist* 19, no. 2 (1998): 145–61.

Berkhout, Peter H. G., et al. "Defining the Rebound Effect." *Energy Policy* 28, nos. 6–7 (2000): 425–32.

Bijsterveld, Karin. *Mechanical Sound: Technology, Culture, and Public Problems of Noise in the Twentieth Century*. Cambridge, MA: MIT Press, 2008.

Brown, Kate. "Gridded Lives: Why Kazakhstan and Montana Are Nearly the Same Place." *American Historical Review* 106, no. 1 (2001): 17–48.

Buiter, Hans. "Constructing Dutch Streets: A Melting Pot of European Technologies." In *Urban Machinery: Inside Modern European Cities*, edited by Mikael Hård and Thomas J. Misa, 141–62. Cambridge, MA: MIT Press, 2008.

Cresswell, Tim. "Towards a Politics of Mobility." *Environment and Planning D: Society and Space* 28 (2010): 17–31.

Cronon, William. *Nature's Metropolis: Chicago and the Great West*. New York: W.W. Norton, 1991.

Dienel, Hans-Liudger, and Helmuth Trischler, eds. *Geschichte Der Zukunft Des Verkehrs: Verkehrskonzepte von Der Frühen Neuzeit Bis Zum 21. Jahrhundert*. Frankfurt am Main: Campus, 1997.

Dimitriou, Harry T., and Ralph Albert Gakenheimer. *Urban Transport in the Developing World: A Handbook of Policy and Practice*. Cheltenham: Edward Elgar, 2011.

Divall, Colin. "Mobilizing the History of Technology." *Technology and Culture* 51, no. 4 (2010) 938–60.

——. "Transport History, the Usable Past and the Future of Mobility." In *Mobilities: New Perspectives on Transport and Society*, edited by Margret Grieco and John Urry, 305–19. Farnham: Routledge, 2011.

Divall, Colin, Julian Hine, and Colin G. Pooley. *Transport Policy: Learning Lessons from History*. Burlington, VT: Ashgate Publishing Company, 2016.

Divall, Colin, and George Revill. "Cultures of Transport: Representation, Practice and Technology." *Journal of Transport History* 26, no. 1 (2005) 99–111.

Edwards, Paul. *A Vast Machine: Computer Models, Climate Data, and the Politics of Global Warming*. Cambridge, MA: MIT Press, 2010.

Ellis, Cliff. "Lewis Mumford and Norman Bel Geddes: The Highway, the City and the Future." *Planning Perspectives* 20, no. 1 (2005): 51–68.

Emanuel, Martin. "Constructing the Cyclist: Ideology and Representations in Urban Traffic Planning in Stockholm, 1930–70." *Journal of Transport History* 33 (2011): 67–91.

——. "Monuments of Unsustainability: Planning, Path Dependence and Cycling in Stockholm." In *Cycling and Recycling: Histories of Sustainable Practices*, edited by Ruth Oldenziel and Helmuth Trischler, 101–21. New York: Berghahn Books, 2015.

European Commission, "Urban Mobility," https://ec.europa.eu/transport/themes/urban/urban_mobility_en (accessed 25 November 2019).

Ewen, Shane. *What Is Urban History?* Cambridge: Polity, 2016.

Geels, Frank W. "A Socio-Technical Analysis of Low-Carbon Transitions: Introducing the Multi-Level Perspective into Transport Studies." *Journal of Transport Geography* 24 (2012): 471–82.

Geels, Frank W., René Kemp, Geoff Dudley, and Glenn Lyons, eds. *Automobility in Transition? A Socio-Technical Analysis of Sustainable Transport*. New York: Routledge, 2012.

Grober, Ulrich. "Von Freiberg nach Rio—Carlowitz und des Begriffs "Nachhaltigkeit."" In *Die Erfindung der Nachhaltigkeit. Leben, Werk und Wirkung des Hans Carl von Carlowitz*, 13–30. Munich: Sächsische Hans Carl von Carlowitz-Gesellschaft, 2013.

Guldi, Jo, and David Armitage. *The History Manifesto*. Cambridge: Cambridge University Press, 2014.

Holden, Erling, Kristin Linnerud, and David Banister. "Sustainable Passenger Transport: Back to Brundtland." *Transportation Research Part A: Policy and Practice* 54 (2013): 67–77.

Hommels, Anique. *Unbuilding Cities: Obduracy in Urban Socio-Technical Change*. Cambridge, MA: MIT Press, 2005.

Hughes, Thomas P. *Networks of Power: Electrification in Western Society, 1880–1930*. Baltimore: Johns Hopkins University Press, 1983.

IPCC, *Climate Change 2014: Synthesis Report*. Geneva, 2015.

Jeekel, Hans. *Inclusive Transport: Fighting Involuntary Transport Disadvantages*. London: Elsevier, 2018.

Kaiser, Wolfram, and Johan W. Schot. *Writing the Rules for Europe: Experts, Cartels, International Organizations*. Houndmills: Palgrave Macmillan, 2014.

Kingsley, Dennis, and John Urry. *After the Car*. Cambridge: Polity Press, 2009.

Klemek, Christopher. *The Transatlantic Collapse of Urban Renewal: Postwar Urbanism from New York to Berlin*. Chicago: University of Chicago Press, 2011.

Koselleck, Reinhart. *Futures Past: On the Semantics of Historical Time*. Cambridge, MA: MIT Press, 1985.

Kröger, Fabian. "Automated Driving in Its Social, Historical and Cultural Contexts." In *Autonomous Driving*, edited by Markus Maurer et al., 41–68. Berlin: Springer, 2016.

Larson, Scott. *"Building Like Moses with Jacobs in Mind": Contemporary Planning in New York City*. Philadelphia: Temple University Press, 2013.

Lintsen, Harry, Frank Veraart, Jan-Pieter Smits, and John Grin. *De Kwetsbare Welvaart van Nederland*. Amsterdam: Prometheus, 2018.

López Galviz, Carlos. *Cities, Railways, Modernities: London, Paris and the Nineteenth Century*. New York: Routledge, 2019.

Low, Nicholas, and Brendan Gleeson. *Making Urban Transport Sustainable*. Basingstoke: Palgrave Macmillan, 2002.

Lundin, Per. *Bilsamhället: Ideologi, expertis och regelskapande i efterkrigstidens Sverige*. Stockholm: Stockholmia, 2008.

Mahoney, James. "Path Dependence in Historical Sociology." *Theory and Society* 29, no. 4 (2000): 507–48.

Marletto, Gerardo. "Car and the City: Socio-Technical Transition Pathways to 2030." *Technological Forecasting and Social Change* 87 (2014): 164–78.

Martens, Karel. *Transport Justice: Designing Fair Transportation Systems*. London: Routledge, 2016.

McShane, Clay, and Joel Tarr. *The Horse in the City: Living Machines in the Nineteenth Century*. Baltimore: JHU Press, 2007.

McShane, Clay. "Transforming the Use of Urban Space: A Look at the Revolution in Street Pavements, 1880–1924." *Journal of Urban History* 5, no. 3 (1979): 279–307.

Mom, Gijs. "The Crisis of Transport History: A Critique, and a Vista." *Mobility in History* 6, no. 1 (2015): 7–19.

Moriarty, Patrick, and Damon Honnery. "Low-Mobility: The Future of Transport." *Futures* 40, no. 10 (2008): 865–72.

Newman, Peter, and Jeffrey R. Kenworthy. *Sustainability and Cities: Overcoming Automobile Dependence*. Washington, DC: Island Press, 1999.

Norton, Peter D. *Fighting Traffic: The Dawn of the Motor Age in the American City*. Cambridge, MA: MIT Press, 2011.

———. "Street Rivals: Jaywalking and the Invention of the Motor Age Street." *Technology and Culture* 48, no. 2 (2007): 331–59.

Oldenziel, Ruth. "Accounting Tricks: How Pedestrians & Cyclists Were Thrown under the Bus, 1910s–1940s." Presentation T2M Philadelphia, 25 September 2014.

Oldenziel, Ruth, Martin Emanuel, A. A Albert de la Bruhèze, and F. C. A Veraart, eds. *Cycling Cities, the European Experience: Hundred Years of Policy and Practice*. Eindhoven: Foundation for the History of Technology, 2016.

Oldenziel, Ruth, and Mikael Hård. *Consumers, Tinkerers, Rebels: The People Who Shaped Europe*. Houndmills: Palgrave Macmillan, 2013.

Oldenziel, Ruth, and Helmut Trischler, eds. *Cycling and Recycling: Histories of Sustainable Practices*. New York: Berghahn Books, 2015.

Ortolano, Guy. "Planning the Urban Future in 1960s Britain." *Historical Journal* 54, no. 2 (2011): 477–507.

Pfister, Christian. "The '1950s Syndrome' and the Transition from a Slow-Going to a Rapid Loss of Global Sustainability." In *Turning Points in Environmental History*, edited by Frank Uekötter, 90–117. Pittsburgh: University of Pittsburgh Press, 2010.

Pflieger, Geraldine, et al. "How Does Urban Public Transport Change Cities? Correlations between Past and Present Transport and Urban Planning Policies." *Urban Studies* 46, no. 7 (2009): 1421–37

Pooley, Colin G. "Landscapes without the Car: A Counterfactual Historical Geography of Twentieth-Century Britain." *Journal of Historical Geography* 36, no. 3 (2010): 266–75.

Radermacher, Franz Josef. "Die Ressourcen der Erde setzen uns Grenzen—vom sächsischen Bergmann Hans Carl von Carlowitz 1713 bis zum neuen Report an den Club of Rome 2052." In *Die Erfindung der Nachhaltigkeit: Leben, Werk und Wirkung des Hans Carl von Carlowitz*, 141–56. Munich: Sächsische Carlowitz-Gesellschaft, 2013.

Rees, William E. "Ecological Footprints and Appropriated Carrying Capacity: What Urban Economics Leaves Out." *Environment and Urbanization* 4, no. 2 (1992): 121–30.

Saunier, Pierre-Yves. "Taking Up the Bet on Connections: A Municipal Contribution." *Contemporary European History* 11, no. 4 (2002): 507–27.

Scott, James C. *Seeing Like a State: How Certain Schemes to Improve the Human Condition Have Failed*. New Haven: Yale University Press, 1998.

Sheller, Mimi. *Mobility Justice: The Politics of Movement in an Age of Extremes*. London: Verso, 2018.

Shove, Elizabeth. "The Shadowy Side of Innovation: Unmaking and Sustainability." *Technology Analysis & Strategic Management* 24, no. 4 (2012): 363–75.

Tarr, Joel Arthur. *The Search for the Ultimate Sink: Urban Pollution in Historical Perspective*. University of Akron Press, 1996.

Trischler, Helmuth, and Martin Kohlrausch. *Building Europe on Expertise: Innovators, Organizers, Networkers*. Houndmills: Palgrave Macmillan, 2014.

Turvey, Ralph. "Horse Traction in Victorian London." *Journal of Transport History* 26, no. 2 (2005): 38–59.

UN-HABITAT. *State of the World's Cities 2010/11: Cities for All: Bridging the Urban Divide*. London: Earthscan, 2008.

United Nations, "About the Sustainable Development Goals," http://www.un.org/sustainabledevelopment/sustainable-development-goals/ (accessed 25 November 2019).

Urry, John. "The 'System' of Automobility." *Theory, Culture & Society* 21, no. 4–5 (2004): 25–39.

Van Lente, Harro. *Promising Technology: The Dynamics of Expectations in Technological Developments*. Enschede: Universiteit Twente, 1993.

Van Lente, Harro, and Arie Rip. "Expectations in Technological Developments: An Example of Prospective Structures to Be Filled In by Agency." In *Getting New Tech-*

*nologies Together*, edited by Cornelis Disco and Bart van der Meulen, 195–220. Berlin: Walter de Gruyter, 1998.

Vasconcellos, Eduardo Alcântara. *Urban Transport, Environment and Equity: The Case for Developing Countries*. London: Earthscan, 2001.

Von Carlowitz, Carl. *Sylvicultura oeconomica oder Haußwirthliche Nachricht und Naturmäßige Anweisung zur Wilden Baum-Zucht,* ed. Joachim Hamberger. Munich: Oekom Verlag, 2013 [1713].

Walks, Alan. *The Urban Political Economy and Ecology of Automobility: Driving Cities, Driving Inequality, Driving Politics*. London: Routledge, 2015.

Williams, Katie. *Spatial Planning, Urban Form and Sustainable Transport*. Aldershot: Ashgate, 2005.

Zylstra, Geoff D. "Whiteness, Freedom, and Technology: The Racial Struggle over Philadelphia's Streetcars, 1859–1867." *Technology and Culture* 52, no. 4 (2011): 678–702.

# SECTION I

⌒⌒

# Selling Unsustainable Urban Mobility

Today urban automobility is considered unsustainable. How did urban automobility come into being? The section "Selling Unsustainable Urban Mobility" presents three chapters that show that cars were never solely conceived as an inevitable development, nor as inherently superior to other mobility modes. They were contested from the start. The authors argue that urban automobility only came about because a coalition of social actors and institutions pushed the car as the most desirable future—even creating its own version of history to suggest that the future would be an inevitable outcome of the past.

Ruth Oldenziel, Pieter van Wesemael, and M. Luísa Sousa trace how transnational experts such as urban planners, city administrators, and road engineers first considered the city accessible to all forms of traffic. Then in the 1920s, when cars were still a rare phenomenon, these expert groups changed course: their urban plans prioritized suburban car drivers commuting to the city over working-class residents. Only in the 1970s did they heed the worldwide critique to bring back the walkable, cyclable, and public transit city. Next, Peter Norton shows how motordom—the U.S. roadbuilding, automobile, and oil lobby—promoted the notion that Americans had a natural "love affair" with the car. The narrative masked the many conflicts between car drivers and pedestrians on the streets. Colin Divall describes two rival mobility systems in British urban regions competing to become the most modern system for the future: a mobility modernity based on cars or based on trains. Local policymakers and activists fought for railroad modernism, but lost out to the car lobby. The subsequent railroad closures made it difficult to achieve more sustainable mobility.

This section demonstrates just how successfully the car's future was sold. At the same time, the unintended consequences underline the ensuing social and ecological price of success that marginalized the more sustainable modes of mobility.

CHAPTER 1

@

# Designing (Un)Sustainable Urban Mobility from Transnational Settings, 1850–Present

Ruth Oldenziel, M. Luísa Sousa, and Pieter van Wesemael

## Introduction

Debates on smart mobility and sustainable cities abound today, with many eyeing the future of 2050. Visions of future mobility solutions for cities, however, have a long history. For almost two centuries, urban planners, policymakers, and social reformers have contemplated how to design healthy and sustainable cities. Urban mobility was also on their minds when vehicular mobility systems emerged, challenging pedestrianism as the norm. Urban planners, confronted with the sheer numbers of people flocking to the cities in the mid-nineteenth century, sought solutions for the ravages wreaked by rapid urbanization. Their solutions to modernize historic city centers included broad boulevards (economic growth), separate middle- and upper-class neighborhoods (social wellbeing), and parks (ecological health)—all aspects of what we nowadays, in the terms introduced by the Brundtland Report, call economic, social, and ecological sustainability.[1]

These nineteenth-century planning pioneers viewed the city as a body, whose separate parts had to function together in order to form a healthy whole. As basis for their designs, they updated the eighteenth-century metaphor likening the city to a body with traffic as the blood flowing smoothly through it. By the early twentieth century, the new experts in road engineering included private mobility (cars) in their core vision for the city, before colliding, during the 1970s environmental crises, with a movement opposing a car-governed society. Since then, critics have resurrected walking and public transit, and reframed cycling, as the three best mobility options for tomorrow's sustainable cities. In the tradition of the countercultural movement, activists have sought to reinstate the street as a shared space, not a conduit for fast traffic. Their visions for 2050 in some respect hark back to the pre-nineteenth-century traditional city.

In this volume, we have many national and local stories about urban mobility and planning ideas that present similar narratives and chronologies. The simultaneity prompts the question of how such ideas emerged at the same time—and spontaneously—throughout the industrializing world. Over the last two decades, a burgeoning scholarship has explained how the simultaneity resulted from the transnational circulation of ideas that shaped international discussions in the twentieth century.[2] When it comes to urban mobility, though, we have a poor understanding of how ideas circulated transnationally or how they became internationally dominant in many continents.[3] This chapter explores how key international experts formed a vision for the future of urban mobility over two centuries. We focus on city administrators, urban planners, and road engineers in transnational settings.

By bringing together three key organizations for the first time in one analytical frame, we seek to recover how these experts defined urban mobility. We examine three transnational platforms that dealt respectively with urban planning, governance, and mobility infrastructures that thus far have been either ignored or not viewed through the lens of urban mobility: the International Federation of Housing and Planning (IFHP, est. 1913), l'Union Internationale des Villes (UIV, est. 1913), and the Permanent International Association for Road Congresses (PIARC, est. 1909).[4] The three international organizations were founded by a generation of experts engaging in the professionalization of their new disciplines. PIARC and IFHP were particularly influential in shaping the debate and setting standards at international, national, and local levels. In particular, we explore the terms by which actors in the past understood what we now call social, economic, and ecological sustainability. While our chapter sets the stage for this book by focusing on the transnational actors and the international circulation of concepts of urban mobility, other contributions in this volume show how local actors appropriated or rejected such ideas and standards. Our chapter is exploratory rather than exhaustive and should be seen as an invitation for further research to understand the paradigm shifts in thinking about sustainable urban mobility.

## From the Pedestrian to the Vehicular City, 1850s–1910s

In the context of European colonialism and U.S. expansionism, the debates about urban mobility were transatlantic and conducted at the world's fairs. Since the 1850s, European and U.S. urban practitioners, social reformers, and civil engineers met at world's fairs to address the twin forces of industrial capitalism and urbanization before exporting their ideas to their colonies.[5] These world exhibitions served as knowledge exchanges and as microcosms of the modern city and its social challenges.[6]

Urban mobility found a stage at the fairs from the start. The exhibits displayed vehicular urban mobility innovations—ranging from the steam locomotive in 1851, and cycles and tricycles in the 1880s, to automobiles, suspension railways (*schwebebahn*), air balloons, and airships in 1900. Such innovations showcased the mechanization of transport through steam (trains, boats, and tractors) and electrical power (subways, trams, trains, elevators, and lifts). By hosting the fairs, organizing cities were transformed into sites of experimentation with new urban transport systems: omnibus corporations were merged, sightseeing boats (*bateaux-mouches*) were introduced, as well as extensive rail systems (both steam train and subway). In dealing with the millions of visitors, the fairs served as a dress rehearsal for how to cope with the millions moving to the cities. There, urban planners such as Eugene Haussmann (in Paris 1867) and Frederick Law Olmsted (in Chicago 1893) showcased their ideas on how to transform historic cities into modern industrial metropolises and how to deal with the millions of people pouring into cities to earn a living.[7] Nineteenth-century fairs, in other words, functioned as living labs for professionals to experiment with urban mobility concepts.

For the mobility of their times, the urban design practitioners developed two related ideas: a logistical system and a recreational network. Haussmann's logistical infrastructure created an urban network of new streets to facilitate the smooth flow of vehicular traffic. Wide boulevards allowed unobstructed flows of both private (carriages and carts) and public vehicles (trams and subways). This vehicle-based planning also resulted in relegating the urban strollers to their own dedicated domain of sidewalks.[8] Smooth vehicular traffic flows (the city's "blood circulation") symbolized the healthy urban economy of goods and people.[9] In the process, though, their street transformed from a social site into a space of logistical flows and economic transactions.

The second mobility design, introduced by Olmsted in the 1860s and 1870s, was a recreational infrastructure of green networks connecting public parks, parkways, and villa parks to calm people's overstressed nerves by bringing the pastoral (nature) into the city. This ecological infrastructure ("the lungs of the city") served as an antidote to the urban evils for people's health and the environment: English-styled parks mimicked nature, offering healthy activities like walking, riding, and boating in scenic landscapes. In today's terms, this pedestrian-based, green urban mobility had more to do with social wellbeing than ecological sustainability.[10] The urban green became the separate space for socialization and community building, now that the streets had been taken over by mobility machines.

Indeed, strict traffic separation between utilitarian (boulevard) and leisure travel (park) became the norm in modern city making and traffic engineering. French urban planner Eugene Hénard, in particular, envisioned the separation of traffic not only by function (work and leisure), but also by mobility mode. At the Paris exhibition grounds in 1900, Hénard experimented by creating space for (individual) vehicular flows on the street level by pushing the rest of the traffic and electric rails underground. He designed space for the millions of visitors' horse-drawn carriages on ground level. An elevated moving walkway (*trottoir roulant*) offered pedestrians a moving panorama over the exhibition—like a real-time movie. In his 1911 Ville Future studies, Hénard systematized these experiments. His vertical street concept introduced a clear traffic hierarchy: private coaches and pedestrians on street level in full view; public transportation of people and goods underground—out of sight.[11] In addition, Hénard developed ring roads and roundabouts for (horse-drawn) vehicles, and though not the first to do so, he also devised traffic rules to prioritize vehicles and discipline other mobility modes.[12]

Haussmann, Olmsted, and Hénard thus contributed to segregating mobility infrastructures according to function (business, work, living, and leisure), and traffic flows according to mobility mode (from trams and trains to carts and pedestrians). Committed to the idea of traffic being the city's lifeblood, the planners still viewed the street as a social and economic conduit rather than a primary mobility site to solve urban congestion. After all, their design strategy of boulevards and park systems aimed to integrate all aspects of urban wellbeing: economic sustainability by creating space for new downtown businesses and facilitating the new industry-based economy; social sustainability by building better housing and public institutions to accommodate the new middle and upper classes of industrial society; and ecological sustainability by improving sanitation, the environment, and recreation (public parks) to boost residents' mental and physical health.[13] Catering to both middle-class and working-class concerns, the planners helped to make modern cities more integrated and sustainable places to live, work, play, and travel.

Although the world exhibitions had been a fertile ground for exchanging transnational knowledge on the challenges facing cities, including

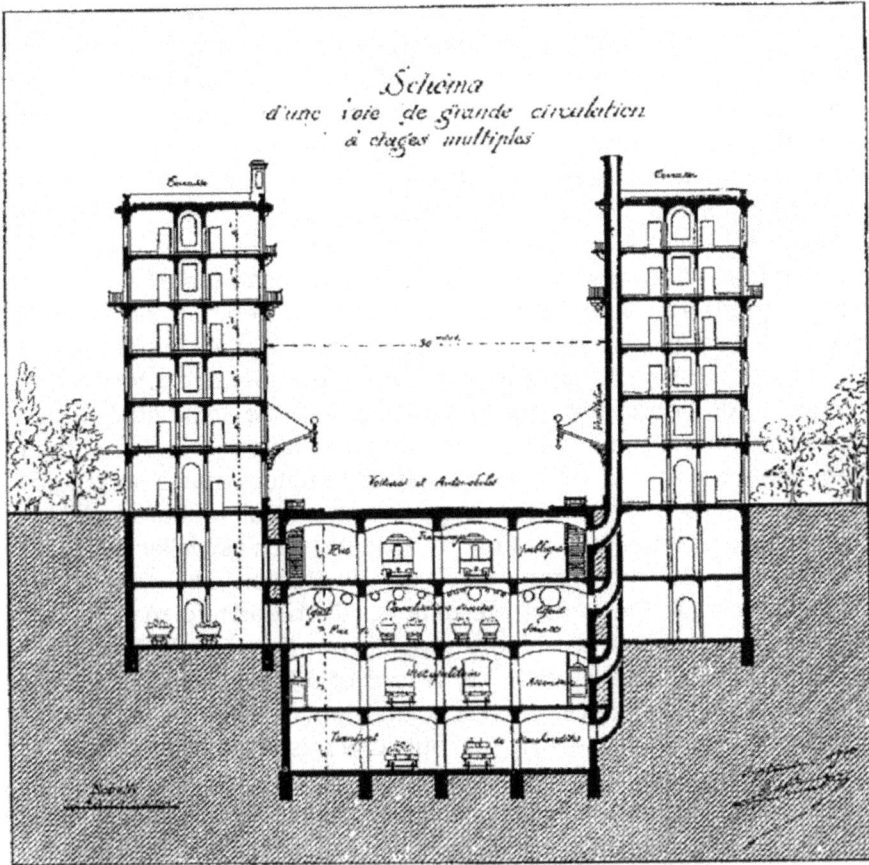

**Figure 1.1.** Eugene Hénard's 1911 street design for the future envisioned a vertical street for segregated urban mobilities with pedestrians and (motorized) coaches on street level, and public transit and transportation of goods underground.

Credit: *Rue future* (Road of the future). Drawing by Eugène Alfred Hénard (1849–1923), published in Eugéne Hènard, "The Cities of the Future," *American City*, January 1911. Work in public domain.

the mobility of people and goods, by the 1910s, the pioneers felt their exchanges called for more permanent—and specialized—international associations.[14] The road engineers founded the Permanent International Association for Road Congresses (PIARC) in 1909. The urban planners established the International Federation of Housing and Planning (IFHP) in 1913.[15] And local city administrators formed l'Union Internationale des Villes (UIV), also in 1913.

From then on, the specialist organizations embedded the transnational exchange of ideas in national institutions and practices. IFHP's urban planners, for example, were increasingly employed in the young planning institutions of the welfare state emerging on both sides of the Atlantic.[16] As a result, their discussions were highly influential in shaping the local region and modern city.[17] PIARC's transnational discussions were also well embedded in the nation-state. Its triennial congresses attracted over a thousand leading engineers working for the state and political elites in all five continents, together with travel and car entrepreneurs looking to create a niche for the new technology: upper-class automobile and touring clubs.[18] PIARC was well connected to high society from the very start. Kings and presidents hosted its congresses before these events started being used as political venues in the hands of Mussolini (1926) and Goebbels (1934). A fair number of aristocrats held leading PIARC positions. UIV, by contrast, despite originating from a vibrant urban international movement, became increasingly marginalized. The international discussions shifted to nation-states and regions instead of cities, and focused on the street as conduit for automobility at the expense of other forms of urban mobility, such as walking.

As urban-based organizations, UIV and IFHP belonged to what Pierre-Yves Saunier calls the "Urban Internationale," a broad reform movement that focused on cities, planning, and social housing.[19] At IFHP, opposing factions hashed out their differing visions of urban planning.[20] By contrast, PIARC was aligned to what scholars identified as the infrastructure state, where civil engineering (or "public works") departments provide society with basic communications, energy, and mobility infrastructures as a public good to foster economic growth for the nation.[21] Nineteenth-century practitioners sought to incorporate economic, social, and ecological aspects of urban sustainability in an integrated vision of the future. The establishment of specialized international organizations in the twentieth century ultimately fragmented that vision.

As we will discuss in the next section, the planners' ideas of separating traffic with dedicated infrastructures for specific road users came to define the street in the twentieth century. The new experts formed specialized knowledge domains of urban planning, urban management, and traffic engineering. Specialization sparked on the one hand a fierce battle between public transit and urban automobility over precious urban public space, and on the other hand the sidelining of pedestrians and cyclists. The horizontal and vertical traffic separation, prioritizing automobility over public transit, pedestrianism, and cycling, also had class and gender implications. Gone was the nineteenth-century vision of integrated boulevards and parks as part of an organic whole, and would not be reinstated until the 1960s. World War I was a watershed moment in the paradigmatic shift.

## Car-Centered City Plans Sideline Nonmotorized Urbanites, 1920s–1970s

Cities had been the drivers of global industrial capitalism in the nineteenth century. After World War I, nation-states took over many of their functions. The collapse of three (Habsburg, Russian, and Ottoman) empires, the suppression of revolutionary movements in many industrializing cities in the wake of the Soviet October Revolution, and the Versailles Treaty reinforced nation-states over empires and cities. Mobility—that is, road mobility—was appropriated as its exclusive domain at an international forum highlighting the nation-state: Paris-based PIARC (1909). Already at PIARC's second congress (Brussels, 1910), the "road problem" was being defined as a "car problem." The organization relegated "other" road users, like horse riders or cyclists, to their own "paths," by technically adapting the road infrastructure to cars.[22] Although PIARC's third congress (London, 1913) discussed the "problem of [road] circulation" from an urban perspective, cities were seen more than anything as obstacles that needed to be bypassed.[23]

PIARC, being exclusively dedicated to mobility, perfectly represented the power shift from the city to nation-state infrastructure. As the organization of roadbuilders, road engineers, and car enthusiasts, PIARC was transnational in orientation, organized nationally, and suburban based. The road engineering community within PIARC—unlike IFHP and UIV— had a profoundly anti-urban outlook. Although PIARC did create subcommittees working on urban traffic, its design principles marginalized pedestrians and cyclists in cities through legal, statistical, financial, and infrastructural means. The institutionalization of the "automobile system" in the interwar period and transnational debates sidelined both cities and nonmotorized road users.

PIARC's proposals for the car-governed future—hammered out in minute detail—before being realized after World War II, were not a forgone conclusion. They were still contested in the interwar period. Before World War I, Belgium's minister of public works and promoter of tramways Auguste Delbeke, as PIARC host, articulated the newly founded organization's grand mission: how the road-building community could make twentieth-century roads fit for old and new traffic "at a low cost." There was an even more pressing issue. Delbeke urged his colleagues to create roads that would be accessible for all—a vision of the street as what we today call a shared space. "You have not only to think of the carriage, the cycle, the motor cycle, the motor car, the electric tramway, the vicinal light railway, you have to think—I implore you—of the dweller of the street and the poor pedestrian."[24] Three years later, PIARC's British host John Burns, a passionate cycling socialist for the London working-class district of Battersea and president of the local governing board, made a similar appeal. Pedestrians needed to be included when developing modern roads. The ultimate goal was to foster a community of road travelers with equal rights and respect for others.[25]

The early calls for equal rights on the road were soon ignored after World War I, however. Instead, PIARC members articulated a vision for automobility. To make that future happen, pedestrians—and cyclists—were excluded by design through a series of technical and highly political interventions throughout the 1920s. The engineers prepared for urban automobility by pushing tram systems underground and lobbying for metro systems and busses, similar to Hénard's proposals. Twentieth-century roads were now designed for a car-dominated future rather than for the pressing needs of growing numbers of pedestrians, cyclists, busses, trams, trucks, handcarts, and the like.[26] These visions of individual motorized mobility came about in spite of the overwhelming—and growing—urban majority of pedestrians, cyclists, and people using public transit over the years. Working in an international setting, the engineers' design principles marginalized and delegitimized pedestrians, cyclists, and handcart drivers as road users. Motorists formed only a tiny fraction of all traffic for many decades. Nevertheless, the car-oriented principles were hammered out and finally set in stone through international standardization procedures and statistical norms after the 1950s. The principles no longer saw the street as a shared space, but were based on separating modalities and facilitating the speed of motorized vehicles.

At the time, the automotive advocates saw themselves as the underdog, promoting the new mobility technology in a world where the railroad dominated in terms of legal frameworks, standardization procedures, and public funds. The contest between the automotive and railroad interests would become an epic struggle in the twentieth century, at least until the 1960s.[27] Engineers, supported by the newly expanded state bureaucracies for transport, prepared solid, labor-intensive, and research-based reports. Their outlining of road problems led to solutions for what social scientists figuratively describe as "path dependency"—a series of decisions becoming entrenched in artifacts and institutions that were difficult to change.[28]

PIARC may not have enforced rules or "worked as a *transfer machine, or synchronizer* of local best practices," but from the viewpoint of public transit interests, pedestrians, and cyclists, the organization was extraordinarily effective in implementing its vision.[29] In the interwar period, PIARC designed a car-oriented blueprint for what became an infrastruc-

**Figure 1.2.** Traffic separation—each type of vehicle needing its own dedicated lane based on speed differences—was lampooned by the British cyclists' union cartoon in 1934 as an untenable design principle.

Credit: Cartoon from *Northampton Chronicle and Echo*, reprinted in *CTC Gazette*, April 1935. Artist unknown.

tural reality in many countries after World War II, based on marginalizing public transit, pedestrians, and cyclists.[30] PIARC rapidly functioned as a well-oiled machine—part of the burgeoning phenomenon of cross-border organizations forming a technocratic internationalism, whereby engineers and scientists positioned themselves as experts, convinced they were better equipped to offer solutions than politicians caught in the wheels of power.[31] Over the twentieth century, these internationally oriented engineers, despite working in highly charged democratic, communist, fascist, and Nazi regimes, developed a remarkably unified set of engineering principles. For one, their technical terms of reference were guided by narrow class concerns.[32] Early on, PIARC adopted the mandate to build dedicated national automotive highways—independent of the existing multifunctional road systems—that excluded other modes of mobility by design.[33] PIARC's discussions about a car-governed future were well underway by 1926. These reached not only UIV city administrator circles but also IFHP urban planners.[34]

In the post-Versailles era, the buildup of nation-states through infrastructures left cities little room to maneuver. On the transnational stage, urban administrators felt the pressure when they tried to organize internationally. New supranational bodies such as the League of Nations considered cities as threats to national sovereignty. Urban administrators established their own international professional organization as part of the "Urban Internationale" movement to promote international socialism. They offered a platform to exchange the best ways to manage socially and economically sustainable cities, believing the city represented the source of good governance and wellbeing.[35] In the words of their historians, "cities, rather than nations, were promoters of global peace and stability."[36] Peace would be achieved by developing "universal best municipal practices" supported by core knowledge shared through transnational circulation. International cooperation was deemed essential.[37] Many UIV founders had deep ties to socialist activism, but soon switched their utopian socialist pedigree to a "technocratic internationalism" as a defense against the political polarization rampant in the wake of World War I.[38]

After the war, UIV members exchanged administrative knowledge, experiences, and data in increasingly pragmatic terms, believing that science and technology could solve problems the cities shared, but they faced increasing marginalization. In 1927, for example, League of Nations committees prevented UIV city administrators from joining national and transnational coalitions. While granting UIV a place on its Permanent Committee of Road Traffic, the League excluded the organization from the Economic Consultative Council, feeling that, as an intergovernmental organization, the League could not give local authorities a legitimacy that might damage the sovereignty of nation-states.[39] State representatives and supranational organizations presented traffic regulations "as economic and political issues that could not be handled by a new association like UIV," historians Bernadin and Gardon argue; the League dismissed UIV as the right organization to regulate automobile traffic or discuss the transnational harmonization of traffic signs.[40] Nationalist dictatorships such as Fascist Italy (1922), Nazi Germany (1933), or Francoist Spain (1939) also had little patience with urban governance.[41] These nation-state biases reflect how mobility issues were framed as national and not urban-specific challenges.

The UIV organization, moreover, barely managed to develop its own set of ideas about people's mobility in the city.[42] It created the Commission for Urban Circulation in July 1927, led by G. De Schulthess, director of the Swiss Union of Local Authorities, who wrote on urban traffic rules and signals, initiated research on traffic lights, and led the European Conference on Road Traffic in 1931.[43] The organization examined how to discipline people's traffic behavior on the street through signals and regulations—issues also discussed by the League's technical committees.[44] More fundamentally, UIV—perhaps unintentionally—participated in sidelining nonmotorized road users in step with the emerging global car-oriented discourse and despite its socialist origins. UIV defined city street problems as car issues. Its focus shifted to managing private motorized mobility away from public transit, marginalizing pedestrians and ignoring cyclists.

We see a similar shift with urban planners. While they had led the way in the nineteenth century, urban planners became followers rather than pioneers in the area of mobility during the twentieth century. Ebenezer Howard, founder of the British Garden City Association, dominated the first IFHP conferences along with his disciples.[45] Originally, Howard firmly embedded his Garden City in rail mobility and public transit. Distances in his Garden City (1902) schemes—with a length of one kilometer between a city's circumference and its historical center—were bridged by canals and urban trains. Connecting radial boulevards (Haussmann) and park networks (Olmsted) with ring roads (Hénard), Howard introduced the novelty of functional zoning. Dedicated urban mobility networks strictly separated industrial from residential mobility, regional from inner-city travel, and "fast" from "slow" traffic.[46]

By the 1920s, the new generation of IFHP urban planners were no longer just focused on the mechanization of public transit, but on private mobility: cars as vehicles for commuting and doing business rather than for touring the countryside. They refocused the debates from mod-

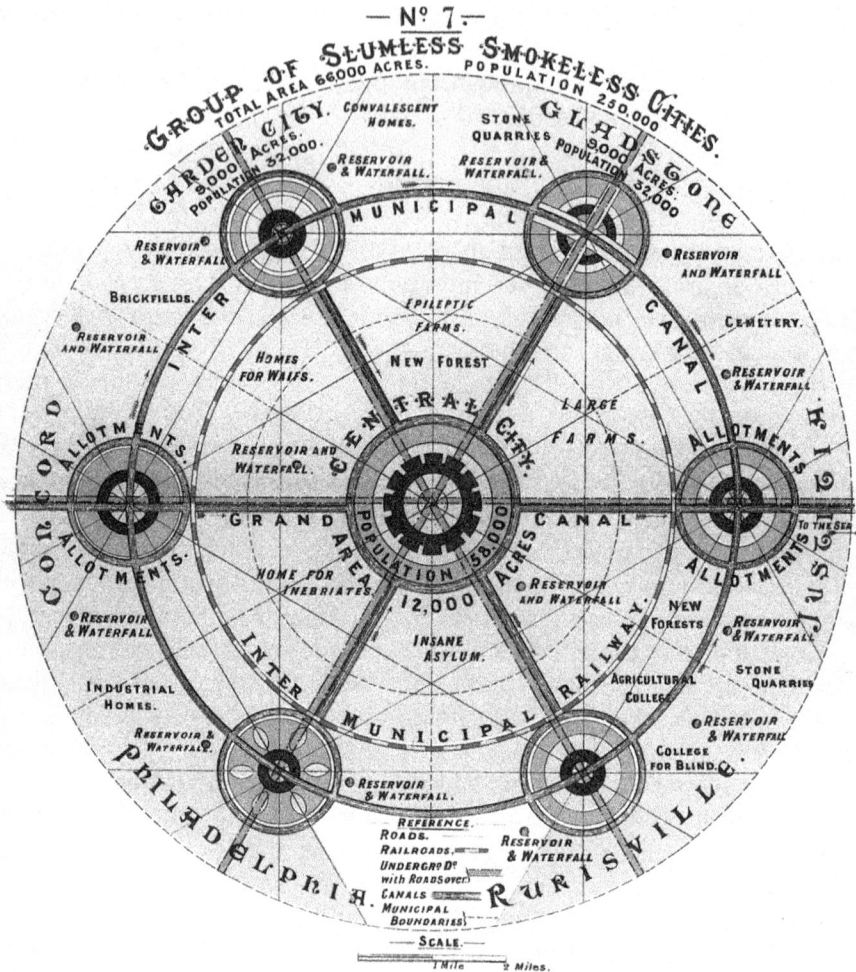

**Figure 1.3.** Ebenezer Howard's garden city design of 1902 based on rail and canal infrastructures.

Credit: Ebenezer Howard, *To-morrow: A Peaceful Path to Real Reform* (London: Swan Sonnenschein & Co., Ltd., 1898). Work in public domain.

ernizing historical cities—which the garden city adepts had considered beyond rescue—to the regional planning of satellite town schemes.[47] At their 1924 conference, IFHP urban planners began to adapt the traditional Garden City schemes to automobility's impact on urban transit and regional planning. Garden City pioneer Raymond Unwin, for instance, began distinguishing thoroughfares and residential streets.[48] Patrick Abercrombie warned that mass automobility, combined with cheap land prices outside the city, would accelerate urban sprawl, like an oil spill infiltrating the region. Based on his work in Florida, John Nolan was alarmed at how Henry Ford's success in creating automobility had turned the suburban ribbon development along the tram rails into urban sprawl, destroying historical villages and landscapes, creating commuter congestion, and shifting economic production away from downtown to the countryside. His solution: decentralize by planning autonomous satellite towns instead of creating business centers connected to bedroom communities by motorways.[49]

The Americans Clarence Stein and Henri Wright, by contrast, advocated "the garden-city of the motor-age," culminating in their design for Radburn, New York.[50] As prominent members of Lewis Mumford's Regional Planning Association of America, they adapted the garden city to the motor age and commuting lifestyle in gendered ways. Neighborhoods—or superblocks with a few hundred households—were built around a green park system close to commercial and social community services. Such neighborhoods were encircled by a ring road, on which car-bound breadwinners (men) commuted from their suburban home to their downtown job. Within the neighborhood, leisure-oriented mobility (walking, cycling, playing, and sport) and a communal green combined with community services would enhance social ties among the new town's residents. Stein and Wright's ring roads—combined with bans on motorized through-traffic and cul-de-sacs for local residents—served to protect the neighborhoods, where women could shop within walking distance, and kids could play and cycle in the streets. The neighborhood design aimed to improve the local economy and people's lives—both their personal and social health—and in modern parlance, the ecological sustainability of the city.

IFHP planners Fritz Schumacher and Thomas Adams fiercely opposed building satellite towns at the expense of historic cities and focused instead on modernizing existing city centers. Each built their ideas on a different mobility system: Schumacher advanced public transit by adapting Howard's scheme, introducing the "finger" concept: the city would extend along public transit lines ("fingers") alternated by green spaces ("lobes") that functioned as the city's "lungs" in between.[51] In Amsterdam, the Van Eesteren group designed a similar plan. Uniquely, its 1934 urban extension plan was partially based on bicycle mobility for cycling distances to the center rather than by public transit or car—a practical design solution given that most workers at that time commuted by bicycle in industrial cities. No other planner applied this mobility scheme.[52]

By contrast, Adams based his revitalization for city centers on cars. The inner city would be modernized by separating work, living, and leisure functions (zoning) and by making the city compact with high-rises (densification). To facilitate business development and accessibility for cars downtown, he pushed other modes underground or upwards. Through the vertical organization of the street, first introduced by Hénard, the engineering profession sought to facilitate automobility. The principle pushed pedestrians and public transit under or above the street.[53]

In spatial terms, in other words, the urban planning discipline developed two mobility paths. On the one hand, for regions, the New Town Movement created separate—and gendered—traffic infrastructures by spreading them over the park landscape. The garden city and neighborhood building schemes separated automobilism (men) outside, and pedestrianism (women and children) inside the new residential areas. On the other hand, for existing cities, these planning movements created central business districts (CBD) combined with urban highways, and prioritized cars by pushing traffic underground or elevating it, thus combining Haussmann's boulevard and Hénard's vertical street. American planner Robert Moses tested both at the New York world's fairs of 1939 and 1964: he reorganized the New York metropolitan region with car parkways, linking suburban residential areas with multilevel downtown business districts in Manhattan through elevated highways, parking lots, mega-malls, and business high-rises around Rockefeller Plaza.[54]

As we have seen, car-oriented planning originated neither from UIV nor IFHP, but from PIARC's international community of road engineers. Between the 1920s and the 1960s, PIARC helped build a transnational mobility paradigm for a car-governed future through the lens of the nation-state. It is important to note that while we often associate car-based suburbanization, central business development, mass-scale automobility, and highways with a typical American tradition, in fact, the international PIARC, IFHP, and UIV discussions about these ideas were transatlantic—at least in the interwar period.[55] When the United States became a global superpower and leading actor in rebuilding Europe after World War II, however, the dynamics and the debates shifted. Never a one-way process of knowledge transfer from the United States to Europe, Americanization involved a complexity of engagement, and appropriation as well as rejection.

Nevertheless, U.S. hegemony was responsible for exporting automobilism to the Global North, reinforced by the emergence of the welfare state.[56] In the postwar era, U.S. planners led the discussions on automobility, traffic engineering, and regional planning. In 1948, American and British road construction and automobile industries established the International Road Federation (IRF) in Washington, D.C., as a commercial alternative to the French-based PIARC, whose engineers were mostly state employees. IRF was involved in Europe's postwar road-building efforts for at least two decades. The French and American organizations, despite their competition, agreed on the building blocks for a postwar car-governed society.[57] PIARC and IRF, supported by the U.S. Marshall Aid programs and the Ford Foundation, offered the building blocks for Europe's efforts to reconstruct destroyed inner cities and later in developing countries.[58]

Local postwar traffic circulation plans were exclusively based on car flows. Yale University's Traffic Engineering program was particularly influential in spreading the car-traffic model worldwide, from Sweden to South Africa.[59] Traffic engineers used forecasting models that no longer counted the throngs of cyclists, for example, simply ignoring them as modes of the past about to die out despite their dominance. They planned them out of existence—and ignored pedestrians as a matter of course. PIARC's Rio de Janeiro congress in 1959—the first time outside the transatlantic world of Europe and the United States—aptly summarized the ever car-oriented paradigm. Traffic had to be separated to allow cars to flow effortlessly through the countryside, reach the city by ring or access roads, and park near the center. Concerning accidents, cars were not seen as dangerous. City cyclists, by contrast, were considered a hazard because they swarmed into cities (Copenhagen), were prone to accidents (France), and reduced the speed of cars (United Kingdom). Separate infrastructures were deemed too expensive unless cyclists outnumbered cars. Few engineers declared their opposition, except for two lone voices: the Brazilian delegate, amazed that there were no public transit discussions, and one Dutch delegate advocating traffic calming, walking, and parking fees, who was horrified that traffic fatalities were presented as an economic cost and benefit analysis.[60] These voices were drowned out by the paradigm considering all engineering problems—and their solutions—in terms of economic growth. And cars were to be the engines of economic growth.

In the postwar period, urban-based UIV followed suit.[61] Its 1949 "Prevention of Road Accidents" debates coincided with the UN Conference on Road and Motor Transport held the same year, where the Convention on Road Traffic and a new Protocol on Road Signs and Signals were agreed on, covering cars almost exclusively.[62] UIV debated how to control and educate nonmotorized road users such as pedestrians (particularly children) and cyclists in order to facilitate automobility, establish standard reporting on road accident statistics, and calculate the economic costs of road accidents for local communities.[63] In the 1950s, the questionnaire to help national members write their reports on traffic congestion presented the rise of urban automobility as inevitable and the compact city as problematic for cars: it would cause "heavy peak hour traffic."[64]

Until the 1960s, IFHP and PIARC members were the key professionals in shaping the welfare state and cities. UIV continued to seek legitimacy as local authorities in international circles of supranational bodies by collaborating with UNESCO (1947) and the UN Economic and Social Council (1949), when the competition became even tougher than before. American organizations such as the Ford Foundation helped fund new international associations, for example, the Council of European Municipalities (Geneva, 1951), which usurped UIV's membership and promoted "European" unity in anti-communist terms.[65] Early on, the international UIV shifted its focus to decolonized Asian and African countries, thus increasing non-Western membership.[66] IFHP and PIARC would follow suit in the 1970s, turning toward decolonized countries when confronted with fierce opposition from activists on American and European city streets.

### Urban Rebellion: The 1960s Walkable, Bikeable, and Public-Transit City

In the late 1960s, a countermovement in the Global North rebelled against the car-oriented urbanism that built downtown businesses districts combined with suburban bedroom communities linked by urban highways. City-based critics rallied against the destruction of historical town and natural landscapes, social neighborhood life and economy, and the environment.[67] They called for social inclusion. The protest against car-oriented planning famously kicked off with a showdown between urban planners Robert Moses and Jane Jacobs in New York's Greenwich Village in 1962. Jacobs criticized Moses's urban highways as examples of "the failure of town planning"—the subtitle of her bestselling book *Life and Death of Great American Cities*.[68] "Vehicularization" of the public domain had killed the local streets and green networks that were vital for socializing, economic transactions, and quality of life. Jacobs's condemnation of urban highways echoed throughout the globe: from Toronto, Halifax, Paris, Toulon, Amsterdam, and Munich, to San Francisco, Sydney, and Melbourne—particularly in low-income neighborhoods that bore the brunt of the grandiose plans. The critics resurrected a vision of the street as a social space (social and economic sustainability) and introduced the bicycle as their new symbol of sustainable urban mobility (ecological sustainability).[69] The U.K. government's Buchanan Report, *Traffic in Towns* (1963), translated the critique into planning terms, introducing concepts such as "traffic integration" (the street as a shared space) and "traffic calming," while holding on to automobility in cities.[70] The planning organizations IFHP, PIARC, and UIV, however, were at a loss when confronted by the protests.

While Colin Buchanan, a road engineer and an architect, already incorporated the emerging critique in *Traffic in Towns*, most in traffic engineering and roadbuilding communities ignored the rising protest to the omnipresence of the car in the city. In their PIARC congresses, the engineers dealt extensively with noise and with air pollution in tunnels, when confronted with the deadly levels of fumes and toxic gases, seeking solutions through ventilation systems already in the 1959 congress. Yet, they considered the issue a technical problem, not an ecological challenge.[71] Only in 1971—a year before the watershed UN conference on the Human Environment in Stockholm—do we see the first cracks appearing in the car-dominated paradigm, when PIARC met behind the Iron Curtain in Prague to interact with socialist-oriented ideas of mobility: public transit was on the agenda for the first time.[72]

In 1971, feeling the heat from social activists, the engineers specifically addressed "public attitudes" and the "pollution factor and effect on planning."[73] Throughout the 1970s, moreover, policymakers faced public outcry over skyrocketing fatal traffic accidents. For the first time, the car was described as an inherent danger for urbanites. General reporter André Saccsyn, a young civil engineer from the University of Brussels, focused on people's demand for a better quality of life. In the PIARC proceedings we find the first endorsement of Jacob's critique of unsustainable urban automobility, by Sune Lindström, professor of city planning at Chalmers Institute of Technology in Gothenburg. While cars were "a necessary tool in modern civilization," Lindström found over 150 thousand fatal accidents and ten to twenty times that number of traffic injuries every year around the world unacceptable. "It is a war of motor traffic against the human population." Traffic engineers needed a new approach, "adapting the traffic environment to people and not people to an unsatisfactory environment" to halve the number of traffic accidents and reduce the "injuries to pedestrians and cyclists by 80 percent."[74] In response, Lindström and other experts kept embracing the principle of traffic separation rather than traffic calming as the best solution. National delegates (Germany, Finland, and Italy) reported on experiments with pedestrian zones to reduce accidents. And while British delegates offered calculations showing that undertunneling urban highways was too costly, their Soviet colleagues found pedestrian underpasses an excellent solution.[75]

In 1971, some delegates seemed to agree with the activists' critique that cars were detrimental to urbanites' health. The general reporter heard accounts of automobility being linked to health problems like cancer. A Polish engineer suggested that car manufacturers had a responsibility for redesigning cars to reduce the environmental impact, in collaboration with the UN—probably in anticipation of the first UN conference on the environment the following year. There were reports from Paris, Madrid, East Berlin, Warsaw, and Prague about car noise and air pollution, though British delegates thought their country's chimneys posed more problems than cars. Most radically, the Belgian reporter argued that automobility ranked second after pedestrianism in creating cities' quality of life. Amid the reporting on pedestrian zones and car-free streets, the French objected strongly to what they felt was PIARC's growing anti-car attitude. They believed that choices between private (cars) and public mobility (public transit) had to be based on rational, economic cost-benefit analyses. Delegates did reflect on the beneficial role of public transit, all agreeing it could mitigate the impact of automobility. Nevertheless, trams were still seen as taking up too much urban space: either they had to go underground (subway) or become a non-rail system (busses) to facilitate the flow of cars.[76]

Ecological sustainability was taken more seriously at PIARC's Mexico City congress (1975), at a time when building and planning professionals faced the consequences of the 1973–74 "oil crisis" and a worldwide rebellion.[77] The urban highways these engineers had been blueprinting for decades ran into local resistance from citizens everywhere when it came to constructing the megaprojects that had been on the drawing board for decades. Moreover, activists throughout the Western world were protesting against technocratic designs, as evidenced by several countries reporting not only on "public attitudes," but also the demand for citizen participation in planning—or what the delegates called "non-expert" planning. The British introduced the notion of "planning from the political angle" through public consultation. The French also responded to "public opinion about quality of life," introducing a national and systematic "Guide to Ecological Constraints" with reference to pedestrians and cyclists. Laymen designing a human-centered city that rejected Le Corbusier's car-oriented manifesto of the Athens Charter caused anxiety among the Austrian delegates; remembering their recent history of Nazism, they warned how conflicts could be politically exploited by populists—now on the political left: "the conflict between man and traffic in an urban environment . . . highlights the attraction of these problems for demagogues and others who can exploit them."[78]

In the mid-1970s, roadbuilders and traffic engineers still perceived environmental concerns outside cities as a matter of balancing road building with natural landscapes for the pleasure of motorists. Within cities, they faced a more direct ecological challenge. For the first time, PIARC engineers had to tackle noise and air pollution head on, because they threatened the quality of life, and consider these issues from the urbanites' perspective. All countries involved in PIARC, with Eastern European engineers in the lead, advocated or had already implemented pedestrian zones on a large scale; cycling made its first appearance, and the question whether cars belonged in cities at all was also addressed.[79] The German delegates considered sustainability a political dilemma: "Where the need for environmental protection conflicts with economic growth, the issues must be decided at the political level." The West German delegates also noted: "Environmental assessment criteria do not yet exist to aid the cost/benefit calculations" for mobility.[80] That said, economic growth was still very much defined in terms of automobility, with most delegates presenting it as both a source of prosperity and a good quality of life. Just its excesses had to be mitigated and solved—if only because engineers faced such a political backlash from the many projects being stalled or even canceled, like the Left Bank of the Seine near Notre Dame.[81] Only in 1979 did the city appear for the first time as a genuine place to live, where traffic had to adapt to its residents rather than vice versa.[82] This moment was short-lived.

IFHP was also slow to respond to the fundamental critique from local grassroots organizations and critics like Jacobs. The organization persisted in advocating car-dependent suburban planning movements (from New Town and Neighborhood Unit to CBD, Urban High Way, and Planned Suburbanization). Preoccupied with reinventing itself after the war because the Nazi regime had taken over the organization, IFHP concentrated on cooperation with the United Nations, and as a UN Habitat affiliate, focused on the Global South and communist Europe.[83] Moreover, IFHP members, many of whom had become policymakers in the welfare state, had strong technocratic predilections. The organization, seemingly tone deaf to local resistance at first, gradually shifted to more fundamental choices for urban transport systems that integrated the region and the city.

In 1963, IFHP planners took the searing critique on board, but were reactive rather than proactive. The organization acknowledged that the American system of suburbs and speedways was detrimental to the regional development of both new towns and city centers: the middle classes were moving away, while "underprivileged and lower-income groups" stayed.[84] At their 1964 conference, IFHP planners admitted traffic congestion could not be solved by building new roads; expanding the public transit system had to reduce car commuting.[85] For their 1966 conference, they invited traffic engineers to discuss ways of solving the negative effects of mass automobility: planning to bring people's daily activities closer together, expanding downtown car parking, and combining highways with regional public transit under the supervision of regional authorities.[86]

Genuine advocacy for pedestrianism—instead of designing for pedestrians in their roles as suburban shoppers going to the city by car—only returned in the 1970s thanks to grassroots movements demanding livable cities.[87] When ecological concerns found their way to urban planning circles in 1977, planners advocated that public transit systems had a role to play in fighting automobility's pollution and fossil-fuel dependency.[88] Here we see for the first time an argument for public transit not to facilitate but to replace urban automobility as the best sustainable option. To rescue the planet, IFHP experts came up with technology-intensive solutions that ignored walking and cycling: light rail and dual mode transit; continuous conveyors; small-capsule systems; car-sharing and dial-a-ride; and even electrical cars. These ideas foreshadowed what was codified in the 1980s as Transit-Oriented Development (TOD): concentrating urban development around hubs of multimodal public transit systems within walking distance would create more compact and sustainable cities. For a brief moment, planners in the West turned to the examples in socialist countries—just as these countries were about to head in the opposite direction to embrace automobility after the Cold War.[89]

The UIV city administrators also had little affinity with grassroots movements in their cities. Not until the early 1970s, when the organization met after the UN Conference on the Human Environment held in Stockholm in June 1972, did the delegates realize that the "ever larger number of motorcars," construction of highways and parking garages, and suburban sprawl were having a similar impact on the human environment as industrialization and urbanization.[90] The international community of city managers (UIV), urban planners (IFHP), and PIARC road engineers moved away from planning in the West when protests erupted against their models, and in the 1980s concentrated on the so-called developing countries instead.

It was not until the end of the Cold War in the 1990s that the road engineering and urban planning community systematically shifted from vehicular transport (cars and public transit) to active mobility (walking and cycling) as the most sustainable mode in cities. Concerned with the outcomes of the UN panel on climate change, PIARC engineers defined city centers as unfit for cars for the first time in 1991, and called for pedestrianism, cycling, and public transit.[91] The urban planners did likewise. In 1993, IFHP turned its back on New Town strategies and embraced historical city centers for their mixed use, small-scale systems and livable streetscapes, by banning cars and trucks and facilitating pedestrians and cyclists.[92] This time, the international experts at IFHP and PIARC were no longer proactive as they had been until 1970, but reactive to the times. Urban-based UIV, by contrast, succeeded in attaining a position that had eluded it for decades, representing cities in international circles. In a reversal of roles, the Council of European Municipalities became the European chapter of UIV in 1990.[93] Fifteen years later, UIV succeeded in collaborating more closely with UN agencies through the United Cities and Local Governments in 2004—a merger of UIV, United Towns Organization, and the Metropolis network that brought together local government leaders and supranational institutions, bypassing national governments.[94] These new alliances between international urban organizations and supranational agencies showed that cities were back in the international arena when it came to sustainability issues, like they had once been in the nineteenth century.

## The Return of the City? Alternative Urban Futures, 1990s and Beyond

In the twentieth century, PIARC and IFHP helped shape the paradigm shift from the walkable city, where all parts had to function together organically, to a view of the city where suburban car mobility dominated and streets were reduced to traffic conduits. PIARC in particular helped by promoting automobility as vital for national economic growth. Over the course of the twentieth century, the international organization of urban administrators UIV was sidelined. The urban policymakers did not manage to develop mobility models that catered to the needs of urban residents, such as walking, cycling, and public transit, despite its allegiance to international socialism and urbanism. Only after an organized countercultural movement's critique put cities at the center of its analysis did the cities and their mobility concerns re-enter the debate in the 1970s. The street re-entered the debate as a place of social interaction and wellbeing—the city as a walkable place. The countercultural movement allowed urban policymakers also to participate in the debate internationally as a major partner. The international urban administrators succeeded particularly at the end of the Cold War, when nation-states were retreating from urban governance and numerous new city networks re-emerged as the alternatives to national agendas—some with major commitments to sustainable urban mobility.

Indeed, a call for cities and urban regions to take their destiny in their own hands once more found a clear voice in the seminal book by Benjamin Barber, *If Mayors Ruled the World: Dysfunctional Nations, Rising Cities.*[95] Barber saw a vital role for mayors and cities in implementing solutions for a sustainable planet—an even more urgent call now that the UN underlined cities rather than nations as the key drivers for change. On the world stage, New York mayor Michael Bloomberg was particularly successful in articulating a leading role for cities and their mayors to create more sustainable urban futures. He appointed as park commissioner Janette Sadik-Khan, whose recent *Streetfight: Handbook for an Urban Revolution* effectively summarized a radical reversal of Moses's car-governed city.[96] *Streetfight* embraces the Placemaking Movement, revisiting the works of Jacobs, Mumford, Howard, and Olmsted to argue that cities are for people, not for cars. Like her colleagues around the world, the commissioner called for transforming the streets and squares of Manhattan once more into commons to be shared for social and economic activities, not as conduits for cars. Cycling and pedestrianism were the driving forces for that goal.

Instead of designing streets based on functional separation, urban and traffic planners advocated the street as a shared space. The Bloomberg administration argued that cars were no longer the undisputed vehicles of economic growth, as the advocates of motordom had contended for decades. In their place, urban livability was the true basis of economic, social, and ecological sustainability. Today's planning movements advocate returning to the more integrated versions of the nineteenth-century city to create places for future sustainable urban development and urban transport. Yet, Bloomberg's vision of the city also included public-private partnership with a new role for corporate interests in urbanism. A key question will be how alternative or non-vehicular approaches will play out in light of public spaces becoming privatized by corporate interests seeking to mine large data sets for commercial gain. Commercial interests—ranging from corporate bike- and car-sharing programs to mobility-as-a-service, and smart-city and mobility information and communication technology innovations such as autonomous driving, tourist apps, and hybrid electric vehicles—promise sustainable urban development. These corporate visions of mobility pose a new challenge for cities in the twenty-first century.

**Ruth Oldenziel**, professor in the history of technology at Eindhoven University of Technology, is editor in chief of *Technology and Culture*. She has published in American, transatlantic, gender, technology, and mobility studies including *Cycling Cities* (coeditor with Martin Emanuel, Adri Albert de la Bruhèze, and Frank Veraart; SHT, 2016), *Cycling and Re-*

*cycling* (coeditor with Helmuth Trischler; Berghahn, 2016), *Consumers, Tinkerers, Rebels* (Palgrave, 2015), *Hacking Europe* (coeditor with Gerard Alberts; Springer, 2014), *Cold-War Kitchen* (coeditor with Karin Zachmann; MIT, 2009), *Gender and Technology* (Hopkins, 2003), *Crossing Boundaries, Building Bridges* (with Karin Zachmann and Annie Canel; Routledge 2000), and *Making Technology Masculine* (AUP, 1999).

**M. Luísa Sousa** is researcher and assistant professor (adjunct) at the Interuniversity Centre for the History of Science and Technology (CIUHCT), Department of Applied Social Sciences, Faculty of Sciences and Technology at NOVA University of Lisbon (Portugal). She is chief editor of *HoST* and a member of T2M's executive committee. Her award-winning publications include works on the history of technology, mobility, and urban planning in Portugal and the former colonies Angola and Mozambique.

**Pieter van Wesemael** is professor of urbanism and urban architecture at Eindhoven University of Technology. His research and teaching include the area of healthy cities, in particular the mutual shaping of public space design and planning, place making, and active lifestyle change. He is interested in developing future strategies for activating environmental design that is informed by historical discourses and practices in active urban mobilities, urban planning, and public space design.

## Notes

Research for this chapter was funded in part by the Foundation for Science and Technology, Portugal (Fundação para a Ciência e a Tecnologia) with the postdoctoral fellowship awarded to M. Luísa Sousa (SFRH/BPD/93517/2013), and through CIUHCT (UID/HIS/00286/2019).

 1. World Commission on Environment and Development, *Our Common Future* (also known as the Brundtland Report) (Oxford: UN, via Oxford University Press, 1987).
 2. The transnational history literature is vast. For an introduction, see Akira Iriye and Pierre-Yves Saunier, eds., *The Palgrave Dictionary of Transnational History* (London: Palgrave, 2009).
 3. In his monumental work, Gijs Mom deals mostly with suburban automobilism and other non-urban mobilities: *Atlantic Automobilism: The Emergence and Persistence of the Car, 1890–1940* (New York: Berghahn Books, 2014), with the second volume forthcoming. Though not explicitly dealing with the transnational circulation of ideas about public transit, the comparative approach of the collection of essays is indispensable: Colin Divall and Winstan Bond, eds., *Suburbanizing the Masses: Public Transport and Urban Development in Historical Perspective* (Aldershot: Ashgate, 2003).

4. Both UIV and PIARC await their historians. For an initial exploration, see Stève Bernardin and Sébastien Gardon, "When Traffic Engineers and Urban Planners Meet: A Search for Transnational Exchanges during the Interwar Period," in *Fourth International Conference of the International Association for the History of Transport, Traffic and Mobility (T2M)* (Marne-la-Vallée, Paris, 2006); we thank Frank Schipper for providing this reference. Gijs Mom, "Building an Infrastructure for the Automobile System; PIARC and Road Safety (1908–1938)," in *23rd PIARC World Road Congress* (Paris, 2007); IFHP has been examined by many others, but not focusing on mobility. M. A. Geertse, "Defining the Universal City: The International Federation of Housing and Town Planning and Transnational Planning Dialogue 1913–1945," Ph.D. diss., VU, Amsterdam, 2012; idem, "Cross-Border Country Planning Dialogue in Interwar Europe," *Sage Open* 5, no. 3 (2015): 1–12; idem, "The International Garden City Campaign: Transnational Negotiations on Town Planning Methods," *Journal of Urban History* 42, no. 4 (2016): 733–52; Phillip Wagner, *Stadtplanung für die Welt? Internationales Expertenwissen 1900–1960* (Göttingen: Vandenhoeck & Ruprecht, 2016); idem, "Facilitating Planning Communication across Borders: The International Federation of Housing and Town Planning in the Interwar Period," *Planning Perspectives*, 31 no. 2 (2016): 299–311; Renzo Riboldazzi, *Un'altra modernità: L'IFHTP e la cultura urbanistica tra le due guerre 1923–1939* (Rome: Gangemi, 2010); idem, "Getting to the Root of the Crisis of Urbanity: The Debate on Urban Open Spaces in the IFHTP Congresses between the Two Wars," *Planum* (May 2012): 1–18; and idem, "The IFHP Congresses between the Wars: A Source for Studies on Modern Town Planning," *Town Planning Review* 84, no. 2 (2013).

5. Pierre-Yves Saunier, "Sketches from the Urban Internationale: Voluntary Societies, International Organizations and US Foundations at the City's Bedside 1900–1960," *International Journal of Urban and Regional Research* 25, no. 2 (2001): 380–403.

6. Pieter van Wesemael, *Architecture of Instruction and Delight: A Socio-historical Analysis of World Exhibitions as a Didactic Phenomenon* (Rotterdam: 010 Publishers, [1997] 2001); Pieter van Wesemael, "World Exhibitions: Didactical Projects towards Real Reform; Advocates and Catalysts of Modern Urban Society, Economy and Metropolis," *Ricerche Storiche* 95, no. 1–2 (2015): 93–103; Pierre-Yves Saunier and Renaud Payre, "Municipalités de tous pays, unissez vous! L'Union Internationale des Villes ou l'Internationale municipale (1913–1940)," *Amministrare* 30, no. 1–2 (1998): 217–39.

7. Charles E. Beveridge and Paul Rocheleau, *Frederick Law Olmsted: Designing the American Landscape* (New York: Universe Publishing, 1998); Witold Rybczynski, *A Clearing in the Distance: Frederick Law Olmsted and North America in the Nineteenth Century* (New York: Scribner, 1999); David H. Pinkney, *Napoleon III and the Rebuilding of Paris* (Princeton: Princeton University Press, 1958); David P. Jordan, "Haussmann and Haussmannisation: The Legacy for Paris," *French Historical Studies* 27, no. 1 (2004): 87–113; Patrice de Moncan, *Le Paris d'Haussmann* (Paris: Les Editions du Mécène, 2012); Lance Jay Brown, David Dixon, and Oliver Gillham, *Urban Design for an Urban Century: Shaping More Livable, Equitable, and Resilient Cities* (Hoboken, NJ: Whiley, 2009), 214. Social Museums also played an important role in these urban planning debates. Van Wesemael, "Architecture of Instruction"; Miriam R. Levin, "Inventing a Modern Paris: The Dynamic Relationship between Expositions, Urban Planning and Museums," *Quaderns d'Història de l'Enginyeria* 12 (2012): 35–56.

8.  Renia Ehrenfeucht and Anastasia Loukaitou-Sideris, "Constructing the Sidewalks: Municipal Government and the Production of Public Space in Los Angeles, California, 1880–1920," *Journal of Historical Geography* 33, no. 1 (2007): 104–24.

9.  Hénard was not the first: working since the 1840s, Hector Horeau devised an elaborate (underground) scheme already in 1869. Nicolas Papayanis, *Planning before Haussmann* (Baltimore, MD: Johns Hopkins University Press, 2004), 209.

10. See chapter by Frank Schipper in this volume.

11. Eugène Hénard, "The Cities of the Future," in *Transactions of the Royal Institute of British Architects, Town Planning Conference London, October 1910* (London: Royal Institute of British Architects, 1911), 345–67.

12. Peter M. Wolf, *Eugène Hénard and the Beginning of Urbanism in Paris, 1900–1914* (The Hague: International Federation of Housing and Planning, 1968).

13. For a definition of sustainability in terms of wellbeing, see chapter by Jan-Pieter Smits and Frank Veraart in this volume.

14. On transnational and transatlantic exchange in urbanism, see Marjatta Hietala, *Services and Urbanization at the Turn of the Century: The Diffusion of Innovations* (Helsinki: Finnish Historical Society, 1987); Helen Meller, *European Cities 1890–1930: History, Culture, and the Built Environment* (New York: Wiley and Sons, 2001); Anthony Sutcliffe, *Towards the Planned City: Germany, Britain, the United States and France 1790–1914* (Oxford: Blackwell, 1981); Daniel Rodgers, *Atlantic Crossings: Social Politics in a Progressive Age* (Cambridge, MA: Harvard University Press, 1998); Van Wesemael, "Architecture of Instruction"; and Anne Rasmussen, "Les Congrès internationaux liés aux Expositions universelles de Paris (1867–1900)," in *Mil neuf cent 7* (1989): 23–44.

15. Van Wesemael, "Architecture of Instruction"; Helen Meller and William Whyte, eds., *Ghent Planning Congress 1913: Premier Congrès International et Exposition Comparée des Villes*, (Abingdon: Routledge, 2014); Helen Meller, "Philanthropy and Public Enterprise: International Exhibitions and the Modern Town Planning Movement, 1889–1913," *Planning Perspectives* 10, no. 3 (1995): 295–310; Wouter van Acker, Michiel DeHaene, and Pieter Uytterhoven, "Tussen stedenbouw en stadsbestuur: de stedententoonstelling van Patrick Geddes en het internationale stedencongres, Gent 1913," in *Op het breukvlak van de moderniteit*, ed. Wouter Van Acker and Christophe Verbruggen, 154–69 (Gent: Snoeck Publishers, 2013).

16. Geertse, "Defining the Universal City"; Wagner, *Stadtplanung*; and Riboldazzi, "The IFHP Congresses between the Wars."

17. Aligned with the welfare state, the IFHP was more influential than CIAM. Riboldazzi, "The IFHP Congresses between the Wars"; Geertse, "Cross-Border Country Planning Dialogue in Interwar Europe."

18.. M. G. Lay, *Ways of the World: A History of the World's Roads and of the Vehicles Who Used Them* (New Brunswick, NJ: Rutgers University Press, 1992), 119.

19. Saunier, "Sketches from the Urban Internationale."

20. For an in-depth analysis of the organization, see Geertse, "Defining the Universal City"; idem, "Cross-Border Country Planning Dialogue in Interwar Europe"; and idem, "The International Garden City Campaign"; Wagner, *Stadtplanung*; idem, "Facilitating Planning Communication across Borders"; Riboldazzi, *Un'altra modernità*; idem, "Getting to the Root of the Crisis of Urbanity"; and idem, "The IFHP Congresses between the Wars."

21. Jo Guldi, *Roads to Power: Britain Invents the Infrastructure State* (Cambridge, MA: Harvard University Press, 2012).
22. Ruth Oldenziel, "Keynote Address. The Vanishing Trick: How Cyclists and Pedestrians were Left Uncounted," *Twelfth International Conference of the International Association for the History of Transport, Traffic and Mobility (T2M)* (Drexel University Philadelphia, 2014); Gijs Mom, "Roads without Rails: European Transnational Freeway Network Building and the Desire for Long-Range Motorized Mobility," *Technology and Culture* 46, no. 4 (2005): 745–72; Ruth Oldenziel and Mikael Hård, *Consumers, Users, Rebels: The People Who Shaped Europe* (London: Palgrave, 2013), chapter 4; Frank Schipper, *Driving Europe: Building Europe on Roads in the Twentieth Century* (Amsterdam: Aksant, 2008), 66–67; Mom, *Atlantic Automobilism*, 27, 49, 95, 577, 622.
23. Stève Bernardin and Sébastien Gardon, "Genèse d'une cause transnationale. Les villes au défi de l'automobile (1908–1938)," in *Séminaire de l'histoire des transports à l'histoire de la mobilité* (Paris I—Paris IV—ENPC, 2007). We thank Stève Bernardin for sharing this text.
24. PIARC, *Minutes of the First Plenary Meeting, Brussels, August 1, 1910* (Paris: PIARC, 1910), 225.
25. PIARC, *Minutes of the Second Plenary Meeting, London* (Paris: PIARC, 1913), 603.
26. The scholarship on automobility is vast. See Christof Mauch and Thomas Zeller, *The World beyond the Windshield: Roads and Landscapes in the United States and Europe* (Athens, OH: Ohio University Press, 2008), and Mom, *Atlantic Automobilism*. See also M. Luísa Sousa, *A mobilidade automóvel em Portugal, 1920–1950* (Lisboa: Chiado Editora, 2016); and idem, "Roads for the 1940 Portuguese Nationality Commemorations: Modernising by Excess in a Context of Scarcity," *Journal of Transport History* 37, no. 2 (2016): 175–93.
27. See also chapter by Colin Divall in this volume.
28. Oldenziel, "Keynote address. The Vanishing Trick."
29. Mom, "Building an Infrastructure for the Automobile System," 22.
30. Theodore M. Porter, "Speaking Precision to Power: The Modern Political Role of Social Science," *Social Research* 73, no. 4 (2006): 1273–94. PIARC positioned itself against the vested railroad interests when policymakers prioritized investing in trains and neglected roads.
31. Johan Schot and Vincent Lagendijk, "Technocratic Internationalism in the Interwar Years: Building Europe on Motorways and Electricity Networks," *Journal of Modern European History* 6, no. 2 (2008): 196–217; Wolfram Kaiser and Johan Schot, *Writing the Rules for Europe: Experts, Cartels, and International Organizations* (Basingstoke: Palgrave Macmillan, 2014).
32. Kaiser and Schot, *Writing the Rules for Europe*; Frank Uekoetter, *The Green and the Brown: A History of Conservation in Nazi Germany* (New York: Cambridge University Press, 2006).
33. Gijs Mom, "Decentering Highways: European National Road Network Planning from a Transnational Perspective," in *Der Moderne Strasse: Planung, Bau und Verkehr vom 18. bis zum 20. Jahrhundert*, ed. Hans-Liudger Dienel and Hans-Ulrich Schiedt (Frankfurt am Main: Campus Verlag, 2010), 77–100, here 82; Mom, "Building an Infrastructure for the Automobile System."
34. Massimo Moraglio, "A Rough Modernization: Landscapes and Highways in Twentieth-Century Italy," in Mauch and Zeller, *The World beyond the Windshield*, 108–24.

35. Since 1928, UIV was also known as IULA or the International Union of Local Authorities. Saunier, "Sketches from the Urban Internationale"; Patrizia Dogliani, "European Municipalism in the First Half of the Twentieth Century: The Socialist Network," *Contemporary European History* 11, no. 4 (2002): 573–96.

36. Stefan Couperus and Shane Ewen, "Whose 'Urban Internationale'? Intermunicipalism in Europe, 1924–36: The Value of a Decentered, Interpretive Approach to Transnational Urban History," in *Cities beyond Borders: Comparative and Transnational Approaches to Urban History*, ed. Nicolas Kenny and Rebecca Madgin (New York: Routledge, 2015), 149–72, here 158 (we thank Shane Ewen for sharing this text); Saunier and Payre, "Municipalités de tous pays, unissez vous!," 3, 4.

37. Couperus and Ewen, "Whose 'Urban Internationale'?," 158.

38. Kaiser and Schot, *Writing the Rules for Europe*.

39. Saunier, "Sketches from the Urban Internationale," 393; Bernardin and Gardon, "When Traffic Engineers and Urban Planners Meet."

40. Bernardin and Gardon, "When Traffic Engineers and Urban Planners Meet," 2, 3, 6, 13.

41. Oscar Gaspari, "Cities against States? Hopes, Dreams and Shortcomings of the European Municipal Movement, 1900–1960," *Contemporary European History* 11, no. 4 (2002): 597–621, here 607.

42. *Tablettes documentaires* since 1921; *Les sciences administratives* in 1925; *L'administration locale* since 1927. Saunier and Payre, "Municipalités de tous pays," 6, 12; Couperus and Ewen, "Whose 'Urban Internationale'?," 156–57.

43. Although De Schulthess collaborated as an expert at the League of Nations fifth session of the Permanent Committee on Road Traffic in 1927 and its tenth session in 1935, he was not accepted as permanent member of the League's Advisory and Technical Committee for Communications and Transit in 1938. Bernardin and Gardon, "When Traffic Engineers and Urban Planners Meet."

44. Schipper, *Driving Europe*; and idem, "Unravelling Hieroglyphs: Urban Traffic Signs and the League of Nations," *Métropoles* 6 (2009): 65–100; Gijs Mom, "Building an Infrastructure for the Automobile System."

45. Ebenezer Howard (president) and Edwart Culpin (secretary) founded IFHP in 1913. Its agenda changed over the years.

46. E. Howard's *To-morrow, A Peaceful Path to Real Reform*, first published in 1898, only included the term Garden Cities in the second 1902 edition: *Garden Cities of To-morrow, a Peaceful Path to Real Reform* (London: Swan Sonnenschein & Co., 1902).

47. Planners were concerned about booming car ownership and commuting. In Great Britain, Pepler (1931) noted that the numbers of cars rose from sixty-seven thousand to two million between 1906 and 1929. For Germany, Adler (1931) described the increase from sixty-four thousand to 660 thousand cars between 1914 and 1930. Policymakers in the department of Seine encompassing Paris observed cars and trucks had increased quicker than public transit (Dautry, 1939). American planners (Simpson, 1939; Lewis and Turner, 1931) also focused on car growth; in Riboldazzi, "Getting to the Root of the Crisis of Urbanity," 6–9. See also Geertse, "Cross-Border Country Planning Dialogue in Interwar Europe," 10.

48. Riboldazzi, "Getting to the Root of the Crisis of Urbanity."

49. John Nolen (IGCTPF, 1923), as cited in Geertse, "Defining the Universal City," 5, 13.

50. Riboldazzi, "Getting to the Root of the Crisis of Urbanity,"12; Francesco Dal Co, "From Parks to the Region: Progressive Ideology and the Reform of the American City," in *The American City: from the Civil War to the New Deal*, ed. Giorgio Ciucci, Francesco Dal Co, Mario Manieri-Elia, and Manfredo Tafuri (Cambridge, MA: MIT, 1979), 143–292.

51. Schumacher (1923: 23), as cited in Geertse, "Cross-Border Country Planning Dialogue in Interwar Europe," 5.

52. Unlike his colleagues, CIAM chairman Van Eesteren was an institutionally well-embedded IFHP urban planner. Ruth Oldenziel, "CIAM and Cycling: Designing for Working-Class Mobility, 1930–1935," manuscript, 2015.

53. Planners like Adams interacted with traffic engineers in the 1920s and 1930s to adapt Olmsted's parkways for suburban regions and Haussmannian boulevards in cities. Renzo Riboldazzi, "Getting to the Root of the Crisis of Urbanity," 6–9.

    On the eve of World War II, city planners included national urbanization and road infrastructure plans at the 1939 IFHP congress for the first time, signifying the rise of national state planning at the expense of cities. Geertse, "Cross-Border Country Planning Dialogue in Interwar Europe," 7.

54. Robert A. Caro, *The Power Broker: Robert Moses and the Fall of New York* (New York: Knopf, 1974); Marshall Berman, *All That Is Solid Melts into Air: The Experience of Modernity* (New York: Viking Penguin, 1988); Hilary Ballon, *Robert Moses and the Modern City: The Transformation of New York* (New York: Norton, 2007); Van Wesemael, "Architecture of Instruction."

55. American regional park systems influenced European planning like Germany's autobahn program, but there were also many exchanges on how to promote best practices in public administration. See especially the 1926 and 1930 PIARC congresses.

56. In the United States, the car industry and autoworkers' unions negotiated many of the building blocks of the welfare state. Nelson Lichtenstein, *The State of the Union: A Century of American Labor* (Princeton: Princeton University Press, 2002); Marie Gottschalk, *The Shadow Welfare State: Labor, Business, and the Politics of Health-Care* (Ithaca, NY: Cornell University Press, 2000); The postwar pacification of labor and capital in post-Nazi Germany was also built on the promises of automobilism. In Sweden, the Social Democratic Party favored automobilism as important for building the welfare state because it combined economic development and free movement. See Pär Blomkvist, "Transferring Technology—Shaping Ideology: American Traffic Engineering and Commercial Interests in the Establishment of a Swedish Car Society, 1945–1965," *Comparative Technology Transfer and Society* 2, no. 3 (2004): 273–302. See also Sébastien Gardon, Arnaud Passalacqua, and Frank Schipper, "Pour une histoire des circulations sur la circulation," *Métropoles* 6 (2009): 1–17; Pierre-Yves Saunier, "Circulations, connexions et espaces transnationaux," *Genèses* 57, no. 4 (2004): 110–26; and idem, "Sketches from the Urban Internationale"; Phillip Wagner, "New Life for American Downtowns? The 1958 International Seminar on Urban Renewal and the Travel of Planning Ideas in the North Atlantic World," *Planning Perspectives* 29, no. 2 (2014): 189–208.

57. Per Lundin, "American Numbers Copied: Shaping the Swedish Postwar Car Society," *Comparative Technology Transfer and Society* 2, no. 3 (2004): 303–27; Gijs Mom, "International Road Federation," in Iriye and Saunier, *The Palgrave Dictionary of Transnational History*, 582–83.

58. Mom, "International Road Federation"; Per Lundin, "Mediators of Modernity: Planning Experts and the Making of the 'Car-Friendly' City in Europe," in *Urban Machinery: Inside Modern European Cities*, ed. Mikael Hård and Thomas J. Misa (Cambridge, MA: MIT Press, 2008), 257–79; Pär Blomkvist, "Roads for Flow— Roads for Peace: Lobbying for a European Highway System," in *Networking Europe: Transnational Infrastructures and the Shaping of Europe, 1850–2000*, ed. Erik van der Vleuten and Arne Kaijser (Sagamore Beach: Science History Publications, 2006), 161–86; Frank Schipper, "Changing the Face of Europe: European Road Mobility During the Marshall Plan Years," *Journal of Transport History* 28, no. 2 (2007): 211–28; Peter Engelke, "Green City Origins: Democratic Resistance to the Auto-Oriented City in West Germany, 1960–1990," Ph.D. diss., Georgetown University, 2011; see also Wagner, "New Life for American Downtowns?"

59. For mass-scale implementation of such car-based local traffic plans, see Per Lundin, "Mediators of Modernity." For their impact on cyclists in particular, see Ruth Oldenziel et al., eds., *Cycling Cities: The European Experience. Hundred Years of Policy and Practice* (Eindhoven: Foundation for the History of Technology and Rachel Carson Center for Environment and Society, 2016), and subsequent studies on Johannesburg, Arnhem-Nijmegen, Munich, The Hague, and Johannesburg in the *Cycling Cities* series: Njogu Morgan, *Cycling Cities: The Johannesburg Experience* (Eindhoven: Foundation for the History of Technology, 2019); Eric Berkers and Ruth Oldenziel, *Cycling Cities: The Arnhem and Nijmegen Experience* (Eindhoven: Foundation for the History of Technology, 2017); Adri A. Albert de la Bruhèze and Ruth Oldenziel, *Cycling Cities: The Munich Experience* (Eindhoven: Foundation for the History of Technology, 2018); Eric Berkers, Frans Botma, and Ruth Oldenziel, *Cycling Cities: The Hague Experience* (Eindhoven: Foundation for the History of Technology, 2018).

60. PIARC, *Second Section—Question 6: The Financing of Road Works and Their Economic Justification, Proceedings Rio de Janiero* (Paris: PIARC, 1959), 273, 274.

61. H. J. D. Revers, *IULA, 1913–1963: The Story of Fifty Years of International Municipal Co-operation* (The Hague: International Union of Local Authorities, 1963), 12. UIV distributed questionnaires in preparation for its meetings. The first congress explicitly addressing mobility issues (on public transit: tramways' municipal companies), slated to be held in Budapest in 1940, was canceled when war broke out. Vereniging van Nederlandse Gemeenten (VNG) Archives, Inventaris nr. 5702, IULA congres 7e Budapest 1940 (uitgesteld). We thank Henk-Jan Dekker for identifying and locating these papers.

62. Howard Roberts, *Prevention of Road Accidents: Digest of the Reports Prepared for the Conference in Geneva, September 1949* (The Hague: International Union of Local Authorities, 1949), 3; Schipper, *Driving Europe*, 227–28.

63. Roberts, *Prevention of Road Accidents*. UIV focused on traffic discipline (education) and regulation, framed from the motorist's point of view, as analyzed by Peter Norton in his "Four Paradigms: Traffic Safety in the Twentieth-Century United States," *Technology and Culture* 56, no. 2 (2015): 319–34.

64. International Union of Local Authorities, *Traffic Congestion in the City Centre: Reports Prepared for the Hague Congress, June 1957* (The Hague: IULA, 1957). The questionnaire explored several strategies for solving traffic congestion: making existing road networks and parking facilities more efficient; closing city

centers to "non-essential motor traffic"; making city centers accessible for heavy traffic by widening roads and adding parking facilities; rebuilding (parts of) cities for automobility; and introducing parking policies.

65. Gaspari, "Cities against States?," 609–13; Dogliani, "European Municipalism," 593–95; Pierre-Yves Saunier, "La toile municipale aux XIXe–XXe siècles: un panorama transnational vu d'Europe," *Urban History Review* 34, no. 2 (2006): 43–56, here 52.

66. Pierre-Yves Saunier, "Selling the Idea of Cooperation. The US Foundations and the European Components of the Urban International (1920s–1960s)," in *American Foundations and Large Scale Research: Construction and Transfer of Knowledge*, ed. Giuliana Gemelli (Bologna: CLUEB, 2001), 219–46; Saunier, "Sketches from the Urban Internationale," 398; idem, "La toile municipale," 53; Dogliani, "European Municipalism," 595; PIARC, *Question VI. The Road within the Environment. Mexico City Congress Proceedings* (Paris: PIARC, 1975).

67. Wagner, "New Life for American Downtowns?"

68. Jane Jacobs, *Life and Death of Great American Cities: The Failure of Town Planning* (New York: Random House, 1961).

69. Zachary Mooradian Furness, *One Less Car: Bicycling and the Politics of Automobility* (Philadelphia: Temple University Press, 2010); Dave Horton, "Environmentalism and the Bicycle," *Environmental Politics* 15, no. 1 (2006): 41–58.

70. Colin Buchanan, *Traffic in Towns* (London: Her Majesty's Stationery Office, 1963); Simon Gunn, "The Buchanan Report, Environment and the Problem of Traffic in Britain," *Twentieth Century British History* 22, no. 4 (2011): 521–42; see the chapter by Colin Divall in this volume. See also Michael Southworth and Eran Ben-Joseph, *Streets and the Shaping of Towns and Cities* (Washington, DC: Island Press, 2013), 117–19.

71. In 1957, PIARC established a technical committee dedicated to the problems with tunnels, gathering detailed information about air pollution. PIARC, *Committee on Road Tunnels. Rio de Janeiro 1959 Reports* (Paris: PIARC, 1959). Their research continued until the Tokyo 1967 congress.

72. See also the chapter by Alexandra Bekasova, Julia Kulikova, and Martin Emanuel in this volume.

73. PIARC, *Urban Street Network. Report, Prague Congress Proceedings* (Paris: PIARC, 1971).

74. Ibid..

75. Ibid.

76. Ibid.

77. On how the energy crisis became known as the "oil crisis," see Timothy Mitchell, *Carbon Democracy: Political Power in the Age of Oil* (London: Verso Books, 2011), chapter 7. For a case study of a local impact of this crisis and of other "automobile debates," together with a political regime transition, see M. Luísa Sousa and Rafael Marques, "Political Transitions, Value Change and Motorisation in 1970s Portugal," *Journal of Transport History* 34, no. 1 (2013): 1–21.

78. PIARC, *Question VI. The Road within the Environment. Mexico City Congress Proceedings* (Paris: PIARC, 1975), 64.

79. PIARC, *The Fifth Question: The Urban Network. Mexico City Congress Proceedings* (Paris: PIARC, 1975).

80. Ibid., 9.

81. Ibid., 24.

82. PIARC, *Vienna Congress Proceedings* (Paris: PIARC, 1979).

83. Wagner, *Stadtplanung*.

84. The conference some months earlier articulated the sentiments that became famous through the Buchanan Report, *Traffic in Towns* (November 1963); Sir Frederick C. Osborn, "Bigger Cities or More Cities? Endeavours, Successes and Failures," IFHP Arnhem, Jubilee Congress, Fifty Years (IFHP, 1963), 23.

85. See IFHP, *Jerusalem, 27th Congress, Report* (IFHP, 1964), 137, which included nine recommendations for regional planning of urbanization and calls for public transit.

86. IFHP's 1966 *Tokyo Congress Report on Urban Transportation and Urban Pattern* listed seven rules for good public transit planning: science-based data; integrating work, living and recreation; creating central business districts with services not available elsewhere; encouraging public transit over private automobility through car parking policies; transferring from car to public transit; optimizing car flows; public transit and private automobility as a coherent system; and applying technological solutions like computational modeling, traffic flow forecasting, and creating traffic governance through a regional transport authority.

87. Pedestrianism was a topic at the IFHP 1976 Helsinki congress (*Proceedings and Papers: Cities for Tomorrow, Directions for Change* [Helsinki: IFHP, 1993], 3) and at a workshop in the Hague organized by V. I. van der Does of the International Federation of Pedestrians. Earlier urban planning discussions on pedestrians saw them as shoppers: Wagner, "New Life for American Downtowns?"; David G. Loth, *The City within a City: The Romance of Rockefeller Center* (New York: W. Morrow, 1966); M. Jeffrey Hardwick, *Mall Maker: Victor Gruen, Architect of an American Dream* (Philadelphia: University of Pennsylvania Press, 2003); Alex Wall, *Victor Gruen: From Urban Shop to New City* (Barcelona: Actor, 2006). On pedestrian activism: Barbara Schmucki, "Against 'the Eviction of the Pedestrian': The Pedestrians' Association and Walking Practices in Urban Britain after World War II," *Radical History Review* 2012, no. 114 (2012): 113–37; Cédric Feriel, "Pedestrians, Cars and the City: From Opposition to Cohabitation," *Metropolitics*, 29 May 2013.

88. IFHP, *Geneva Congress: Towards a More Humane Urban Technology. Topic Transportation*, Vol. 1: *Papers and Proceedings* (IFHP, 1977).

89. See several interesting examples in Bekasova, Kulikova, and Emanuel, this volume.

90. International Union of Local Authorities, *Local Government and the Environment* (The Hague: IULA, 1972).

91. Kurt Suter, "Environment and Roads: Preface," *PIARC Marrakesh Congress* (Paris: PIARC, 1991).

92. IFHP, *Proceedings and Papers: Cities for Tomorrow, Directions for Change*.

93. Gaspari, "Cities against States?," 619–20.

94. Pierre-Yves Saunier, "United Cities and Local Government" in Iriye and Saunier, *The Palgrave Dictionary of Transnational History*, 1065–66. See also Saunier, "La toile municipale," 52.

95. Benjamin Barber, *If Mayors Ruled the World: Dysfunctional Nations, Rising Cities* (New Haven: Yale University Press, 2013).

96. PlaNYC is a plan launched in 2007 to prepare the city of New York for one million new residents, strengthen the economy, and expand and modernize its public infrastructure as a sustainable and resilient city. Janette Sadit-Kahn

and Seth Solomonow, *Streetfight: Handbook for an Urban Revolution* (New York: Penguin Random House, 2016). Cycling was central to that vision. Jen Petersen, "Whose Streets? Paving the Right to the City," Ph.D. diss., New York University, 2011.

# Bibliography

Albert de La Bruhèze, Adri A., and Ruth Oldenziel. *Cycling Cities: The Munich Experience*. Eindhoven: Foundation for the History of Technology, 2018.

Ballon, Hilary. *Robert Moses and the Modern City: The Transformation of New York*. New York: Norton, 2007.

Barber, Benjamin. *If Mayors Ruled the World: Dysfunctional Nations, Rising Cities*. New Haven: Yale University Press, 2013.

Bekasova, Alexandra, Julia Kulikova, and Martin Emanuel. "State Socialism and Sustainable Urban Mobility: Alternative Paths in St. Petersburg since the 1880s." In this volume.

Berkers, Eric, and Ruth Oldenziel. *Cycling Cities: The Arnhem and Nijmegen Experience*. Eindhoven: Foundation for the History of Technology, 2017.

Berkers, Eric, Frans Botma, and Ruth Oldenziel. *Cycling Cities: The Hague Experience*. Eindhoven: Foundation for the History of Technology, 2018.

Berman, Marshall. *All That Is Solid Melts into Air: The Experience of Modernity*. New York: Viking Penguin, 1988.

Bernardin, Stève, and Sébastien Gardon. "Genèse d'une cause transnationale. Les villes au défi de l'automobile (1908–1938)." In *Séminaire de l'histoire des transports à l'histoire de la mobilité*. Paris I—Paris IV—ENPC, 2007.

———. "When Traffic Engineers and Urban Planners Meet: A Search for Transnational Exchanges during the Interwar Period." *Fourth International Conference of the International Association for the History of Transport, Traffic and Mobility (T2M)*. Marne-la-Vallée, Paris, 2006.

Beveridge, Charles E., and Paul Rocheleau. *Frederick Law Olmsted: Designing the American Landscape*. New York: Universe Publishing, 1998.

Blomkvist, Pär. "Roads for Flow—Roads for Peace: Lobbying for a European Highway System." In *Networking Europe: Transnational Infrastructures and the Shaping of Europe, 1850–2000*, edited by Erik van der Vleuten and Arne Kaijser, 161–86. Sagamore Beach: Science History Publications, 2006.

———. "Transferring Technology—Shaping Ideology: American Traffic Engineering and Commercial Interests in the Establishment of a Swedish Car Society, 1945–1965." *Comparative Technology Transfer and Society* 2, no. 3 (2004): 273–302.

Brown, Lance Jay, David Dixon, and Oliver Gillham. *Urban Design for an Urban Century: Shaping More Livable, Equitable, and Resilient Cities*. Hoboken, NJ: Wiley, 2009.

Buchanan, Colin. *Traffic in Towns*. London: Her Majesty's Stationery Office, 1963.

Caro, Robert A. *The Power Broker: Robert Moses and the Fall of New York*. New York: Knopf, 1974.

Couperus, Stefan, and Shane Ewen. "Whose 'Urban Internationale'? Intermunicipalism in Europe, 1924–36: The Value of a Decentered, Interpretive Approach to Transnational Urban History." In *Cities beyond Borders: Comparative and Trans-*

*national Approaches to Urban History*, edited by Nicolas Kenny and Rebecca Madgin, 149–72. New York: Routledge, 2015.

Dal Co, Francesco. "From Parks to the Region, Progressive Ideology and the Reform of the American City." In *The American City, from the Civil War to the New Deal*, edited by Giorgio Ciucci, Francesco Dal Co, Mario Manieri-Elia, and Manfredo Tafuri, 143–292. Cambridge, MA: MIT, 1979.

De Moncan, Patrice. *Le Paris d'Haussmann*. Paris: Les Editions du Mécène, 2012.

Divall, Colin. "Railway Modernism Losing Out: Lessons from an English Conurbation, 1955–1975." In this volume.

Divall, Colin, and Winstan Bond, eds. *Suburbanizing the Masses: Public Transport and Urban Development in Historical Perspective*. Aldershot: Ashgate, 2003.

Dogliani, Patrizia. "European Municipalism in the First Half of the Twentieth Century: The Socialist Network." *Contemporary European History* 11, no. 4 (2002): 573–96.

Ehrenfeucht, Renia, and Anastasia Loukaitou-Sideris. "Constructing the Sidewalks: Municipal Government and the Production of Public Space in Los Angeles, California, 1880–1920." *Journal of Historical Geography* 33, no. 1 (2007): 104–24.

Engelke, Peter. "Green City Origins: Democratic Resistance to the Auto-Oriented City in West Germany, 1960–1990." Ph.D. diss., Georgetown University, 2011.

Feriel, Cédric. "Pedestrians, Cars and the City: From Opposition to Cohabitation." *Metropolitics*, 29 May 2013.

Furness, Zachary Mooradian, *One Less Car: Bicycling and the Politics of Automobility*. Philadelphia: Temple University Press, 2010.

Gardon, Sébastien, Arnaud Passalacqua, and Frank Schipper. "Pour une histoire des circulations sur la circulation." *Métropoles* 6 (2009): 1–17.

Gaspari, Oscar. "Cities against States? Hopes, Dreams and Shortcomings of the European Municipal Movement, 1900–1960." *Contemporary European History* 11, no. 4 (2002): 597–621.

Geertse, M. A. "Cross-Border Country Planning Dialogue in Interwar Europe." *Sage Open* 5, no. 3 (2015): 1–12.

———. "Defining the Universal City: The International Federation of Housing and Town Planning and Transnational Planning Dialogue 1913–1945." Ph.D. diss., VU, Amsterdam, 2012.

———. "The International Garden City Campaign: Transnational Negotiations on Town Planning Methods." *Journal of Urban History* 42, no. 4 (2016): 733–52.

Gottschalk, Marie. *The Shadow Welfare State: Labor, Business, and the Politics of Health-Care*. Ithaca, NY: Cornell University Press, 2000.

Guldi, Jo. *Roads to Power: Britain Invents the Infrastructure State*. Cambridge, MA: Harvard University Press, 2012.

Gunn, Simon. "The Buchanan Report, Environment and the Problem of Traffic in Britain." *Twentieth Century British History* 22, no. 4 (2011): 521–42.

Hardwick, M. Jeffrey. *Mall Maker: Victor Gruen, Architect of an American Dream*. Philadelphia: University of Pennsylvania Press, 2003.

Hénard, Eugène. "The Cities of the Future." In *Transactions of the Royal Institute of British Architects, Town Planning Conference London, October 1910*, 345–367. London: Royal Institute of British Architects, 1911.

Hietala, Marjatta. *Services and Urbanization at the Turn of the Century: The Diffusion of Innovations*. Helsinki: Finnish Historical Society, 1987.

Horton, Dave. "Environmentalism and the Bicycle." *Environmental Politics* 15, no. 1 (2006): 41–58.

Howard, Ebenezer. *Garden Cities of To-morrow, a Peaceful Path to Real Reform.* Presented as the second edition of *To-morrow, A Peaceful Path to Real Reform.* 1898. London: Swan Sonnenschein & Co., 1902.

———. *To-morrow, A Peaceful Path to Real Reform.* London: Swan Sonnenschein & Co., 1898.

International Federation for Housing and Planning (IFHP). *Geneva Congress: Towards a More Humane Urban Technology. Topic Transportation,* Vol. 1: *Papers and Proceedings.* IFHP, 1977.

———. *Helsinki Congress, Proceedings and Papers.* IFHP, 1976.

———. *Jerusalem, 27th Congress, Report.* IFHP, 1964.

———. *Proceedings and Papers: Cities for Tomorrow, Directions for Change.* Helsinki: IFHP, 1993.

———. *Tokyo Congress Report on Urban Transportation and Urban Pattern.* IFHP, 1966.

International Union of Local Authorities. *Local Government and the Environment.* The Hague: IULA, 1972.

———. *Traffic Congestion in the City Centre: Reports Prepared for The Hague Congress, June 1957.* The Hague: IULA, 1957.

Iriye, Akira, and Pierre-Yves Saunier, eds. *The Palgrave Dictionary of Transnational History.* London: Palgrave, 2009.

Jacobs, Jane. *Life and Death of Great American Cities: The Failure of Town Planning.* New York: Random House, 1961.

Jordan, David P. "Haussmann and Haussmannisation: The Legacy for Paris." *French Historical Studies* 27, no. 1 (2004): 87–113.

Kaiser, Wolfram, and Johan Schot. *Writing the Rules for Europe: Experts, Cartels, and International Organizations.* Basingstoke: Palgrave Macmillan, 2014.

Lay, M. G. *Ways of the World: A History of the World's Roads and of the Vehicles Who Used Them.* New Brunswick, NJ: Rutgers University Press, 1992.

Levin, Miriam R. "Inventing a Modern Paris: The Dynamic Relationship between Expositions, Urban Planning and Museums." *Quaderns d'Història de l'Enginyeria* 12 (2012): 35–56.

Lichtenstein, Nelson. *The State of the Union: A Century of American Labor.* Princeton: Princeton University Press, 2002.

Loth, David G. *The City within a City: The Romance of Rockefeller Center.* New York: W. Morrow, 1966.

Lundin, Per. "American Numbers Copied: Shaping the Swedish Postwar Car Society." *Comparative Technology Transfer and Society* 2, no. 3 (2004): 303–27.

———. "Mediators of Modernity: Planning Experts and the Making of the 'Car-Friendly' City in Europe." In *Urban Machinery. Inside Modern European Cities,* edited by Mikael Hård and Thomas J. Misa, 257–79. Cambridge, MA: MIT Press, 2008.

Mauch, Christof, and Thomas Zeller. *The World beyond the Windshield: Roads and Landscapes in the United States and Europe.* Athens, OH: Ohio University Press, 2008.

Meller, Helen. *European Cities 1890–1930: History, Culture, and the Built Environment.* New York: Wiley and Sons, 2001.

———. "Philanthropy and Public Enterprise: International Exhibitions and the Modern Town Planning Movement, 1889–1913." *Planning Perspectives* 10, no. 3 (1995): 295–310.

Meller, Helen, and William Whyte, eds. *Ghent Planning Congress 1913: Premier Congrès International et Exposition Comparée des Villes.* Abingdon: Routledge, 2014.

Mitchell, Timothy. *Carbon Democracy: Political Power in the Age of Oil.* London: Verso Books, 2011.

Mom, Gijs. *Atlantic Automobilism: The Emergence and Persistence of the Car, 1890–1940.* New York: Berghahn Books, 2014.

———. "Building an Infrastructure for the Automobile System; PIARC and Road Safety (1908–1938)." In *23rd PIARC World Road Congress.* Paris: PIARC, 2007.

———. "Decentering Highways: European National Road Network Planning from a Transnational Perspective." In *Der Moderne Strasse: Planung, Bau und Verkehr vom 18. bis zum 20. Jahrhundert*, edited by Hans-Liudger Dienel and Hans-Ulrich Schiedt, 77–100. Frankfurt am Main: Campus Verlag, 2010.

———. "International Road Federation." In Iriye and Saunier, *The Palgrave Dictionary of Transnational History*, 582–83.

———. "Roads without Rails: European Transnational Freeway Network Building and the Desire for Long-Range Motorized Mobility." *Technology and Culture* 46, no. 4 (2005): 745–72.

Moraglio, Massimo. "A Rough Modernization: Landscapes and Highways in Twentieth-Century Italy." In Mauch and Zeller, *The World beyond the Windshield*, 108–24.

Morgan, Njogu. *Cycling Cities: The Johannesburg Experience.* Eindhoven: Foundation for the History of Technology, 2019.

Norton, Peter. "Four Paradigms: Traffic Safety in the Twentieth-Century United States." *Technology and Culture* 56, no. 2 (2015): 319–34.

Oldenziel, Ruth. "CIAM and Cycling: Designing for Working-Class Mobility, 1930–1935." Manuscript, 2015.

———. "Keynote Address. The Vanishing Trick: How Cyclists and Pedestrians Were Left Uncounted." *Twelfth International Conference of the International Association for the History of Transport, Traffic and Mobility* (T2M), Drexel University, Philadelphia, 2014.

Oldenziel, Ruth, Martin Emanuel, Adri A. Albert de la Bruhèze, and Frank Veraart, eds. *Cycling Cities: The European Experience. Hundred Years of Policy and Practice.* Eindhoven: Foundation for the History of Technology and Rachel Carson Center for Environment and Society, 2016.

Oldenziel, Ruth, and Mikael Hård. *Consumers, Users, Rebels: The People Who Shaped Europe.* London: Palgrave, 2013.

Osborn, Sir Frederick C. "Bigger Cities or More Cities? Endeavours, Successes and Failures." IFHP Arnhem, Jubilee Congress, Fifty Years. IFHP, 1963.

Papayanis, Nicolas. *Planning before Haussmann.* Baltimore, MD: Johns Hopkins University Press, 2004.

Petersen, Jen. "Whose Streets? Paving the Right to the City." Ph.D. diss., New York University, 2011.

Permanent International Association for Road Congresses (PIARC). *Committee on Road Tunnels. Rio de Janeiro 1959 Reports.* Paris: PIARC, 1959.

———. *The Fifth Question: The Urban Network. Mexico City Congress Proceedings.* Paris: PIARC, 1975.

———. *Minutes of the First Plenary Meeting, Brussels, August 1, 1910.* Paris: PIARC, 1910.

———. *Minutes of the Second Plenary Meeting, London.* Paris: PIARC, 1913.

———. *Prague. Proceedings*. Paris: PIARC, 1971.
———. *Question VI. The Road within the Environment. Mexico City Congress Proceedings*. Paris: PIARC, 1975.
———. *Second Section—Question 6: The Financing of Road Works and their Economic Justification. Proceedings Rio de Janeiro*. Paris: PIARC, 1959.
———. *Urban Street Network. Report, Prague Congress Proceedings*. Paris: PIARC, 1971.
———. *Vienna Congress Proceedings*. Paris: PIARC, 1979.
Pinkney, David H. *Napoleon III and the Rebuilding of Paris*. Princeton: Princeton University Press, 1958.
Porter, Theodore M. "Speaking Precision to Power: The Modern Political Role of Social Science." *Social Research* 73, no. 4 (2006): 1273–94.
Rasmussen, Anne. "Les Congrès internationaux liés aux Expositions universelles de Paris (1867–1900)." In *Mil neuf cent 7* (1989): 23–44.
Revers, H. J. D. *IULA, 1913–1963: The Story of Fifty Years of International Municipal Co-operation*. The Hague: International Union of Local Authorities, 1963.
Riboldazzi, Renzo. "Getting to the Root of the Crisis of Urbanity: The Debate on Urban Open Spaces in the IFHTP Congresses between the Two Wars." *Planum* (May 2012): 1–18.
———. "The IFHP Congresses between the Wars: A Source for Studies on Modern Town Planning." *Town Planning Review* 84, no 2 (2013).
———. *Un'altra modernità: L'IFHTP e la cultura urbanistica tra le due guerre 1923–1939*. Rome: Gangemi, 2010.
Roberts, Howard. *Prevention of Road Accidents: Digest of the Reports Prepared for the Conference in Geneva, September 1949*. The Hague: International Union of Local Authorities, 1949.
Rodgers, Daniel. *Atlantic Crossings: Social Politics in a Progressive Age*. Cambridge, MA: Harvard University Press, 1998.
Rybczynski, Witold. *A Clearing in the Distance: Frederick Law Olmsted and North America in the Nineteenth Century*. New York: Scribner, 1999.
Sadit-Kahn, Janette, and Seth Solomonow. *Streetfight: Handbook for an Urban Revolution*. New York: Penguin Random House, 2016.
Saunier, Pierre-Yves. "Circulations, connexions et espaces transnationaux." *Genèses* 57, no. 4 (2004): 110–26.
———. "La toile municipale aux XIXe–XXe siècles: un panorama transnational vu d'Europe." *Urban History Review* 34, no. 2 (2006): 43–56.
———. "Selling the Idea of Cooperation. The US Foundations and the European Components of the Urban International (1920s–1960s)." In *American Foundations and Large Scale Research: Construction and Transfer of Knowledge*, edited by Giuliana Gemelli, 219–46. Bologna: CLUEB, 2001.
———. "Sketches from the Urban Internationale: Voluntary Societies, International Organizations and US Foundations at the City's Bedside 1900–1960." *International Journal of Urban and Regional Research* 25, no. 2 (2001): 380–403.
———. "United Cities and Local Government." In Iriye and Saunier, *The Palgrave Dictionary of Transnational History*, 1065–66.
Saunier, Pierre-Yves, and Renaud Payre. "Municipalités de tous pays, unissez vous! L'Union Internationale des Villes ou l'Internationale municipale (1913–1940)." *Amministrare* 30, no. 1–2 (1998): 217–39.
Schipper, Frank. "Changing the Face of Europe: European Road Mobility during the Marshall Plan Years." *Journal of Transport History* 28, no. 2 (2007): 211–28.

———. *Driving Europe. Building Europe on Roads in the Twentieth Century*. Amsterdam: Aksant, 2008.

———. "Green Urban Spaces and Sustainable Mobility: Parks as Pockets of Persistence since the 1830s." In this volume.

———. "Unravelling Hieroglyphs: Urban Traffic Signs and the League of Nations." *Métropoles* 6 (2009): 65–100.

Schmucki, Barbara. "Against 'the Eviction of the Pedestrian': The Pedestrians' Association and Walking Practices in Urban Britain after World War II." *Radical History Review* 2012, no. 114 (2012): 113–37.

Schot, Johan, and Vincent Lagendijk. "Technocratic Internationalism in the Interwar Years: Building Europe on Motorways and Electricity Networks." *Journal of Modern European History* 6, no. 2 (2008): 196–217.

Smits, Jan-Pieter, and Frank Veraart. "Toward a Long-Term Measurement System of Sustainable Urban Mobility." In this volume.

Sousa, M. Luísa. *A mobilidade automóvel em Portugal, 1920–1950*. Lisboa: Chiado Editora, 2016.

———. "Roads for the 1940 Portuguese Nationality Commemorations: Modernising by Excess in a Context of Scarcity." *Journal of Transport History* 37, no. 2 (2016): 175–93.

Sousa, M. Luísa, and Rafael Marques. "Political Transitions, Value Change and Motorisation in 1970s Portugal." *Journal of Transport History* 34, no. 1 (2013): 1–21.

Southworth, Michael, and Eran Ben-Joseph. *Streets and the Shaping of Towns and Cities*. Washington, DC: Island Press, 2013.

Sutcliffe, Anthony. *Towards the Planned City: Germany, Britain, the United States and France 1790–1914*. Oxford: Blackwell, 1981.

Suter, Kurt. "Environment and Roads: Preface." *PIARC Marrakesh Congress*. (Paris: PIARC, 1991).

Uekoetter, Frank. *The Green and the Brown. A History of Conservation in Nazi Germany*. New York: Cambridge University Press, 2006.

Van Acker, Wouter, Michiel DeHaene, and Pieter Uytterhoven. "Tussen stedenbouw en stadsbestuur: de stedententoonstelling van Patrick Geddes en het internationale stedencongres, Gent 1913." In *Op het breukvlak van de moderniteit*, edited by Wouter Van Acker and Christophe Verbruggen, 154–69. Gent: Snoeck Publishers, 2013.

Van Wesemael, Pieter. *Architecture of Instruction and Delight: A Socio-historical Analysis of World Exhibitions as a Didactic Phenomenon*. Rotterdam: 010 Publishers, [1997] 2001.

———. "World Exhibitions: Didactical Projects towards Real Reform; Advocates and Catalysts of Modern Urban Society, Economy and Metropolis." *Ricerche Storiche* 95, no. 1–2 (2015): 93–103.

Vereniging van Nederlandse Gemeenten (VNG) Archives, Inventaris nr. 5702, IULA congres 7e Budapest 1940 (uitgesteld).

Wagner, Phillip. "Facilitating Planning Communication across Borders: The International Federation of Housing and Town Planning in the Interwar Period." *Planning Perspectives* 31, no. 2 (2016): 299–311.

———. "New Life for American Downtowns? The 1958 International Seminar on Urban Renewal and the Travel of Planning Ideas in the North Atlantic World." *Planning Perspectives* 29, no. 2 (2014): 189–208.

———. *Stadtplanung für die Welt? Internationales Expertenwissen 1900–1960*. Göttingen: Vandenhoeck & Ruprecht, 2016.

Wall, Alex. *Victor Gruen: From Urban Shop to New City.* Barcelona: Actor, 2006.

Wolf, Peter M. *Eugène Hénard and the Beginning of Urbanism in Paris, 1900–1914.* The Hague: International Federation of Housing and Planning, 1968.

World Commission on Environment and Development, *Our Common Future* (also known as the Brundtland Report) (Oxford: UN, via Oxford University Press, 1987).

CHAPTER 2

## History as Motordom's Tool of Agenda Legitimation
### Twentieth-Century U.S. Urban Mobility Trajectories

Peter Norton

### Introduction

A century ago, many urban mobility futures were possible in the United States. Though there were already millions of motor vehicles, the pursuit of the drive-anywhere, drive-only city, even if only as an ideal, would have seemed absurd. Relatively sustainable mobilities, above all walking and mass transit, were essential for American cities at that time, and the future appeared to include both as major and enduring components of urban transportation. Though not called "sustainable," such mobilities were valued as spatially and economically efficient. Hence the automobile's eventual priority in urban transportation was not originally on history's trajectory. Nevertheless, in the ensuing decades, more sustainable futures were foreclosed, in part because versions of history were deployed to legitimize less sustainable alternatives. Instead of sustainability, automobile enterprises promoted a version of progress according to which there can never be stasis or sufficiency, but only "ever-new horizons"—General Motors' favorite metaphor of the 1930s and 1940s. The pursuit of such a future required versions of the past that were consistent with it.

The status quo has momentum, and diverting it takes force. The status quo has long favored the drive-anywhere, drive-only city, and its momentum has confined today's most visible efforts to improve the sustainability of urban mobility within the strict constraints of this inherited model. Technology, we hear, will make car dependency more sustainable.[1] But if we can escape the status quo's confines, far more possibilities come into view. Among the groups that want to divert the status quo's momentum, the advantage goes to those who first articulate a vision of the future and align it with the predominant values of the present. But before they can induce others to follow this path, they must justify the change of course, legitimize the new path, and make it the right path to follow. To do this, they must align it with history's trajectory. If this trajectory is inconvenient, history can be rewritten as needed.

Beginning in the 1920s, the American automobile industry developed the first and most visible popular histories of the automobile in the United States, and its histories have predominated ever since. They served to justify a radical, expensive, and elusive effort to reconstruct cities to accommodate the vehicle least suited to them. In the American city of 1920, automobiles were newcomers and often blamed for causing traffic congestion and pedestrian casualties. In cities large and small, urban mobility above all meant streetcars and walking. Reconstruction coincided with industry's efforts to change the norms of street use, laws, and engineering standards so that cities would welcome automobiles. In response, diverse automotive interest groups, including manufacturers, dealers, and automobile clubs, recognizing common threats and shared interests, organized a collective effort. Among themselves and in the press, the coalition was sometimes known as *motordom*. Motordom told versions of history that celebrated progress in transportation while redefining it as the ever-expanding reach of cars and motor roads.

The technique of history telling was an important but generally unappreciated development in the new field of public relations and the new enterprise of the full-service advertising agency. Beginning in the twentieth century, public relations professionals learned to arrange not only facts, but hopes, anxieties, and fantasies, casting them as parts in dramas whose internal coherence made them credible. By applying the vanities, the insecurities, and the cognitive biases of audiences, public relations could better persuade than crude boasts or lies. To promote the automobile city, motordom developed an account of American culture as essentially a car culture, united by the values of independence and freedom.[2] Motordom used history as a means to legitimize this new car culture by giving it an American genealogy.

The pioneer and enduring leader in history-telling within American motordom was General Motors (GM). Among the many variations on the technique that GM and others in motordom practiced, three from GM serve here as representatives of their periods. The first story, introduced in 1932 and evolving over the following two decades, was an account of technological inventiveness yielding a "new necessity" that delivered social progress to all. The second, originating in 1961, began when the social progress story had become vulnerable. It sidestepped growing criticism of automobiles' depredations by celebrating cars as the free and spontaneous expression of American culture—a "love affair" that was frankly irrational but which, as the free choice of a free people, could not be suppressed. Finally, elements of both stories were united in 2003 in a more complex account that presents America as a car culture, where rational self-interest and raw enthusiasm favored the automobile.

All three stories were presented with extraordinary inventiveness at lavish expense, challenging us to consider the purposes that justified such efforts by a manufacturer in business not to tell history, but to sell vehicles. The stories' durability and pervasiveness also press us to consider their effects on others' attempts to understand the extreme car dependency of most of the United States—even its cities. Such influence may be direct, in works that accept car culture or rational self-interest as leading explanations, but it may also be indirect, in works where an opposing argument is largely a product of the position it rejects. These challenges are directed above all to those who seek a more sustainable mobility future, because history is a trajectory. Those who would deflect this trajectory in favor of a different future must begin by reconsidering the past that defines this trajectory. Motordom's ventures into history were such efforts, and others interested in divergent futures can learn from the example.[3]

## Motordom: The First Historians of the Automobile in America

Today we are still immersed in a received history of the automobile in America that gives us undue confidence in what we know. There are also subversive counternarratives, but in presenting an opposing account they, too, are influenced by the predominant history. A vast scholarly history has been somewhat freer of the predominant history, but its social influence has been slight. The predominant history, by contrast, has reached mass audiences. It is mostly accurate in detail, but selective in misleading ways. This makes it both more intractable and more influential.

The predominant histories are diverse, but, since their origins in the 1920s and 1930s, they have developed persistent themes. In the predominant account, the automobile, while attractive to people worldwide, has had a special resonance in American culture, which welcomed it as liberating. Traffic fatalities were high, but Americans tolerated them. A "car culture" developed, attracting people of all classes. Cities evolved to accommodate the demands of this culture: drive-ins, motels, and suburbs were responses to cars' popularity. Roads were congested, especially after World War II, and roadbuilding was merely a necessary response to the popularity of the automobile. Later generations were troubled by the disappearance of the streetcar and by the destruction that came with the urban interstates, but at the time these developments were generally accepted as the price of progress. Americans' enthusiasm for cars was not always rational, and experts often criticized the costs to cities, to the environment, and to human lives, but as a free society the United States was guided more by popular preference than by experts' judgments. Today we may recognize excesses that were much less apparent then. We have corrected some of these excesses already, and through technological innovation—especially driverless cars—we will adapt car culture to new standards of spatial efficiency, sustainability, and safety. Or so the typical accounts say.[4]

Motordom cast itself only a bit part in this drama. Its story omits its own prolonged and strenuous effort to adapt the city to the automobile. Beginning in the 1920s, it redirected blame for danger from speed to recklessness. It redirected blame for pedestrian casualties from cars to careless pedestrians. It redirected blame for congestion to low speed limits, insufficient street and road networks, and obstructive streetcars. By the late 1920s, motordom was developing a vision of the automobile, and the automobile city, as the inevitable future. The trajectory of history put a motor age utopia just over the horizon, in the city of tomorrow: a drive-anywhere city where all congestion was due to insufficient road capacity, all injuries were due to carelessness and inadequate roads, and those who questioned these things were cranky throwbacks from another age.

Popular histories put the future automobile city on this historical trajectory. They appeared in countless variations across all media. Three of the most influential examples, spaced decades apart from each other, can stand in for the rest. Though the first two are largely forgotten today, all three were among the most widely seen works of popular history ever presented, each reaching audiences of millions. Though all three are closely associated with General Motors, other members of motordom contributed to this history as well.

## The New Necessity

One of the first in motordom to see strategic value in history-telling was Charles F. Kettering of General Motors. Kettering united skills in engineering, management, and public relations. In 1920 he was hired as vice president of GM's research division. With Alfred P. Sloan and other GM leaders, Kettering was an innovator in market strategy, guiding the company to pass Ford by the late 1920s and become the world's largest corporation.

In 1928, just as GM was racing ahead of Ford, Chicago began to plan a world's fair for 1933.[5] GM's exhibit featured a working Chevrolet assembly line. But Kettering had more in mind. He wanted to tell history in a way that would justify an unlimited future for the car. He sketched this history with a GM colleague, Allen Orth, in a breezy little book published in 1932, when the automobile industry was reeling from the Depression. Called *The New Necessity: The Culmination of Progress in Transportation*, it was one in a series of books published for the Century of Progress exposition in advance of its opening.[6] In 1929, just before the Depression, Kettering had warned that sustainable demand for products required manufacturers to "keep the consumer dissatisfied."[7] In response to the Depression, GM committed itself to this kind of economic sustainability, in part by promising a better future. To align this future with the past, GM told histories of the automobile. Kettering and Orth's book included a history of the automobile in America that would evolve into motordom's version of history.

The major themes of this account would become the established history of the automobile in America. According to the authors, following the display of a Benz automobile at the Chicago World's Fair of 1893,

> America was bitten by a new bug—the automobile. Americans were quick to recognize the possibilities of the automobile—it seemed to represent transportation in its most desirable form, possessing speed and exclusiveness. But the conservatives were there too—gazing humorously at the snorting buggy careening up Main Street, or smiling in a self-satisfied manner as they drove their smart turnouts past a horseless buggy stranded by the wayside.[8]

Kettering and Orth thus introduced the most persistent stock characters of a historical drama: an enthusiastic, younger majority of future-minded auto enthusiasts, opposed by a retrograde class of skeptical conservatives.

By the 1910s, Americans of all classes, rural and urban, "had decided they liked the automobile. It was just the thing they had always wanted. It possessed individuality and utility and so they bought automobiles by the thousands."[9] Here we get another persistent theme of the received history. After some resistance from older and more rural segments of the population, Americans embraced the car. Mass-production Fords erased the class resentments of the previous decades, when only the rich could afford one. Well before 1920, Americans across social and geographical space were united in this enthusiasm. Soon the automobile "evolved from luxury to a necessity—a necessity not to any specific class but to everybody."[10]

*New Necessity*'s omissions are significant. Automobiles were intensely controversial in their first decades, especially in cities. Kettering and Orth never mention pedestrians or their resentments. In their only reference to safety, they reassure readers by noting improvements such as four-wheel brakes and better headlights, while admitting "one factor that the manufacturers cannot control. That is the peculiarly constructed piece of apparatus which sits immediately behind the steering wheel. He (or she) is responsible for more than ninety per cent of the accidents."[11]

In *The New Necessity*, the motor age was a consequence of Americans' demand for cars. They demanded drivable roads too. Road construction in and out of towns was a response to drivers' demands, not an inducement to demand. Once Americans embraced the car, "then the logical thing happened. It was expecting too much of these thousands of motorists to keep themselves confined to the narrow limits of the city's streets. . . . So they began to grumble, demanded automobile roads, and got them."[12] Demand for motor roads preceded the supply: "The process started when people began to demand highways for their automobiles."[13]

Kettering and Orth traced this "logical thing" to their present, 1932, where it justified change. "A man buys a car that will travel sixty miles an hour with ease, but if he makes a trip to a town sixty miles away, it takes him two hours to get there. Why? Because he has to pass through a dozen small towns and through the busiest street in every town." But "if the country were really built for automobiles, it would be possible to travel along an express highway around the busy streets of all the towns at the possible speed of sixty miles an hour."[14] Following history's trajectory, the next "logical thing" was express motor highways. Where would the logical thing lead? Kettering and Orth predicted: "Someday in the not too far distant future a great express highway will traverse the continent and compared to the capacity of the highway of today, it will carry an almost fabulous stream of traffic, travelling well over a mile a minute."[15] When paved roads "have covered every logical course and when an automobile can travel these roads with maximum speed and safety, then we can truthfully say that the automobile can do nothing further to liberalize the people of the world."[16] This was a manifesto for the drive-anywhere future, and history was its justification. With this agenda, motordom would tell this version of history, reaching mass audiences.

By itself, *The New Necessity*'s influence was limited. Several newspapers printed reviews.[17] GM's exhibit at the Century of Progress was scant on history. But eventually the book's message found new and enduring forms that reached many millions. After the fair closed in 1934, Kettering persuaded GM to keep some of the displays and add more for a road show. America had gone to the world's fair—now the world's fair would go to America. Eight large, custom-made, futuristic road vehicles called "Streamliners" would carry the exhibits and serve as displays themselves. They were like large buses except that they had no windows; instead, their sides opened to display wonders of science and engineering for local audiences across the country. Each stop was an event, like the events that public relations pioneer Edward Bernays recommended as means to attract publicity. GM called the traveling show the Parade of Progress. These tours were repeated intermittently until the last ended in 1956.[18]

The first Parade of Progress, carried in nine Streamliners plus numerous support vehicles, toured the country from 1936 to 1940. Like GM's exhibit at the Century of Progress, this tour made little use of history. But GM revived the Parade of Progress in 1940–41, following its spectacular Futurama exhibit at the New York World's Fair of 1939–40. Twelve new "Futurliners," which replaced the Streamliners, took select exhibits to small-town America. This time the emphasis on the future was complemented by an extraordinary new exhibit on the past, built specially for the Parade of Progress. The version of history depicted in *Our American Crossroads* aligned with the version of the future that GM more famously presented in its colossal Futurama exhibit.[19]

*Our American Crossroads* occupied the full length of one Futurliner. Through a big glass panel, fairgoers saw a large, detailed diorama of an ordinary village circa 1900, about which a recorded voice reminisced. The actor who recorded it, Parker Fennelly of Maine, played New England codgers on the radio and in the movies. In 1939, Fennelly acted in the first radio performance of Thornton Wilder's play *Our Town*. Wilder's story was set in the imaginary little New Hampshire town of Grover's Corners, following the hopes and heartbreaks of generations of residents from 1901 to 1938, the year the play was first performed. The play includes a narrator called the "stage manager," who talks the audience through the story. It was huge success, winning a Pulitzer Prize.

*Our American Crossroads* imitated *Our Town*, this time with Fennelly's voice narrating as an unseen stage manager. Grover's Corners was now Pleasant Corners. In *Our Town*, the stage manager remembers the 1904 arrival of the automobile in Grover's Corners without affection: "And now they're bringing in these auto-mo-biles, best thing to do is just stay home. Why I can remember when dogs used to sleep in the middle of the street all day, and nothing ever come to disturb'm."[20] Similarly, in *Crossroads*, Fennelly represented the most skeptical audience for twentieth-century innovation: the small-town old-timer.

As viewers looked over the details of the large diorama, Fennelly described Pleasant Corners as a rural backwater. But soon the magic starts. First a horseless carriage appears—a little model moving along a slot on the dirt road. Fennelly describes the skeptical response—which turns out to be justified as the car breaks down. The locals taunt the unfortunate motorist: "Better get a horse!" But the car's practical advantages soon convert locals.

Time in the exhibit passes at about four years a minute, while the diorama changes in astonishing ways. Hidden electric motors rotate segments of the scene. The dirt road rolls over; now it's a paved road busy with automobiles. A general store rolls over; now a modern variety store is next to it. A field rolls over; now there are houses. A new school and a new steel bridge appear too. Progress is made visible. By the 1920s, the once sleepy crossroads is a bustling stretch of highway, where people can get ahead. As the story ends, the town's main street—a dirt track in 1900—has become a busy four-lane highway. There was a striking vividness to the eleven-minute scene. The electromechanical wizardry of the display made it a popular attraction, watched with fascination by millions.

*Crossroads* toured the United States with the Parade of Progress in 1941, ceasing in December after the U.S. entered World War II. By then, according to GM's estimates, over twelve million people had seen it.[21] The Parade, including *Crossroads*, resumed the tour in 1953, continuing almost without interruption for over three years, and reaching eight million people in 148 towns and cities in thirty-five states and three Canadian provinces.[22] Newspaper accounts indicate that *Crossroads* was a big draw, and it became the only major exhibit from the tour to remain on public display after 1956. The Chicago Museum of Science and Industry exhibited it from then until 2001, when it moved to the General Motors Heritage Center in Sterling Heights, Michigan.

## The Love Affair

On 28 June 1956, the Parade of Progress arrived in Spokane, Washington. It was the show's final stop. The next day, President Eisenhower signed the Federal-Aid Highway Act of 1956, establishing the funding mechanism that would transform the interstate highways from a formal designation for a national network composed mostly of two-lane roads into a system of freeways that cut through America's cities. Within cities the massive projects were often destructive and controversial. Many welcomed them enthusiastically, but many others decried them. By the late 1950s, urban interstates and the drive-anywhere city were under attack.

While most critics were local, coming from all walks of life, the few who found national audiences tended to be from a more exclusive intellectual set, predominantly from the urban northeast. They cast Americans as irrational idolaters, sacrificing themselves financially and bodily to the automobile.[23] Lewis Mumford and John Keats (a writer of popular humor) best represent the new narrative; William H. Whyte and Jane Jacobs offered variants that engaged in less demonization of the car and more celebration of a model of streets—small in scale, diverse in character and use—long-since rejected by highway engineers. To these critics, the innovation of the automobile did not negate the enduring values of equity, sociability, and civic engagement that depended upon urban fabrics. In effect, their critique was based on a version of social sustainability that clashed with motordom's economic sustainability effort to secure a perpetually growing market for new cars. The journalist and freelance writer John Keats specialized in light fare, leavening biting sarcasm with sketchy cartoons. In 1956 Keats ridiculed suburbia in *The Crack in the Picture Window*. After the 1956 Highway Act, he followed with *The Insolent Chariots* (1958), which made fun of the chrome-adorned excesses of the era's cars. Both were big sellers, and both decoupled the automobile's place in American life from the celebration of progress.

Keats' publisher, Lippincott, advertised *Insolent Chariots* as "All about America's Love Affair with the Automobile."[24] Three years later, through a different channel, this metaphor would become the favorite thesis for the rise of the automobile in the United States. Until then it was almost unknown. Bergen Evans, an English professor known as the host of CBS TV's *The Last Word*, had used it once to disparage Americans' idolatry of the automobile in a 1954 book attacking hokum.[25] It was used again in an unsigned editorial in the Rochester *Democrat and Chronicle*.[26] This time the phrase was intended merely to express the popularity of the automobile, which justified accommodating it even though it "requires billions in highway and other expenditures" and "gives our cities their biggest headaches." Weeks later, on Valentine's Day, a GM ad campaign depicted interlinked hearts carved in a tree trunk: in one was "U.S.A.," in the other "Chevy." The copy described the relationship as "the longest love affair since automobiles began."[27] In 1961, IBM's *Think* magazine ran an article celebrating "Our Love Affair with the Automobile."[28]

Following the cluster of criticism in the late 1950s, motordom needed an answer. The "love affair" metaphor, already in evidence in the Chevrolet ad campaign, would serve the purpose. If Americans have a love affair with the automobile, and if the affair began in the car's early days, before organized motordom existed, then extraordinary efforts to accommodate cars were due to mass preferences and cultural constants, not motordom's agendas. The "love affair" explanation, if accepted, would make a rational defense of the car's utility or cost efficacy unimportant. If the automobile was the free choice of a free people, then America, as a free society, would adopt it. In a free society, experts find the best way to implement the people's choices, but it is not their place to judge them. Versions of automobile history could explain the rise of the automobile in America as a love affair, and in so doing justify extraordinary efforts to accommodate the car (love will find a way) without requiring rational justification (love is blind). Motordom could present versions of history that would justify the enormous and expensive highway projects then underway.

The "love affair" explanation had the virtue of being at least half true. Most people welcomed the chance to buy a car once they could afford one. Even though many such purchases had less to do with affection than with circumstances where there were few alternatives, there was a kind of affection for cars for delivering their purchasers from isolation. But there was hostility too. The antagonism was particularly widespread in cities, where it was unmissable in the daily newspapers. The half-truth in the "love affair" explanation concealed the untold story of the real antagonism to cars that was common in American cities in the 1910s and 1920s, and that persisted later—especially in response to the major urban highway projects of the 1950s and 1960s.

In the television age, a rich visual history of Americans' love affair with the automobile would not require an elaborate electromechanical diorama. It could be presented simultaneously to millions on prime-time television. NBC had a suitable vehicle. In 1955 NBC-TV launched *Project 20*, a series of fifty-minute "telementaries" (documentaries for television).[29] In 1959 NBC announced it was working on a *Project 20* telementary, "the story of America's love affair with the automobile."[30] The program would be aired as an episode of the *Du Pont Show of the Week*. Du Pont then owned a 23 percent share in General Motors, to which it sold paints and fabrics.[31] In 1957 the Supreme Court found Du Pont in violation of antitrust for this arrangement, but two years later Du Pont secured a federal court's permission to retain its GM shares on condition that it would forego its corporate voting rights.[32]

Sponsors' influence over scripts was no secret; the sponsors themselves admitted it. Testifying to the Federal Communications Commission, Gail Smith, GM's director of advertising, dis-closed that GM did not permit depictions of drunk driving, though he was not specific about the scripts GM had changed.[33] Some writers, notably Rod Serling, complained about sponsors' influence.[34] In spring 1961, NBC began heavily advertising an episode of the *Du Pont Show of the Week*. In every ad, "Merrily We Roll Along" was described as "the story of America's love affair with the automobile."[35] After months of reminders, all of them using the "love affair" metaphor, NBC finally broadcast "Merrily" Sunday evening, 22 October. The telementary bore resemblances to *Our American Crossroads*. This time the narrator was Groucho Marx. Like Parker Fennelly, Groucho made light of the early automobile's failings and the consequent low expectations. He described the restrictions these skeptics imposed on the automobile, sometimes in misleading ways. He summarized Great Britain's Red Flag Act of 1865, which required steam road locomotives to be preceded by a man carrying a red flag, but transposed the setting to America at the beginning of the automobile age.[36] The people behind such restrictions came off as ridiculous luddites.[37]

As in *Crossroads*, however, the car's attractions soon overwhelmed such stuffy resistance. By the 1920s, "our culture, like our economy, was on wheels." "We were so in love with the automobile," Groucho explained. In fifty-one minutes, Groucho used the words "love affair" repeatedly, and developed the metaphor: in this couple, the car was the "girl"; the American driver, the man. It was the "great American romance between a man and his car." Americans had a "burning love affair with the automobile." It began early, when "the motor car was being treated like the new girl in town." Then followed "the long honeymoon with our new sweetheart." From the wheel of a 1961 Chevrolet convertible on a Los Angeles freeway, Groucho concluded: "Our romance with the automobile—it's still going on. Our honeymoon ended (along with a few other things) in 1929, but we're still very much married to Lizzie. We don't always know how to get along with her, but you certainly can't get along without her." Groucho, then on his own third marriage, paused, then added, "And if that isn't marriage I don't know what is."

Soon after the broadcast, motordom took up the "love affair" thesis by this name, and helped establish it. It has remained in circulation ever since. In 1962 every known reference to the "love affair" came from people connected to motordom. Richard Latham, an industrial designer with Raymond Loewy Associates who designed GM's Scenicruiser bus for Greyhound, used the "love affair" thesis in a public lecture in May 1962. According to a reporter's summary, Latham explained that "the American public is in love with the automobile." The thesis shields the car from its critics: "Critics of the automobile overlook the fact that the 'Great American Love Affair' with the automobile has made such a difference in the lives of millions of people that they are willing to overlook or ignore its faults."[38] "Merrily" was rebroadcast nationally in August 1962; advertisements again called it the story of Americans' love affair with the car. That November, Michael Schwartz, chairman of the executive committee of the Chicago Automobile Show, attributed the success of auto shows to Americans' "60-year love affair" with the automobile.[39] Months later *Petroleum Today*, the American Petroleum Institute's magazine, published an article about the early history of the automobile in America under the title "Start of a Love Affair." The author, Christy Borth, was the retired assistant to the managing director of the Automobile Manufacturers Association, and was known within the industry as its unofficial historian. According to Borth, "The relationship of the American and his car is illogical because it is a love affair."[40]

Beginning in 1963, the "love affair" phrase began to appear in news items without help from motordom. Reporters used the term as if it was just an expression—an untraceable bit of folk wisdom. By the mid-1960s it had passed into the lexicon of social commentary, where it has remained as a supposed artifact of "conventional wisdom."[41] In the light of the "love affair" thesis, critics of the car could seem elitist, antidemocratic, and out of touch. "Merrily" was too plebeian in style, too elementary in content, to attract intellectual discussion. Intellectuals—critics of the automobile and others—ignored it. Strangely, however, its mantra gradually became the most widely accepted and the single most common explanatory metaphor for the automobile in American life. By this standard, the film must rank as one of motordom's greatest public relations successes. Both among intellectuals and in the popular press, "Americans' love affair with the automobile" and close variants have remained a ubiquitous presence in discussions of the automobile.[42]

The automobile's critics accepted the notion at least as much as its defenders, unwittingly assuming the role in which the film cast the car's critics: as backward-looking enemies of fun. Indeed the thesis was so successful with the car's critics that the car's defenders have even mistakenly attributed it to them. As Joel Schwartz of the American Enterprise Institute sees it: "From the perspective of the automobile's critics, Americans have an irrational love affair with the automobile."[43] Defending cars, Schwartz contends that preference for them is universal, independent of culture, and economically rational—and in so doing he inadvertently undermines the dual moral of the "Merrily" fable—that the love affair and the "car culture" that go with it are distinctly American, and accommodation of the car at any expense requires no rational defense.

"Americans' love affair with the automobile" is neither self-evident truism, nor organic folk wisdom, nor cultural theory—though it has been presented as all three. It is a masterstroke of public relations, an invention for a distinct purpose: to make car-dependent design normal design.

## America on the Move

There is irony in the fact that the originators of the "love affair" thesis invested so much effort, ingenuity, and money into telling it. If Americans took to the car naturally, eagerly, and universally, it is strange that the story required such an investment. But the "love affair" thesis was not the only account of the automobile's priority. It emerged against an environment of growing criticism—not of the car itself but of the extent to which it was accommodated, and of the car's social and environmental costs. As such criticism continued and evolved, the "love affair" thesis evolved too.

In 1973 a U.S. Senate subcommittee began to investigate anticompetitive practices in the U.S. automobile industry. Some alleged there was too little competition; senators were considering legislation to restore it. General Motors was under particular scrutiny for monopolistic practices. The subcommittee summoned Bradford Snell, a young lawyer, as expert witness. In a long statement, Snell blamed the decline in urban mass transit on "a relentless campaign to destroy America's rail and bus systems."[44] In support of his statement, he submitted a long report documenting the use of a holding company created by General Motors and other corporations to buy up street railways and replace them with inferior bus services.[45]

Snell's proof was a version of history. His account was the antithesis of the predominant "love affair" histories, those in the vein of *Our American Crossroads* and "Merrily We Roll Along." It was also riddled with defects. He had evidence to connect the early demise of several struggling urban electric railways to a deliberate effort by some corporations in motordom to replace them with buses, but this was no explanation of the automobile city.[46] Snell answered motordom's versions of history with one that reflected the same errors in mirror image. If it was not a "love affair," then it was a betrayal. If the love object was not the automobile, then it was the streetcar. If motordom was not the hero, then it was the villain.

Nevertheless, in simplified forms, Snell's history thrived. Mainstream press publications and television programs persistently retold it as if it was reliable. Numerous errors of fact were overlooked. Through a 1988 Hollywood movie, *Who Framed Roger Rabbit?*, a version of it reached millions.[47] Such attention demands explanation. Snell's thesis served an unmet need. The predominant explanation—the love affair—was too incredible for too many people. Millions of Americans did not own or want cars, but the "love affair" thesis said they did. Millions who did own cars resorted to them from necessity, not choice or "love." Many could name loved ones killed or maimed in crashes. Many more had lost a neighborhood to an expressway or parking lots. They did not recognize themselves, their communities, or their experiences in the love affair's account of eager enthusiasm for cars, or in the caricature of cars' critics as cranks. The "love affair" thesis was too crude to satisfy all who heard it, and those it dissatisfied were hungry for an alternative.

General Motors answered Snell in a long rebuttal.[48] Numerous scholars joined in the corrections over the ensuing decades. None of these rejoinders attracted anything like the audiences that Snell's popularizers achieved. In 1996 the PBS television program *POV* nationally aired a fifty-five-minute documentary called *Taken for a Ride*, which presented the Snell thesis as sound.[49] Snell himself appears in the program as an interview subject. For the first time, critics of the policy priority for automobiles were commanding more popular attention for their cause than the advocates of the automobile.

General Motors needed some kind of reply for a mass audience. In 1997, a year after *Taken for a Ride*, it got an opportunity when the Smithsonian Institution's National Museum of American History was looking for sponsors for a lavish redesign of its Hall of Transportation as a new permanent exhibit. GM took the opportunity to promote a new telling of the history of the automobile in America. Like *Crossroads* and "Merrily," this history would be for the millions. It would be subtler than its predecessors, but consistent with the "love affair" thesis in attributing the drive-everywhere city ultimately to popular choice.

The National Museum of American History had exhibited historic cars in its Hall of Transportation since 1964. As a part of the Smithsonian Institution, the museum enjoyed unmatched prestige among history museums in the United States. Nevertheless, its automobile exhibit was rather stodgy; the cars were simply displayed alone, as museum pieces. In the 1990s its directors wanted something that would not merely display cars but put them in context. In 1997 Congress voted the museum $3 million as "seed money" to start a project that would raise $21 million more.

At the time, the Smithsonian was reeling from a recent international controversy over the presentation of historical objects in thought-provoking exhibitions that told stories, evoked eras, captured perspectives, and sometimes even challenged visitors—exactly what was proposed for the new transportation exhibit. The Smithsonian's National Air and Space Museum had proposed to include artifacts and images of bombed Hiroshima with the nose section of *Enola Gay*, the B-29 bomber that had dropped an atomic bomb on that city. Widespread protest led to five redrafts of the exhibit, its cancellation, and the resignation of the director of the National Air and Space Museum in May 1995. *Enola Gay* was put on display, but as an object, not an exhibit. It was a fiasco for the Smithsonian.[50] The National Museum of American History had no desire to repeat it.

Among donors to the transportation exhibit, General Motors took an early and wide lead. In 2001 the museum announced that GM had agreed to give $10 million. In second place, at $5 million, was the American Automobile Association.[51] GM publicly insisted on one condition: the Hall of Transportation would become the General Motors Hall of Transportation. The history museum had never named an exhibit hall for a company. But GM insisted, and with $10 million at stake, the Smithsonian's board of regents relented.[52]

The decision was controversial. The project director, Steven Lubar, accepted it as the cost of doing business, but admitted that "many staff members were unhappy."[53] In a *New York Times* ad, critics damned the deal, citing the Snell thesis among the grounds for their opposition.[54] Later, 170 scholars signed a petition urging the museum not to "let donors influence both the nature and content of exhibitions." Lubar and others who had worked so hard to put the exhibit together, confident in their position that GM had neither sought influence on the exhibit's contents nor would be granted any, chafed at being "lectured" by scholars who had fallen for Snell's flawed thesis.[55]

Yet even if GM's direct influence on the content was "zero" (as a GM spokesman stated),[56] it was generally consistent with the love affair thesis. Before the Smithsonian even began its search for donors for its new exhibit, this interpretation of automotive history was by far the best established, in and out of academia, and was hence likely to be evident in the exhibit's contents with or without GM's direct influence.

On 30 September 2003, weeks before the new exhibit opened to the public, the museum held an exclusive gala reception for dignitaries in the newly named General Motors Hall of Transportation. The event was named "America's Love Affair with the Automobile." The exhibit itself, called *America on the Move*, opened on 22 November, when the museum introduced its general theme: "This major exhibition examines how transportation—from 1876 to 1999—has shaped our American identity from a mostly rural nation into a major economic power, forged a sense of national unity, delivered consumer abundance, and encouraged a degree of social and economic mobility unlike that of any other nation of the world." In a generally favorable review, the historian Zachary Schrag noted a more specific theme: "Changes in transportation were the products of choices by regular people."[57] The description would have applied with equal validity to *Our American Crossroads* and to "Merrily We Roll Along."

At the exhibit, Schrag found that "the trope of progress is still visually dominant."[58] He noted the very low profile of traffic's death toll and of public policy that promoted driving. But as Schrag observed, the grimmer aspects of automobile history are not absent. Segregation and racial discrimination, white flight, and the devastation of black neighborhoods by interstate highways are all acknowledged. But according to the exhibit, as Schrag noticed, the causal agents are mass preferences. This is most apparent in the segment of the exhibit about streetcars, which features Washington, D.C., as its example city. Exhibit designers knew that many visitors would be acquainted with the Snell thesis, which was most relevant to this part of the exhibit. Visitors would notice the ubiquity of streetcars in cities throughout the first half of the twentieth century. Some acknowledgment of streetcars' disappearance from the vast majority of cities was needed. No object is used for this purpose, but through a remarkable signboard on a wall, the museum does ask what some visitors would surely be asking—and perhaps answering, with the help of a popular version of the Snell thesis: "What Happened to Streetcars?" This question figures prominently at the top of the sign.

In three short paragraphs, the sign provides the answers: consumer choice, driven by streetcars' obsolescence. It explains: "The limitations of streetcar systems, government and corporate policies and actions, consumer choice, and the development of alternatives—especially the bus and the car—helped make trolleys obsolete." Four factors were in play: technology, public policy, corporate strategy, and mass preferences. Although the relative importance of these factors is a matter of disagreement, the exhibit does not shrink from evaluating them and choosing a winner.

Technology mattered, according to the sign, particularly for reasons of comfort and cost. "Buses began replacing trolleys in the 1910s. Many commuters considered buses a modern, comfortable, even luxurious replacement for rickety, uncomfortable trolleys." In fact, comfort varied widely on both streetcars and buses; crowding, rather than vehicle type, was the greatest factor. The sign continues: "Buses made business sense for transit companies; they were more flexible and cheaper to run than streetcars." This, too, is a problematic contention, and its validity changes with time and according to the regulatory environment.

Even after World War I, when the operating expenses of electric railways rose sharply, we find streetcars operating at less expense than buses, and street railways treating buses not as alternatives to streetcars but as supplements. For example, one expert, recommending buses to street railways, advised them to use buses to feed passengers to streetcar lines, but cautioned that "the community must be prepared to pay a higher rate for motor-bus than for modern trolley transportation." Specifically, "the cost of a seat-mile on a bus is from 1½ to 2 times as great as for up-to-date street car operation."[59] Though the relative cost efficacy of buses improved, the sign ignores the policy factors influencing this trend. The case for the bus's superiority turns out to be a blind alley; ultimately it attributes change to a mass preference specifically for private automobiles, at the expense of buses as well as streetcars.

The sign bravely addresses the Snell thesis directly: "In a few cities, auto and auto-supply companies, including General Motors, Firestone Tire and Rubber Company, and Standard Oil of California, bought an interest in transit companies and encouraged the conversion from streetcar to bus." However, this alternative explanation is rather easily dismissed: "But many cities made the choice to switch without this influence." This is the only corporate strategy the text considers, and the sign relegates it to a bit part. Public policy is not addressed at all, despite its extraordinary importance in the transformation. In other areas of the exhibit, visitors can learn about some of the policies that promoted car-dependent suburbs. But they do not learn that streetcars were strictly regulated in ways that constrained revenues and drove up costs. Visitors reading this sign would have to be forgiven for supposing that these factors were unimportant in the declining service standards that led many to give up on them.

According to the sign, the decisive factor was mass preference. "Most importantly, Americans chose another alternative—the automobile. The car became the commuter option of choice for those who could afford it, and more people could do so." To the extent that there was such a choice, it occurred amid public policies that prioritized moving cars over all other modes of transportation—policies that constituted a de facto war on motor vehicle congestion at all cost. The alert visitor can piece this together from elements of the exhibit, but the sign itself treats the preferences as essential and independent of policy. The sign concludes: "As in most cities, the majority of D.C.-area residents prefer to drive alone in their cars from their homes to their workplaces." Practice under given conditions is interpreted as essential preference.

In this and other ways, *America on the Move*'s messages prominently include the love affair thesis, retold for a new generation. Like *Our Amer-*

*ican Crossroads* and "Merrily We Roll Along," it is a compound story of multiple threads, including skepticism of the automobile, doubts about the pride of place it won, and mistakes along the way. *America on the Move* pays more attention to the costs and to the missteps than its predecessors. But like them, it ultimately credits the triumph of the automobile to its universal appeal, to America's distinctively car-friendly culture, and above all to Americans' choices.

As scholars, the exhibit's designers were acquainted with revisionist history and acknowledged it in some of the content. But as public museum professionals, they were also in the business of designing an exhibit that reflected the public's tastes, that avoided offense to the constituencies it depended upon, and that could raise questions about the established history while also largely accepting it. Though critics of the GM gift warned that "corporate money in Washington generally does not come without a price,"[60] GM had only to be confident that the Smithsonian would not actually rewrite the established history that GM and others in motordom had already written. By the 1990s this history was consistent with the prevailing scholarship and with the public's expectations. Hence the museum did not have to conform to GM's expectations. To present a history that legitimized the automobile's extraordinary priority, GM only needed the museum to present the mainstream, popular history that motordom had been promoting for sixty years.

### Conclusion

*Our American Crossroads*, "Merrily We Roll Along," and *America on the Move* are mutually consistent versions of history that were developed and promoted at great expense by a business committed to shareholder value. Though its material interests were in the present and the future, GM recognized that the legitimacy of the future it wanted depended upon its alignment with history's trajectory. Hence it made itself the single most visible history teller of the automobile in America. But of course such kinds of storytelling were not limited to GM, to the automobile, or to the United States. Particularly after World War II, they reached overseas, extending U.S. economic, cultural, and political influence. Uniting such efforts were promises of better futures justified in part by constructed, selective histories.[61]

There is danger in pursuing new values, such as sustainability, within the framework of a status quo that created the problems sustainability is intended to address. Sustainability, approached via a status quo that too uncritically accepts that automobile dependency is the product of mass preferences, rational economic choice, or a cultural "love affair" with cars, may give us a future of more energy-efficient urban sprawl enabled by connected autonomous vehicles, without duly considering other possibilities. Autonomous vehicles may indeed be useful tools in a more sustainable future, but we can't find their optimum role if dubious assumptions, whose origins we've forgotten, prevent us from making a fair review of the possibilities.

Proponents of more sustainable urban mobility are often frustrated by an attachment to automobiles that, to them, may appear positively strange. Where they see obvious dependency, defenders of the status quo see freedom. When they say they offer new choices, their audiences hear new constraints. When they speak of opportunities, others perceive threats. Such difficult experiences are encounters with the momentum of history's trajectory, which will grant new ideas a hearing only within the terms imposed by the status quo. But American motordom demonstrated that history's trajectory can be shifted, and the work begins in the past. New histories, written without the influence of the agendas of the status quo's defenders, can show new possibilities beyond the unfavorable framing the status quo would give them. To uncover new future possibilities, we may best begin by recovering lost histories.

**Peter Norton** is associate professor of history in the Department of Engineering and Society at the University of Virginia. He is the author of *Fighting Traffic: The Dawn of the Motor Age in the American City* (MIT Press). His article "Street Rivals: Jaywalking and the Invention of the Motor Age Street," published in *Technology and Culture*, won the Abbott Payson Usher Prize of the Society for the History of Technology.

## Notes

1. On such claims of "technological promise" and the commitments they promote, see Harro van Lente, "From Promises to Requirement," in *Contested Futures: A Sociology of Prospective Techno-Science*, ed. Nik Brown, Brian Rappert, and Andrew Webster (London: Routledge, 2000).
2. Peter Norton, "Of Love Affairs and Other Stories," in *Incomplete Streets: Processes, Practices, and Possibilities*, ed. Stephen Zavestoski and Julian Agyeman (London: Routledge, 2015), 17–35.
3. The technique has applications far beyond urban mobility. During the so-called "redemption" of the South by white segregationists in the 1880s and 1890s, historians, notably William Archibald Dunning of Columbia University, wrote histo-

ries characterizing the preceding Reconstruction era governments as disasters. Because these historians blamed black voters, their histories justified disenfranchisement and segregation. Popularized versions of this history reached a mass audience; see John David Smith and J. Vincent Lowery, eds., *The Dunning School: Historians, Race, and the Meaning of Reconstruction* (Lexington: University of Kentucky Press, 2013). Carter G. Woodson condemned the Dunning school and its popularizers as "rewriters of history" in *The Mis-Education of the Negro* (Washington, DC: Associated Publishers, 1933), ch. 8. As a reformer born of former slaves, Woodson made it his life's purpose to recover Africans' and African Americans' history, in part to serve a better future.

4. The "typical accounts" are superabundant. The three examples examined in this chapter are taken as representative of a vast body of popular work.

5. As Oldenziel, Sousa, and Van Wesemael (this volume) have shown, the significance of world's fairs changed markedly over their first century, but their importance persisted. As they lost their stature as forums of expertise, they gained importance as legitimizers of corporate consumerism and image building. On the world's fairs of particular significance here, see Robert W. Rydell, *World of Fairs: The Century-of-Progress Expositions* (Chicago: University of Chicago Press), 1993.

6. Charles F. Kettering and Allen Orth, *The New Necessity: The Culmination of Progress in Transportation* (Baltimore: Williams and Wilkins, 1932).

7. Charles F. Kettering and Allen Orth, "Keep the Consumer Dissatisfied," *Nation's Business* 17 no. 1 (1929): 30–31, 79.

8. Kettering and Orth, *The New Necessity*, 6.

9. Ibid., 18.

10. Ibid., 14–15.

11. Ibid., 30.

12. Ibid., 18.

13. Ibid., 26.

14. Ibid., 20–21.

15. Ibid., 123.

16. Ibid., 21–22.

17. "The New Necessity," *New York Times Book Review*, 10 July 1932, 10; "The New Necessity," *Cincinnati Enquirer*, 24 July 1932, section 4, 2; "Book Visualizes Future of World," *Salt Lake Telegram*, 26 July 1932; E. Y. Watson (North American Newspaper Alliance), "Auto Makers Looking for New Ideas for Transformed Age to Follow Readjusted Position," *Great Falls* [Montana] *Tribune*, 11 September 1932, 6; E. Y. Watson, "Auto Seen as Fourth Necessity," *Hartford Courant*, 11 September 1932, part 4, 7; E. Y. Watson, "Huge Progress Lines Horizon," *Los Angeles Times*, 11 September 1932, part 6, 3.

18. Nathaniel Robert Walker, "American Crossroads: General Motors' Midcentury Campaign to Promote Modernist Urban Design in Hometown U.S.A.," *Buildings and Landscapes: Journal of the Vernacular Architecture* Forum 23 no. 2 (fall 2016), 89–115; "'Circus of Science' Will Tour the Country," *Science News Letter* 29 no. 775 (Feb. 15, 1936), 101–02.

19. Futurama has received extensive scholarly attention. On its specific use as a means of "selling the unsustainable city," see Dolores Hayden, "'I Have Seen the Future': Selling the Unsustainable City" (Urban History Association presidential address, 2010), *Journal of Urban History* 38 no. 1 (Jan. 2012): 3–15.

20. Thorton Wilder, *Our Town: A Play in Three Acts*, 1938, Act II.

21. "G.M. Show Is Coming," *State Journal* (Lansing, MI), 9 July 1953, 29.
22. "Parade of Progress Spends Night Here," *Daily Missoulian* (Missoula, MT), 7 July 1956, 2.
23. As Robert Staughton Lynd and Helen Merrell Lynd famously documented, even in 1929 many Americans' attachment to their automobiles was already controversial; one minister in "Middletown" (Muncie, Indiana) denounced it as "auto-mobilitis." Lynd and Lynd, *Middletown: A Study in American Culture* (New York: Harcourt, Brace, and World, 1929), 259.
24. *New York Times*, 30 November 1958.
25. Bergen Evans, *The Spoor of Spooks and Other Nonsense* (New York: Knopf, 1954).
26. *Democrat and Chronicle* (Rochester, NY), 28 January 1956.
27. The ad appeared in numerous newspapers 14 February 1956; e.g., *Detroit Free Press*.
28. Ken Purdy, "Our Love Affair with the Automobile," *Think* (IBM) 27, no. 9 (1961): 14–18.
29. Audrey Bishop, "Television News and Notes," *Baltimore Sun*, 11 December 1955.
30. WROC-TV, "'Our American Heritage' Sunday Nights" (advertisement), *Democrat and Chronicle* (Rochester, NY), 20 September 1959.
31. Robert F. Freeland, *The Struggle for Control of the Modern Corporation: Organizational Change at General Motors, 1924–1970* (Cambridge: Cambridge University Press, 2001), 4.
32. Austin C. Wehrwein, Du Pont to Keep Its Stock in G.M., but Loses Votes," *New York Times*, 3 October 1959.
33. Drew Pearson, "Big Business Censors Networks" (Washington Merry Go Round), *Daytona Beach Morning Journal*, 24 October 1961.
34. Chris Yogerst, "Rod Serling's Vast Promised Land: Battling Sponsors, Debating the FCC, and Fighting for Mature Television, 1959–1966," *Historical Journal of Film, Radio, and Television* 38, no. 4 (2018): 828–42.
35. See, e.g., NBC, "Laughter USA" (advertisement), *New York Times*, 17 September 1961.
36. On the so-called Red Flag Act of 1865, see "Locomotives on Roads," *The British Almanac* (London, 1866), 199–200.
37. NBC Television, "Merrily We Roll Along," produced and directed by Robert L. Bendick, *Du Pont Show of the Week*, 22 October 1961.
38. "Auto Design Is Subject of Arts Lecture," *Cincinnati Enquirer*, 5 May 1962.
39. Fred Olmsted, "Its Show Sell, Chicago Says," *Detroit Free Press*, 21 November 1962.
40. Christy Borth, "Start of a Love Affair," *Chicago Tribune*, 27 October 1963; originally published in *Petroleum Today*.
41. Joel Schwartz, "The Social Benefits and Costs of the Automobile," in *21st Century Highways: Innovative Solutions to America's Transportation Needs*, ed. Wendell Cox, Alan Pisarski, and Ronald D. Utt (Washington, DC: Heritage Foundation, 2005), ch. 2, here 39.
42. Norton, "Of Love Affairs and Other Stories," esp. 30.
43. Schwartz, "Social Benefits and Costs," 37.
44. Bradford Snell, "Statement of Bradford C. Snell before the United States Senate Subcommittee on Antitrust and Monopoly," 26 February 1974, 1.
45. Bradford Snell, "American Ground Transport: A Proposal for Restructuring the Automobile, Truck, Bus, and Rail Industries," 26 February 1974, United States

Senate, Committee on the Judiciary, Subcommittee on Antitrust and Monopoly (Washington: U.S. Government Printing Office, 1974).

46. Snell at least drastically overstated what his evidence could show. See Zachary Schrag, "'The Bus Is Young and Honest': Transportation Politics, Technical Choice, and the Motorization of Manhattan Surface Transit, 1919–1936," *Technology and Culture* 41 no. 1 (2000): 51–79, here 53–54.

47. Robert Zemeckis, dir., *Who Framed Roger Rabbit*, written by Jeffrey Price and Peter S. Seaman, Touchstone Pictures and Amblin Entertainment, 1988.

48. General Motors Corporation, "The Truth about 'American Ground Transport': A Reply by General Motors," United States Senate, Committee on the Judiciary, Subcommittee on Antitrust and Monopoly (Washington: U.S. Government Printing Office, 1974).

49. Martha Olson and Jim Klein, *Taken for a Ride* (documentary), New Day Films, 1996.

50. Otto Mayr, "The Enola Gay Fiasco: History, Politics, and the Museum," *Technology and Culture* 39 no. 3 (1998): 462–73.

51. Elaine Sciolino, "Smithsonian Museum Close to Naming a Hall for G.M.," *New York Times*, 19 July 2001, A14.

52. Sciolino, "Smithsonian Museum Close."

53. Steven Lubar, "The Making of 'America on the Move' at the National Museum of American History," *Curator* 47, no.1 (2010): 19–51.

54. Florence Fund, "Taken for a Ride: General Motors' Money Will Corrupt Smithsonian History" (advertisement), *New York Times*, 16 September 2001, sec. 4, 11.

55. Lubar, "The Making of 'America on the Move.'"

56. Sciolino, "Smithsonian Museum Close."

57. Zachary M. Schrag, "America on the Move" (review), *CRM: The Journal of Heritage Stewardship* (National Park Service) 3 no.1 (2006): 116–17, here 116.

58. Ibid., 117.

59. Walter Jackson (consultant on bus and car service, Mount Vernon, New York), "Motor-Busses Will Aid Better City Development," *American City* 23 (July 1920), 49–52, here 49, 51.

60. Lubar, "The Making of 'America on the Move.'"

61. On twentieth-century American depictions of the future, see Joseph J. Corn, ed., *Imagining Tomorrow: History, Technology, and the American Future* (Cambridge, MA: MIT Press, 1986); Joseph J. Corn and Brian Horrigan, *Yesterday's Tomorrows: Past Visions of the American Future* (Baltimore: Johns Hopkins University Press, 1984). On promises of a better future contributing to postwar American consumerism, see Cynthia Lee Henthorn, *From Submarines to Suburbs: Selling a Better America, 1939–1959* (Athens, GA: Ohio University Press, 2006). For techniques that extend American economic, cultural, and political influence abroad during the Cold War, see Robert H. Haddow, *Pavilions of Plenty: Exhibiting American Culture Abroad in the 1950s* (Washington, DC: Smithsonian Institution Press, 1997); Walter L. Hixson, *Parting the Curtain: Propaganda, Culture, and the Cold War, 1945–1961* (New York: St. Martin's Press, 1997); and Ruth Oldenziel and Karin Zachmann, eds., *Cold War Kitchen: Americanization, Technology, and European Users* (Cambridge, MA: MIT Press, 2009), esp. ch. 3: Cristina Carbone, "Staging the Kitchen Debate: How Splitnik Got Normalized in the United States," 59–81.

# Bibliography

Carbone, Cristina. "Staging the Kitchen Debate: How Splitnik Got Normalized in the United States." In *Cold War Kitchen: Americanization, Technology, and European Users*, edited by Ruth Oldenziel and Karin Zachmann, 59–81. Cambridge, MA: MIT Press, 2009.

Corn, Joseph J., ed. *Imagining Tomorrow: History, Technology, and the American Future*. Cambridge, MA: MIT Press, 1986.

Corn, Joseph J., and Brian Horrigan. *Yesterday's Tomorrows: Past Visions of the American Future*. Baltimore: Johns Hopkins University Press, 1984.

Evans, Bergen. *The Spoor of Spooks and Other Nonsense*. New York: Knopf, 1954.

General Motors Corporation. "The Truth about 'American Ground Transport': A Reply by General Motors." In *The Industrial Reorganization Act: Hearing before the Subcommittee on Antitrust and Monopoly of the Committee on the Judiciary, United States Senate, Ninety-Third Congress, Second Session on S. 1167*, Part 4A, Appendix to, Part 4. Washington, DC: U.S. Government Printing Office, 1974.

Haddow, Robert H. *Pavilions of Plenty: Exhibiting American Culture Abroad in the 1950s*. Washington, DC: Smithsonian Institution Press, 1997.

Hayden, Dolores, "'I Have Seen the Future': Selling the Unsustainable City" (Urban History Association presidential address, 2010). *Journal of Urban History* 38, no. 1 (2012): 3–15.

Henthorn, Cynthia Lee. *From Submarines to Suburbs: Selling a Better America, 1939–1959*. Athens, GA: Ohio University Press, 2006.

Hixson, Walter L. *Parting the Curtain: Propaganda, Culture, and the Cold War, 1945–1961*. New York: St. Martin's Press, 1997.

Kettering, Charles F. and Allen Orth, "Keep the Consumer Dissatisfied," *Nation's Business* 17 no. 1 (1929): 30–31, 79.

——. *The New Necessity: The Culmination of Progress in Transportation*. Baltimore: Williams and Wilkins, 1932.

Lubar, Steven. "The Making of 'America on the Move' at the National Museum of American History." *Curator* 47, no. 1 (2010): 19–51.

Lynd, Robert Staughton, and Helen Merrell Lynd. *Middletown: A Study in American Culture*. New York: Harcourt, Brace, and World, 1929.

Mayr, Otto. "The Enola Gay Fiasco: History, Politics, and the Museum." *Technology and Culture* 39, no. 3 (July 1998): 462–73.

Norton, Peter. "Of Love Affairs and Other Stories." In *Incomplete Streets: Processes, Practices, and Possibilities*, edited by Stephen Zavestoski and Julian Agyeman, 17–35. London: Routledge, 2015.

Oldenziel, Ruth, and Karin Zachmann, eds. *Cold War Kitchen: Americanization, Technology, and European*. Cambridge, MA: MIT Press, 2009.

Rydell, Robert W. *World of Fairs: The Century-of-Progress Expositions*. Chicago: University of Chicago Press, 1993.

Schrag, Zachary M. "America on the Move" (review). *CRM: The Journal of Heritage Stewardship* (National Park Service) 3, no.1 (2006): 116–17.

——. "'The Bus Is Young and Honest': Transportation Politics, Technical Choice, and the Motorization of Manhattan Surface Transit, 1919–1936." *Technology and Culture* 41 no. 1 (2000): 51–79, here 53–54.

Schwartz, Joel. "The Social Benefits and Costs of the Automobile." In *21st Century Highways: Innovative Solutions to America's Transportation Needs*, edited by

Wendell Cox, Alan Pisarski, and Ronald D. Utt, ch. 2. Washington, DC: Heritage Foundation, 2005.

Smith, John David, and J. Vincent Lowery, eds. *The Dunning School: Historians, Race, and the Meaning of Reconstruction*. Lexington: University of Kentucky Press, 2013.

Van Lente, Harro. "From Promises to Requirement." In *Contested Futures: A Sociology of Prospective Techno-Science*, edited by Nik Brown, Brian Rappert, and Andrew Webster. London: Routledge, 2000.

Walker, Nathaniel Robert. "American Crossroads: General Motors' Midcentury Campaign to Promote Modernist Urban Design in Hometown U.S.A." *Buildings and Landscapes: Journal of the Vernacular Architecture Forum* 23, no. 2 (2016): 89–115.

Woodson, Carter G. *The Mis-education of the Negro*. Washington, DC: Associated Publishers, 1933.

Yogerst, Chris. "Rod Serling's Vast Promised Land: Battling Sponsors, Debating the FCC, and Fighting for Mature Television, 1959–1966." *Historical Journal of Film, Radio, and Television* 38, no. 4 (2018): 828–42.

# CHAPTER 3

# Railway Modernism Losing Out

## Lessons from an English Conurbation, 1955–1975

### Colin Divall

## Introduction

This chapter aims to inform today's cultural politics of sustainable urban mobility. Recognizing that radical political and social change is driven as much, if not more, by emotions than dry, "rational" debate, activists such as George Monbiot emphasize the importance of popular story-telling "that learns from the past, places us in the present and guides the future." Successful stories—that resonate with a critical number of citizens—provide an alternative to the dominant, half-remembered assumptions and narratives that maintain current ways of life and stymie our imaginations when it comes to the future.[1] For example, while mainstream transport planners acknowledge the need to rapidly reduce greenhouse gas emissions, not much changes. This is because popular opinion, as well as political and policy paradigms, are imbued with norms—for instance about the value and meaning of travel time—that rule out the radical measures that would make a real difference.[2] People cannot conceive of more sustainable ways of living and moving. Hence a cultural politics of sustainable urban mobilities involves developing stories that will engage, convince, and inspire enough of us—as scholars, policy analysts, decision-makers, and above all citizens—to dream of, and work toward, a future that otherwise seems impossible.

Some in the vanguard of transport and mobility studies recognize the importance of storytelling. Jon Shaw and Iain Docherty sketch a more sustainable future for U.K. transport by following the fictional Smith family on a trip.[3] Similarly, transition analysts and activists use storylines to indicate qualitative pathways toward less carbon-intensive patterns of mobility.[4] Although such efforts, along with transport studies, acknowledge the past's bearing on the present and future, historians are rarely part of the team.[5] This is a missed opportunity. So as well as fellow historians, this chapter is addressed to sympathetic academics and actors in the policy complex: decision-makers (including politicians) and policy analysts in government, and their agencies, business corporations, and pressure (or advocacy) groups, who can be persuaded that history plays a more important role in "thinking change" and can then tell stories that inspire popular support for radical reform.[6]

This chapter focuses on the first task: exemplifying the kind of historical insights (or usable past) needed for compelling stories. More particularly, it is an exercise in hindsight, an analysis of how debates from the mid-1950s to the mid-1970s still affect transport and land-use policy in a fast-developing urban region of southern England. I thus review how today's policy complex construes and constructs the relationship between the three dimensions—environmental, social, and economic—of "sustainable" urban mobility. Because a comprehensive critique is not feasible here, I focus on the "strong" (environmental and social) aspects of sustainability, particularly greenhouse gas emissions, as indicators of the policy complex's wider commitment to change in South East Dorset.[7]

Why this particular region? Like many other countries across Europe and elsewhere in the Global North, postwar Britain contained a wide variety of urban forms—some old, some new—but all struggling to adapt their mobility systems to changing economic and social circumstances. As well as the existing industrial conurbations, garden cities, and ancient market towns, the 1950s and 1960s witnessed, for example, the planned development of what became extensive new settlements like Milton Keynes. For at least two decades after World War II, British cities and towns enjoyed sufficient autonomy from central government for local planners and politicians to develop ideas about urban mobility that were particular to their areas: while the overall trend toward automobility is undeniable, alternatives were quite often discussed and even, at least in part, put into practice.[8] However, one common urban form emerging (in Britain) from the 1950s has not been studied in much detail: the multi-polar region with a fairly small, densely populated urban core predating motor vehicles, surrounded by a peri-urban belt of many peripheral, semi-rural, as well as more conventionally suburban, settlements highly dependent on autos both for access to the core as well as trips between them. South East Dorset is one such area, although it is by no means unique—for example, a zone of perhaps forty kilometers surrounding the ancient city of Oxford shares many of these characteristics.[9]

Thus by suggesting what historical insights could offer the cultural politics of sustainable urban mobility in South East Dorset, I hope to encourage others to research similar regions in the United Kingdom and, allowing for the inevitable national differences, in other countries. This study exemplifies three of the usable past's dimensions: as a contested process in which today's patterns of urban mobility and thinking about them developed; as a realm of path dependencies that locked in dominant ways of moving and (apparently) constrained future possibilities; and as a deposit of lost visions about the future that could be excavated to inspire fresh thinking and storytelling.

## The South East Dorset Conurbation

First, an outline of the modern urban region occupying the southeastern corner of Dorset, a small county on the southern English coast. With a population of 475 thousand, South East Dorset is a polycentric conurbation consisting of a built-up area along the coast, with several outlying towns, separated from each other and the urban core by statutorily protected green spaces. The core incorporates the historic towns of Poole in the west and Christchurch in the east, with the Victorian resort of Bournemouth between. The main satellites lie a maximum of twenty-five kilometers from the core, including Ringwood, which is excluded from the official "travel-to-work" area because it is just inside the adjacent county of Hampshire. As the U.K.'s largest conurbation not administered as a city, local government is divided. Until April 2019, Poole and Bournemouth were unitary authorities, responsible since 1997 for local transport and land-use planning. Christchurch and the outlying districts (except Ringwood) came under Dorset County Council, which dealt with local transport planning; land use was the responsibility of the next tier down, the district councils. These divisions dated back to reorganization in 1974, when Christchurch, historically part of Hampshire, moved into Dorset, along with the then self-governing county borough of Bournemouth (ceremonially part of Hampshire), and the district councils were created from many smaller ones. The trunk road and railway networks are the responsibility of two national government agencies, Highways England and Network Rail, which take strategic guidance from the ministerial Department for Transport.

Although this fragmentation has historically hindered policy making, the situation has improved. From April 2019, the three coastal towns formed a single unitary authority (Bournemouth, Christchurch, and Poole Council), while the other district councils in Dorset merged into a similar authority (Dorset Council), replacing Dorset County Council, leaving only Ringwood outside the two councils' remit. Before this, Dorset County Council and the two unitary authorities (Poole, Bournemouth) had been working closely for some years; their joint fifteen-year (2011–26) strategic local transport plan, LTP3, published in 2011, still covers the entire South East Dorset conurbation (plus the rest of Dorset), except for the small part in Hampshire; the first (and only) review was published in November 2014, while Implementation Plan 3, 2017–20, came out in May 2017.[10] The third and most comprehensive iteration of a nationally mandated plan published in 2001, LTP3 is the first to include ambitious, detailed targets for greenhouse gas reductions.[11] It is based on a very thorough review, the South East Dorset Multi-Modal Transport Study, by international consultants Atkins Transport Planning and Management, and published in April 2012.[12]

These are weighty documents, and while sheer length does not guarantee a credible strategy in this "multi-centred, high car-dependant conurbation," the local authorities are jointly committed to the environmental and social dimensions of sustainable mobility, while recognizing the political imperative for economic growth.[13] LTP3's five goals include "[r]educing the overall level of emissions of carbon dioxide and other greenhouse gases from travel and transport," as well as "[p]romoting equal opportunities, including access to services, with the desired outcome of achieving a fairer society."[14] The former goal is particularly commendable given that the United Kingdom's internationally leading statutory commitment to slashing domestic greenhouse gas emissions by 2050 (by at least 80 percent against the 1990 level) no longer sets targets for transport.[15] The comparatively dense population in the conurbation's core makes it attractive to pursue lower-carbon initiatives. Projects since 2011 have promoted active modes (walking, cycling) and public transport (buses), along with measures to deter car usage. As part of Implementation Plan 2 (2014–17), Three Towns Travel, a GBP18 million package to "improve sustainable travel facilities in and around Poole, Bournemouth and Christchurch" and "provide viable alternatives to car travel and lead to increased modal shifts to sustainable travel modes," was completed in March 2015 and judged a major success.[16] Implementation Plan 3 aims to further encourage a modal shift by combining similar soft measures and infrastructural improvements.

So far, so good. But how soon will personal mobility within the conurbation become environmentally sustainable?[17] We cannot expect a wholesale transition before LTP3 ends in 2026. Nevertheless, Dorset's policy complex needs to acknowledge the continuing—indeed increasing—urgency. Unfortunately, as detailed later, powerful institutions in the region are re-envisioning the future, putting much greater emphasis on economic factors. By looking back fifty years or more, when the "sustainability" of personal mobility in the area was also under debate, we can get a better sense of how cultural politics frames the policy complex's thinking.

## Contested Mobilities, Lock-ins, and Missed Opportunities

Mechanized transport will never be as sustainable in environmental (or social) terms as walking and cycling, but in any urban area more than a few kilometers across, it will be both functionally and economically necessary. Not everyone is fit enough to move under their own power, and for these people mechanized transport is essential. Thus the issue, both now and in the past, is how to mix mechanized modes—buses, trams, trains, cars, and motorcycles—and provide acceptable trade-offs (and synergies) between the environmental, social, and economic dimensions of sustainability. What is "acceptable" is fundamentally a matter of political judgment and the balance between personal and mass transport. Despite the rapid rise in urban motoring in the Global North after 1945, public transport remained important, particularly in Europe, where urban morphology had long been shaped by mass transit. But what kind of public transport has been, and might continue to be, significant? Railways have played an important part in shaping urban regions since the mid-nineteenth century. Although railways have never been regarded as easily sustainable, since World War II many countries, including the United States, argue that under some circumstances, urban and suburban railways can be more sustainable, particularly in environmental and social terms, than alternative modes. Their capacity to bypass roads congested with cars and trapped buses is a particularly attractive feature.[18]

I explore how these trends played out in the United Kingdom through debates at two geopolitical levels, the national and the regional, and how people moved into, out of, and around the conglomeration rapidly developing in South East Dorset from the mid-1950s and, when the county border lay between Poole and Bournemouth, South West Hampshire. This story reflects the general postwar enthusiasm for automobility, leading to major road schemes in and around the conurbation and high car-dependency in the 1960s and 1970s. Dorset's present-day politicians and policy analysts are well aware of these facts. They also know there used to be several railway lines in the region, whereas now there is only one, the London mainline through the urban core. Until 1964–66, three secondary routes served the towns and villages to the north of what even then was the continuously built-up coastal zone (map 3.1). While today's South East Dorset conurbation is typical in that most public transport is by bus, there is little doubt that had these railways survived, they would be well used to access both the urban core and destinations beyond in a free-flowing, low-carbon way.[19] It is highly unlikely they will ever reopen. This is a classic example of historical

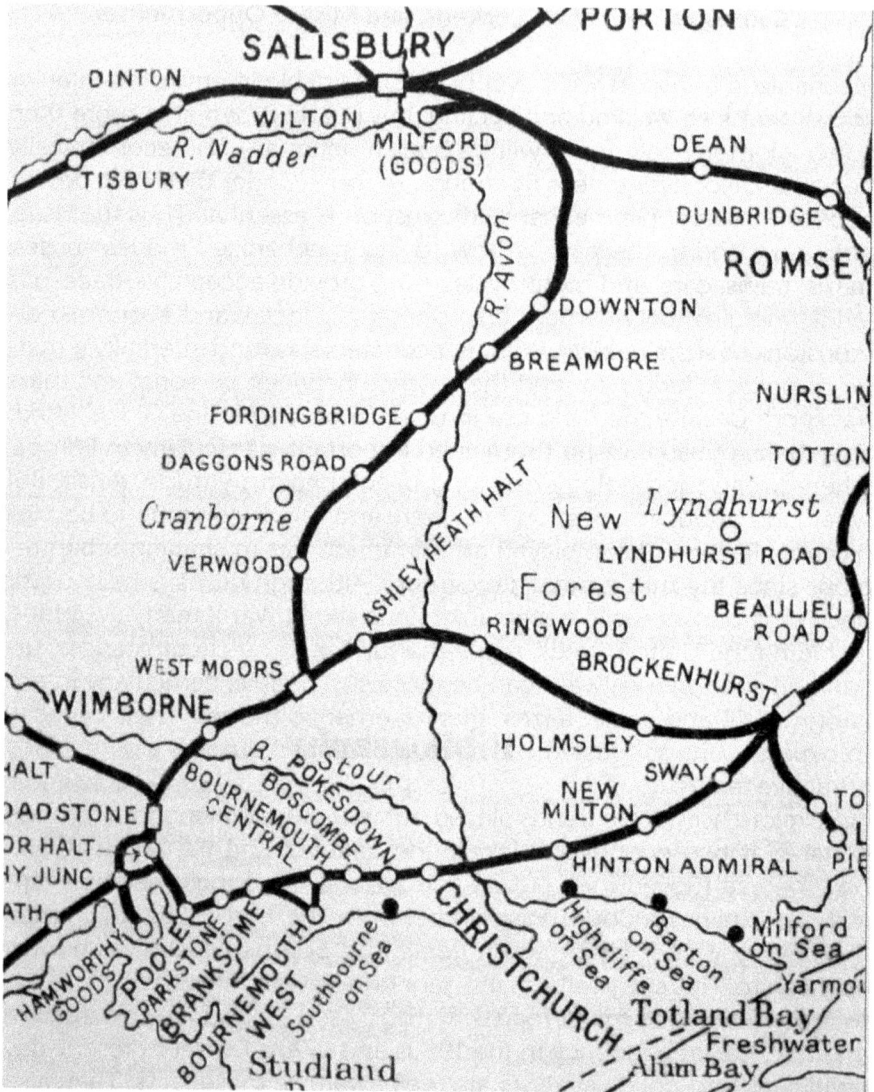

**Map 3.1.** Railways in South East Dorset and South West Hampshire, ca. 1960.
Adapted from Southern Railway general system map, 1939.

path-dependency and lock-in: once the secondary lines had closed, the physical integrity of their track beds destroyed, and major highways built instead, it became impossible to even imagine they could be re-instated. Some in Dorset's policy complex do not need fresh lessons in this basic lock-in: they know from hard-won experience that over the long term, seemingly once-sound policies and decisions can turn out badly.[20]

The fuller story, however, is more complex and nuanced, and the historical *process* of framing the terms in which debates considered the (lack of a) future for these lines holds lessons about today's struggle for sustainability. First, and most obviously, we note that opponents of the dominant discourse of urban automobility couched their arguments in ways prefiguring many of today's concerns. While activists in the 1960s lost these battles, with hindsight we can see that they "won" the war on the long-term environmental and social unsustainability of urban automobility, and the desirability to keep open the possibility of passenger trains as an arguably more socially inclusive, and certainly lower-carbon, congestion-busting mode. Timescales were critical here: short-term politics *and* popular opinion defeated vague ideas about what might only be achieved over decades. This missed opportunity should give today's policy complex pause for thought: do present-day debates also risk prematurely dismissing the arguments of subaltern groups, repeating the mistake of precluding long-term flexibility? Second, and more subtly, by understanding the cultural politics of a key concept, "modernization," in terms of which the political and policy battles of the 1960s were fought, we become sensitized to the ways certain actors in South East Dorset are diluting LTP3's commitment to the strong dimensions of sustainable urban mobility.

## "Modernization," the Beeching Report, and the Buchanan Report

The headline story of how South East Dorset became so car-dependent stems from two studies facilitated by the 1957–64 Conservative government: the nationalized British Railway Board's *The Reshaping of British Railways* (the Beeching Report, published in March 1963), and the Ministry of Transport working group's *Traffic in Towns: A Study of the Long Term Problems of Traffic in Urban Areas* (the Buchanan Report, November 1963).[21] Both reports, named after their principal authors, were delivered to the controversial yet influential minister of transport from 1959 to 1964, Ernest Marples. Their contents, or more accurately the different values they expressed, framed debates about the future of personal mobility: the likely findings had been favorably trailed in the press and in political circles for months before publication. Moreover, although published eight months after Beeching, the Buchanan Report was secretly revealed to Marples by July 1963, just as the first railway closure proposals were posted—including those in South East Dorset / South West Hampshire.[22]

The Beeching report, proposing widespread railway closures (the "Beeching Axe"), is still notorious in the United Kingdom, while only experts know of the Buchanan Report. In international terms, Beeching's analysis resonated with the kind of thinking that had led to numerous withdrawals of passenger trains in the United States before World War II, but it was chiefly the product of debates within British Railways and central government in the 1950s. Despite international interest, most European governments did not start similar large-scale rationalization programs for several decades.[23] By contrast, the Buchanan Report constituted a British response to the emerging transnational critique of mass urban motorization voiced by North American authors such as Kevin Lynch and Jane Jacobs, and it would become influential in European countries such as Sweden, Italy, Norway, Denmark, the Netherlands, and Germany.[24]

Despite very different policy framings and presentation—Buchanan's attractive, jargon-free, and richly illustrated layout contrasted very favorably with Beeching's rather dour, heavy text—both reports emphasized "modernization." The concept had quickly become central to British political and policy discourse after 1945 as the country struggled to rebuild its economy: modernization was the (only) way forward. Its usefulness for framing debates about urban mobilities, thus garnering support among elite, expert, and popular audiences, lay in the fact that it was a portmanteau—a term whose meaning could be reconfigured (or even emptied) to suit different, even contradictory, policies. While mainly economic growth informed these debates, notions of social equity and environmental sustainability were also in play.

The Beeching Report was as much a product as the Buchanan Report was of the very rapidly growing levels of car ownership and usage in late 1950s' Britain, both a key symbol and measure of social, economic, and even cultural modernization. To (be seen to) drive was to be part of the modern way of living, to be someone in a modernizing society. This was in line with other European capitalist countries; however, for fifteen years after World War II, Britain's economic difficulties had hampered ambitious plans, approved in 1946, for inter-urban motorway construction on the scale found in Germany. Urban road building lagged even further behind other European (let alone North American) cities. From 1947, U.K. local authorities were obliged to prepare development plans (with a twenty-year horizon) that included proposals for all-purpose ring roads to keep through-traffic out of city centers and radial "spokes" to ease flows between central and outer districts—ideas that were common elsewhere in Europe. However, very little construction took place, which, combined with car ownership levels far in excess of immediate postwar predictions, led to intolerable urban traffic congestion in the late 1950s.[25]

Beeching focused on the railways' lack of economic "sustainability." Buchanan's concern with urban congestion certainly addressed cities' economic viability, but also, and more radically, the mounting social and environmental costs of automobility.[26] By 1960, the railways' financial losses were seen as unaffordable in senior government circles (the Cabinet) and the national bureaucracy or civil service (Whitehall). Beeching sought to return the railways to profit by identifying passenger services—such as inter-urban expresses—that would pay despite growing automobility, while closing the rest, notably rural stopping trains and even many suburban commuter lines (the "Axe"). This initial program would take only a few years, though the report's wider analysis looked forward about two decades, a typical timespan for planners then.[27] In contrast, Buchanan tried to reconcile growing public, policy, and political concerns about increasing urban congestion, expecting that the demand for cars and roads to drive them on would increase relentlessly. The timescale here was exceptional—four to five decades.[28]

If Buchanan's concern for social and environmental sustainability was not entirely novel in the international context, his analysis of an urban district's "environmental capacity" to absorb motor traffic certainly was. In historian Simon Gunn's view, the report demonstrated for the first time in the United Kingdom (and elsewhere) that modernist urban renewal and environmental awareness need not be mutually exclusive.[29] While hailing mass-scale ownership of cars as socially desirable and politically inevitable, Buchanan warned that unregulated motoring would wreck the social and physical fabric of towns and cities that had never been designed for cars. The challenge was to fit growing numbers of vehicles into old spaces while enhancing urban life. Several new insights underpinned the proposed solutions. First, motor traffic *within* towns had much more complex flows than assumed, as people moved between their homes, shops, workplaces, and social facilities; new roads were needed to maintain this door-to-door convenience. But the social and environmental costs of even existing motor traffic were too high: traffic caused congestion, death and injury through "accidents," noise, poor air quality, as well as multiple visual intrusions, such as parked vehicles, cluttered streets, the aesthetic degradation of architectural and historic vistas, and so on. Buchanan's understanding of "environment" therefore expressed not only an urban district's aesthetic value, but also its "environmental capacity" defined by the permitted volume of motor traffic, without precluding the "civilised urban life" appropriate to each district's industrial, commercial, or residential character.[30]

The report's novelty lay in suggesting that whole towns be rebuilt over forty years to ensure each district had appropriate traffic flows. Buchanan's conservationist thrust was therefore necessarily coupled with a modernist insistence on radically rebuilding urban spaces with highways designed to deal with the anticipated levels of traffic. Towns would adopt a cellular structure in which a network of free-flowing "distributor highways" served the different zones, including residential and amenity "environmental areas" where motor traffic was heavily restricted or even banned outright.[31] Modern conurbations would be oases of civilized living surrounded by (and, in Buchanan's view, nurtured by) free-flowing motor traffic.

Yet Buchanan acknowledged that public transport had to continue as an adjunct to automobility: the number of public-transport vehicles "depends largely upon the extent to which the public does or does not switch its travelling habits to private cars."[32] The report also argued that making public transport cheaper could minimize car usage "for the main movements . . . in larger cities."[33] Railways were dismissed as largely irrelevant because "events [had] passed far beyond the point at which it would have been possible to revert" to them. However, in drawing lessons from Europe and the United States, Buchanan did acknowledge the potential of both light- and heavy-rail (including undergrounds) for commuting.[34]

Finally, Buchanan recommended that urban redevelopment should accord with the "much needed integration" of transport and land-use planning, supported by comprehensive studies.[35] Other influential figures went further. The steering group appointed by Marples to oversee Buchanan's work (the Crowther committee) argued that the appropriate geographical scale for this kind of planning was the region, not just the particular city or town. In an international context, this was scarcely a new idea: the planning of New York as a metropolitan region dates back to at least the 1920s. In Britain, like elsewhere in Europe (Stockholm being a good example), similar practices developed only after World War II; however, by the early 1960s, regional planning was regarded as a panacea across much of the continent.[36]

Despite this growing political enthusiasm, British regional planning was still weak, largely reactive, and fragmented, with limited strategic powers divided between central and local government. Nationally, the Ministry of Transport, the Ministry of Housing and Local Government, and the Board of Trade oversaw different elements; by mid-1963, new government-appointed regional study groups were starting to coordinate work—notably in the southeast region designated for "London overspill" (shifting people out of London). Otherwise, responsibility for transport and land-use planning remained divided between the principal local authorities: the county councils and the equivalent county-borough councils. Their strategic powers over land use, expressed in county development plans, had to be approved by the Ministry of Housing and Local Government. Nevertheless, as "highway authorities" these councils controlled road building and improvements (Ministry of Transport grants were available for some of the cost) apart from the national trunk-road and motorway network—the Ministry of Transport's responsibility. The Crowther committee caustically noted that this arrangement resulted in "co-ordination of the negative kind that provides opportunity for representations to be made . . . [and] it is not the sort . . . from which new initiatives can be born."[37] It therefore recommended establishing powerful regional development agencies to plan and enact "urban modernisation" programs.[38]

The immediate reaction to the Buchanan Report was largely positive, with broad agreement in the general and specialist press, in professional circles, and even among motoring pressure groups over the analysis, diagnosis, and proposals. The chief opposition came from transport economists, who argued (correctly, it turned out) that Buchanan had overestimated the likely growth of car usage in cities, and who favored measures such as road-pricing that would act as a deterrent by imposing a direct cost on drivers.[39] In the short term, Marples secured the Ministry of Housing and Local Government's support for Buchanan's main proposals, along with a large increase in the roads budget and the formation of a cross-ministerial Urban Planning Group to advise local authorities; from January 1964, the Ministry of Transport progressively required these highway authorities to justify new urban-road schemes by carrying out land-use/transport surveys. Things did not change much when Labour came to power in October that year. In 1965, the new government set up more regional study groups to cover all of England, and gave them, along with their executive boards, wider responsibilities as Economic Planning Councils. However, despite being given the task of drawing up comprehensive regional transport plans, these authorities never had the extensive planning and executive powers envisaged by Crowther.[40]

The Beeching Report was very different in tone, substance, and intent. Here "modernization" functioned to garner public support (or at least acquiescence) for a closure program already decided in principle if not in detail. The debate about secondary railways in the late 1950s and early 1960s was conducted at two geopolitical levels: in secret, within the Cabinet and Whitehall, where closure in pursuit of short-term financial savings was the default; and more openly in the regions, where objections from user groups and local government admitted the possibility of minor concessions. To understand "modernization" in this way, as key to the cultural politics of railway policy, is not to say that the

Beeching Axe was without merit; but it does show how powerful, elite groups shaped and rhetorically deployed popular values and attitudes to deflect scrutiny of their semicovert policies. In contrast, as detailed shortly, while protesters argued for the "modernization" of South East Dorset / South West Hampshire's secondary railways in ways that resonate with today's concern for strong sustainability, in the face of the values and judgments informing the Buchanan Report, they were far too weak to win the popular debate, let alone make any impression on the policies of shadowy national elites.

Charles Loft demonstrates the critical importance of "modernization" in framing, shaping, and popularizing government railway policy from the mid-1950s and through the 1960s, surviving the switch from Conservative to Labour government. While initially supportive of large-scale railway investment through the 1955 Modernisation Plan, senior Conservative politicians and the Treasury had decided by 1958–59 that the system's finances were unsustainable: spiraling capital costs were paralleled by rapidly mounting operating losses. By 1960, government policy had switched decisively in favor of road investment, and a semicovert policy review within Whitehall was moving toward a decision to withdraw many passenger services and concentrate limited funds on improving the rest.[41]

The railways' shrinking, more specialized future was widely and publicly extolled as "modernization." For example, in 1960, the prime minister argued, "The industry must be of a size and pattern suited to modern conditions and prospects . . . , the railway system must be remodelled to meet current needs, and the modernisation plan must be adapted to this new shape."[42] Such rhetoric allowed the remodeling of the railways to be presented as an opportunity for positive change, rather than a highly problematic exercise to make them profitable, which moreover threatened the Conservatives' growing commitment to regional planning. The Beeching Report adopted this sloganizing—the quote above was included in the report's foreword—although its dry, technocratic presentation demanded a good deal of work by ministers, Whitehall, and the British Railways Board to carry political and public opinion once it was published in March 1963. While the report's analysis and detailed proposals quickly ran into controversy, this initial public launch went very well, so much so that it served as a template for Buchanan.[43]

Thus, as far as secondary services were concerned, the political reality was that as early as 1959–60, railway modernization no longer required a strong case for particular withdrawals, but rather for individual reprieves.[44] This logic was not made public, although plenty of activists and commentators assumed that something similar was at work.

Moreover, central government made it much more difficult to mount effective campaigns against individual proposals. The public and any interested body could object through the Transport Users' Consultative Committees, regional consumer bodies that had vetoed some closures and delayed others in the 1950s; however, these powers were removed in 1962. The minister of transport now unequivocally decided whether to withdraw a passenger service, acting on advice from senior ministerial officials. They, in turn, relied heavily on the recommendations of the appropriate Transport Users' Consultative Committee, limited to considering the ill-defined notion of "hardship" to users, and the measures—normally additional bus services—that might alleviate this. However, central government recognized that factors such as regional development or urban congestion might be sufficient to refuse closure. Local authorities and other officials, as well as voluntary bodies, could therefore make representations directly to the minister of transport. So, too, could other Whitehall departments, such as regional planning, defense, and agriculture. Matters were discussed by a secret cross-departmental Whitehall committee, chaired by a senior Ministry of Transport official, which then made a recommendation to the minister.[45] However, this arrangement was open to the same kind of criticism leveled at regional planning by the Crowther committee: it was reactive and often worked without a clear view of the wider, long-term issues.

All of this applied to any closure proposal. But urban (including suburban) railways were a slightly different case. Despite Buchanan's dismissive attitude, other influential voices in Whitehall were more positive about the railways' potential to alleviate traffic congestion (and by implication its associated social and environmental costs), and successfully lobbied Beeching to exclude from his report some loss-making suburban services in major conurbations such as Glasgow and Manchester. Many others went into the closure process and were often bitterly and sometimes successfully opposed.[46]

## Modernization, Sustainability, and South East Dorset's Railways

How did this national politics of "modernization" play out in South East Dorset / South West Hampshire? To what extent did political, policy, and public discourse reflect issues we should now regard as being about sustainability? What follows is not a comprehensive account: it focuses on British Railways' proposals, announced in June and July 1963, to close the three secondary passenger services to the north of the coastal belt.

British Railways' timing was deeply unfortunate in terms of Dorset County Council's bold proposals, dating from its County Development Plan of 1955, to greatly expand South East Dorset's population over the next twenty years.[47] By May 1963, the potential increase was even larger, as the Ministry of Housing and Local Government was debating whether some of London's overspill should be settled in districts through which the threatened railways ran. How were people to move around? As late as 1963, Dorset County Council was still planning only fairly modest highway schemes to address predicted congestion over the next twenty years in and around Poole, Dorset's part of the urban core.[48] Neighboring authorities had other ideas; in particular, the County Borough of Bournemouth was already well advanced with major highway plans anticipating Buchanan's prescriptions.[49] Fragmented governance also made it more difficult to develop a coherent response to British Railways' proposals; several county councils were involved, for while one train service ran for about half its length through Hampshire, another ran briefly through that county and then Wiltshire, and the third, the Somerset & Dorset, ran extensively through both its eponymous counties. Nor was Whitehall's marginally more favorable attitude to (sub)urban railways any help as British Railways, the Ministry of Transport and the Transport Users' Consultative Committees for the South West and the South East classified all three services as rural, despite terminating in Bournemouth, the urban core's center. This was reasonable since the lines ran through few densely populated areas, and were not heavily used by commuters.[50]

Not surprisingly, scarcely anyone denied British Railways' case that the services were financially unviable. Modernization—or the lack of it—was thus a major issue for the railways' proponents. Certainly the irregular, infrequent service of old-fashioned, steam-hauled carriages was far removed from the electric or diesel-powered suburban trains found in the big cities, or the contemporary car or bus. The key was what the future might bring— in the context of the growing conurbation. What might "modernization" mean for mobility into, out of, and around the region? Was there a viable alternative to the constrained automobility that was shortly to be made public by Buchanan, but was already being debated locally? This battle over the imagined future concerned not just what a "modernized" train service might look like, but also geography (how extensive did the conurbation have to become to need trains?) and timescales (how long would it take to grow to this point?).

To take the first point: the Transport Users' Consultative Committee public hearings, local newspaper editorials, articles and letters, interventions from community and business leaders, and pamphlets from advocacy groups provide ample evidence of a well-informed body of opinion arguing for the immediate modernization of the railways' infrastructure, trains, working practices, and service patterns. Although "modernization" meant different things to different people, it ultimately amounted to experiments where revenue might grow and costs decline sufficiently to reduce financial losses to an acceptable level. Most suggestions involved trying out improvements that were already common elsewhere in the United Kingdom or abroad: for example, using diesel trains, destaffing or closing lightly used stations, removing surplus tracks, simplifying signaling, or improving timetables.[51] These suggestions usually had short-term, conservative goals: that over five years, a better but cheaper-to-run train service would attract more passengers to fundamentally the same traffic flows.

This conservative modernization struggled to make headway against the sheer scale of existing losses. Almost no one suggested that the trains could be made to turn a profit. Instead, the public battle shifted to the terrain of "social accounting," now called cost-benefit analysis, where the issues of strong sustainability were raised. Cost-benefit analysis was just starting to be used to justify building urban infrastructure, like London's Victoria underground line, where operating losses would be more than compensated by wider social and economic benefits. The Ministry of Transport began to recognize the potential of cost-benefit analysis for quantitatively assessing the viability of suburban rail services, although there was insufficient expertise to deliver detailed studies in the timescale demanded by Beeching's national politics.[52]

In Dorset and Hampshire, objectors cited the various advantages of (particularly new) trains over cars and buses that made them more sustainable in social and environmental terms. Dorset County Council argued in terms that today would amount to the claim that women, the elderly, and children were being discriminated against because they were far less likely than men to have access to cars, and that buses did not always provide an equivalent service to trains. Another powerful argument was that trains were safer than road transport, so that once the costs—human, social, and financial—of road "accidents" (that is, crashes) were reckoned, the railways' financial losses became far less significant. Traffic congestion in the urban core was also widely cited as a reason for keeping the trains: Dorset County Council argued that road traffic in and around Poole was already higher than average, while central government grants for investment in new highways were inadequate.[53] Quite apart from the Ministry of Transport's blanket refusal to consider delaying the closure program so that the railways could undergo a cost-benefit analysis, it is hard to believe that existing passenger num-

bers were high enough to tip the balance. Even the argument that urban congestion could only get worse was not a definitive point in favor
of "sustainable" trains over "unsustainable" cars (and buses). The same
argument could be used for investing in urban highways, the course of
action anticipated in Bournemouth.

Nonetheless, Dorset County Council's plans for the conurbation
meant a case could be made for keeping the trains as a partial alternative to automobility. These questions were key: What did the future
hold? How big would the conurbation become? How long would it take
to develop? How would employment, housing, and recreation be distributed? Would new patterns of land use encourage people to move
around the conurbation in economically, socially, and environmentally
sustainable ways, or deter them from doing so? In other words, would
the "modern," late-twentieth-century conurbation develop as, at best,
a space of partly constrained automobility augmented by chiefly road-
based public transport, or as one where trains were the backbone to
a comprehensive and arguably more sustainable system of personal
mobility?

Given the tenor of national debates, the latter argument was lost almost as soon as it was made, despite Dorset County Council's persua-
sive appeals to the Ministry of Transport. As already noted, the Ministry
of Housing and Local Government was toying with developing South
East Dorset / South West Hampshire for London overspill; the numbers
seemed to require railways, and by September 1963, Dorset County
Council was including outlying settlements such as the market town
of Wimborne and the rural village of Verwood, both with threatened
railway stations, in its vision of the developing conurbation, predicting
that the population would exceed 250 thousand by 1981. The council
argued that it was "utter folly" to close lines for which there might be
"great demand" within just a decade.[54]

The Ministry of Transport could not entirely ignore these arguments,
particularly since the prospect of accommodating London overspill had
raised the question more generally of what, if any, railway provision was
needed to mitigate road congestion, particularly from commuting.[55] But
Whitehall did not take very seriously the prospect of overspill as far west
as Dorset, and so the closure proposals were discussed, in secret, only
by the ministry's cross-departmental committee. For the two shorter
routes, which closed in May 1964, one meeting was enough. The other
line (Somerset & Dorset), which eventually closed in March 1966 when
Labour was in power, proved more of a problem for unrelated reasons,
and the delay allowed Dorset County Council to return repeatedly to
urban expansion. The council hoped that Labour's electoral commit-

ment in 1964 to halt major closures until regional, multimodal transport plans had been completed would give the new South West Economic Planning Council time to acknowledge the line's potential. However, Marples's replacement as minister, Tom Fraser, was unable to hold the Cabinet to this promise in the face of the urgent need for further retrenchment; and while the regional Economic Planning Council proved reluctant to rubber stamp the ministry's closure program, it saw no merit in keeping this particular route.[56]

In all these instances, Dorset County Council's case was weakened by a lack of consistent support from local politicians and authorities; they broadly favored road transport or, at best, equivocated over the advantages of trains. The tone of the secret debates within Whitehall was captured by the South East Transport Users' Consultative Committee report of November 1963, arguing (while accepting "they were not really qualified to judge"!) that despite recent population growth, it was "unlikely" that future development would be "seriously prejudiced" by withdrawing trains. The Ministry of Housing and Local Government's brief advice was similar; while confirming that population growth along the railway to the urban core's north was likely to be "large" over the next twenty years, these new settlements were not intended for London-bound commuters and so trains were not needed—cars and buses could handle travel within the conurbation. Thus Dorset County Council's arguments were summarily dismissed: Whitehall was not going to spend national taxes on reprieving these secondary railways. By the time Labour's 1968 Transport Act had introduced subsidies for loss-making passenger trains, all three secondary railways were closed and the tracks partly dismantled.[57]

These decisions were not, of course, determined by the cultural politics of "modernization" alone. The power to define what modernization meant in the context of urban mobility was entangled with the power to imagine the South East Dorset / South West Hampshire conurbation's future in terms of geographical extent, developmental timescale, socioeconomic patterns of land use, and hence the ways people would travel. Sustainability was fairly prominent in these debates, both nationally and regionally, in public and in secret; however, the argument for railways as a socially and environmentally sustainable, congestion-busting mode seemed only remotely plausible over the long term—even then depending on assumptions about land use and traffic that ran counter to the strong tide of political and public opinion in favor of (constrained) automobility. Over the forty-plus years envisaged by the Buchanan Report, Dorset County Council was proved to be largely "right," partly for a reason not even the council predicted: the development of long-distance commuting eastward, even as far as London. But it proved impossible to conjure up an imaginary future convincingly enough to overcome the secretive central government complex of politicians and senior civil servants, determined to slash British Railways' "unsustainable" losses as quickly as possible.

Even Buchanan's radical attempt to reconcile the automobility of a "car-owning democracy" with environmental considerations did not survive the short-term electoral and economic cycles of 1960s' British politics. Certain elements were selectively taken up by politicians, nationally and regionally, and urban planners, supported by a critical degree of public opinion. By European standards, the United Kingdom's former low levels of urban road construction made a degree of catching up inevitable: the issue was not whether, but when and how, highways would be planned and built. Following Buchanan, integrated transport and land-use studies became a major factor shaping urban mobilities during the 1960s and 1970s, not least in South East Dorset and South West Hampshire.[58]

Bournemouth had already been planning major highways before the region's railway closures; similarly, Hampshire County Council's objections to these had probably been motivated by the hope of being bought off by bigger highway grants. Dorset County Council quickly fell into line. Once the trains had gone in 1964 and 1966, public protest quickly died down, and, starting in 1965, the three authorities worked together to prepare a comprehensive land-use/transport study for the conurbation. Published in 1967 and looking forward about thirty years, the study proposed satisfying a predicted doubling of road traffic by 1981 largely through large-scale highway construction, although it noted that traffic management and possibly parking restrictions might be more appropriate in small parts of the urban core. It also supported maintaining and even developing the bus network to alleviate congestion. This, at least, was consistent with Buchanan's philosophy, although the study—like most in the United Kingdom—demonstrated little, if any, systematic enthusiasm for his ideas on environmental capacity.[59]

A year later, in 1968, Labour's Transport Act contained provisions for reviving urban public transport, chiefly through creating powerful Passenger Transport Authorities in several of the older industrial conurbations; these had capital and revenue spending powers. But South East Dorset / South West Hampshire was not yet large enough to have such a body. Nevertheless, by the mid-1970s, local policy had moved a little more in favor of public transport, perhaps reflecting the national shift in public opinion against destructive highway building: by 1974 (when Bournemouth and Christchurch moved into Dorset), all capital spending following the 1967 study had been on roads. In 1976, South East Dorset's revised transport study protected a length of dismantled railway for possible use as a light-rail route. This protection lasted only five years, however, and by 1989 critical lengths of ex-railway infrastructure had been lost to building, demolition, or conversion to roads.[60] The rumble of trains would never again trouble the conurbation's residents.[61]

## Concluding Remarks: Lessons Learned?

What are the lessons for today's cultural politics of sustainable urban mobility? First, that it is essential to tell compelling stories about life and travel several decades later in towns and cities that are socially, environmentally, and economically sustainable, for our imagination and spirit need sustenance in the struggle to achieve systematic change, especially when powerful interests threaten to dilute the strong definition of "sustainability." Here, history helps by showing that over the long term, weaker voices were proved "right" about keeping open options for more socially inclusive, lower-carbon modes of transport. Timescales matter—it is all too easy to give up on the future in the face of apparently overwhelming short-term challenges. Second, that governance matters: follow the money and look for the geopolitical boundaries when assessing who is defining the terms of debate. And finally (partly to reiterate the first point), no one concerned with policy making—whether mainstream or radical—should ignore popular culture: change, especially systematic change, is almost impossible if it flies in the face of popular opinion.

Given South East Dorset's half-century of venerating the auto, LTP3's positive vision and good intentions were probably never enough to develop with sufficient urgency ways of moving that are socially equitable and would help prevent climate breakdown. The situation becomes worse when, as hinted earlier, new political and policy actors enter the arena, because the relationship between the social, environmental, and economic dimensions of sustainability is once again redefined. Who are these actors, and what are their priorities?

The good news is that political/policy debates are more transparent than fifty years ago—these paragraphs depend on documents that would have been secret in the 1960s. While the Department for Transport and the Treasury still wield considerable power over urban-transport policy and spending, they are more willing to listen to (but not necessarily act upon) dissenting arguments. The balance between central government and the regions is also no longer quite as one-sided: some central government finance for regional transport infrastructure is now devolved to an organization founded in 2016, the Dorset Local Enterprise Partnership.[62] The not-so-good news is that this partnership is not a conventional democratic body where members are either directly elected or represent organizations to which they have been elected by citizens. Although local-authority politicians form a majority, unelected representatives of business and other interest groups such as tertiary educational establishments also have a vote. Inevitably, their priorities weigh heavily in the partnership's deliberations.[63] Its "overarching aim is to create more jobs and drive economic growth in Dorset."[64] In 2014, the partnership drew up the county's Strategic Economic Plan, which in turn heavily shaped the priorities for LTP3's Implementation Plan 3 (2017–20).[65]

Although "sustainability" has lost much of its critical edge in policy and academic discourse, it arguably remains as important for persuading the public of the wisdom of policy initiatives as "modernization" was in the 1950s and 1960s. Certainly, the strategic plan's 2016 iteration proclaims that by 2033, "Dorset will be Britain's most sustainable Core City-Region."[66] But the cultural politics of "modernity" in the 1960s suggests we should carefully scrutinize what the Dorset Local Enterprise Partnership means in terms of urban mobility. An initial reading of its plan is encouraging: there are welcome references to "sustainable transport hubs, the widespread use of sustainable transport options, ensur[ing] sustainable access and travel," and "major transport infrastructure with minimal impact on the environment."[67] From an environmental point of view, matters then take a turn for the worse. Most importantly, there does not seem to be any reference to rapidly driving down transport's *absolute* greenhouse gas emissions. Indeed, LTP3's (2011) commitment to reducing the "overall level" becomes the much weaker aim of reducing per capita emissions from road transport (a performance indicator taken from LTP3). This relative decoupling is a sleight of hand: absolute emissions can increase even as the per capita measure comes down—if, for example, some people drive farther while the population increases among those, such as the young and elderly, who tend to drive less. And it ignores the likely impact on other modes—for instance, the near certainty that improved road access to Bournemouth airport will encourage more carbon-intensive flying.[68] In short, history suggests that while the enterprise partnership emphasizes "sustainability" because the term resonates strongly with wider political and public opinion, it is redefining the concept so that environmental (and perhaps social) considerations do not hamper the stronger imperative "to create jobs and drive economic growth." Implementation Plan 3's rubric almost admits as much: "the focus will be on employment and the economy whilst continuing to address wider LTP goals as part of the delivery program."[69] Economic "sustainability" trumps all else.

At least the historical problems of fragmented regional governance have largely been alleviated, although Hampshire County Council's exclusion from LTP3 suggests that boundaries still matter: traffic flows into, out of, and around the conurbation do not observe county borders. At the moment, Dorset's two local authorities do not control certain regional transport services (particularly trains), mirroring the division between national direction and regional acquiescence found in the Beeching/Buchanan era.[70] But even here, change is in the air: it is possible that a new subnational transport body for the southwest region (the counties of Dorset, Somerset, and, still farther west, Devon and Cornwall) will be established to develop and perhaps later deliver strategic transport plans.[71] If so, it will be worth looking in more detail at Labour's regional planning authorities in the 1960s, not least because then, as potentially now, the South East Dorset / South West Hampshire conurbation was divided between the bodies responsible for southwest and southeast England.

But none of this will count for anything if there is no popular support for environmentally and socially sustainable forms of urban transport. Popular opposition to closing South East Dorset / South West Hampshire's railways was muted and ineffective, partly because of the wider public's enthusiasm for urban automobility. Central governments both reacted to and encouraged this; even at the regional level, Dorset County Council did not wish to see trains replace urban highways and motoring so much as offer a supplementary alternative. Individuals and voluntary organizations who steadfastly argued throughout the late 1960s and into the 1970s that urban automobility would prove self-defeating, and that environmentally and socially more sustainable options should be kept open, remained a small, if growing, minority. In the long run, they were (mostly) right: but is the public today fundamentally any less enamored of the car than in the 1960s?

So here, perhaps, is the chief role for historians of the usable past: to broad- (and narrow) cast the stories of imagined futures like those in South East Dorset / South West Hampshire that now, with fifty years' hindsight, seem so desirable, yet at the time were a hopelessly lost cause. We all need encouragement to dream, to conjure up futures that seem utopian but might be achievable if we keep imagining, hoping, and acting. The policy vanguard knows this, but the battle for popular opinion and political clout demands stories from the past, even, or perhaps particularly, about "lost" causes, to help spur fresh thinking about the future. Collectively, we need to reimagine our relationship to mobility so we can dwell in urban spaces in ways we value and enjoy, partly because they are more socially equitable and environmentally sustainable. This chapter does not provide neat answers from the past about how to do this; it suggests that further research might provide a deeper and more nuanced appreciation of how history can help us be more imaginative—not only in thinking about sustainable living but also in how we use stories to help achieve it. While any transition will be achieved only by combining collective politics and personal practice, without the insights of (cultural) history, we make ourselves needlessly short-sighted.

**Colin Divall**, professor emeritus of railway studies at the University of York, U.K., was head of the Institute of Railway Studies & Transport History from its founding jointly with the National Railway Museum in 1995. He now splits his time between research on the history of rural transport in England's West Country and campaigning for better facilities for walkers and cyclists in the small Dorset market town where he lives.

## Notes

1. George Monbiot, *Out of the Wreckage: A New Politics for an Age of Crisis* (London: Verso, 2017).
2. Moshe Givoni and David Banister, "Mobility, Transport and Carbon," in *Moving Towards Low Carbon Mobility*, ed. Moshe Givoni and David Banister (Cheltenham, MA: Edward Elgar, 2013), 7–9. See also Marlene Freudendal-Pedersen, "Structural Stories, Mobility and (Un)freedom," in *Social Perspectives on Mobility*, ed. Thyra Uth Thomsen, Lise Drewes Nielsen, and Henrik Gudmundsson (Aldershot: Ashgate, 2005), 29–45.
3. John Shaw and Iain Docherty, *The Transport Debate* (Bristol: Polity Press, 2014). See also John Sutton, *Gridlock: Congested Cities, Contested Policies, Unsustainable Mobility* (London: Routledge, 2015), xiv–xviii.
4. For example, Glenn Lyons, "Transport Analysis in an Uncertain World," *Transport Reviews* 36, no. 5 (2016): 553–57; Glenn Lyons and Cody Davidson, "Guidance for Transport Planning and Policymaking in the Face of an Uncertain Future," *Transportation Research Part A* 88 (2016): 104–16; Robin Hickman and David Banister, *Transport, Climate Change and the City* (Abingdon: Routledge, 2014), 65–92; Moshe Givoni, "Alternative Pathways to Low Carbon Mobility," in Givoni and Banister, *Low Carbon Mobility*, 209–30; Tim Schwanen, "Sociotechnical Transition in the Transport System," in Givoni and Banister, *Low Carbon Mobility*, 231–54; John Grin, Jan Rotmans, and Johan Schot, with Frank Geels and Derk Loorbach, *Transitions to Sustainable Development: New Directions in the Study of Long Term Transformative Change* (London: Routledge, 2010); David Ban-

ister, Dominic Stead, Peter Steen, Jonas Åkerman, Karl Dreborg, Peter Nijkamp and Ruggero Schleicher-Tappeser, *European Transport Policy and Sustainable Mobility* (London: Spon Press, 2000), 111–73.

5. For example, Carmen Hass-Klau, *The Pedestrian and the City* (New York: Routledge, 2015), 1–104; Hickman and Banister, *Transport*, 1– 63, 94–107; Stephen Glaister, June Burnham, Handley Stevens and Tony Travers, *Transport Policy in Britain*, 2nd ed. (Houndmills: Palgrave Macmillan, 2006), 1–41; Geoff Vigar, *The Politics of Mobility: Transport, Environment and Public Policy* (London: Spon Press, 2002), 42–65; David Starkie, *The Motorway Age: Road and Traffic Policies in Post-War Britain* (Oxford: Pergamon Press, 1982); John Grant, *The Politics of Urban Transport Planning: An Analysis of Transportation Policy Formulation in Three UK County Boroughs between 1947 and 1974* (London: Earth Resources, 1977).

6. Givoni and Banister, "Mobility," 10.

7. Sutton, *Gridlock*, 24–33.

8. For example, Simon Gunn, "The Rise and Fall of British Urban Modernism: Planning Bradford, Circa 1945–1970," *Journal of British Studies* 49, no. 4 (2010): 849–69; idem, "Ring Road Birmingham and the Collapse of the Motor City Ideal in 1970s Britain," *Historical Journal* 61, no. 1 (2018): 227–48; Guy Ortolano, "Planning the Urban Future in 1960s Britain," *Historical Journal* 54, no. 2 (2011): 477–507; Otto Saumarez Smith, "Central Government and Town-Centre Redevelopment in Britain, 1959–1966," *Historical Journal* 58, no. 1 (2015): 217–44.

9. Sutton, *Gridlock*, 17–20; Hickman and Banister, *Transport*, 140–75; John Michael Thompson, *Great Cities and their Traffic* (London: Gollancz, 1977).

10. Bournemouth Borough Council, Borough of Poole, Dorset County Council (BBC etc.), *Bournemouth, Poole and Dorset Local Transport Plan 3: Strategy Document 2011–2026* (Dorchester: Dorset County Council, 2011); *Bournemouth, Poole, Dorset Local Transport Plan 3: First Progress Report 2011 to 2014* (Dorchester: Dorset County Council, 2014); *LPT3 Implementation Plan 2017 to 2020* (Dorchester: Dorset County Council, 2017).

11. LTP1 (July 2001) covered the coastal urban core; LTP2 (2006) included the wider South East Dorset Travel to Work Area. BBC etc., *South East Dorset Provisional Local Transport Plan 2006–11* (Bournemouth: Bournemouth Borough Council, 2005).

12. Atkins Transport Planning and Management, *South East Dorset Multi-Modal Transport Study: Final Report* (n.p., 2012), retrieved 6 October 2017, https://www.dorsetcouncil.gov.uk/roads-highways-maintenance/documents/improvements-and-transport-planning/south-east-dorset-multi-modal-transport-study.pdf. Budgeted at GBP2.3 million, the study took nearly four years to complete. It was prepared in conjunction with the three local authorities, then-existing regional bodies (the Government Office for the South West, the South West Regional Development Agency, and South West Councils), the Highways Agency (predecessor to Highways England), and the national Department for Transport. BBC etc., *Bournemouth, Poole and Dorset Local Transport Plan 3: Appendices* (Dorchester, 2011), 21–22. A surprising omission was Network Rail.

13. BBC etc., *Implementation Plan*, 15.

14. Dorset County Council, *Bournemouth, Poole and Dorset Local Transport Plan 3: Dorset Passenger Transport Strategy* (Dorchester: Dorset County Council, 2016), 4. See also BBC etc., *Bournemouth, Poole and Dorset: Local Transport Plan 2011 to 2026: Summary Document* (Dorchester: Dorset County Council, 2011), 6, 8.

15. Dorset County Council, *Bournemouth, Poole and Dorset LTP3 2011–2026: Low Carbon Travel Strategy (Draft)* (Dorchester: Dorset County Council, 2011), 4; Sutton, *Gridlock*, 24–25.

16. BBC etc., *Implementation Plan*, 2, 12–15; Bournemouth Borough Council, *Three Towns Travel* (2017), retrieved 2 October 2017, https://www.bournemouth.gov .uk/travelandtransport/projectsconsultationslocaltransportplans/ThreeTowns Travel/ThreeTownsTravel.aspx; Department for Transport, *Impact of the Local Sustainable Transport Fund: Summary Report: Moving Britain Ahead* (London: DfT, 2017).

17. As elsewhere in this book, mobility refers chiefly to the movement of people—although we must recognize that the circulation of materials, goods, and waste is equally important for the sustainable city. Markus Hesse, *The City as a Terminal: The Urban Context of Logistics and Freight Transport* (London: Routledge, 2008); Jian Liu, "Supply Chains," in Givoni and Banister, *Low Carbon Mobility*, 148–65; James Macmillen, "Mobility as a Complex System: Key Elements and Interactions," in Givoni and Banister, *Low Carbon Mobility*, 193, 197, 200–1.

18. Colin Divall and Winstan Bond, eds., *Suburbanizing the Masses: Public Transport and Urban Development in Historical Perspective* (Aldershot: Ashgate, 2003); Ralf Roth and Marie-Noëlle Polino, eds., *The City and the Railway in Europe* (Aldershot: Ashgate, 2003); Jack Simmons, *The Railway in Town and Country, 1830–1914* (Newton Abbot: David & Charles, 1986); John Kellett, *The Impact of Railways on Victorian Cities* (London: Routledge & Kegan Paul, 1969); Robert Cervero, "Transit-Oriented Development and the Urban Fabric," in *Sustainable Railway Futures: Issues and Challenges*, ed. Becky P. Y. Loo and Claude Comtois (Farnham: Ashgate, 2015), 75–93; Linna Li and Becky P. Y. Loo, "The Promotion of Social Equity through Railways," in Loo and Comtois, *Sustainable Railway Futures*, 129–44.

19. Chris Austin and Richard Faulkner, *Disconnected: Broken Links in Britain's Rail Policy* (Addlestone: Oxford Publishing, 2015), 50, 125–26, 132; Association of Train Operating Companies (ATOC), *Connecting Communities: Expanding Access to the Rail Network* (London: ATOC, 2009), 16, 19.

20. BBC etc., *Local Transport Plan 3*, 23, 78–79.

21. British Railways Board (BRB), *The Reshaping of British Railways* (London: Her Majesty's Stationery Office, 1963); Ministry of Transport (MoT), *Traffic in Towns: A Study of the Long Term Problems of Traffic in Urban Areas* (London: Her Majesty's Stationery Office, 1963).

22. Simon Gunn, "The Buchanan Report, Environment and the Problem of Traffic in 1960s Britain," *Twentieth Century British History* 22, no. 4 (2011): 531–33; Charles Loft, *Government, the Railways and the Modernization of Britain: Beeching's Last Trains* (London: Routledge, 2006), 75, 90, 101–4; Starkie, *Motorway Age*, 37–40.

23. Gregory Thompson, *The Passenger Train in the Motor Age: California's Rail and Bus Industries, 1910–41* (Columbus: Ohio State University Press, 1994); Terry Gourvish, *British Railways 1948–73: A Business History* (Cambridge: Cambridge University Press, 1986), 1–304; Loft, *Beeching's Last Trains*, 16–73; Ralf Roth and Colin Divall, eds., *From Rail to Road and Back Again? A Century of Transport Competition and Interdependency* (Farnham: Ashgate, 2015).

24. Gunn, "Buchanan Report," 522, 542; Carmen Hass-Klau, *Pedestrian*, 92; Martin Emanuel, "Where Public Transit Eclipses Cycling," in *Cycling Cities: The European Experience*, ed. Ruth Oldenziel, Martin Emanuel, Adri Albert de la Bruhèze,

and Frank Veraart (Eindhoven: Foundation for the History of Technology, 2016), 149–59, here 154; Banister, *Transport Planning*, 26.

25. Hass-Klau, *Pedestrian*, 80–87; Peter Merriman, *Driving Spaces: A Cultural-Historical Geography of England's M1 Motorway* (Oxford: Blackwell, 2007), esp. 23–73, 162–86; David Jeremiah, *Representations of British Motoring* (Manchester: Manchester University Press, 2007), 163–239; Starkie, *Motorway Age*, 1–30; Barbara Schmucki, "Cities as Traffic Machines: Urban Transport Planning in East and West Germany," in Divall and Bond, *Suburbanizing the Masses*, 149–70.
26. Loft, *Beeching's Last Trains*, 56–59; Gunn, "Buchanan Report," 523–24.
27. Loft, *Beeching's Last Trains*, 53–89.
28. Gunn, "Buchanan Report," 525–28.
29. Ibid., 522–23.
30. Ibid., 530–31; MoT, *Traffic in Towns*, 35–37, 39–40, 44–52, 191, 203–13.
31. Gunn, "Buchanan Report," 530–31; MoT, *Traffic in Towns*, 14–23, 33–52; Barbara Schmucki, "'If I Walked on My Own at Night I Stuck to Well Lit Areas': Gendered Spaces and Urban Transport in 20th Century Britain," *Research in Transportation Economics* 34 (2012): 82–83.
32. MoT, *Traffic in Towns*, 26.
33. Ibid., 25, 194, 195; Loft, *Beeching's Last Trains*, 58; Starkie, *Motorway Age*, 42–45.
34. MoT, *Traffic in Towns*, 24, 26, 37–38, 175, 177, 184, 186.
35. Ibid., 193.
36. Peter Hall, *Cities in Civilization: Culture, Innovation, and Urban Order* (London: Weidenfeld & Nicolson, 1998), 782–802, 861–70; Tomas Ekman, "Vision in Solid Form: A Comparison between Two Solutions to the Traffic Problem in Stockholm, 1941 and 1992," in Divall and Bond, *Suburbanizing the Masses*, 171–86.
37. Geoffrey Crowther et al. "Report of the Steering Group," in MoT, *Traffic in Towns*, para. 42.
38. Ibid., para. 49.
39. David Rooney, "The Political Economy of Congestion: Road Pricing and the Neo-Liberal Project," *Twentieth Century British History* 25, no. 4 (2014): 633–43.
40. Gunn, "Buchanan Report," 525, 531–33; Loft, *Beeching's Last Trains*, 91, 114–20; Vigar, *Politics of Mobility*, 45–46; Banister, *Transport Planning*, 24–27; Starkie, *Motorway Age*, 37–40, 62–63; Grant, *Urban Transport Planning*, 48–49.
41. Loft, *Beeching's Last Trains*, 53–94; Gourvish, *British Railways*, 307–74, 389–460.
42. BRB, *Reshaping*, 1.
43. Loft, *Beeching's Last Trains*, 93–94, 101–2.
44. Ibid., 73.
45. Ibid., 23, 31–32, 46–47, 58, 64–65, 80–82.
46. Ibid., 8–11, 87, 91, 94–96, 106, 112, 153.
47. Dorset County Council, *County Development Plan: Written Statement* (Dorchester: Dorset County Council, 1964).
48. Ibid., 5, 12–13.
49. "B'mth Ahead in Plans," *Bournemouth Evening Echo*, 28 November 1963.
50. MoT, "Withdrawal of Unremunerative Services: Southern Region: Somerset & Dorset Line" (1962–64), MT124/769; Brockenhurst–Ringwood–Bournemouth (1963–68), MT124/775; Salisbury–Fordingbridge–Bournemouth" (1963–71), MT124/777; all in The National Archives, Kew, Surrey.
51. Branch Line Reinvigoration Society (BLRS), *The Somerset & Dorset Railway* (London: BLRS, 1962); idem, *Unprofitable Lines? A Financial Study of Certain Railway Passenger Services in Somerset, Hampshire and Dorset* (London: BLRS, 1963);

David St. John Thomas, *The Rural Transport Problem* (London: Routledge & Kegan Paul, 1963), 21–35, 127–29, 135–43, 150–57, 166–71; Gerard Fiennes, *I Tried to Run a Railway* (London: Ian Allan, 1967), 114–20.

52. Loft, *Beeching's Last Trains*, 84–85, 87, 94, 112.

53. MoT, "Somerset & Dorset Line"; "Brockenhurst–Ringwood–Bournemouth"; "Salisbury–Fordingbridge–Bournemouth."

54. Dorset County Council, Economic Development Committee minutes (1963–65), DCC/A/29/1 in the Dorset History Centre, Dorchester; MoT, "Brockenhurst–Ringwood–Bournemouth."

55. Loft, *Beeching's Last Trains*, 91, 95.

56. Ibid., 114–20; MoT, "Somerset & Dorset Line"; Department of Economic Affairs, "Railways (Closures): Somerset & Dorset Line" (1965–67), EW22/64 in The National Archives. Kew, Surrey.

57. MoT, "Somerset & Dorset Line"; "Brockenhurst–Ringwood–Bournemouth"; "Salisbury–Fordingbridge–Bournemouth"; Loft, *Beeching's Last Trains*, 122–28.

58. Gunn, "Buchanan Report," 533–42; Starkie, *Motorway Age*, 39–41, 59–60, 62–70.

59. Dorset County Council, Hampshire County Council, Bournemouth County Borough, *First Report on a Land Use and Transportation Study of South-East Dorset and South-West Hampshire* (1967), D.1459/7/5 in the Dorset History Centre, Dorchester; Vigar, *Politics of Mobility*, 45–46; Hass-Klau, *The Pedestrian*, 92–94.

60. Colin Divall, "The 'Old Road': Reusing, Interpreting and Commemorating an Abandoned Railway in Southern England, 1964–2015," in *New Uses for Old Railways*, ed. Anne McCants, Eduardo Beira, José Manuel Lopes Cordeiro, Paulo B. Lourenço, and Hugo Silveira Pereira (n.p.: Createspace Independent Publishing Platform, 2016), 210–14.

61. Technological innovation (new at any rate to the United Kingdom) in the shape of tram-trains running on both heavy- and light-rail tracks offers a distant prospect of a greater role for rail. BBC etc., *Local Transport Plan 2006–11*, 40; *Local Transport Plan 3*, 75, 79–80; *Implementation Plan 3*, 39–48.

62. The Dorset Local Enterprise Partnership started to shadow the Wessex Multi Area Partnership from 2011. BBC etc., *Local Transport Plan 3*, 7, 12, 14–16; Dorset Local Enterprise Partnership (DLEP), "Governance," DLEP website, 2018, retrieved 25 July 2018, http://dorsetlep.co.uk/governance.

63. This is partly why central government wants Local Enterprise Partnerships, a point privately confirmed to me by a Whitehall official. See also Sutton, *Gridlock*, 52, note 3.

64. DLEP, "Dorset is Alive with Opportunities," DLEP website, 2018, retrieved 25 July 2018, http://dorsetlep.co.uk/.

65. DLEP, *Transforming Dorset: Strategic Economic Plan* (n.p., 2014), retrieved 25 July 2018, http://dorsetlep.s3.amazonaws.com/SEP%20Pics%20&%20Docs/6342%20LEP%20Strategic%20Economic%20Plan%20v3%20LOW%20RES.pdf; *A Strategic Economic Vision for Dorset* (n.p., 2016), retrieved 25 July 2018, http://dorsetlep.s3.amazonaws.com/Documents/DLEP%20Vision%202016%20LOWRES.pdf; BBC etc., *Implementation Plan*, 1, 7.

66. DLEP, *Strategic Economic Vision*, 3.

67. Ibid., sections 1.2, 1.6.

68. BBC etc., *Local Transport Plan 3*, 111; *Implementation Plan 3*, 56–57.

69. BBC etc., *Implementation Plan 3*, 40.

70. BBC etc., *Local Transport Plan 3*, 73–75.

71. "Economic Boost for County as Dorset to Be Granted More Powers to Deal with Transport," *Dorset Echo*, 31 May 2018, Retrieved 23 July 2018 http://www.dorsetecho.co.uk/news/16260425.display/.

# Bibliography

## Archival Sources

Dorset History Centre, Dorchester, Dorset.
Dorset County Council. *County Development Plan: Written Statement*, 1964. D.1405/2/2/1.
Dorset County Council. Economic Development Committee minutes, 1963–65. DCC/A/29/1.
Dorset County Council, Hampshire County Council, Bournemouth County Borough. *First Report on a Land Use and Transportation Study of South-East Dorset and South-West Hampshire*, 1967. D.1459/7/5.
The National Archives, Kew, Surrey.
Department of Economic Affairs. "Railways (Closures): Somerset & Dorset Line" (1965–67). EW22/64.
Ministry of Transport. "Withdrawal of Unremunerative Services: Southern Region: Somerset & Dorset Line" (1962–64). MT124/769;
"Brockenhurst–Ringwood–Bournemouth" (1963–68). MT124/775;
"Salisbury–Fordingbridge–Bournemouth" (1963–71). MT124/777.

## Published Sources

Association of Train Operating Companies (ATOC). *Connecting Communities: Expanding Access to the Rail Network*. London: ATOC, 2009.
Atkins Transport Planning and Management. *South East Dorset Multi-Modal Transport Study: Final Report*. 2012. Retrieved 6 October 2017, https://www.dorsetcouncil.gov.uk/roads-highways-maintenance/documents/improvements-and-transport-planning/south-east-dorset-multi-modal-transport-study.pdf.
Austin, Chris, and Richard Faulkner. *Disconnected: Broken Links in Britain's Rail Policy*. Addlestone: Oxford Publishing, 2015.
Banister, David. *Transport Planning*. 2nd edition. London: Spon Press, 2002.
Banister, David, Dominic Stead, Peter Steen, Jonas Åkerman, Karl Dreborg, Peter Nijkamp, and Ruggero Schleicher-Tappeser. *European Transport Policy and Sustainable Mobility*. London: Spon Press, 2000.
Bournemouth Borough Council. *Three Towns Travel*. 2017. Retrieved 2 October 2017, https://www.bournemouth.gov.uk/travelandtransport/projectsconsultationslocaltransportplans/ThreeTownsTravel/ThreeTownsTravel.aspx.
Bournemouth Borough Council, Borough of Poole, Dorset County Council. *Bournemouth, Poole and Dorset: Local Transport Plan 2011 to 2026: Summary Document*. Dorchester: Dorset County Council, 2011.
——. *Bournemouth, Poole and Dorset Local Transport Plan 3: Appendices*. Dorchester: Dorset County Council, 2011.
——. *Bournemouth, Poole, Dorset Local Transport Plan 3: First Progress Report 2011 to 2014*. Dorchester: Dorset County Council, 2014.

——. *Bournemouth, Poole, Dorset Local Transport Plan 3: LPT3 Implementation Plan 2017 to 2020*. Dorchester: Dorset County Council, 2017.

——. *Bournemouth, Poole and Dorset Local Transport Plan 3: Strategy Document 2011–2026*. Dorchester: Dorset County Council, 2011.

——. *South East Dorset Provisional Local Transport Plan 2006–11*. Bournemouth: Bournemouth Borough Council, 2005.

Branch Line Reinvigoration Society (BLRS). *The Somerset & Dorset Railway*. London: BLRS, 1962.

——. *Unprofitable Lines? A Financial Study of Certain Railway Passenger Services in Somerset, Hampshire and Dorset*. London: BLRS, 1963.

British Railways Board. *The Reshaping of British Railways*. London: Her Majesty's Stationery Office, 1963.

Cervero, Robert. "Transit-Oriented Development and the Urban Fabric." In *Sustainable Railway Futures: Issues and Challenges*, edited by Becky P. Y. Loo and Claude Comtois, 75–93. Farnham: Ashgate. 2015.

Crowther, Geoffrey, et al. "Report of the Steering Group." In MoT, *Traffic in Towns: A Study of the Long Term Problems of Traffic in Urban Areas*, [v–xiv]. London: Her Majesty's Stationery Office, 1963.

Department for Transport (DfT). *Impact of the Local Sustainable Transport Fund: Summary Report: Moving Britain Ahead*. London: DfT, 2017.

Divall, Colin. "The 'Old Road': Reusing, Interpreting and Commemorating an Abandoned Railway in Southern England, 1964–2015." In *New Uses for Old Railways*, edited by Anne McCants, Eduardo Beira, José Manuel Lopes Cordeiro, Paulo B. Lourenço, and Hugo Silveira Pereira, 205–27. N.p.: Createspace Independent Publishing Platform, 2016.

Divall, Colin, and Winstan Bond, eds. *Suburbanizing the Masses: Public Transport and Urban Development in Historical Perspective*. Aldershot: Ashgate, 2003.

Dorset County Council. *Bournemouth, Poole and Dorset Local Transport Plan 3: Dorset Passenger Transport Strategy*. Dorchester: Dorset County Council, 2016.

——. *Bournemouth, Poole and Dorset LTP3 2011–2026: Low Carbon Travel Strategy (Draft)*. Dorchester: Dorset County Council, 2011

Dorset Local Enterprise Partnership. "Dorset is Alive with Opportunities." 2018. Retrieved 25 July 2018, http://dorsetlep.co.uk/.

——. "Governance." 2018. Retrieved 25 July 2018, http://dorsetlep.co.uk/govern ance/.

——. *A Strategic Economic Vision for Dorset*. N.p.: Dorset Local Enterprise Partnership, 2016. Retrieved 25 July 2018, http://dorsetlep.s3.amazonaws.com/Docu ments/DLEP%20Vision%202016%20LOWRES.pdf.

——. *Transforming Dorset: Strategic Economic Plan*. N.p.: Dorset Local Enterprise Partnership, 2014. Retrieved 25 July 2018, http://dorsetlep.s3.amazonaws .com/SEP%20Pics%20&%20Docs/6342%20LEP%20Strategic%20Economic%20 Plan%20v3%20LOW%20RES.pdf.

Ekman, Tomas. "Vision in Solid Form: A Comparison between Two Solutions to the Traffic Problem in Stockholm, 1941 and 1992." In *Suburbanizing the Masses: Public Transport and Urban Development in Historical Perspective*, edited by Divall and Bond, 171–86.

Emanuel, Martin. "Where Public Transit Eclipses Cycling." In *Cycling Cities: The European Experience: Hundred Years of Policy and Practice*, edited by Ruth Oldenziel, Martin Emanuel, Adri Albert de la Bruhèze, and Frank Veraart, 149–59. Eindhoven: Foundation for the History of Technology, 2016.

Fiennes, Gerard. *I Tried to Run a Railway*. London: Ian Allan, 1967.

Freudendal-Pedersen, Marlene. "Structural Stories, Mobility and (Un)freedom." In *Social Perspectives on Mobility*, edited by Thyra Uth Thomsen, Lise Drewes Nielsen, and Henrik Gudmundsson, 29–45. Aldershot: Ashgate, 2005.

Givoni, Moshe. "Alternative Pathways to Low Carbon Mobility." In *Moving Towards Low Carbon Mobility*, edited by Moshe Givoni and David Banister, 209–30. Cheltenham, MA: Edward Elgar, 2013.

Givoni, Moshe, and David Banister. "Mobility, Transport and Carbon." In *Moving Towards Low Carbon Mobility*, edited by Givoni and Banister, 1–12.

Glaister, Stephen, June Burnham, Handley Stevens, and Tony Travers. *Transport Policy in Britain*. 2nd edition. Houndmills: Palgrave Macmillan, 2006.

Grant, John. *The Politics of Urban Transport Planning: An Analysis of Transportation Policy Formulation in Three UK County Boroughs between 1947 and 1974*. London: Earth Resources, 1977.

Grin, John, Jan Rotmans, and Johan Schot, with Frank Geels and Derk Loorbach. *Transitions to Sustainable Development: New Directions in the Study of Long Term Transformative Change*. London: Routledge, 2010.

Gourvish, Terry. *British Railways 1948–73: A Business History*. Cambridge: Cambridge University Press, 1986.

Gunn, Simon. "The Buchanan Report, Environment and the Problem of Traffic in 1960s Britain." *Twentieth Century British History* 22, no. 4 (2011): 521–42.

——. "Ring Road Birmingham and the Collapse of the Motor City Ideal in 1970s Britain." *Historical Journal* 61, no. 1 (2018): 227–48

——. "The Rise and Fall of British Urban Modernism: Planning Bradford, circa 1945–1970." *Journal of British Studies* 49, no. 4 (2010): 849–69.

Hall, Peter. *Cities in Civilization: Culture, Innovation, and Urban Order*. London: Weidenfeld & Nicolson, 1998.

Hass-Klau, Carmen. *The Pedestrian and the City*. New York: Routledge, 2015.

Hesse, Markus. *The City as a Terminal: The Urban Context of Logistics and Freight Transport*. London: Routledge, 2008.

Hickman, Robin, and David Banister. *Transport, Climate Change and the City*. Abingdon: Routledge, 2014.

Jeremiah, David. *Representations of British Motoring*. Manchester: Manchester University Press, 2007.

Kellett, John. *The Impact of Railways on Victorian Cities*. London: Routledge & Kegan Paul, 1969.

Li, Linna, and Becky P. Y. Loo. "The Promotion of Social Equity through Railways." In *Sustainable Railway Futures: Issues and Challenges*, edited by Becky P. Y. Loo and Claude Comtois, 129–44. Farnham: Ashgate. 2015.

Liu, Jian. "Supply Chains." In *Moving Towards Low Carbon Mobility*, edited by Givoni and Banister, 148–65.

Loft, Charles. *Government, the Railways and the Modernization of Britain: Beeching's Last Trains*. London: Routledge, 2006.

Lyons, Glenn. "Transport Analysis in an Uncertain World." *Transport Reviews* 36, no. 5 (2016): 553–57.

Lyons, Glenn, and Cody Davidson. "Guidance for Transport Planning and Policy-making in the Face of an Uncertain Future." *Transportation Research Part A* 88 (2016): 104–16.

Macmillen, James. "Mobility as a Complex System: Key Elements and Interactions." In *Moving Towards Low Carbon Mobility*, edited by Givoni and Banister, 190–205.

Merriman, Peter. *Driving Spaces: A Cultural-Historical Geography of England's M1 Motorway.* Oxford: Blackwell, 2007.

Ministry of Transport. *Traffic in Towns: A Study of the Long Term Problems of Traffic in Urban Areas.* London: Her Majesty's Stationery Office, 1963.

Monbiot, George. *Out of the Wreckage: A New Politics for an Age of Crisis.* London: Verso, 2017.

Ortolano, Guy. "Planning the Urban Future in 1960s Britain." *Historical Journal* 54, no. 2 (2011): 477–507.

Roth, Ralf, and Colin Divall, eds. *From Rail to Road and Back Again? A Century of Transport Competition and Interdependency.* Farnham: Ashgate, 2015.

Roth, Ralf, and Marie-Noëlle Polino, eds. *The City and the Railway in Europe.* Aldershot: Ashgate, 2003.

Rooney, David. "The Political Economy of Congestion: Road Pricing and the Neo-Liberal Project." *Twentieth Century British History* 25, no. 4 (2014): 628–50.

Schmucki, Barbara. "Cities as Traffic Machines: Urban Transport Planning in East and West Germany." In *Suburbanizing the Masses: Public Transport and Urban Development in Historical Perspective*, edited by Divall and Bond, 149–70.

——. "'If I Walked on My Own at Night I Stuck to Well Lit Areas': Gendered Spaces and Urban Transport in 20th Century Britain." *Research in Transportation Economics* 34 (2012): 74–85.

Schwanen, Tim. "Sociotechnical Transition in the Transport System." In *Moving Towards Low Carbon Mobility*, edited by Givoni and Banister, 231–54.

Shaw, John, and Iain Docherty. *The Transport Debate.* Bristol: Polity Press, 2014.

Simmons, Jack. *The Railway in Town and Country, 1830–1914.* Newton Abbot: David & Charles, 1986.

Smith, Otto Saumarez. "Central Government and Town-Centre Redevelopment in Britain, 1959–1966." *Historical Journal* 58, no. 1 (2015): 217–44.

Starkie, David. *The Motorway Age: Road and Traffic Policies in Post-War Britain.* Oxford: Pergamon Press, 1982.

Sutton, John. *Gridlock: Congested Cities, Contested Policies, Unsustainable Mobility.* London: Routledge, 2015.

Thomas, David St. John. *The Rural Transport Problem.* London: Routledge & Kegan Paul, 1963.

Thompson, Gregory. *The Passenger Train in the Motor Age: California's Rail and Bus Industries, 1910–41.* Columbus: Ohio State University Press, 1994.

Thompson, John Michael. *Great Cities and Their Traffic.* London: Gollancz, 1977.

Vigar, Geoff. *The Politics of Mobility: Transport, Environment and Public Policy.* London: Spon Press, 2002.

# SECTION II

⮐

# Recovering Sustainable Mobilities of the Past

Without a doubt, walking is our most sustainable form of mobility, closely followed by cycling. Yet most studies have ignored the continuing importance of walking and cycling practices. In the section "Recovering Sustainable Mobilities of the Past," the authors introduce new research methods and issues to prove that pedestrians and cyclists may have slipped under the radar, but have never really disappeared. To see them anew as a more sustainable future, researchers need to do some creative detective work: looking for clues through alternative sources, such as diaries and photographs, that can recover the historical traces of their existence.

Colin Pooley uses diaries to trace what walking meant for people in the United Kingdom. Importantly, he shows that walking—humankind's most normal way to get around until very recently—was seen as "abnormal" once cars entered the city. Franck Cochoy, Roland Canu, and Cédric Calvignac use street photographs from Toulouse, France, to discover what kind of devices pedestrians chose to carry consumer goods. Their research reveals something that policymakers and scholars have simply overlooked: when it comes to delivering goods, pedestrians are trucks without wheels, and are accustomed to lugging lots of stuff around. Finally, through historical photographs, Tiina Männistö-Funk discovers that cyclists and pedestrians were everywhere in the Finnish city of Turku. These were mostly women conducting activities near home—activities that scholars and policymakers have ignored. Their space was soon given away to car infrastructures. This evidence points to the social injustices that urban planning created when favoring motorists.

In short, this section reveals the histories of walking and cycling, emphasizing their importance for conceiving more sustainable mobility futures that include the existing practices in walkable and cyclable cities.

CHAPTER 4

# Pedestrian Stories
## *Recovering Sustainable Urban Mobility*
### Colin Pooley

## Introduction

Walking is the most sustainable form of transport for most short journeys and can form part of many longer multimode trips. It requires few resources, has low-level impact on the environment compared to other travel modes, and is accessible to most people. It thus meets the basic criteria of both environmental and social sustainability.[1] In the past, walking was the taken-for-granted form of movement for many journeys. However, current transport policies in most countries rarely view travel on foot as a form of transport that needs to be planned, and only minimal provision is made for pedestrians.[2] In this chapter, I draw on examples from Britain to demonstrate the historical significance of walking as a form of transport, and to chart the reasons for its relative neglect and decline. I argue that recognizing the significance of the pedestrian in urban transport systems, together with the provision of improved infrastructures, could contribute significantly to a more sustainable future for urban mobility. Although the examples are drawn from Britain, the argument equally applies to most countries where automobiles dominate the transport system.

For most of human history, pedestrians have formed the main traffic in both urban and rural areas. Some people had access to animal-powered transport, and waterways were important in certain locations, but the default travel mode in urban areas was walking. From the mid-nineteenth century, wealthy nations expanded their urban public transport systems with omnibuses, suburban railways, and trams, thus increasing the mobility options. Private transport by bicycle and motor car gradually became available, but these remained the preserve of the relatively affluent well into the twentieth century. Although private or public powered transport now dominates urban streets all over the world, travel on foot continues to be important for both urban and rural areas in many poorer countries.[3]

Definitive data on walking as a transport mode are hard to come by (see below), but reliable estimates show that in the first decade of the twentieth century, approximately half of all travel to and from work in Britain was on foot, and walking probably formed a larger proportion of trips undertaken for other everyday purposes such as shopping, visiting friends, and children traveling to and from school. The sharpest decline in walking to work occurred in the 1920s, as people switched to cycling and public transport, and then in the 1960s due to increased car use.[4] By 2015, walking accounted for barely 10 percent of the journeys to and from work, though some 22 percent of all trips (for any purpose) recorded in the British National Travel Survey were on foot.[5] This is broadly similar to many other Western European countries, but significantly higher than in North America and Australia, where walking accounts for less than 10 percent of all travel.[6] Not only is walking by far the most environmentally sustainable and accessible option, but also walking for everyday trips and for leisure can contribute to good health, increased sociability, and community cohesion. Walking is also the most socially inclusive form of urban transport. For those with limited time for leisure activities, walking for everyday travel can be particularly important as a route to such benefits. As walking has declined, so too has the sustainability of urban travel, while the environmental impacts of transport have increased. Consequently, those unable to access the dominant transport modes have experienced transport-related social exclusion.[7]

There is substantial social science literature on walking as an activity, but this tends to focus disproportionately on walking as a leisure activity (especially in the open countryside and on mountains), on the performativity of walking, and on the kinesthetic experience of traveling on foot. There is also literature on the perceived risks of walking, especially for women.[8] In contrast, everyday (or utility) walking undertaken as part of normal daily life is a relatively neglected topic.[9] This chapter focuses on the practical dilemmas of everyday urban walking, the ways these have changed over time, and the policies that might encourage more people to walk on a daily basis. The theory supporting this research is drawn from the field of mobility studies, where the so-called "new mobilities paradigm" has highlighted the role of mobility in constructing and executing most aspects of everyday life.[10] There has been extensive reworking and development of the original ideas, but all the research within this framework places the human experience of movement center stage rather than simply as the process of moving from one location to another.[11] So far, there has been only limited interaction between mobilities theory and transport studies, with even less consideration of historical trends.[12] By focusing on the changing role of walking in Britain's urban transport since the 1890s, this chapter adds to the growing literature.

I now turn to the sources of data for studying the history of everyday walking in Britain, and examine their problems of use. I then develop an argument that the marginalization and decline of walking for everyday travel in Britain over the past century are the result of three main processes operating in unison: the changing norms of travel behavior that have evolved over time; the changes in personal circumstances and family structures that have affected how people travel; and the altered perceptions of risks that walkers may encounter in the street. A range of personal testimonies traces the historical trends in each process, along with the policies proposed that could make walking easier and more desirable, and thus reverse the long-run and widespread decline in everyday walking that has occurred in Britain and elsewhere.

### Sources of Evidence: Recovering Past Sustainable Urban Mobility

Walking is all but invisible in many sets of transport statistics, and this obscures its potential significance in creating more sustainable urban mobility practices. I argue that better understanding of the role of walking in the past can help to focus attention on this most sustainable form of travel. For instance, walking (and, for that matter, cycling) is excluded from Eurostat data on passenger road transport,[13] and the United Kingdom's Department for Transport did not begin publishing separate statistics on walking (and cycling) until 2012.[14] These were derived from the "Active People's Survey" carried out by Sport England since 2006. Although these data provide insights into utility walking, the main focus is sport and active leisure.[15] According to data for 2014–2015, utility walking in Britain is increasing slightly, with 25 percent of the people surveyed stating they walk at least five times a week for utility purposes. As yet these data are limited, and it is hard to know if this is a sustained reversal of a previous downward trend.[16] The British National Travel Survey (NTS), which does provide some data on all travel modes from 1965 to the present, shows that the proportion of all trips undertaken on foot dropped from 34.8 percent in 1975/6 to 22 percent in 2015. The NTS definition of walking trips, however, has changed over time; for instance, its first survey in 1965 excluded all trips under one mile (1.6 km). Unsurprisingly, the extent to which people walk for everyday purposes varies from place to place, largely dependent on the proximity of relevant services. Thus, utility walking in rural areas is low (though leisure walking is more common), while in urban areas where more people live close to the services and amenities they use, travel on foot is more common. This is the case in most parts of the world; for instance, 32 percent of all travel in London is undertaken on foot, the same as in Bangalore. The equivalent figure for New York is 39 percent (higher than most U.S. cities); for Paris it is 47 percent, and 27 percent in Shanghai.[17]

While some information exists on walking as a travel mode, none of the sources gives us any insights into the experience of traveling on foot in urban areas. To understand how and why people do (or do not) walk for everyday travel, we need to dig beneath the bare statistics to uncover the motivations, barriers, and experiences related to walking in cities. Accounts of city walking can be gained from a number of sources. Interviews and oral history testimonies are useful for the recent past, although all such data, especially oral history, is dependent on both the interviewee's memory and the interviewer's skill.[18] Ideally, what is needed are first-hand accounts provided at (or close to) the time when travel took place: personal diaries written up on a daily basis can provide such insights. Diaries also have their limitations as historical sources for everyday travel: they were mostly written by more educated and affluent members of society; young women were more likely to keep diaries than other demographics; and we have no way of knowing how the writer selected what to include or exclude. It is also likely that the most mundane activities (such as everyday walking) were under-recorded in favor of more unusual events. Nonetheless, diaries can provide significant insights into aspects of everyday travel (including walking) that are missing from other data.[19] Both oral history and diary evidence feature in this chapter, albeit limited to a small number of individual informants who cannot be considered representative of a larger population.

I also wanted to find personal testimonies of walking from a larger sub-set of the population. The records of London's Central Criminal Court (the Old Bailey) from 1674 to 1913 are available online and provide detailed testimonies from victims, witnesses, and those accused of a wide range of crimes in London.[20] Because much crime was committed on the streets, the accounts of what occurred (especially from witnesses and victims) also provide evidence of who was on the streets at different times of day, as well as what they were doing.[21] This chapter uses sample data from these records for the years 1891, 1901, and 1911 to gain a wider perspective on the experience of walking. These data also contain biases. Most crime was committed at night, so the testimonies are dominated by those on the streets after dark. Moreover, it is not possible to judge the truthfulness of statements, even though all were given under oath. However, these data have been widely used, and their reliability assessed, for studying criminality, and there is no reason to doubt the veracity of statements made by witnesses or victims regarding their daily movements on the street.[22] In the following sections, selected quotes illustrate my argument. Although, as with all qualitative data, the representativeness of such quotes cannot be fully assessed, and statistical representativeness is not the purpose of such research,[23] the quotes selected are drawn from a very much larger set of information available and represent themes and experiences that occurred repeatedly in the data.

## The Normality of Walking

Walking for everyday travel is most common in societies and time periods that fulfill two conditions: first, where many people have limited options regarding how they travel due to the lack of technological development or access to the transport technologies available; and, second, where travel on foot is perceived as the normal and taken-for-granted means of getting from one place to another. For instance, two centuries ago, the development of and access to motorized transport (both public and private) were more limited in all countries of the world.[24] In this section, I focus on the extent to which walking continued to be viewed as normal in British cities as the options for travel increased both through new technologies and less restricted access. The majority of people feel more comfortable when conforming to the social norms of the society in which they live: they are reluctant to stand out from the crowd and may fear ridicule (or worse) if they are seen to transgress.[25] In most rich countries today, the perceived norm for much everyday travel is the automobile, leading to the dominant culture of automobility discussed at length in the mobilities literature.[26] A century ago, this was very different: walking would have been the only available form of travel for most people, and movement on foot would have been the taken-for-granted option for much urban travel. Gradually, while public and private motorized transport expanded, the normality of walking decreased.

Statements given at the Old Bailey trials in London show the extent to which pedestrians filled the streets of Britain's cities in the late nineteenth and early twentieth centuries. Men, women and children of all ages and social classes walked at most times of the day and night as they went about their everyday business. The Old Bailey data obviously just record those who encountered a criminal offence. These would have been a tiny minority of all pedestrians on the streets at any one time—and it is certainly not the intention of this paper to suggest that walking the streets of London in the early twentieth century was dangerous—but there is no reason to doubt that those who encountered criminality (as witness or victim) were a reasonably representative cross-section of a larger pedestrian population. The following testimonies illustrate the range of persons on the streets of London around 1900, and some of the activities in which they were engaged.[27]

In March 1891, Frederick Monroe was witness to a crime as he was returning home from posting a letter just before midnight:

> I am a Wesleyan minister, living in John Wesley's Home, 47, City Road—on the night of 3rd March, about a quarter to twelve, I had been to the post, and on my return I saw a gentleman walking on the other side of the road, and suddenly saw seven or eight men leap out of the shadow of a building and knock him down on the pavement.[28]

Although popping out on foot to post a letter would also be commonplace today, venturing onto the streets late at night was clearly normal for this gentleman. It was equally normal for people to walk home after an evening's entertainment, as stated in November 1891 by Alfred Hawthorne, who took a deliberately long route home, entailing a two-hour walk (presumably for the exercise and fresh air, though this is not specified): "I live at 52, Dean Street, Islington—on this Saturday I went to Sadler's Wells about seven o'clock, and left about a quarter to ten, and went for a walk round by Chapel Street, Islington, and then got home about a quarter to twelve."[29] Although most of the offenders recorded in the Old Bailey data were male, statements from witnesses and victims show that women of every social class were also present on the streets of London. In April 1901, Florence Brown was walking home from work in the evening when she was assaulted:

> I am single—I live at Rothschild Villas, Acton, with my mother, and am a waitress—I have known the prisoner about two years, and have been keeping company with him—last August I became engaged to him—we often had quarrels, but nothing very serious ... on Saturday, April 20th, I was going home about 8.45 p.m., and saw him following me—I asked him where he was going—he said he was coming to see me—he had rather a disappointed look on his face, as if he did not want me to see him—we walked towards the gate next to our house.[30]

Lady Anne Carson was accosted by boys while walking near her home in Knightsbridge:

I am the wife of Sir Edward Carson, and live at 39, Rutland Gate—between 1 and 2 p.m. on August 14th I was walking by Rutland Gate—it was raining—I had an umbrella in one hand and my dress and purse in the other—the purse was attached to my wrist by a steel chain—four or five boys came along—the prisoners were three of them—Snell stopped and seized my purse—I tried to hold it for some time, and tried to push him off with my umbrella—the others stood by—they did not molest me so far as violence was concerned.[31]

Children also walked the streets without adult company, as exemplified by the case of Harry Pracey who was accosted when walking home from school with his younger brother in February 1911:

On February 3 I left school with my brother Albert at 4.30 p.m. I met prisoner in Hornsey Road; he asked me where the Oxford coffee shop was, and I and my brother showed it him; he took us inside and gave us tea and cake. After staying there a little while prisoner took us both by the hand to a yard where he got some bottles, which he changed for money at a beershop. He then led us up Highbury Hill to Upper Street, where he again gave us tea and cake at a coffee shop. He said he had been a soldier and had been all over the world. I did not want to go with him, but he held our hands and I was frightened. He took us to the Embankment, where he spoke to a woman. A policeman then spoke to us.[32]

Evidence from these data suggests that in the late nineteenth and early twentieth century, the streets of London were, indeed, teeming with pedestrians. Men, women, and children of all social classes and ages passed each other on the streets, and thoroughfares were busy until late into the night. Most people had few alternatives for undertaking their everyday journeys, but even the rich (such as Lady Carson) also walked alone at times. The city was also configured in such a way that most everyday needs could be met within walking distance of home, though longer journeys on foot were also undertaken from time to time, as in the case of James Nash, who walked some twenty miles (32 km) in November 1910, presumably to seek work in London: "On November 25, at 1 a.m., I was standing at a coffee stall by the Elephant and Castle, having just walked from Hatfield, when Jackson offered me a cup of coffee and gave me sixpence to get a lodging."[33] For most people in early-twentieth-century London, walking was the normal means of moving from place to place.

In the twenty-first century, while some people do walk regularly, for many this activity has become an uncommon and unusual form of transport: even one that can be seen as transcending the bounds of normality. Our study of walking and cycling in four English cities demonstrated this, with one respondent stating quite simply: "You feel unusual walking."[34] Another said, "The whole thing with transport and not having a car, I do feel like a second-class citizen, there's definitely a sense that as a pedestrian and a cyclist, you are definitely second-class citizens."[35] It is hard to pin down when this change occurred, as it was a gradual progression over almost a century.[36] In the 1920s and 1930s, walking continued to be quick, cheap, and convenient for some, as evidenced by a female respondent who lived in Manchester in the 1930s: "I soon decided to get up a bit earlier and walk because . . . . I was paying . . . half a crown for tram fares, and I thought I can't even save up to go home. So I started walking to work and walking back."[37] For others, however, the combination of improved public transport, greater availability and lower cost of bikes, and increasing separation of homes from workplaces as industry relocated from city centers to peripheral locations meant that travel by bus, tram, train, or bike became much more practical. This is illustrated by two respondents in Glasgow and Manchester: "No, not [walking] to work because you would have to leave too early in a morning. The subway was so quick and it was so cheap";[38] "Oh no. No it [walking] would have taken too long. Five miles, it would have taken an hour and a half. . . . The bike was so much quicker."[39]

The extent to which car travel supplanted walking (and much public transport use and cycling) was different for males and females, and also occurred gradually during the twentieth century. Until the 1950s, car use was generally limited in Britain.[40] It was the increased complexity of travel and the greater distances involved that often forced people to either buy a car or use an existing car more for utility journeys rather than restricting its use mainly to leisure travel, which was more common in the first half of the twentieth century. Moreover, 86 percent of British households were still without a car in 1951.[41] These points are neatly encapsulated by two Manchester respondents: "If you had access to a car at that stage . . . you would have used that for leisure only. It would not have occurred to you to use it for work."[42] "Yes, I got my first car in 1954 . . . I didn't want a car to travel through Manchester to get to Blackley, but I knew when I was offered this job at Alderley Edge, that I would have to do it because there was no cross-country transport at all. It was just hopeless, so I decided to have a car."[43] Once it became normal to use a car for traveling to work, its use for most other journeys—even short ones—was likely to follow, to the detriment of walking or public transport as the main travel mode. Women learned to drive much later than men, and, until the 1990s, most women who traveled by car were in the passenger seat. Whereas 69 percent of all British men held a driving license by 1975, only 29 percent of women had one. It was not until the early 1990s that more than half of all the women in Britain could drive, and, at that time, only 37 percent of women aged 60 to 69 had a driving license, compared to 81 percent of men. The proportion of men with a driving license has remained at about 80 percent until the present day, with some 68 percent of women now being able to drive.[44] Using a car for most travel has become the norm for a substantial majority of the British population. Despite the previously mentioned small increase in recorded utility walking in recent years, due mainly to growing health and environmental concerns, it is too early to know if this will be sustained—for most people walking is mainly for recreation and pleasure.[45]

## The Convenience of Walking

In many respects, walking is the easiest and most convenient form of transport. It is cheap, needs no special equipment or planning, and can be undertaken to at least some extent by most people of any age. It is also the only means of moving from place to place that has not changed in terms of its speed of travel, ease, and accessibility. The main factors that might discourage walking—such as the need to carry luggage, inclement weather, or simple fatigue—have also not altered significantly over time. It is thus not the changes in walking itself that have led to its decline—arguably improvements in human nutrition as well as outdoor clothes and footwear should have made walking easier and more attractive—but rather the changes in the external environment and associated alternative modes of transport. The most important of these is the expansion of other transport modes, together with the fact that people have to travel longer distances to fulfill their everyday needs. Other factors also play a role, especially with respect to the decline in walking, even for short trips, in urban areas. In 2015, 7 percent of trips by car in Britain were less than one mile (1.6 km), and 25 percent were less than two miles (3.2 km), distances that many people could walk if necessary.[46] Numerous factors can contribute to the unwillingness of many people to walk even short distances. These include changing lifestyle choices, increased female workforce participation, expanded everyday action spaces, greater educational choices for children, more sedentary lifestyles, and unhealthy eating habits, plus the general perceptions of busyness that lead many people to see the car as the easiest and most convenient mode of transport for almost all journeys. However, I argue that many of these lifestyle factors are not in themselves new; lifestyles in the twenty-first century are in fact as compatible with everyday walking (and public transport, which usually entails a walk to a bus/tram stop or train station) as they were in the past. Some people definitely build walking into their everyday travel: in 2015, some 20 percent of men over age seventeen, and 32 percent of women, did not have a driving license, and 25 percent of British households did not have access to a car.[47]

It is hard to argue that individuals and households in the past were not as busy and as pressed for time as people are today. For instance, in the early twentieth century, working hours were, for the most part, longer than today; domestic duties were much more time consuming; and families were on average larger.[48] Men and women would find most hours of the day filled with work, domestic duties, or child care, yet they had no alternative but to walk for most of their everyday needs. At times, they would carry heavy loads; the weather would be as unpredictable as today; and they were undoubtedly often tired. What has probably changed most dramatically is the extent to which most people now expect to be able to achieve most tasks (including travel) quickly, and also anticipate that they will have a substantial amount of leisure time. The ability to travel quickly by car helps to facilitate both of these desires. While most activities in urban areas could still be undertaken perfectly well by a combination of walking and public transport, the desire to minimize travel time and to maximize leisure time appears to have become paramount. Again, it is hard to pin down a date at which such changes occurred: they were both gradual and segmented with significant differences in gender, age, social class, and location. Selected examples from personal diaries and oral history testimonies illustrate some dimensions of this shift.

The everyday pressures of balancing work and domestic duties in the 1920s are clearly illustrated by Annie Rudolph, who lived in London. She was seventeen when she kept a diary, and during this period her mother died unexpectedly. As the eldest female at home, she was required to take on most of the housework and care of her younger siblings, together with continuing to assist in her father's shop and study part-time at college. Her long diary entry for Sunday, 25 May 1923 sums up her mood and how she was juggling her commitments:

> Little book I am miserable . . . I was up this morning before 8—(I used to roll down about 8.45 or 9)—washed the children—combed their hair—gave them breakfast and got them off to school. It was about 9 o'clock that I was able to have a cup of tea myself. Then I put a soup on the gas for father, Mark and myself for the shop—Then I ran up to make the beds, and dusted—went out shopping—cleaned the place round. The children don't care for soup so I had to make them potatoes and veal cutlets. I have to prepare meat and kosher it the previous day. While this was cooking I boiled some lockshen [noodles] for the soup. Dinner was ready by 12.15.

Whilst the kids were eating I poured the soup into bottles, packed them and ran off to the shop—There I put on the gas to warm up and made dinner—then I washed up, being finished all that by about 3.—Then swept round, typed some letters, saw to book keeping—then it was time for tea— made that quickly then ran home to cook another dinner for Esther, of potatoes, steak—and pudding—then it was time to wash the kids—gave them supper and sent them to bed. Then father came home and wanted his supper—*then* I was able to sit down—it's now 10 o'clock—have just sat down. This today and every day.[49]

Despite these commitments, Annie traveled everywhere either on foot or public transport, including to and from her father's shop, which was four miles (6.5 km) from their home, a journey which she undertook on foot and tram. Indeed, she saw walking as a way of relaxing even when tired, as stated in her entry for 23 July 1923: "I'm so tired in the evenings that I'm glad to be at home. Sometimes when I have an hour to spare I go for a walk—but I'm mostly indoors."[50]

Some thirty years later, Gillian Caldwell (born 1937) was living in Edinburgh, initially studying and then working in an office. Most of her travel was by public transport (bus, tram, or train), though she sometimes walked for leisure or when public transport failed to materialize, and most trips by public transport would have entailed some walking. She did not drive herself but she had several male friends who did, and motoring was clearly the most attractive option for her. The fact that everyday utility walking was something she did rarely is clearly suggested by her diary entry for 19 April 1955: "This wonderful weather is tout incroyable. Every morning is a joy to wake up to & so I walked to the office this morning. It was so lovely I shall do it again."[51] Her life was not especially busy (neither study nor work seemed especially demanding), and she spent a large amount of her time on leisure activities in coffee houses, at the cinema, and excursions out of Edinburgh. She had grown up in rural Cumbria (Eskdale), with limited access to public transport, so maybe this factor led her to spend as little time as possible as a pedestrian. Her attitude to what she deemed unwarranted walking is perhaps best summed up by her entry for 28 December 1953, when she was back in Eskdale for Christmas: "Uncle Stuart and I went for a walk this afternoon—I was literally forced to go! All these town dwellers have an absolute mania for walking."[52]

Whereas Gillian Caldwell seemed to have quite negative attitudes toward walking (at least when she deemed it inappropriate), many twenty-first century respondents suggested that they would like to walk more, but a combination of their commitments and family obligations made that difficult. Three interviewees from Leeds, Worcester, and

Leicester have typical responses: "I enjoy walking—always have done—but we don't have time to do it."[53] "With the demands of family and work and everything, there's not much time or energy [for walking]."[54] "[When you have children] you don't have any sleep and you just can't do it. You can't get up at half six every day and go to work."[55]

Although it is not possible to generalize from a small number of individual stories, these examples do demonstrate the variety of responses about everyday walking, and that the pressures of life in the past were often as great, or greater, than they are today. Convenience and lifestyle constraints may be excuses for not walking more, but, in reality, the individual impacts of so-called time-space compression are rather less than is sometimes suggested.[56] The present-day reluctance to walk may relate more to negative attitudes regarding travel on foot (as expressed by Gillian Caldwell, even in the 1950s) than to any actual time pressures or lifestyle constraints.

### The Risks of Walking

It is sometimes suggested that we live in a risk society, where people are highly concerned about a wide range of potential global and more local threats.[57] One aspect is the perceived dangers inherent in traveling, be they from terrorism or disease when undertaking global travel, or from traffic or assault closer to home.[58] Heightened perceptions of risk have particularly influenced present-day attitudes toward walking, with many respondents in a recent survey citing their concerns about (often unspecified) dangers as reasons for restricting the amount, location, and timing of walking. Two examples illustrate this point clearly: "If I want to go to the Post Office, there's one quite close but I'll take the car because I don't like walking through the estate. ... I feel very vulnerable walking some places because I can't run."[59] "I know the good areas and the bad areas in the city and I always make sure I am walking with someone, or that I am walking at the right time."[60] Paradoxically, such attitudes that limit walking can further increase perceptions of risk as streets busy with pedestrians are almost always safer (and, crucially, perceived to be safer) than those that are deserted. Traditional street designs, where people and traffic can flow easily, are also the safest environments for pedestrians.[61] Dangerous traffic was only rarely cited as a risk to pedestrians, though it was seen as inconvenient and causing an unpleasant walking environment. In contrast, cyclists frequently cited traffic as the risk that gave them the greatest concern. Despite the perception of risk when walking today, I argue that there is little evidence that being a pedestrian has become any more dangerous over time. More probably it was in the past, when many more people walked regularly and traffic was less regulated, that the streets presented greater risks to pedestrians.[62]

The Old Bailey records from around 1900 show that the streets were not crime free, and that traveling on foot posed risks at any time of the day or night (though most crimes were committed after dark). The testimonies of diarists suggest that such risks did not significantly affect people's willingness to travel on foot (or by any other means). Although the diarists record some difficult and potentially risky encounters, there is little evidence that they altered their behavior or routes accordingly. Ida Berry (born 1884) kept a diary between 1902 and 1907 while living with her family in south Manchester. She traveled extensively (both alone and with friends or relatives) around the urban area on foot, by bicycle, and on various forms of public transport and never encountered any dangers or significant inconveniences other than punctures on her bike and the effects of weather and fatigue. There is no evidence that she ever adjusted her walking routes or times to take account of perceived risks. One short quote from her diary entry for 28 April 1905 is typical: "Maud and I walked as far as 'Owens College' and back as far as Fallowfield. We were tired."[63] In London in the 1920s, Annie Rudolph had slightly more encounters that might be deemed risky—or at least gave her concern at the time—but she brushed them off lightly, and there is no evidence that such occurrences altered her behavior in any way. Most such encounters were with men offering unwanted attention, as in these two instances recorded on 8 January and 12 December 1923:

> Had a most annoying experience this evening. I was returning from evening school. On my ownsome of course. I heard quick foot marks behind me, and a voice said "do you mind if I walk with you? I'm going your way!" I got the wind up and crossed the road, but *would* you believe it, he crossed over too. Isn't it absurd to walk zig-zag to avoid someone one doesn't know, so I said "I don't know you and don't *want* to know you. If you don't skiddadle—in other words vamoose—I'll call someone." So he said "Now don't talk like that kid. I want to know you." But I turned my nose up and flew!!! Positively.[64]

> I almost fainted with horror the other day. I was up West with my friend—we were strolling along looking into the shops. I was walking with my hand swinging limply. Suddenly I felt another hand touch mine—and squeeze it—I gasped—and turned. It was an old man about over 50—I went all colours—and clasping my friend—I flew along until we were a long distance from there—I was horrified. Whenever I am up West I walk—looking neither to the right or the left—It's beastly—but that's how it is.[65]

Oral history interviews with respondents who were ten or eleven years old in the 1940s also revealed incidents where children were placed in positions of harassment and potential danger. Many respondents—predominantly female, but some male—gave similar accounts of being approached by men in inappropriate ways. However, these were not experiences that affected their behavior or prevented them from walking and playing outside either in groups or alone. In most cases, children did not tell either their parents or anyone else in authority, but simply dealt with the experience and learned from it. One example from Lancaster in the late-1940s is typical:

> If any men approached us—we were often flashed at, even in those days. . . . Well, you knew it was wrong and you kept well away from them, but we would be half-frightened and half laugh[ing]. We knew to keep away from them. . . . An RAF chap stopped me and offered me money to go down on't (this was when I was going down into town shopping for me mother) offered me money to go down onto the canal with him. I didn't know what for, but I knew it was wrong. But I still got the shopping, and took it back home. So I wasn't so frightened, but I just knew it was wrong. . . . And I don't think that I ever told my parents, because sex wasn't ever talked about.[66]

In contrast, when we talked to children who were age ten or eleven around the year 2000, the responses were rather different. None of the children interviewed had actually encountered any dangers or potentially threatening situations, but most (both boys and girls) stated that they were not allowed out alone and that their opportunities for walking and outdoor play were restricted by their parents because of unspecified fears of molestation or abduction. Two examples are typical: "And there's a massive big field to play football, but there's no one to play football with. And no one takes me, 'cause I can't go on my own, too dangerous. . . . Because someone could nab me. . . . Um, we're both [respondent and mother] worried about that."[67] "Because my mum says there's people hang around who we're not supposed to like. . . . You don't know what they're doing sometimes. . . . It's the same reason as I'm not allowed to go down to the field on my own, there's people around that are a bit loopy.[68]

There is no evidence that the actual risks to children or adults have increased over time. Increased CCTV surveillance and awareness of inappropriate behavior toward women and children may have actually reduced such risks, but the perceptions of risk have increased considerably, leading to self-imposed and parent-imposed restrictions on everyday mobility on foot. It has been suggested that media coverage of rare events, which then become normalized within society, is partly to blame; certainly the impact of all forms of media—most notably internet-based social media—has been marked over the past two decades, but social networks operating within communities are probably equally influential in shaping social norms.[69] To return to an earlier theme, restricting walking because of perceived risks—from strangers, traffic, or unspecified causes—has become normal. Parents who transcend these norms and allow their offspring to play out or walk alone in the neighborhood may be seen as bad parents, even though there is no evidence of real risk. Such "paranoid parenting," as it has been dubbed, can severely restrict children's freedom to get exercise in an outdoor environment, may restrict their ability to develop independence and manage risk, and leads to increased car use as children are ferried everywhere by parents.[70]

## Conclusions and Solutions

The qualitative data used here cannot serve as a basis for generalizations about a wider population. It does, however, provide important insights into the travel experiences and processes of change taking place within society as the usual means of moving from place to place transformed over the twentieth century. It may also be the only way to acquire long-term data on the experience of everyday walking. The changes were both gradual and segmented, with important differences in gender, age, social class, and location. The ways decisions about everyday travel were made in the past, and may still be made in the present, vary for each individual depending on factors such as journey purpose, time of day, companions, luggage, and weather. Large-scale travel surveys and censuses may be misleading as they erase the diversity of individual experiences that necessarily exist. If such diverse experiences and expectations are not recognized in transport planning, the policies to promote walking can be ineffective or generate unintended consequences. Uncovering often hidden aspects of past urban mobility can provide usable histories that inform present-day transport policy and lead to more sustainable urban futures.

In current surveys, most people state that they enjoy walking for leisure and recognize that walking is a valuable form of exercise that can contribute to good health. A quote from a respondent in Worcester illustrates this point: "I think the walking beats everything. And actually, if I ever do get a little bit of time, I really enjoy walking."[71] As motorized private transport came to dominate everyday travel, rates of walking fell markedly over the past century. However, the enjoyment factor, coupled with increased awareness of the health benefits of exercise and the environmental impacts of cars, has recently led to a slight increase in the amount of walking both for leisure and utility purposes in Britain, though as yet the gains are limited. If the trends of the past hundred years are to be reversed, we need to recognize fully the reasons why people walk only rarely, and implement policies that counteract past processes. I argue that any policy to reverse the long-term decline in urban walking, and thus promote more environmental and social sustainability in urban travel, must have three main objectives: first, make walking feel safe by increasing pavement space, restricting traffic, improving pedestrian road crossings, ensuring good lighting, maintaining pavements well by clearing them of leaves, ice, and snow when appropriate, and removing unnecessary street clutter that can obstruct pedestrians. Second, cities must be planned to make walking feel as easy and convenient as possible so that people can access most services and facilities relatively close to home, thus minimizing the need for longer journeys. Third, and partly as a result of the previous strategies, walking must be normalized within society. If there are more people on the streets, if taking a car only a short distance to collect a newspaper or post a letter is deemed unusual (or even unacceptable), then it may be easier to establish travel on foot for short trips in urban areas as a societal norm to which most people would happily subscribe. For longer trips, walking to a bus/tram stop or railway station would also become the norm.

Such changes are not difficult and do not require large expenditures (especially compared to the costs of new road schemes or even dedicated cycle routes, which are garnering support). In Britain, policymakers have been persistently reluctant to commit expenditure explicitly targeted at improving the urban environment for walking. Pedestrians are perceived as making few demands on the urban environment; too often, implemented policies are aimed at restricting pedestrian flows and channeling them through particular routes to achieve smoother traffic flows, rather than make walking feel easy, safe, and normal. Increasing the footfall on urban streets not only benefits individuals' health and enhances the urban environment through reduced pollution and congestion, but also benefits society through greater sociability and community interaction. Some argue that the more people on the streets, the greater the incentive for others to join them, and for walking to become the travel mode of choice for short trips in urban areas. A transition to a more sustainable urban transport system can be facilitated through greater awareness of past travel behaviors, while the social, economic, environmental, and health costs of not achieving such a transition are almost certainly far greater than producing a more sustainable transport future.

**Colin Pooley** is Emeritus Professor of Social and Historical Geography in the Environment Centre and the Centre for Mobilities Research (Ce-MoRe), Lancaster University, U.K. His research focuses on the social geography of Britain and continental Europe since 1800, with recent projects examining residential migration, everyday mobility, and sustainable travel. Publications include *Mobility, Migration and Transport: Historical Perspectives* (Palgrave Pivot, 2017) and *Promoting Walking and Cycling: New Perspectives on Sustainable Travel* (Policy Press, 2013). His current research is on the recovery of everyday mobilities (especially walking) from diaries and other life writing.

## Notes

The material for this paper is drawn from projects undertaken with many collaborators and funders. These include Jean Turnbull, who conducted oral history interviews for the project "The Journey to Work in Britain since c1890," funded by the Leverhulme Trust; Jean Turnbull and Mags Adams, who conducted interviews for the ESRC-funded project "Changing Patterns of Everyday Mobility"; Tim Jones, Miles Tight, Dave Horton, Griet Scheldeman, Caroline Mullen, Ann Jopson, and Emanuele Strano, who worked on the EPSRC-funded project "Understanding Walking and Cycling"; and Marilyn Pooley, who assisted with transcribing diaries. I thank them all for their input to this research.

1. David Banister, *European Transport Policy and Sustainable Mobility* (London: Spon Press, 2000); David Banister, "The Sustainable Mobility Paradigm," *Transport Policy* 15, no. 2 (2008): 73–80.
2. This point was made by Rod Tolley as long ago as 1990, and circumstances have not changed significantly since then: Rodney Tolley, *The Greening of Urban Transport: Planning for Walking and Cycling in Western Cities* (London: Belhaven Press, 1990).
3. Gina Porter, "Living in a Walking World: Rural Mobility and Social Equity Issues in Sub-Saharan Africa," *World Development* 30, no. 2 (2002): 285–300; Colin Pooley, *Mobility, Migration and Transport: Historical Perspectives* (London: Palgrave, 2017).
4. Colin Pooley, Jean Turnbull, and Mags Adams, *A Mobile Century? Changes in Everyday Mobility in Britain in the Twentieth Century* (Aldershot: Ashgate, 2005).
5. Department for Transport (DfT), *National Travel Survey 2015* (London: National Statistics, 2016), retrieved 12 September 2017, https://www.gov.uk/government/statistics/national-travel-survey-2015.
6. David Bassett et al., "Walking, Cycling, and Obesity Rates in Europe, North America, and Australia," *Journal of Physical Activity & Health* 5 no. 6 (2008): 795–814; Colin Pooley et al., "Policies for Promoting Walking and Cycling in England: A View from the Street," *Transport Policy* 27 (2013): 66–72.

7.  David Ogilvie et al., "Promoting Walking and Cycling as an Alternative to Using Cars: Systematic Review," *British Medical Journal* 329 (2004): 763–66; David Ogilvie et al., "Interventions to Promote Walking: Systematic Review," *British Medical Journal* 334 (2007): 1204–7; Colin Pooley et al., *Promoting Walking and Cycling: New Perspectives on Sustainable Travel* (Bristol: Policy Press, 2013); Colin Pooley, "Mobility, Transport and Social Inclusion: Lessons from History," *Social Inclusion* 4, no. 3 (2016): 100–9.

8.  See, for example, Rebecca Solnit, *Wanderlust: A History of Walking* (London: Verso, 2001); Tim Ingold, "Culture on the Ground: The World Perceived through Feet," *Journal of Material Culture* 9, no. 3 (2004): 315–40; John Wylie, "A Single Day's Walking: Narrating Self and Landscape on the South West Coast Path," *Transactions of the Institute of British Geographers* 30, no. 2 (2005): 234–47; Katrin Lund, "Seeing in Motion and the Touching Eye: Walking over Scotland's Mountains," *Etnofoor* 18, no. 1 (2005): 27–42; Tim Ingold and Jo Vergunst, eds., *Ways of Walking: Ethnography and Practice on Foot* (Aldershot: Ashgate, 2008); Jennie Middleton, "Stepping in Time: Walking Time and Space in the City," *Environment and Planning A* 41, no. 8 (2009): 1943–61; Hayden Lorimer, "Walking: New Forms and Spaces for Studies of Pedestrianism," in *Geographies of Mobilities: Practices, Spaces, Subjects*, ed. Tim Cresswell and Peter Merriman (Farnham: Ashgate, 2011), 19–34.

9.  Exceptions include Jennie Middleton, "The Promotion of London as a 'Walkable City' and Overlapping Walks of Life," in *Regenerating London: Governance, Sustainability and Community in a Global City*, ed. Rob Imrie et al. (Abingdon: Routledge, 2009), 192–211; Peter Norton, "Street Rivals: Jaywalking and the Invention of the Motor Age Street," *Technology and Culture* 48, no. 2 (2007): 331–59; Peter Norton, "Urban Mobility without Wheels: A Historiographical Review of Pedestrianism," in *Mobility in History: The State of the Art in the History of Transport, Traffic and Mobility*, ed. Gijs Mom, Gordon Pirie, and Laurent Tissot (Neuchâtel: Editions Alphil, 2009), 111–15; Peter Norton, *Fighting Traffic: The Dawn of the Motor Age in the American City* (Boston: MIT Press, 2011; Pooley et al. "Policies for Promoting Walking and Cycling."

10. John Urry, *Sociology beyond Societies: Mobilities for the Twenty-First Century* (London: Routledge, 2000); John Urry, *Mobilities* (Cambridge: Polity, 2007); Mimi Sheller and John Urry, "The New Mobilities Paradigm," *Environment and Planning A* 38, no. 2 (2006): 207–26.

11. See for example: Tim Cresswell, *On the Move: Mobility in the Modern Western World* (New York: Routledge, 2006); Tim Cresswell and Peter Merriman, *Geographies of Mobilities: Practices, Spaces, Subjects* (Farnham: Ashgate, 2011); Peter Merriman, *Mobility, Space and Culture* (London: Routledge, 2012); Peter Merriman et al., "Mobility: Geographies, Histories, Sociologies," *Transfers* 3, no. 1 (2013): 147–65.

12. Recent attempts to fill this gap include Colin Divall and George Revill, "Cultures of Transport: Representation, Practice and Technology," *Journal of Transport History* 26, no. 1 (2005): 99–111; Gijs Mom et al., "Towards a Paradigm Shift? A Decade of Transport and Mobility History," in Mom, Pirie, and Tissot, *Mobility in History: The State of the Art*, 13–40; Jon Shaw and Markus Hesse, "Transport, Geography and the 'New' Mobilities," *Transactions of the Institute of British Geographers* 35, no. 3 (2010): 305–12; Margaret Grieco and John Urry, eds., *Mobilities: New Perspectives on Transport and Society* (Farnham: Ashgate, 2011); Colin Divall et al., eds., *Transport Policy: Learning Lessons from History* (Farnham: Ashgate, 2016); Pooley, *Mobility, Migration and Transport*.

13. Eurostat. Transport Statistics, 12 September 2017, retrieved 12 September 2017, http://ec.europa.eu/eurostat/web/transport/overview.
14. Department for Transport (DfT), *Walking and Cycling Statistics* (London: DfT, 2016), retrieved 12 September 2017, https://www.gov.uk/government/collecti ons/walking-and-cycling-statistics#historical-data-tables.
15. Sport England, Active People Interactive, retrieved 12 September 2017, http://activepeople.sportengland.org/.
16. Department for Transport (DfT), *Local Area Walking and Cycling: 2014–2015* (London: DfT, 2016), Retrieved 12 September 2017, https://www.gov.uk/govern ment/statistics/local-area-walking-and-cycling-in-england-2014-to-2015.
17. Land Transport Authority, "Passenger Transport Mode Shares in World Cities," *Journeys* 12 (2014): 54–64.
18. Karen Fields, "What One Cannot Remember Mistakenly," *Oral History* 17, no. 1 (1989): 44–53; Robert Perks, *Oral History: Talking about the Past* (London: Historical Association, 1992); Donald Ritchie, *Doing Oral History* (Oxford: Oxford University Press, 2014).
19. Robert Fothergill, *Private Chronicles: A Study of English Diaries* (London: Oxford University Press, 1974); P. Lejeune, *On Diary* (Honolulu: University of Hawaii Press, 2009); Colin Pooley and Marilyn Pooley, "'Mrs Harvey came home from Norwich . . . her pocket picked at the station and all her money stolen': Using Life Writing to Recover the Experience of Travel in the Past," *Journal of Migration History* 1, no. 1 (2015): 54–74.
20. *The Proceedings of the Old Bailey, London's Central Criminal Court, 1674–1913*, Oldbaileyonline.org, retrieved 12 September 2017, https://www.oldbaileyonline .org/.
21. See, for instance, Peter K. Andersson, "'Bustling, Crowding, and Pushing': Pickpockets and the Nineteenth-Century Street Crowd," *Urban History* 41, no. 2 (2014): 291–310.
22. Robert Shoemaker, "The Old Bailey Proceedings and the Representation of Crime and Criminal Justice in Eighteenth-Century London," *Journal of British Studies* 47, no. 3 (2008): 559–80; Heather Shore, "The Reckoning': Disorderly Women, Informing Constables and the Westminster Justices, 1727–33," *Social History* 34, no. 4 (2009): 409–27; Peter King, "Ethnicity, Prejudice, and Justice: The Treatment of the Irish at the Old Bailey, 1750–1825," *Journal of British Studies* 52, no. 2 (2013): 390–414.
23. David Silverman, *Doing Qualitative Research: A Practical Handbook* (London: Sage Publications, 2013).
24. Harold J. Dyos and David Aldcroft, *British Transport: An Economic Survey from the Seventeenth Century to the Twentieth* (Leicester: Leicester University Press, 1969); Tomas Errázuriz, "When Walking Became Serious: Reshaping the Role of Pedestrians in Santiago, 1900–1931," *Journal of Transport History* 32, no. 1 (2011): 39–65; Norton, *Fighting Traffic*; Gijs Mom, *Atlantic Automobilism: Emergence and Persistence of the Car, 1895–1940* (New York: Berghahn Books, 2014).
25. Maria Lapinski and Rajiv Rimal, "An Explication of Social Norms," *Communication Theory* 15, no. 2 (2005): 127–47; Cristina Bicchieri and Ryan Muldoon, "Social Norms," *Stanford Encyclopedia of Philosophy* (Stanford: Stanford University Press, 2011), retrieved 12 September 2017, https://stanford.library.sydney.edu.au/archives/spr2012/entries/social-norms/.
26. Mimi Sheller and John Urry "The City and the Car," *International Journal of Urban and Regional Research* 24, no. 4 (2000): 737–57; John Urry, "The 'System' of Automobility," *Theory, Culture and Society* 21, no. 4–5 (2004): 25–39;

Mike Featherstone et al., _Automobilities_ (London: Sage, 2005); Jim Conley, _Car Troubles: Critical Studies of Automobility and Auto-Mobility_ (Aldershot: Ashgate, 2009).

27. Seventy-nine testimonies relating to 1891, 1901, and 1911 have been extracted as part of a project examining walking from Old Bailey Data from 1801–1911.
28. _Proceedings of the Old Bailey_ (hereafter OB), Ref: t18910406-333.
29. OB Ref: t18911116-59.
30. OB Ref: t19010513-371.
31. OB Ref: t19010910-584.
32. OB Ref: t19110228-12.
33. OB Ref: t19110110-9.
34. Data from EPSRC-funded Understanding Walking and Cycling (hereafter UWAC) project, 2009–11, interview with "Eliza," Leeds. See Pooley et al., _Promoting Walking and Cycling_.
35. Data from UWAC project 2009–11, interview with "Jim," Lancaster.
36. Data used in the following section comes from oral history testimonies collected as part of a project on the journey to work in twentieth-century Britain, funded by the Leverhulme Trust. For further information see Pooley et al., _A Mobile Century_.
37. Oral history interview with respondent RJ16, female, Manchester, 1930s.
38. Oral history interview with respondent RJ52, female, Glasgow, 1930s.
39. Oral history interview with respondent RJ24, male, Manchester, 1940s.
40. Particularly when compared to the United States. See Mom, _Atlantic Automobilism_.
41. DfT, _National Travel Survey 2015_.
42. Oral history interview with respondent RJ04, male, Manchester, 1950s.
43. Oral history interview with respondent RJ15, female, Manchester, 1950s.
44. DfT, _National Travel Survey 2015_.
45. Pooley et al. _Promoting Walking and Cycling_.
46. DfT, _National Travel Survey 2015_. There are no long-run data that allow detailed analysis of changes in journey length by car over time.
47. DfT, _National Travel Survey 2015_.
48. John Stevenson, _British Society, 1914–45_ (Harmondsworth: Penguin, 1984); Arthur Marwick, _British Society since 1945: The Penguin Social History of Britain_ (Harmondsworth: Penguin, 2003).
49. Diary of Annie Rudolph, Bishopsgate Institute Archive, London (GDP/31).
50. Diary of Annie Rudolph, Bishopsgate Institute Archive, London (GDP/31).
51. Diary of Gillian Caldwell, Bishopsgate Institute Archive, London (GDP/1).
52. Diary of Gillian Caldwell, Bishopsgate Institute Archive, London (GDP/1).
53. Data from UWAC project 2009–11, interview with "Jack" and "Deidre," Leeds.
54. Data from UWAC project 2009–11, interview with "Percy," Worcester.
55. Data from UWAC project 2009–11, interview with "Cassie," Leicester.
56. David. Harvey, _The Condition of Modernity: An Enquiry into the Origins of Cultural Change_ (Oxford: Blackwell, 1989), 284–307.
57. Ulrich Beck, _Risk Society: Towards a New Modernity_ (London: Sage, 1992); Ulrich Beck, "The Terrorist Threat World Risk Society Revisited," _Theory, Culture & Society_ 19, no. 4 (2002): 39–55.
58. Laurie Pickup, "Hard to Get Around: A Study of Women's Travel Mobility," in _Women in Cities: Gender and the Urban Environment_, ed. Jo Little, Linda Peake, and Pat Richardson (London: Macmillan, 1988), 98–116; Mayer Hillman, John Adams, and John Whitelegg, _One False Move_ (London: Policy Studies Institute,

1990); Raoul Bianchi, "Tourism and the Globalisation of Fear: Analysing the Politics of Risk and (in) Security in Global Travel," *Tourism and Hospitality Research* 7, no. 1 (2006): 64–74.

59. Data from UWAC project 2009–11, interview with "Jen," Worcester.
60. Data from UWAC project 2009–11, interview with "Anju" and "Pooja," Leicester.
61. Bill Hillier, "Can Streets Be Made Safe?," *Urban Design International* 9, no. 1 (2004): 31–45.
62. Bill Luckin, "War on the Roads: Traffic Accidents and Social Tension in Britain, 1939–45," *Clio Medica* 41 (1997): 234–54; Bill Luckin and David Sheen, "Defining Early Modern Automobility: The Road Traffic Accident Crisis in Manchester, 1939–45," *Cultural and Social History* 6, no. 2 (2009): 211–30.
63. Diary of Ida Berry, Bishopsgate Institute Archive, London (GDP/28).
64. Diary of Annie Rudolph, Bishopsgate Institute Archive, London (GDP/31).
65. Diary of Annie Rudolph, Bishopsgate Institute Archive, London (GDP/31).
66. Data from ESRC-funded project on changing patterns of everyday mobility (hereafter CPEM). See Pooley et al., *A Mobile Century*. Oral history interview with "Teresa," born 1937, Lancaster.
67. Data from CPEM project, Oral history interview with "Chris," born 1992, Salford.
68. Data from CPEM project, Interview with "Dean," born 1990, Morecambe.
69. Steven Kohm et al., "The Impact of Media on Fear of Crime among University Students: A Cross-National Comparison 1," *Canadian Journal of Criminology and Criminal Justice* 54, no. 1 (2012): 67–100; Yvonne Jewkes, *Media and Crime* (London: Sage, 2015).
70. Frank Furedi, *Paranoid Parenting* (Harmondsworth: Penguin, 2001); R. Pain, "Paranoid Parenting? Rematerializing Risk and Fear for Children," *Social & Cultural Geography* 7, no. 2 (2006): 221–43.
71. Data from UWAC project 2009–11, interview with "Percy," Worcester.

## Bibliography

Andersson, Peter K. "'Bustling, Crowding, and Pushing': Pickpockets and the Nineteenth-Century Street Crowd." *Urban History* 41, no. 2 (2014): 291–310.

Banister, David. *European Transport Policy and Sustainable Mobility*. London: Spon Press, 2000.

———. "The Sustainable Mobility Paradigm." *Transport Policy* 15, no. 2 (2008): 73–80.

Bassett, David, John Pucher, Ralph Buehler, Dixie Thompson and Scott Crouter. "Walking, Cycling, and Obesity Rates in Europe, North America, and Australia." *Journal of Physical Activity & Health* 5, no. 6 (2008): 795–814.

Beck, Ulrich. *Risk Society: Towards a New Modernity*. London: Sage, 1992.

———. "The Terrorist Threat World Risk Society Revisited." *Theory, Culture & Society* 19, no. 4 (2002): 39–55.

Bianchi, Raoul. "Tourism and the Globalisation of Fear: Analysing the Politics of Risk and (in) Security in Global Travel." *Tourism and Hospitality Research* 7, no. 1 (2006): 64–74.

Bicchieri, Cristina, and Ryan Muldoon. "Social Norms." In *Stanford Encyclopedia of Philosophy*. Stanford: Stanford University Press, 2011. Retrieved 12 September 2017, https://stanford.library.sydney.edu.au/archives/spr2012/entries/social-norms/.

Conley, Jim, ed. *Car Troubles: Critical Studies of Automobility and Auto-Mobility*. Aldershot: Ashgate, 2009.

Cresswell, Tim. *On the Move: Mobility in the Modern Western World*. New York: Routledge, 2006.

Cresswell, Tim, and Peter Merriman. *Geographies of Mobilities: Practices, Spaces, Subjects*. Farnham: Ashgate, 2011.

Department for Transport (DfT). *Local Area Walking and Cycling: 2014–2015*. London: DfT, 2016. Retrieved 12 September 2017, https://www.gov.uk/government/statistics/local-area-walking-and-cycling-in-england-2014-to-2015.

——. *National Travel Survey 2015*. London: National Statistics, 2016. Retrieved 12 September 2017, https://www.gov.uk/government/statistics/national-travel-survey-2015.

——. *Walking and Cycling Statistics*. London: DfT, 2016. Retrieved 12 September 2017, https://www.gov.uk/government/collections/walking-and-cycling-statistics#historical-data-tables.

Divall, Colin, Julian Hine, and Colin Pooley, eds. *Transport Policy: Learning Lessons from History*. Farnham: Ashgate, 2016.

Divall, Colin, and George Revill. "Cultures of Transport: Representation, Practice and Technology." *Journal of Transport History* 26, no. 1 (2005): 99–111.

Dyos, Harold J., and Derek Aldcroft. *British Transport: An Economic Survey from the Seventeenth Century to the Twentieth*. Leicester: Leicester University Press, 1969.

Errázuriz, Tomas. "When Walking Became Serious: Reshaping the Role of Pedestrians in Santiago, 1900–1931." *Journal of Transport History* 32, no. 1 (2011): 39–65;

Eurostat. Transport Statistics. Retrieved 12 September 2017, http://ec.europa.eu/eurostat/web/transport/overview.

Featherstone, Mike, Nigel Thrift, and John Urry. *Automobilities*. London: Sage, 2005.

Fields, Karen. "What One Cannot Remember Mistakenly." *Oral History* 17, no. 1 (1989): 44–53.

Fothergill, Robert. *Private Chronicles: A Study of English Diaries*. London: Oxford University Press, 1974.

Furedi, Frank. *Paranoid Parenting*. Harmondsworth: Penguin, 2001.

Grieco, Margaret, and John Urry, eds. *Mobilities: New Perspectives on Transport and Society*. Farnham: Ashgate, 2011.

Harvey, David. *The Condition of Modernity: An Enquiry into the Origins of Cultural Change*. Oxford: Blackwell, 1989.

Hillier, Bill. "Can Streets Be Made Safe?" *Urban Design International* 9, no. 1 (2004): 31–45.

Hillman, Mayer, John Adams, and John Whitelegg. *One False Move*. London: Policy Studies Institute, 1990.

Ingold, Tim. "Culture on the Ground: The World Perceived through Feet." *Journal of Material Culture* 9, no. 3 (2004): 315–40.

Ingold, Tim, and Jo Vergunst, eds. *Ways of Walking: Ethnography and Practice on Foot*. Aldershot: Ashgate, 2008.

Jewkes, Yvonne. *Media and Crime*. London: Sage, 2015.

King, Peter. "Ethnicity, Prejudice, and Justice: The Treatment of the Irish at the Old Bailey, 1750–1825." *Journal of British Studies* 52, no. 2 (2013): 390–414.

Kohm, Steven, Courtney Waid-Lindberg, Michael Weinrath, Tara O'Connor Shelley, and Rhonda Dobbs. "The Impact of Media on Fear of Crime among University Students: A Cross-National Comparison." *Canadian Journal of Criminology and Criminal Justice* 54, no. 1 (2012): 67–100.

Land Transport Authority. "Passenger Transport Mode Shares in World Cities." *Journeys* 12 (2014): 54–64.

Lapinski, Maria, and Rajiv Rimal. "An Explication of Social Norms." *Communication Theory* 15, no. 2 (2005): 127–47.

Lejeune, Philippe. *On Diary*. Honolulu: University of Hawaii Press, 2009.

Lorimer, Hayden. "Walking: New Forms and Spaces for Studies of Pedestrianism." In *Geographies of Mobilities: Practices, Spaces, Subjects*, edited by T. Cresswell and P. Merriman, 19–34. Farnham: Ashgate, 2011.

Luckin, Bill. "War on the Roads: Traffic Accidents and Social Tension in Britain, 1939–45." *Clio Medica* 41 (1997): 234–54;

Luckin, Bill, and David Sheen. "Defining Early Modern Automobility: The Road Traffic Accident Crisis in Manchester, 1939–45." *Cultural and Social History* 6, no. 2 (2009): 211–30.

Lund, Katrin. "Seeing in Motion and the Touching Eye: Walking over Scotland's Mountains." *Etnofoor* 18, no. 1 (2005): 27–42.

Marwick, Arthur. *British Society since 1945: The Penguin Social History of Britain*. Harmondsworth: Penguin, 2003.

Merriman, Peter. *Mobility, Space and Culture*. London: Routledge, 2012.

Merriman, Peter, Rhys Jones, Tim Cresswell, Colin Divall, Gijs Mom, Mimi Sheller, and John Urry. "Mobility: Geographies, Histories, Sociologies." *Transfers* 3, no. 1 (2013): 147–65.

Middleton, Jennie. "The Promotion of London as a 'Walkable City' and Overlapping Walks of Life." In *Regenerating London: Governance, Sustainability and Community in a Global City*, edited by Rob Imrie, Loretta Lees, and Mike Raco, 192–211. Abingdon: Routledge, 2009.

———. "Stepping in Time: Walking Time and Space in the City." *Environment and Planning A* 41, no. 8 (2009): 1943–61.

Mom, Gijs. *Atlantic Automobilism: Emergence and Persistence of the Car, 1895–1940*. New York: Berghahn Books, 2014.

Mom, Gijs, Colin Divall, and Peter Lyth. "Towards a Paradigm Shift? A Decade of Transport and Mobility History." In *Mobility in History: The State of the Art in the History of Transport, Traffic and Mobility*, edited by Gijs Mom, Gordon Pirie, and Laurent Tissot, 13–40. Neuchâtel: Editions Alphil, 2009.

Norton, Peter. *Fighting Traffic: The Dawn of the Motor Age in the American City*. Boston: MIT Press, 2011.

———. "Street Rivals: Jaywalking and the Invention of the Motor Age Street." *Technology and Culture* 48, no. 2 (2007): 331–59.

———. "Urban Mobility without Wheels: A Historiographical Review of Pedestrianism." In *Mobility in History: The State of the Art in the History of Transport, Traffic and Mobility*, edited by Gijs Mom, Gordon Pirie, and Laurent Tissot, 111–15. Neuchâtel: Editions Alphil, 2009.

Ogilvie, David, Matt Egan, Val Hamilton, and Mark Petticrew. "Promoting Walking and Cycling as an Alternative to Using Cars: Systematic Review." *British Medical Journal* 329 (2004): 763–66.

Ogilvie, David, Charles E. Foster, Helen Rothnie, Nick Cavill, Val Hamilton, Claire F. Fitzsimons, and Nanette Mutrie. "Interventions to Promote Walking: Systematic Review." *British Medical Journal* 334 (2007): 1204–7.

Pain, Rachel. "Paranoid Parenting? Rematerializing Risk and Fear for Children." *Social & Cultural Geography* 7, no. 2 (2006): 221–43.

Perks, Robert. *Oral History: Talking about the Past*. London: Historical Association, 1992.

Pickup, Laurie. "Hard to Get Around: A Study of Women's Travel Mobility." In *Women in Cities: Gender and the Urban Environment*, edited by Jo Little, Linda Peake, and Pat Richardson, 98–116. London: Macmillan, 1988.

Pooley, Colin. *Mobility, Migration and Transport: Historical Perspectives*. London: Palgrave, 2017.

———. "Mobility, Transport and Social Inclusion: Lessons from History." *Social Inclusion* 4, no. 3 (2016): 100–9.

Pooley, Colin, Dave Horton, Griet Scheldeman, Caroline Mullen, Tim Jones, Miles Tight, Ann Jopson, and Alison Chisholm. "Policies for Promoting Walking and Cycling in England: A View from the Street." *Transport Policy* 27 (2013): 66–72.

Pooley, Colin, Tim Jones, Miles Tight, Dave Horton, Griet Scheldeman, Caroline Mullen, Ann Jopson, and Emanuele Strano. *Promoting Walking and Cycling: New Perspectives on Sustainable Travel*. Bristol: Policy Press, 2013.

Pooley, Colin, and Marilyn Pooley. "'Mrs Harvey came home from Norwich … her pocket picked at the station and all her money stolen': Using Life Writing to Recover the Experience of Travel in the Past." *Journal of Migration History* 1, no. 1 (2015): 54–74.

Pooley, Colin, Jean Turnbull, and Mags Adams. *A Mobile Century? Changes in Everyday Mobility in Britain in the Twentieth Century*. Aldershot: Ashgate, 2005.

Porter, Gina. "Living in a Walking World: Rural Mobility and Social Equity Issues in Sub-Saharan Africa." *World Development* 30, no. 2 (2002): 285–300.

*The Proceedings of the Old Bailey, London's Central Criminal Court, 1674–1913*. Oldbailyonline.org. Retrieved 12 September 2017, https://www.oldbaileyonline .org/.

Ritchie, Donald. *Doing Oral History*. Oxford: Oxford University Press, 2014.

Shaw, Jon, and Markus Hesse. "Transport, Geography and the 'New' Mobilities." *Transactions of the Institute of British Geographers* 35, no. 3 (2010): 305–12.

Sheller, Mimi, and John Urry. "The City and the Car." *International Journal of Urban and Regional Research* 24, no. 4 (2000): 737–57.

———. "The New Mobilities Paradigm." *Environment and Planning A* 38, no. 2 (2006): 207–26.

Silverman, David. *Doing Qualitative Research: A Practical Handbook*. London: Sage Publications, 2013.

Shoemaker, Robert. "The Old Bailey Proceedings and the Representation of Crime and Criminal Justice in Eighteenth-Century London." *Journal of British Studies* 47, no. 3 (2008): 559–80.

Shore, Heather. "The Reckoning': Disorderly Women, Informing Constables and the Westminster Justices, 1727–33." *Social History* 34, no. 4 (2009): 409–27.

Solnit, Rebecca. *Wanderlust: A History of Walking*. London: Verso, 2001.

Sport England. "Active People Interactive." Retrieved 12 September 2017, http://activepeople.sportengland.org/.

Stevenson, John. *British Society, 1914–45*. Harmondsworth: Penguin, 1984.

Tolley, Rodney. *The Greening of Urban Transport: Planning for Walking and Cycling in Western Cities*. London: Belhaven Press, 1990.

Urry, John. *Mobilities*. Cambridge: Polity, 2007.

———. *Sociology beyond Societies: Mobilities for the Twenty-First Century*. London: Routledge, 2000.

———. "The 'System' of Automobility." *Theory, Culture and Society* 21, no. 4–5 (2004): 25–39.

Wylie, John. "A Single Day's Walking: Narrating Self and Landscape on the South West Coast Path." *Transactions of the Institute of British Geographers* 30, no. 2 (2005): 234–47.

# CHAPTER 5

# Load Story

## *A Century of Pedestrian Logistics in Toulouse*

### Franck Cochoy, Roland Canu, and Cédric Calvignac

## Introduction

Walking is not only about people moving.[1] It is also about what people carry when they are walking. In this chapter, we address the history of the latter practice of carrying things, or what we term "pedestrian logistics," by capturing street life in a French city over a century. We observe a striking paradox. On the one hand, the practice of moving things on foot is ubiquitous: it can be seen everywhere in the public space, in pictures of street life, and, as seen in Colin Pooley's contribution to this volume, even in criminal court cases. Perhaps counterintuitively, given the emphasis of the dominant discourse on motorization, people still find it practical and rational to transport stuff on foot. This practice plays a key role in how people behave in the street. From a global perspective, moreover, pedestrian transport is also more sustainable than motorized transport because it reduces travel distances, saves energy, and avoids pollution. Goods movement represents 20–30 percent of the vehicle kilometers traveled in urban areas.[2]

Ordinary people and experts alike are not fully aware of the importance of pedestrian transport. People do things like shopping without really caring or realizing that they themselves are acting as vehicles for transportation. The topic is unknown to mobility experts, who lack both the interest and the appropriate methods to observe and access people's daily pedestrian logistics. Our contribution aims to fill this gap. We show what tactics pedestrians have embraced to carry their goods and belongings. For this purpose, we present an innovative method that utilizes historical photographs to capture mundane and otherwise hidden practices. Since these hidden practices are, in our opinion, just as important as infrastructures and high-tech objects for supporting sustainable practices such as walking, our method therefore helps to recover usable pasts.

Why urban studies have paid so little attention to pedestrians and their carrying practices is puzzling. After all, walking is the most accessible and widely shared mode of transportation. While pedestrians dominate in the streets, official traffic surveys focus on motorists, motorcyclists, public transit passengers, and—at times—cyclists, who often undertake intermodal journeys combining vehicle and pedestrian travel. These modes of transit nearly always involve some amount of walking before or after a journey. Even driving a car includes walking: to get to and from the car, for example. This simple observation leads us to rephrase our question: why has so little attention been paid to the most common—and most sustainable—mode of transport of all? State or municipal policies have been based on developing collective solutions embodied by broad access infrastructures for almost a century in the industrializing world, as Oldenziel, Sousa, and Van Wesemael remind us in their contribution to this volume. Moreover, according to the same authors, local authorities had little say and no access to large funds, and were generally marginalized; they often had to delegate urban development to nationally oriented engineers and architects, whose preference for large infrastructures biased and restricted their actions. Urban planning is a long-term process focusing on motor vehicle traffic control and infrastructure (transport networks, urban furniture, and landscape design).[3] By focusing on the infrastructural dimensions of urban development, be it for car or pedestrian control, most research ignores the mundane equipment used by pedestrians for their mundane mobility.[4]

That said, people, experts, and planners are becoming more aware of the benefits of walking. The policy aim to achieve "walkable cities" is growing.[5] European city planners have been creating downtown pedestrianization policies for both shopping and improved livability. More recently, bicycles are attracting welcome and special policy attention, as policymakers have come to appreciate them for their efficient, healthy, and ecological benefits. Nevertheless, the increase in nonmotorized transportation modes like walking and cycling has often gone hand in hand with infrastructure-only-based approaches: an exclusive focus on solutions such as pedestrian zones and self-service bicycle stations. This reductionism has led to missed policy opportunities. Unbuilding car-centered cities to create pedestrian infrastructures takes many years—if not decades—while a transformation in personal pedestrian accessories can be much faster. Such temporal discrepancies call for the development of ordinary and personalized pedestrian equipment alongside infrastructural and/or collective facilities. The level of comfort of people's urban experience depends considerably on the quality of interaction with low-tech equipment, such as a ledge on which to place a bag, a hook for hanging up belongings or clothes, spaces large enough to accommodate a person carrying many loads, bags that can be sufficiently adapted to pedestrian transport and changing uses, and handles or straps designed to improve comfort. These elements are often neglected, even though they have always been important.[6]

Low-tech and straightforward solutions are undoubtedly a promising prospect.[7] They can influence people's choice of transport mode. They can encourage urban residents to make better use of city centers. For instance, by relocating certain activities, such as food supply, to the city center, residents may contribute to an urban development of densification that experts consider environmentally far more sustainable than suburbanization. Such rearrangement may lower the number of motorized shopping trips to large suburban commercial areas. Here again, citizens will reassess their practices according to the comfort they experience.

Our sociohistorical study has two goals. Firstly, we show to what extent pedestrian traffic has changed over the centuries (modular distribution), as well as the nature and number of items pedestrians carry or use (personal belongings and individual accessories). Second, we show that urban residents have not waited until public authorities provided technical assistance to adapt their own "vehicular agency."[8] We have unearthed historical data to conduct a two-step study of how low-tech pedestrian equipment has evolved. Our methodology recovers an aspect of urban mobility that so far has mostly been hidden. We conclude by discussing the benefits of such a retrospective study.

## Logistical Details: Mundane Accessories and Fleeting Gestures

Because historians tend to focus on written testimonies and texts, they often cannot account for tacit, mundane, and fleeting gestures. After all, ordinary people do not think to write about the routines at the heart of their daily lives. This omission can be rectified by shifting from history to archaeology: seeking the material traces of "unwritten" behaviors. Such traces exist, particularly in photographs.[9] Photography has the remarkable ability to capture movements instantly, "freeze" life as it is lived, and save the ephemeral past as if it was part of an eternal present. To account for the history and importance of pedestrian logistics, we relied on an archive with hundreds of photographs dating back to the nineteenth century of the streets of Toulouse, a large city in southwest France. By conducting a statistical analysis, we show how pedestrian logistics evolved from the tension between fashion and function. Over time, more people in Toulouse came to carry increasingly more items, while surprisingly still being able to keep their hands free.

Our methodology combines archaeology, ethnography, and statistics.[10] We have selected three key sites in Toulouse city center: Rue d'Alsace-Lorraine, a large Haussmannian street that crosses the center of Toulouse from north to south (see figure 5.1); Place du Capitole, the main square and site of Toulouse city hall; and Allées Lafayette, a site which includes a square and crossroads, with cafés, movie theaters, and a pedestrian area. The three sites—though very different in terms of architecture, infrastructure, and social function—are all key locations close to the city center. These sites have been repeatedly photographed at different times in history. Our selection draws comparisons over four distinct periods: the early twentieth century, the interwar period, the 1950s–1960s, and the present. The photographic material comes from four different sources. We consulted the archives of two major photographers: Eugène Trutat (1840–1910), who photographed Toulouse around 1900, and Jean Dieuzaide (1921–2003), who photographed different aspects of the city after World War II.[11] To cover the interwar period, we relied on the Labouche collection, a database of thirty thousand postcards. Finally, we documented the current situation in Toulouse by taking our own photographs of the major sites previously selected from the other archives.

Our study is based on systematic observation and coding photographs, and thus falls within the practice of "quantitative observation." This approach relies on and renews a methodology that, though not widely used, is quite common in social sciences. It was pioneered in *The Unemployed in Marienthal*, by Lazarsfeld et al., who, like us, counted passers-by in a town's main street. They drew subtle analyses of social rhythms, showing how the local population was affected when the region's main textile factory closed.[12] Since then, the method has been used by several authors in the interactionist tradition, including Howard Becker, who eloquently justified this approach as a valuable research tool in his *Sociological Work*.[13] William Whyte recorded videos of New York plazas and analyzed them statistically to trace the relationship between urban design and people's behavior in terms of gathering, sitting, etc.[14]

We drew inspiration from this sociological tradition to implement our own: coding all the observable elements in what we call an "observiaire" (a term combining observation and questionnaire).[15] We identified and integrated many variables in our "observiaire": number and gender of people, number and type of bags, how bags are carried, postures, pace of movement, and the types of interaction between pedestrians and vehicles, etc. All in all, we coded six hundred pedestrians, fifty for each of the three sites over the four periods.[16]

For the purposes of our investigation, we designed two different "observiaires": the first grid to measure the observable traffic and identify the modes of transit, and the second grid to describe pedestrians and their accessories. After carefully "reading" our collection of photographs, we established the variables for each grid. The coded units in the first grid are the photographs themselves. For each, we noted the name of the site and then the type (cars, bicycles, public transit, and pedestrians), the state (moving or parked), and the number of vehicles. We also noted the number of people observable in each picture by counting the visible "heads" restricted to pedestrians: we excluded people on trams and bicycles or in cars from the count and treated them as an integral part of these vehicles. We used this information later to account for the evolution of the various modes of transit—including pedestrians.

The second grid coded pedestrians and their accessories. Unlike the previous grid, the coded unit is the person, not the picture. We did not code everyone visible in each photograph, only those with at least one hand visible. This criterion enabled us to describe what people were carrying or not carrying, allowing for the inevitable problem of hidden faces of bodies that appear in two-dimensional representations. This solution obviously underestimates the number of pedestrians with accessories: because this bias remains constant over time and place, it does not affect the robustness of our findings. We also excluded certain professionals, such as police officers, shopkeepers wearing aprons, and people sitting beside or walking with a bicycle. Every person who met our criteria was identified with the number of the photograph and allocated a separate number inserted in the image with Photoshop, then described in the grid (figure 5.1). Filling in these details led us to study our material systematically and repeatedly, paying equal attention to each "vehicle unit."[17] Besides recording actors, we also noted some rare scenes that seemed significant to us.

In conjunction with our quantitative survey, we conducted a qualitative ethnography of what was observed and how this evolved. Despite the typical conflict between qualitative and quantitative methods, we believe that quantitative analysis is better when based on a precise description of what is counted, whereas qualitative analysis is better if there is a strong sense of proportion. If we had decided not to count details, such as the type and number of items carried by each pedestrian, we would probably have missed some unique and significant events. For instance, when coding the various persons who appear in a large picture of Alsace-Lorraine Street, we noticed that two men were tipping their hats: this observation wonderfully illustrates both the capacity of photography to unwittingly retrieve the essence of life and, in this par-

| Name | Label | Values |
|------|-------|--------|
| City | City | {1, Gothenburg}... |
| Photo_number | Photo | None |
| Person_number | Person | None |
| Site | Site | {1, Capitol}... |
| Era | Era | {1, Before WWI} |
| Site_activity | Site activity | {1, Market} |
| Gender | Gender | {1, Male}... |
| Age | Age | {1, Adult}... |
| Pace | Pace | {0, Immobile}... |
| Orientation | Orientation | {1, Face}... |
| Position | Position | {0, Sidewalk}... |
| Hat | Hat | {0, No}... |
| Number_of_visible_arms | Arms | None |
| Plain_bag | Plain bag | None |
| Handbag | Handbag | None |
| Basket | Basket | None |
| Rolling_basket | Rolling basket | None |
| Box | Box | None |
| Clothing | Clothing | None |
| Naked_object | Naked object | None |
| Wrapped_object | Wrapped object | None |
| Unidentified_object | Unidentified object | None |
| Backpack | Backpack | None |
| Briefcase_school_bag | Briefcase, school bag | None |
| Suitcase | Suitcase | None |

**Figure 5.1.** Coding photographs according to criteria such as what pedestrians were carrying.

© Conseil général de la Haute-Garonne, Archives départementales, Labouche collection, 26_FI_31555_000159.

**Figure 5.2.** This 1900s photograph illustrates social interaction in the form of two men greeting each other by tipping their hats when crossing the main street in Toulouse.

© Conseil général de la Haute-Garonne, Archives départementales, Labouche collection, 26 FI 31555 TP 003040 0001.

ticular case, the former polite way of acknowledging each other in the city (figure 5.2).

Systematically observing and coding pedestrian logistics over a century showed historical variations that reveal the use of different modes of transportation and different ways of carrying belongings, bags, and other containers. Our analysis includes the major urban developments that channeled the various vehicle flows as analyzed by infrastructural studies as well as pedestrian accessories and their use. We extended the classic approach describing the modal split and its social, economic, and environmental consequences by closely observing the hand-to-hand contact between human and nonhuman actors that form the same vehicle unit. Our approach helps to recover otherwise ignored mobilities (walking), as well as the fine-grained details of pedestrian mobility.

## Evolution of the Visual Modal Split

The images of two famous sites in Toulouse (Lafayette and Capitole) in the early twentieth (figure 5.3, left) and twenty-first centuries (figure 5.3, right) give us a glimpse of the transformations that have imprinted a

**Figure 5.3.** *Top:* Lafayette area, comparing 1903 and 2011. *Bottom:* Capitol Square, comparing 1911 and 2011.

*Top left:* © Conseil général de la Haute-Garonne, Archives départementales, Labouche collection, 26 FI 31555 71. *Bottom left:* 26 FI 31555 335. *Top and bottom right:* © Roland Canu.

century of urban life, both in terms of the city's morphological evolution and the nature of the flows that bring it to life. It is easy to see, for example, how much the demarcation between sidewalks and streets have progressively differentiated traffic principles. We have observed how any ambiguity regarding the zones reserved for motor vehicles and for pedestrians has been removed over time. Around 1900, pedestrians in Toulouse walked almost as much on the street (44 percent) as on the sidewalk (56 percent). Today it is almost 100 percent on the sidewalk. This observation is consistent with the outcome of international regulations aimed at facilitating motorized traffic and disciplining pedestrians.[18] In the Toulouse case, this observation is also reinforced by the fact that two of the three sites are now pedestrian or semi-pedestrian zones.

We also observed—confirming scholarship on nonmotorized traffic— how pedestrians became more disciplined, while other modes of transit gradually gained more ground in the city center.[19] Over the four periods, there were numerous vehicles and in various forms: public or private, motorized or not, with two or four wheels. Having distinguished four generic categories of vehicles (public transit, cars, bicycles, and motorcycles/scooters), we measured—for each period and for each site—the space occupied by each category, by relating the number of vehicles in

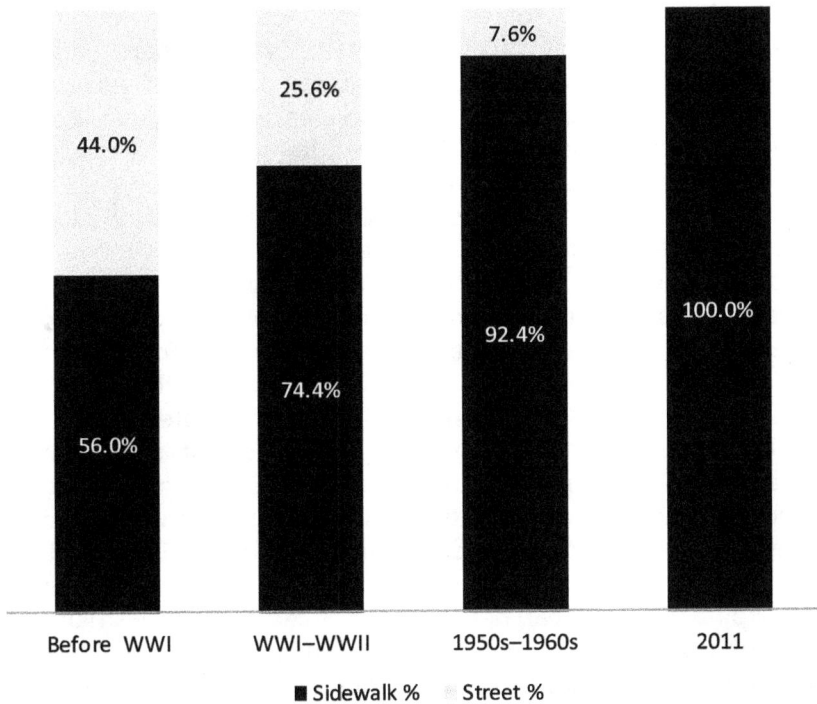

**Figure 5.4.** The proportion of pedestrians walking on the sidewalks or streets in the four periods. Only the people parallel to the sidewalk are counted as pedestrians walking on the sidewalk. We thus did not count the people stepping from the sidewalk to cross the street.

each category to the number of pedestrians in the pictures. The result is what we might call a "visual modal split" (based on close examination of the photographs), using the number of visible pedestrians as reference point.

Before World War I, public transit was the most visible form of vehicle in the city.[20] Lagging behind large French cities since the early nineteenth century, Toulouse adopted public transit only in 1863, with three horse-drawn tramlines.[21] Two additional innovations at the turn of the two centuries—railways in 1887 and electric trams in 1906—established the importance of public transit for downtown traffic.

Of the three sites, the Capitole area prioritized public transit throughout the first half of the twentieth century, with stops for two of the three tramlines, kiosks with controllers' offices, and passenger waiting rooms. The decline we observed in public transit after World War II (0.064 vehicles per pedestrian between the two wars, compared to only 0.037

between 1950 and 1970) represents two distinct times: an initial period, marked by the removal of tramways in 1957, when experts sought to free up space for cars and use buses instead of trams. These car-oriented measures were also in response to cars' lure of greater flexibility, as well as consumers' enthusiasm for the automobile.[22] The next period corresponds with the construction of two subway lines (in 1993 and in 2007). Our analysis should therefore mitigate the impression of a continuous decline (0.0088 vehicles per pedestrian in 2011): today public transit in Toulouse no longer operates in the pedestrianized center but on the outskirts, and no longer moves above ground but underground.

Figure 5.5 shows the huge rise, since the interwar period, in the number of cars on the city's streets. Automobility required the adoption of contradictory strategies: policymakers initially facilitated its development by widening the streets, by deploying traffic lights to facilitate car flows at the expense of pedestrian flows, and by building numerous parking lots (outside or underground: Capitole Square first welcomed cars before moving them down to a concealed, five-floor underground facility). Then came the countermovement of sustainable urban planning, of safeguarding historic urban heritage, and of dedicated pedestrian areas. Consequently, motorized vehicles have been gradually evicted from the city center. In Toulouse, the pedestrianization dynamics have spread from two points (Capitole and Alsace-Lorraine) and followed two axes (Taur, Saint-Rome, and Filatiers, as well as Alsace-Lorraine Street).[23] The

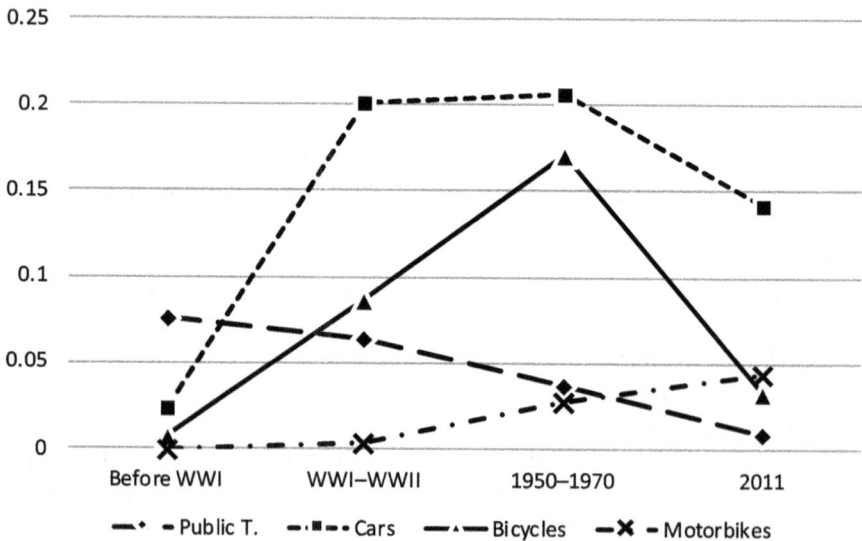

**Figure 5.5.** The number of vehicles per head of Toulouse's population in each period.

general notion that cars were favored and taking over the city space rests largely on an illusion, at least for the city center.[24] Our findings show that not only were there many countermeasures, but also that whatever the increase in number of cars, pedestrians still outnumbered them, no matter the number of passengers in the cars.

We also want to draw attention to the surprising observation in figure 5.5 of the variation in bicycle use on the street. The number of bicycles increased in the first part of the twentieth century, soon reaching a level comparable to cars (0.17 bicycles versus 0.2 cars per pedestrian). What is most intriguing in our observations, however, is the subsequent decline in transporting goods by bicycle. The decline of the latter practice was steep from the 1970s, with the ongoing rise of the automobile and the new French connotation of bicycles being associated with the poorest working classes.[25] Eventually, the city's redevelopment of infrastructure and traffic systems encouraged the return of cycling. In 2011, Toulouse city council voted for a "Bike Plan 2011–2020;" two years later, the city had 508 kilometers of cycle paths and 253 bicycle rental stations.[26] In addition, car access to the city center has declined sharply. This is in line with the current discourse about cities of the future inevitably excluding cars from their centers through the adoption of sustainable urban development policies. These transformations are reflected in a distinct increase in cycling around Toulouse, particularly after 2005.[27]

This infrastructural development of the city was paralleled by the evolution of bicycles. On closer inspection, we see that the morphology of twenty-first-century two-wheelers is quite different from that of the twentieth century.[28] And these differences matter: depending on the bicycles' shape and accessories, cycling and transportation practices vary, and thus redefine the urban experience. Whereas bicycles were generic and quite visible before World War I, they diversified afterward, and were customized for certain activities. Since World War II, various types of equipment adapted bicycles for transporting diverse objects. The first equipment was added to the rear of bicycles, in the form of the luggage rack. Of the bicycles we observed between 1950 and 1970, 39.8 percent had this device. In comparison, only 5.1 percent had a front basket. Today, two-thirds of the observed bicycles have at least one piece of equipment (such as front basket, bag, luggage rack, or child seat). Contrary to the observations between 1950 and 1970, these accessories now fit more easily on the front of bikes. No doubt the technical standards of shared bicycle schemes are part of this transition: bike-share operators all equip their bicycles with a front basket, a standardized accessory that enables cyclists and pedestrians to take part in intermodal transportation.

How did pedestrian mobility evolve in the city center in our sample? Over the twentieth century, the number of people walking in downtown Toulouse has increased considerably: the average number of pedestrians we see in each picture has risen from forty (before World War I) to over a hundred (2011). The densification of human flows seems to be related to two changes. The first change is demographic. Toulouse today is a metropolis of southwest France, with a steep rise in population, from nearly 150 thousand residents in 1900 to 450 thousand now, combined with a late growth of its suburbs since the 1970s. In the late 1990s, however, the city experienced the demarcation of pedestrian zones in the center, reserving 7,900 meters of streets for pedestrians. We observe transformations at street level that are just as spectacular as those at the urban planning level. These changes imply new relationships between people and their accessories, as well as between fashion and function.

## The Transformation of Carrying Devices and Practices

The transformation in pedestrian equipment mostly relates to its function for transporting loads, specifically consumer goods. This evolution is related to "consumer logistics."[29] We now turn to a major aspect of the sustainable city: improving pedestrian facilities and equipment aimed at relocating food supply in the city center. Let us first go back in time to examine how buyers and sellers organized their supplies. On the one hand, consumer logistics is a purpose-oriented, functional, and rational activity. It was even more so a century ago: at a time when merchants did not provide their customers with bags, people had to anticipate where to go, for what purpose, and with which containers. Shopping with the family required careful planning, and usually involved a baby carriage and a personal shopping basket.[30]

In other words, going to the market was a matter of logistics, both for the merchants, who had to prepare the right types of baskets to display their goods and take care of home deliveries, and for the shoppers, who needed to take their own containers to carry items. It was impossible to trace any name on the diverse containers, as these remained the property of their respective owners. The containers used by both supply and demand sides were plain and opaque, with no inscription revealing their origin. As such, they were just containers—neutral vehicles, without the power to redefine goods and advertise their origin, which modern packaging introduced much later. Consequently, foods were qualified only through tasting or discussing them, unlike packaged goods, which appeared in later years, and are qualified through delegated text inscriptions and "test" procedures (nutritional charts, brand names, and so on).[31]

On the other hand, the urban experience of strolling around meant that planned and unplanned journeys coexisted within the city. As people wandered in the city purposelessly, their behavior as well as their personal accessories framed their availability to other emerging serendipitous experiences, such as shopping.

Most of us consider moving around with our hands free as universal behavior, enabling us to instantly engage in social interaction (like shaking hands and waving) and/or shopping. But it is not. In his famous study on body techniques, the French anthropologist Marcel Mauss highlighted sleeping as one of the most physical activities.[32] When we sleep, we loosen social norms as well as self-control, abandoning ourselves to pure biological forces. Mauss showed that social norms and cultural frames surrounding sleep still remain surprisingly significant: in different parts of the world, how people sleep varies considerably, depending on the place and culture, the equipment used (e.g., pillows and blankets) as well as the position (e.g., lying, standing, and on horseback). Walking follows a similar pattern. While sleeping modes changed in the Maussian account, ways of walking also changed over time.[33] In the left photo in figure 5.6, we clearly see that three of the four men are walking with their hands behind their backs. Far from appearing accidental and random, this behavior can be measured and dated: walking with one or both hands behind your back was very common in the early twentieth century, when 9 percent of men did so. This behavior progressively disappeared in the following decades. Despite appearances, hands were not fully available for other uses such as consumer logistics. Sometimes people's hands were busy holding their accessories. In the right part of figure 5.6, two women and one man are holding parasols, while another

**Figure 5.6.** Pedestrians changed the way they held their hands.
© Conseil général de la Haute-Garonne, Archives départementales, Labouche collection. *Left:* 26 FI 31555 71; *right:* 26 FI 31555 185.

man is walking with a cane. In fact, 17 percent of pedestrians used such accessories before World War I, but here again such habits vanished in the following decades. Why?

## Did Fashion or Function Dictate Consumer Logistics?

Part of the explanation is the increase in the number of items carried. It is hard to tell, however, whether the changing fashions helped people to use their hands for other purposes, or whether the need to carry things forced people to abandon previously fashionable behavior. The historical trend is indeed that of the generalization and intensification of consumer logistics. Pedestrians' average loads increased continuously from the early twentieth century (figure 5.7).[34]

Several factors contributed to such an evolution. For one, people's purchasing power increased. We observe a massive increase in the number of women carrying handbags while walking. Moreover, suppliers reduced home deliveries, shifting the burden to individual consumers. More generally, the development of consumer society, the corresponding specialized retail outlets, and the overall democratization of class society have played a part. The combined phenomena multiplied the

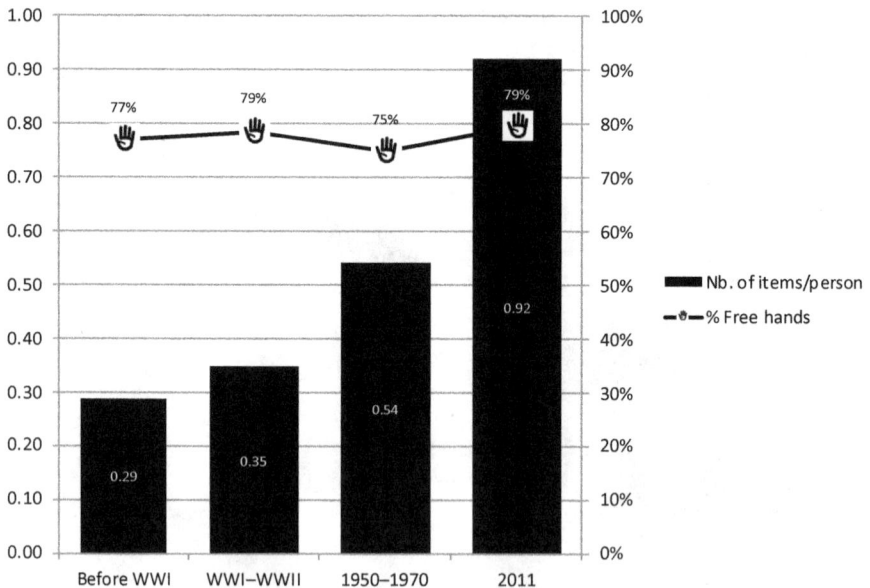

**Figure 5.7.** The number of items (excluding accessories) that each person in Toulouse carried and the proportion of free hands.

number of bags and items carried. Before democratization in the 1920s reduced the number of servants shopping on behalf of their employers in the early hours of the day, most people seen in the streets at other times had lighter loads. Over the next decades, however, the disappearance of servants was paralleled by a continuous increase of pedestrians' loads.

It is also interesting to note that the increase in pedestrians' loads did not stop their hands being available for duties other than carrying things: surprisingly, while the average pedestrian load tripled over the century (from 0.29 items per person to 0.92), the proportion of free hands in the same population remained astonishingly high and stable, between 75 percent and 79 percent. How did people manage to carry more things on their body without needing more hands? To solve this puzzle, we need to examine the evolution of carrying techniques and equipment.

## A Shift in Carrying Techniques and Accessories

The technical and physical way pedestrians carry loads has undergone a transformation. As figure 5.8 shows, notable changes took place in how loads were distributed between three main areas of pedestrians' bodies: hands, arms (on elbow and under arm), and upper body (shoul-

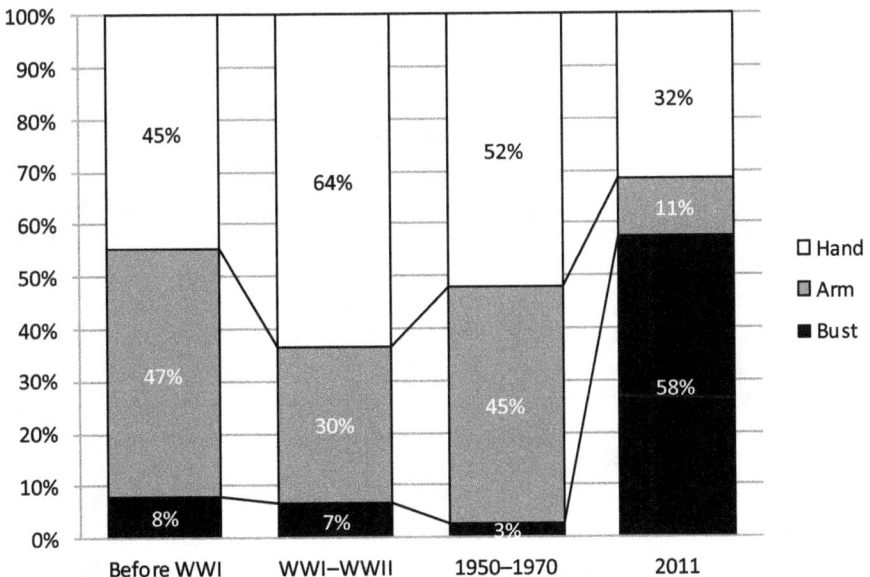

**Figure 5.8.** The evolving ways of carrying items in hands, in arms, or using bust (including back and shoulders).

ders and backs). Before World War I, 45 percent of items and bags were carried in hands and 47 percent on or under arms. Until the 1980s, arms and hands remained for more than 90 percent of pedestrians the main way to carry goods. After the interwar period, especially handbags (45 percent) began to be carried less in the hand or under the arm than on the elbow, largely driven by fashion, such as the promotion of the Coco Chanel 2.55 bag in February 1955 (as the name implies).

During the first three periods, people rarely transported items on their shoulders and backs (less than 10 percent). By contrast, a dramatic shift occurred from 1950 to 1970 and in the early twenty-first century, when hands and arms became more free (today, only 32 percent and 11 percent, respectively). The shoulders and back are regularly used to carry various loads (almost 60 percent of items/bags), thanks to the introduction of shoulder straps and backpacks. Even though such devices have been available for a long time, their use by pedestrians was very limited in the postwar boom. It was not until the 1980s that fashion captured these accessories and legitimated them as indispensable urban containers. The backpack, given the developments we identified, has certain logistical and circulatory a priori advantages—in addition to freeing the hands—that highlight its current popularity. Backpacks favor an unplanned management of objects (both in terms of number and weight) and help maneuver interactions with other pedestrians (flow densities and the risks associated with friction and collisions). Backpacks also help in coping with infrastructures that are ill suited to containers that protrude. In contrast with bulky bags carried on the side of the body, backpacks help when taking an escalator, stepping into a shop, or slipping into a dense crowd. This general trend requires more investigation.

The 78 percent rate of "bust carriage" in figure 5.9 includes various locations on the body, depending on what is carried. People carry almost 80 percent of personal bags on their shoulders or back, whereas they carry more than 90 percent of commercial bags in their hands. This is because people already use their back or shoulders to carry their personal belongings when shopping. Moreover, shopping bags are rarely equipped with straps, and shops do not offer any containers that can be carried on our backs. In this respect, sellers are apparently more than a century out of date in terms of consumer-friendly technologies. As we have seen, consumers tried to carry more things while keeping their hands as free as possible and consequently adopted shoulder bags and backpacks. Retailers encouraged them, but in an ambiguous way: they have helped customers to increase their loads by providing them with free bags, which did not exist in the past. However, unlike personal bags,

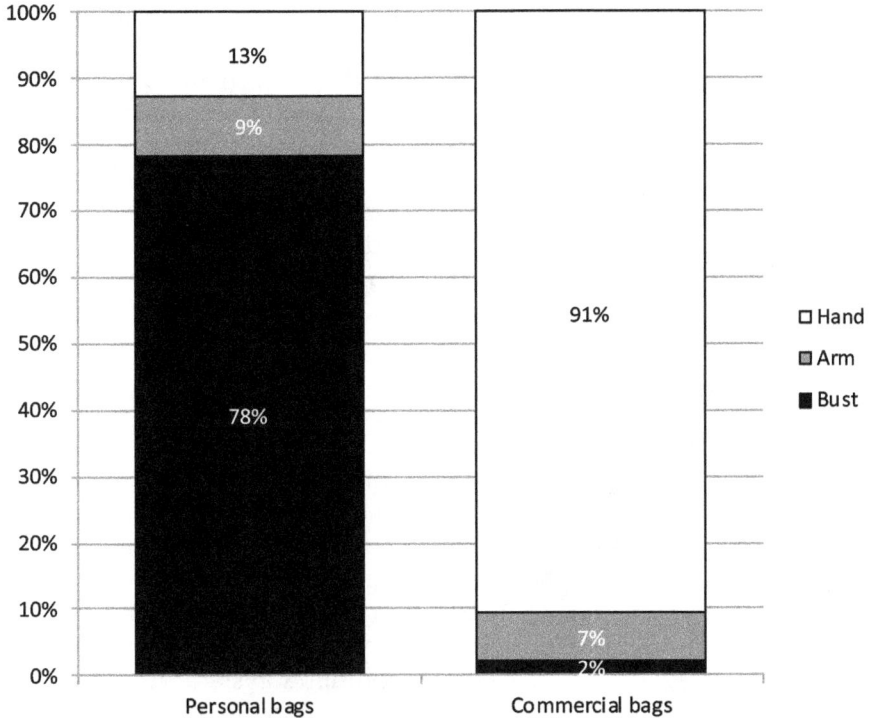

**Figure 5.9.** Ways of carrying personal and commercial bags in 2011. This chart is based on a video-assisted observation of one thousand pedestrians on two days in Toulouse city center.

these containers cannot be carried on the shoulder or on the back. This ambivalence is well illustrated in figure 5.10, where a young woman is carrying her handbag on her shoulder while trying to hold a commercial bag elsewhere. She has moved the latter onto her elbow, probably because the strap is too short to reach her shoulder. In doing so, she is keeping her hands free for other activities: talking on the phone, using her hand to protect her eyes from the sunlight.

The lessons from this "story of carrying" are clear: if we want people to behave in a more sustainable way, favor pedestrian rather than motorized logistics, use their feet rather than their cars, wander in the city center rather than travel in the suburbs, we will have to consider the hidden aspects of consumer logistics, care about minor social and material details, and offer actors more sustainable solutions. Recently, some companies seem to have understood the problem and are taking advantage of it, for instance by promoting "organic" bags with

**Figure 5.10.** A young woman using her arms and hands to carry multiple items, talk on the phone, and shade her eyes. © Roland Canu.

straps long enough to be carried on the shoulder.[35] However, consumer logistics is much more than mere container and marketing innovations. History shows that consumer logistics involves the general organization of the city; the interaction between humans, containers, and things; and thus proper human-accessory assemblages as well as suitable public policies.

## Conclusion

The contributions of our chapter are five-fold. The first is methodological: the statistical analysis of a picture series gives mobility historians a means of encapsulating mundane and forgotten practices that written data cannot capture. The second contribution stems from the first: our proposed approach challenges the "infrastructure reductionism" that previous urban planning studies favor at the risk of overlooking the abundant urban design practices that often resist, evolve, or challenge existing equipment. The third contribution is the rich set of otherwise-hidden pedestrian practices and devices that our studies uncover. In other words, if history can explore "roads-not-taken" (as discussed in this volume's introduction), it can also reveal "roads-that-were-taken-but-remained-invisible." We have argued that—even though the preponderance of auto-focused statistical data would suggest otherwise—pedestrians never ceased to be a part of the urban transit landscape, and have even remained by far the most populous part of it. We have shown that if high-tech objects—ranging from trains to planes—matter, we should also focus on smaller and individual items, like all sorts of bags and accessories. Pedestrians, far from passively adjusting to available urban frameworks or transportation devices, have demonstrated an incredible ability to develop innovative behavior, notably by shifting container types: they favored bags with straps and backpacks that helped them to carry more goods efficiently without hampering their freedom of movement. Fourth, our historical study of pedestrian logistics confirms that, as relevantly suggested by this book's introduction, the past is "usable" and must be used. Discovering that human mobility practices and individual transportation devices matter as much as (or even more than) large urban schemes should lead city planners to take the former more into account when designing the latter. Last, but not least, our study shows the sheer load of human-transported goods that is ignored in all forecasts and surveys that are biased toward truck deliveries.[36] This finding shows that transportation is not only a matter of vehicles transporting people or goods, but also a matter of people carrying things themselves. Taking this point into account could be key for the development of a more accurate approach when calculating urban sustainability and consumer goods.

Alongside the specific inherent challenges of implementing smooth and efficient intermodality—transport regulation, global pricing, coordinating timetables, launching mobile apps for instant bus, metro, and tram information—other challenges emerge. These include the customization of urban transportation services, as well as the need to remodel individual and collective equipment to ensure better matching. This effort should focus on adjusting devices—individual and collective, public and private, low-tech and high-tech—and helping pedestrians cope with the difficulties they experience when carrying their belongings, bags, or containers. Intermodal concerns would then no longer be the end point of sustainable development initiatives, but rather the starting point for new reflection on the connection between elementary units (pedestrians) and more complex transportation networks.

Sociotechnical solutions that alleviate walking activities could well be the "tipping point" toward sustainable urban mobility.[37] Reintroducing comfortable practices should stimulate more of the population to take up urban walking or at least adopt soft modes of transportation. The backpack is a shining example, providing a satisfactory solution to the growing number of bags and items people carry. We still need to find an equivalent for the shopping bag that will achieve greater comfort for conducting more sustainable consumer logistics (even though easing consumption is a problem in itself from a sustainable perspective). These efforts, combined with infrastructure investments by public actors, if coordinated, should achieve the adoption of more environmentally friendly behavior. To make such behavior happen, we will also have to rely on the cultural echoes of these technical incentives: urban residents will have to commit to the cause of developing a more sustainable city in order to truly appreciate the changes in technical devices at their disposal and use them sustainably.

**Franck Cochoy**, professor of sociology at the University of Toulouse Jean Jaurès and a researcher at LISST-CNRS, works in economic sociology, looking at the human and technical mediations that frame or equip the relationship between supply and demand. His research projects include packaging, self-service, shopping carts, and consumer logistics. He is the author of several books, including *On the Origins of Self-Service* (Routledge, 2015) and *On Curiosity, the Art of Market Seduction* (Mattering Press, 2016). His recent articles were published in *Applied Mobilities, Economy and Society, Environment and Planning A, Mobilities,* and *Visual Studies.*

**Roland Canu**, a lecturer in sociology at the University of Toulouse Jean Jaurès and a member of CERTOP-CNRS (UMR 5044), works in economic sociology, focusing on the sciences and technologies employed in the advertising industry over the past century. His most recent work analyzes subliminal and innovation advertising.

**Cédric Calvignac**, lecturer in sociology at the University of Albi (France) and a member of CERTOP-CNRS (UMR 5044), works at the crossroads of science and technology studies (STS) and economic sociology. His research focuses on the description and analysis of sociotechnical systems in different collective actions, ranging from the prosaic (e.g., urban walking equipment and techniques) to high tech (e.g., design, development, and adoption of citizen Wi-Fi networks, electronic sales platforms, and mobile tourism applications).

## Notes

This chapter is an outcome of a collective Swedish-French Urbanet-ANR project launched by Daniel Normark and continued by Helene Brembeck, Johan Hagberg, Niklas Hansson, Ulrika Holmberg (CFK, University of Gothenburg, Sweden), Florence Brachet (EHESS, Paris), Cédric Calvignac, Roland Canu, Franck Cochoy (head for France), Anaïs Daniau, Michèle Lalanne, Claire Thébault, and Jean-Sébastien Vayre (CERTOP, CNRS, and University of Toulouse, France). During the research, one of the authors benefitted from the support of the Center for Retailing, School of Business, University of Gothenburg, Sweden. The chapter borrows elements from previous publications: Roland Canu and Franck Cochoy, "Places et déplacements : une archéologie statistique de la logistique piétonne (Toulouse, XXe–XXIe siècles)," *Flux* 88 (2012): 19–33; Franck Cochoy, Cédric Calvignac, and Roland Canu, "Bärandets historia. Den vindlande vägen mot en hållbar fotgängarlogistik (Toulouse, 1900–2011)," *Kulturella Perspektiv* 3, no. 4 (2013): 7–14; Franck Cochoy, Cédric Calvignac, and Roland Canu, "Load Story: La logistique piétonne à Toulouse," *Mondes sociaux, Magazine des sciences humaines et sociales toulousaines*, 2 December 2014, updated 19 December 2018; Franck Cochoy, Johan Hagberg, and Roland Canu, "The Forgotten Role of Pedestrian Transportation in Urban Life: Insights from a Visual Comparative Archaeology (Gothenburg and Toulouse, 1825–2011)," *Urban Studies* 52, no. 12 (2015): 2267–86.

1. Tim Edensor, "Walking in Rhythms: Place, Regulation, Style and the Flow of Experience," *Visual Studies* 25, no. 1 (2010): 69–79.

2. Laetitia Dablanc, "Goods Transport in Large European Cities: Difficult to Organize, Difficult to Modernize," *Transportation Research Part A* 41, no. 3 (2007): 280–85.

3. In their contribution to this volume, Oldenziel, Sousa, Van Wesemael show that car boosters have successfully advocated and lobbied public authorities and budgets to prepare societies for automobility. See also Peter Norton: in his book *Fighting Traffic*, the author shows that to favor automobiles, American cities developed aggressive policies aimed at delegitimizing pedestrians as primary users of the streets. Peter Norton, *Fighting Traffic: The Dawn of the Motor Age in the American City* (Cambridge, MA: MIT Press, 2008). For similar evidence and arguments, see also Barbara Schmucki, "Against 'the Eviction of the Pedestrian': The Pedestrians' Association and Walking Practices in Urban Britain after World War II," *Radical History Review* 114 (2012): 113–37; Patrick Fridenson, "La société française et les accidents de la route, 1890–1914," *Ethnologie française* 21, no. 3 (1991): 307–13; Peter W. J. Bartrip, Peter "Pedestrians, Motorists, and No-Fault Compensation for Road Accidents in 1930s Britain," *Journal of Legal History* 31, no. 1 (2010): 45–60.

4. See, e.g., Olivier Coutard, Richard Hanley, and Rae Zimmerman, "The Social Diffusion of Large Technical Systems," in *Mobile Technologies of the City*, ed. Mimi Sheller and John Urry (London: Routledge, 2005); Mike Featherstone, Nigel Thrift, and John Urry, eds., "Automobilities," *Theory, Culture and Society* 21, no. 4–5 (2004): 1–284.

5. Mary Soderstrom, *The Walkable City: From Haussmann's Boulevards to Jane Jacobs Streets and Beyond* (Montréal: Véhicule Press, 2008); Carmen Hass-Klau, *The Pedestrian and the City* (London: Belhaven Press, 1990).

6. To be fair, urban planners are interested in pedestrian equipment, but only if it appears to be "smart." Indeed, the only pedestrian equipment that public actors have recently invested in is the smartphone; see Mimi Sheller and John Urry, eds., *Mobile Technologies of the City* (London: Routledge, 2005).

7. Philippe Bihouix, *L'âge des low tech. Vers une civilisation techniquement soutenable* (Paris: Seuil, 2014).

8. Cédric Calvignac and Franck Cochoy, "From 'Market Agencements' to 'Vehicular Agencies': Insights from the Quantitative Observation of Consumer Logistics," *Consumption Markets & Culture* 19, no. 1 (2016): 133–47.

9. John Collier and Malcom Collier, *Visual Anthropology: Photography as a Research Method* (Albuquerque: University of New Mexico Press, 1986); Jon Prosser, ed., *Image-Based Research: A Sourcebook for Qualitative Researchers* (London: Falmer Press, 1998).

10. Roland Canu, Cédric Calvignac, Franck Cochoy, and Johan Hagberg, "Visual Archeology of Pedestrian Logistics in Urban Mobility," paper presented at Traffic Safety, City Planning and Social Justice: A Symposium on Sustainable Urban Mobility, Chalmers University of Technology, Gothenburg, Sweden, 5 October 2017.

11. See Hanna Diamond, "The Return of the Republic: Crowd Photography and the Liberation in Toulouse 1944–45," *French Politics, Culture and Society* 37, no. 1 (2019): 90–116.

12. Paul Lazarsfeld, Marie Jahoda, and Hans Zeisel, *Marienthal: The Sociography of an Unemployed Community* (Chicago: Aldine, Atherton, 1971 [1933]).

13. Howard S. Becker, *Sociological Work: Method and Substance* (New Brunswick: Transaction Books, 1977).

14. William Whyte, *The Social Life of Small Urban Spaces* (Washington, DC: The Conservation Foundation, 1980).

15. Franck Cochoy, "Calculation, Qualculation, Calqulation: Shopping Cart's Arithmetic, Equipped Cognition and Clustered Consumers," *Marketing Theory* 8, no. 1 (2008): 15–44.

16. For a similar approach but different in its focus on geographical distribution, see Männistö-Funk's chapter in this volume.

17. Erving Goffman, *The Presentation of Self in Everyday Life* (New York: Anchor Books, 1959).

18. See Ruth Oldenziel, Martin Emanuel, Adri A. Albert de la Bruheze, and Frank Veraart, eds., *Cycling Cities: The European Experience: Hundred Years of Policy and Practice* (Eindhoven: Foundation of the History of Technology, 2016).

19. On sidewalks and disciplining pedestrians, see Nicholas Blomley, *Rights of Passage: Sidewalks and the Regulation of Public Flow* (New York: Routledge, 2011); Peter D. Norton, "Street Rivals: Jaywalking and the Invention of the Motor Age Street," *Technology and Culture* 48, no. 2 (2007): 331–59.

20. Union des Transports Publics Urbains et Régionaux (UTPUR), *Les transports collectifs et la ville* (Paris: Celse, 1969).

21. Michel Taillefer, *Nouvelle histoire de Toulouse* (Toulouse: Privat, 2002).

22. On Toulouse, see François Bordes, "Les précurseurs toulousains, 1839–1861," Midi-*Pyrénées patrimoine*, hors-série (June 2010): 16–24. Vincent Kaufmann, Jean-Marie Guidez, Françoise Mermoud, and Jean-Louis Couderc, *Les citadins face à l'automobilité. Étude compare des agglomérations de Besançon, Grenoble, Toulouse, Berne, Genève et Lausanne* (Lyon: Dossier Certu, 1998). For the more general pattern, see Oldenziel et al., *Cycling Cities*.

23. For a detailed history of public transportation in Toulouse, see Robert Marconis and Julie Vivier, *150 ans de transports publics à Toulouse* (Toulouse: Privat, 2010).

24. Our study is focused on data from selected places in the city center. However, as Männistö-Funk relevantly points out in the following chapter, the modal share in a few select places in a city may be a poor indicator of the full city's modal split. Local newspaper and archival sources on Toulouse suggest real problems of urban traffic jams in the 1960s and 1970s, an issue that clearly persists in suburban parts of the conurbation today.

25. Marc Rivere, "D'une écologie politique à une économie médiatique. Toulouse, Genève, Saragosse" (Ph.D. thesis in Géographie Aménagement, Université Toulouse, 2009), 39.

26. Thomas Simonian, "Vélo à Toulouse: le Plan et la Fête / Les élus veulent 'assurer le tempo,'" *Le Journal Toulousain*, 12 June 2013, accessed 7 September 2018, https://www.lejournaltoulousain.fr/societe/velo-a-toulouse-le-plan-et-la-fete-les-elus-veulent-assurer-le-tempo-23247.

27. Nevertheless, the presence of bicycles in the city center remains far from the post–Second World War peak. The motorization of two-wheeled vehicles par-

tially explains this difference. Two-wheeled motorcycles now outnumber bicycles (0.0443 motorcycles versus 0.335 bicycles per individual). Indeed, as Toulouse and its suburbs expand, it has become faster and less tedious for individuals living in the suburbs to opt for the engines that require no physical effort and move at greater speed. In the city center, other means of transport have taken over, in particular the metro. Toulouse's new dimensions justify less use of the bicycle downtown: whereas the residents in the center and nearby suburbs prefer the metro, those living beyond prefer motorized vehicles that make travel easier, especially when transporting loads.

28. Cochoy et al., "Bicycles, Cyclists and Loads."
29. Kent Granzin and Kenneth Bahn, "Consumer Logistics: Conceptualization, Pertinent Issues and a Proposed Program for Research," *Journal of the Academy of Marketing Science* 17, no. 1 (1989): 91–101.
30. See Johan Hagberg and Daniel Normark, "From Basket to Shopping Bag," *Journal of Historical Research in Marketing* 7, no. 4 (2015): 452–75.
31. Franck Cochoy, "Making People Buy and Eat Differently. Lessons from the Modernization of Small Independent Grocery Stores in the Early Twentieth Century," *Review of Agricultural, Food and Environmental Studies* 99, no. 1 (2018): 15–35.
32. Marcel Mauss, "Techniques of the body," *Economy and Society* 2, no. 1 (1973): 70–88.
33. For an outstanding account of the social construction of walking, see Elizabeth Shove and Mika Pantzar, "Consumers, Producers and Practices: Understanding the Invention and Reinvention of Nordic Walking," *Journal of Consumer Culture* 5, no. 1 (2005): 43–64.
34. Except accessories like canes and parasols.
35. E.g., this bag offered by PromoGreen: "Sac Épaule Publicitaire Natur'l," PromoGreen.fr, accessed 7 September 2018, http://www.promogreen.fr/sac-ecolo gique-sac-epaule-publicitaire-natur-l-p11752.html.
36. This point calls for further reflections about the statistical criteria and measurement of sustainability efforts; see Jan Pieter Smits and Frank Veraart's contribution to this volume.
37. Malcom Gladwell, *The Tipping Point: How Little Things Can Make a Big Difference* (Boston: Little, Brown and Company, 2002).

## Bibliography

Becker, Howard S. *Sociological Work: Method and Substance*. New Brunswick: Transaction Books, 1977.

Bartrip, Peter W. J. "Pedestrians, Motorists, and No-Fault Compensation for Road Accidents in 1930s Britain." *Journal of Legal History* 31, no. 1 (2010): 45–60.

Bihouix, Philippe. *L'âge des low tech. Vers une civilisation techniquement soutenable.* Paris: Seuil, 2014.

Blomley, Nicholas. *Rights of Passage: Sidewalks and the Regulation of Public Flow*. New York: Routledge, 2011.

Bordes, François. "Les précurseurs toulousains, 1839–1861." *Midi-Pyrénées patrimoine*, hors-série (June 2010): 16–24.

Calvignac, Cédric, and Franck Cochoy. "From 'Market Agencements' to 'Vehicular Agencies': Insights from the Quantitative Observation of Consumer Logistics." *Consumption Markets & Culture* 19, no. 1 (2016): 133–47.

Canu, Roland, Cédric Calvignac, Franck Cochoy, and Johan Hagberg. "Visual Arche-
ology of Pedestrian Logistics in Urban Mobility." Paper presented at Traffic Safety,
City Planning and Social Justice: A Symposium on Sustainable Urban Mobility,
Chalmers University of Technology, Gothenburg, Sweden, 5 October 2017.

Canu, Roland, and Franck Cochoy. "Places et déplacements: Une archéologie statistique de la logistique piétonne (Toulouse, XXe–XXIe siècles)." _Flux_ 88 (2012):
19–33.

Cochoy, Franck. "Calculation, Qualculation, Calqulation: Shopping Cart's Arithmetic, Equipped Cognition and Clustered Consumers." _Marketing Theory_ 8, no. 1
(2008): 15–44.

———. "Making People Buy and Eat Differently. Lessons from the Modernization of
Small Independent Grocery Stores in the Early Twentieth Century." _Review of
Agricultural, Food and Environmental Studies_ 99, no. 1 (2018): 15–35.

Cochoy, Franck, Cédric Calvignac, and Roland Canu. "Bärandets historia. Den vindlande vägen mot en hållbar fotgängarlogistik (Toulouse, 1900–2011)." _Kulturella
Perspektiv_ 3, no. 4 (2013): 7–14.

———. "Load Story: La logistique piétonne à Toulouse." _Mondes sociaux, Magazine
des sciences humaines et sociales toulousaines_, 2 December 2014, updated 19
December 2018, http://sms.hypotheses.org/3100.

Cochoy, Franck, Johan Hagberg, and Roland Canu. "The Forgotten Role of Pedestrian Transportation in Urban Life: Insights from a Visual Comparative Archaeology (Gothenburg and Toulouse, 1825–2011)." _Urban Studies_ 52, no. 12 (2015):
2267–86.

Cochoy, Franck, Johan Hagberg, Daniel Normark, Hélène Ducourant, Ulrika Holmberg, and Cédric Calvignac. "Bicycles, Cyclists and Loads: A Comparative Analysis of Cycling Practices in Gothenburg and Toulouse." _Applied Mobilities_ (2017),
1–25.

Collier, John, and Malcom Collier. _Visual Anthropology: Photography as a Research
Method_. Albuquerque: University of New Mexico Press, 1986.

Coutard, Olivier, Richard Hanley, and Rae Zimmerman. "The Social Diffusion of Large
Technical Systems." In _Mobile Technologies of the City_, edited by Mimi Sheller
and John Urry. London: Routledge, 2005.

Dablanc, Laetitia. "Goods Transport in Large European Cities: Difficult to Organize,
Difficult to Modernize." _Transportation Research Part A_ 41, no. 3 (2007): 280–85.

Diamond, Hanna. "The Return of the Republic: Crowd Photography and the Liberation in Toulouse 1944–45." _French Politics, Culture and Society_ 37, no. 1 (2019):
90–116.

Edensor, Tim, "Walking in Rhythms: Place, Regulation, Style and the Flow of Experience." _Visual Studies_ 25, no. 1 (2010): 69–79.

Featherstone, Mike, Nigel Thrift, and John Urry, eds. "Automobilities." _Theory, Culture
and Society_ 21, no. 4–5 (2004): 1–284.

Fridenson, Patrick. "La société française et les accidents de la route, 1890–1914." _Eth-
nologie française_ 21, no. 3 (1991): 307–13.

Gladwell, Malcom. _The Tipping Point: How Little Things Can Make a Big Difference_.
Boston: Little, Brown and Company, 2002.

Goffman, Erving. _The Presentation of Self in Everyday Life_. New York: Anchor Books,
1959.

Granzin, Kent, and Kenneth Bahn. "Consumer Logistics: Conceptualization, Pertinent
Issues and a Proposed Program for Research." _Journal of the Academy of Marketing Science_ 17, no. 1 (1989): 91–101.

Hagberg, Johan, and Daniel Normark. "From Basket to Shopping Bag." *Journal of Historical Research in Marketing* 7, no. 4 (2015): 452–75.

Hass-Klau, Carmen. *The Pedestrian and the City*. London: Belhaven Press, 1990.

Kaufmann, Vincent, Jean-Marie Guidez, Françoise Mermoud, and Jean-Louis Couderc. *Les citadins face à l'automobilité. Étude comparée des agglomérations de Besançon, Grenoble, Toulouse, Berne, Genève et Lausanne*. Lyon: Dossier Certu, 1998.

Lazarsfeld, Paul, Marie Jahoda, Hans Zeisel. *Marienthal: The Sociography of an Unemployed Community*. Chicago: Aldine, Atherton, 1971 (1933).

Marconis, Robert, and Julie Vivier. *150 ans de transports publics à Toulouse*. Toulouse: Privat, 2010.

Mauss, Marcel. "Techniques of the body." *Economy and Society* 2, no. 1 (1973): 70–88.

Norton, Peter. *Fighting Traffic: The Dawn of the Motor Age in the American City*. Cambridge, MA: MIT Press, 2008.

——. "Street Rivals: Jaywalking and the Invention of the Motor Age Street." *Technology and Culture* 48, no. 2 (2007): 331–59.

Oldenziel, Ruth, Martin Emanuel, Adri A. Albert de la Bruheze, and Frank Veraart, eds. *Cycling Cities: The European Experience: Hundred Years of Policy and Practice*. Eindhoven: Foundation of the History of Technology, 2016.

Prosser, Jon, ed. *Image-Based Research: A Sourcebook for Qualitative Researchers*. London: Falmer Press, 1998.

Rivere, Marc. "D'une écologie politique à une économie médiatique. Toulouse, Genève, Saragosse." Ph.D. thesis in Géographie Aménagement, Université Toulouse, 2009.

Schmucki, Barbara. "Against 'the Eviction of the Pedestrian': The Pedestrians' Association and Walking Practices in Urban Britain after World War II." *Radical History Review* 114 (2012): 113–37.

Sheller, Mimi, and John Urry, eds. *Mobile Technologies of the City*. London: Routledge, 2005.

Shove, Elizabeth, and Mika Pantzar. "Consumers, Producers and Practices: Understanding the Invention and Reinvention of Nordic Walking." *Journal of Consumer Culture* 5, no. 1 (2005): 43–64.

Soderstrom, Mary. *The Walkable City: From Haussmann's Boulevards to Jane Jacobs Streets and Beyond*. Montréal: Véhicule Press, 2008.

Taillefer, Michel. *Nouvelle histoire de Toulouse*. Toulouse: Privat, 2002.

Union des Transports Publics Urbains et Régionaux (UTPUR). *Les transports collectifs et la ville*. Paris: Celse, 1969.

Whyte, William. *The Social Life of Small Urban Spaces*. Washington, DC: The Conservation Foundation, 1980.

# CHAPTER 6

◔◕

# Recovering Sustainable Mobility Practices
## A Visual History of Turku's Streetscape 1950–1980

Tiina Männistö-Funk

## Introduction

Data and sustainability are closely linked issues. Often, large technological systems producing unsustainable outcomes also produce socially unequal power relations.[1] Such power inequalities contribute to producing biased data. After all, institutions that exploit most resources—and often cause most harm—also leave the most visible traces, readily available for historians to study. One such case is urban mobility. Motorization, car-centered traffic planning, and the marginalization of non-motorized modes have been historically linked to the inequality between powerful networks and institutions, and the less powerful, less visible groups that often bear the brunt of unsustainable systems.[2] In the past century or so, powerful elites involved in urban mobility have produced statistics and data sets that document motorized modes and leave non-motorized modes in the shadow—even though these represent the large majority who depend on such modes for their daily lives.

This chapter sheds light on the long history of underrepresented mobility groups. It shows how historical analysis helps us to understand the relationship between data, power, and sustainability. Along with my methodological contribution to this analysis, I introduce visual tools for quantifying and analyzing urban mobility. As I argue, the use of photographs can recover information about the more sustainable mobility practices—walking and cycling—that are rarely visible in most statistical and written data. Photographs provide another framework: they fix things in time and space, and allow for new interpretations. I have studied the empirical case of the Finnish city Turku between the 1950s and the 1970s, using visual sources to compare them with the available statistics and to concentrate on the geographical distribution of different modes of mobility. My method can be compared with the statistical analysis of visual sources that Cochoy, Canu, and Calvignac describe in their chapter. These are all ideas and models for different quantitative uses of pictures as sources.

Based on the patterns revealed in the visual analysis, I discuss the way in which gender, age, and socioeconomic background shape issues of social and environmental sustainability. The first section starts by discussing the possibilities that visual data offers. The second section compares findings based on visual data with existing statistical data, and the third section outlines the changes in mobility seen in the visual data. Based on these findings, the fourth section reflects on the connections between social and environmental unsustainability.

In recent years, there has been growing interest in the embodied and practical aspects of everyday mobility. Unlike earlier transport studies, such scholarship has studied urban cyclists' and pedestrians' social practices from a cultural perspective. Such studies have been closely aligned with the multidisciplinary "new mobilities paradigm," which highlights social and spatial questions such as power and identity.[3] These studies are often based on ethnographic observations. Using cultural geography, they highlight the meanings of places, for example, or employ Henri Lefebvre's notion of rhythms.[4]

The paradox of historical research is that common activities of everyday life in the past are often the most difficult activities to study. Daily practices—while omnipresent—tend to leave few researchable traces. Historian David Edgerton has proposed a history of technology-in-use that would make "a whole invisible world of technologies" visible. Such an approach leads to "a rethinking of our notion of technological time, mapped as it is on innovation-based timelines."[5] In the history of mobility, such an alternative perspective of mobility practices can challenge, problematize, and complement the picture presented by the statistical modal split as we now know it. It might also show that the most common modes in use are also the most overlooked and persistent—especially in the case of walking.

Everyday cycling and walking are only marginally visible in written sources and archival materials. Bicycle historian Nicholas Oddy has remarked that as cycling ceased to be a fashionable upper-class hobby in the late nineteenth century, and became a mundane, anonymous activity, it also no longer left a paper trail.[6] Through alternative sources, recent cycling historians have increased our knowledge of urban cycling in the period between 1900 and 1970s to fill this gap.[7] The historical research on pedestrians is even more dismal. Pedestrians' activities usually only appear in written historical sources in relation to complaints, except for the fashionably strolling late-nineteenth century flaneurs, who are overrepresented in the historiography of walking.[8] While we still know relatively little about the most common cycling practices in the past compared to automobility, we know even less about pedestrians, who have dominated our urban pasts. Together with Colin Pooley's chapter, in which he studies past pedestrian practices through diaries, we demonstrate that recovering those practices is not only possible, but also informs the present quest for more sustainable mobility practices in an important way.

## Visual Sources to Study Past Everyday Mobility

My experience with visual sources of past urban mobilities comes from a project studying the history of the street space and mobility in the city of Turku—one of Finland's largest cities.[9] Turku, situated at the mouth of the Aura River on Finland's west coast, has a compact city center with a grid plan of some six square kilometers.[10] I have studied a hundred years of the city's traffic history, using the source material of photographic street views from the photograph archive of the Turku Museum Centre. The archive holds a collection of over a million photographs, negatives, and slides depicting Turku, ranging from the oldest photograph taken in Finland in 1842 to present-day photographs. For my research, I analyzed all the street views in the grid-plan area, either with a street in the background/foreground or as the main subject, and at least one vehicle or person in the street. These criteria generated over 3,500 photographs. The majority of these, just under 3,000 photographs, date from the 1950s to the early 1980s, the time frame of this chapter.

The selected photographs were taken by a multitude of photographers for a number of reasons, ranging from artistic and journalistic to personal and documentary. More often than not, their main purpose was something other than documenting traffic. Intended subjects were mostly bringing into focus specific buildings or general scenes and views of the city. A section of the pictures, especially in the 1950s and the 1960s, was taken by the museum employees to document buildings that were to be demolished. Photographs taken for newspapers and books are also included, as well as photographic collections of associations and city departments—for example, the department responsible for urban infrastructure. While mainly aiming to document a different subject entirely, many of these photographs show a stretch of one or several streets with people and vehicles moving or standing in them. I therefore consider them as sources of past mobilities. However, using photographs as sources requires special care.

Photographs are often seen as problematic sources: they are subjective pictures with a limited scope and focus, shaped by the conventions, practices, and interests of their time.[11] At the same time, they can appear very seductive, seeming to open a window to the past.[12] The seductiveness can be traced to the indexical nature of photography. This is the special relationship between the subject and the picture, where the former imprints itself on the latter. Despite this technical indexicality, a photograph cannot directly explain the meaning of its subject.[13] In his handbook on photographs as sources for historians, German historian Jens Jäger points out the danger of only seeing in photographs what we already know.[14] This problem arises when we look at both present-day pictures and historical photography. In the latter case, the material and cultural context needed to analyze photographic information calls for a large body of knowledge about the place, time, and culture in which the photograph was initially produced. This is in line with the contextualizing approach that photographic research has taken since the 1990s.[15] The necessary context is often seen as a compilation of literature and written sources. In the case of large photographic collections like the one I have used in my study, photographs themselves can add to the contextual understanding of certain features of the street space and their changes over time. Such features include the amount of space, as well as the number, actions, and diversity of various street-users, types of materials, and objects in the space.

Contextual information is also necessary to determine the documentary value of a photograph. Economic, aesthetic, and personal motivations, as well as the intended use of a picture, always influence its documentary qualities—and thus the ways it can serve as a historical source.[16] The time of year and day a photograph is taken, along with the photographic technology and visual conventions of the culture and era, have greatly influenced the scenes captured by any photographer. For example, there was an overrepresentation of summer pictures in the photographic collection I analyzed. Also, the purpose of photographing and the choices made by the photographer regarding the cropping and focus of the picture quite crucially limit and steer the things shown in the resulting photograph. In many cases, the presence of a photographer might also have affected the things and persons we see in the photograph. Actual staging appears to have been quite rare in the case of street photographs. Nevertheless, it is likely that when taking pictures of certain buildings, the photographer might have either waited until there were no pedestrians in the picture or, equally, waited for someone to come into the picture. Even the most unremarkable shots are products of a string of decisions that affect their content.

Photographic research—historical and otherwise—has often focused on the activity, point-of-view, and motivation of the photographer as a historical participant in cultural production, or in photographs as part of a cultural imagery of certain topics.[17] This perspective is not especially valuable when using photographs to gain insight into mundane everyday practices, as these are seldom the main topic of photographs, even snapshots.[18] It is exactly these mundane practices that I seek in my source material, to study the history of pedestrian and cyclist mobility in Turku. I argue that my research was possible thanks to the unintended and technically original material revealed in many photographs. The famous cultural critic Walter Benjamin coined the term "optical unconscious" to describe how a camera sees the world differently from a human eye and can thus show even the most common phenomena in a new way, or highlight such phenomena that are otherwise too unremarkable, quick, or scattered to be observed.[19] In mobility research, for example, the amount and patterns of pedestrian mobility can be such scattered phenomena, often deemed too unremarkable to observe or document.

On the other hand, photographs have the apparent drawback of being immobile, only showing one frozen moment in time, making it impossible to study, for example, the speed of different street-users or their style of movement. Especially the late nineteenth-century technological solutions for photography were still too slow to capture fast-moving objects sharply, or at all, and the same is even true with some twentieth-century photography, although to a lesser degree. In many photographs of Turku before the 1950s, fast-moving cars and cyclists, sometimes even the fastest pedestrians, appear only as a blur. In contrast, since the late 1960s, especially journalistic and documentary photographs of Turku's streets have been taken to emphasize the new phenomenon of mass-motorization and capture dynamic pictures of car traffic.

The methodology for studying everyday activities from visual sources comes more from anthropology and archaeology than from classical historical research. In their contribution to this volume as elsewhere, Franck Cochoy and his coauthors have used photographs of streetscapes in Gothenburg and Toulouse to code and quantify the changes in pedestrian habits of carrying, their accessories, and their physical practices—what they call pedestrian logistics.[20] This chapter provides a more multimodal slant, including the geographical dispersion and social inequality of mobility. However, my approach to visual sources is similar to Cochoy and coauthors. Like them, I argue that even though the relationship between pictures and reality is complicated and open to discussion, photographs can be extremely useful in the way they freeze physical and material details, often as unintended content. The photographs never show the entire "truth" of the past, nor give access to unbiased reality. In this they are similar to written sources: they cannot tell us all about "how it actually has been" because this knowledge is not attainable. However, some of the specifics of visual sources can be used not only to read things about the past that other kinds of sources might not contain, but also to see these things from diverse perspectives. Thousands of frozen moments of street life and traffic, captured for different reasons by different types of photographers, can significantly complement our perception of how urban mobility has changed, and, by showing the parallel changes in street space and the use of space by different modes, help us understand why it changed.

## Visual Sources Capture the Modal Split of the Moment

For my research, I mapped the various moving and parked vehicles visible in the photographs by time and place, creating point maps of different years or decades to discover quantitative and geographic patterns. As the number of photographs and also their locations vary from year to year, an absolute quantitative analysis was not possible. Fortunately, their large total number and distribution over a long period in a compact geographic area enabled me to analyze and compare the shares of different types of mobility at different times and also map popular routes or traffic nodes. In addition to vehicles, I also marked pedestrians on the point maps, where possible according to gender, based on the visual data.

The information gleaned from the visual sources can complement the statistics, but does not give the same kind of information as a modal split based on traffic counts. On the other hand, the changes in modal split based on traffic counts do not tell the whole story of the situation on the street. The individual picture sources allow us to study in great detail "the modal split of the moment"—in other words, the share of modes on a specific street at a given moment—plus the compilation of these splits at specific moments. Compared with more conventional modal split data, the pictures highlight the various modes' space, experience, and possibilities on the street. Examining the images in detail provides another opportunity to consider the difference between modes. For example, cars tend to be significantly larger, heavier, and noisier than cyclists and pedestrians, making the presence of one car a very different material phenomenon than that of one bicycle or pedestrian. Furthermore, although parked cars do not move, they still take up space on the street in a way that the modal split does not measure.

Individual street photographs not only show us what various urban areas looked like at different times and with different modal splits; they also allow us to analyze the situation, especially the slower modes. "The modal split of the moment" is more decisive for cyclists' and pedestrians' experience of a street than the modal split of an hour, a day, or a year, because the modes coexisting in the same space at any given moment affect each other's possibilities directly. Those who move under their own power are unprotected against sensory and physical influences and spend more time on the streets per covered distance than motorized street-users. Both these aspects make them more exposed to the influences of coexisting modes during the "modal split of the moment" when they are on the street.

French historian and literature scholar Michel de Certeau argues in his classic essay on everyday life that the essence of pedestrian practices cannot be studied by mapping pedestrian routes.[21] This might be true for cultural, social, and personal meanings, and the experiences of walking. Mapping pedestrianism and bicycle use can, however, complement the statistical data we have on historical and present-day traffic and mobility. We currently have very few statistics on the ratios of pedestrian and bicycle traffic in Turku historically. This is a typical situation. By the time traffic planning had emerged as an important individual field, integrating statistics and traffic counts by the 1950s and 1960s, cycling had long been labeled a dying mode that did not call for special attention.[22] Thus in Finland, like elsewhere, many traffic counts were not designed to inform about cycling.[23] Traffic planners' aim worldwide became to shape cities into car-cities. Their mantra was efficiency, measured in terms of passenger cars.[24] The leading urban planning principle of high-modernist efficiency is perhaps best symbolized by Le Corbusier's *The Radiant City*, published in 1933. While he was not the inventor of car flows, he visually celebrated the free flow of traffic and promoted a functional segregation. The traditional multipurpose city streets needed to be cleared for motorized traffic.[25] Though cyclists dominated in many European streets at the time, modernist planning often ignored cycling altogether. It also aimed to minimize walking, making it as efficient as possible, for example by planning short distances to parking lots and bus stops or using technical devices like lifts and, to a lesser extent, moving walkways.[26]

In planning and related data collection, the focus was directed overwhelmingly toward motorized modes. After World War II, European traffic planning was generally more diverse than its American equivalent, as many of Europe's historic city centers restricted the growth potential for car traffic.[27] In the interwar period, Finnish road planners had taken influences from Nordic countries and central and southern Europe, but just before the war they began going on study trips also to the United States.[28] Like their European colleagues, Finnish postwar planners were heavily influenced by the American traffic-planning models that prioritized automobility and sought to facilitate high-volume car traffic corridors also in the city centers.[29] The most prominent Finnish example of car-city planning was the 1968 Smith-Polvinen plan that would have brought a massive network of highways into downtown Helsinki.[30] Between its commissioning in 1965 and release in 1968, the negative effects of motorized traffic had become part of the public discussion. The extremely car-centered solutions suggested by the plan raised immediate negative reactions and made it later into a symbol of the whole modernist city planning in Finland, even though they were never carried out to the extent suggested.[31] The plan brings also the general neglect of nonmotorized modes into view, describing car traffic and public transit in great detail, but only mentioning pedestrians twice: once as a factor disturbing motorized traffic and once in a modal split of commuter transportation.[32] Similar tendencies were present in other, less dramatic, city and traffic plans of the 1950s and 1960s, leading to limited knowledge about nonmotorized modes or ignoring information that concerned them, as can be seen in the case of Turku discussed below.

The city of Turku has not organized systematic traffic counts, instead implementing ad hoc counts only for specific planning purposes. My research covers a period of a hundred years, and I came across only two traffic counts in the grid-plan area that included data on pedestrians and cycling. For the city and traffic plan published in 1952, a traffic count was undertaken on two days in September 1948 on one of the bridges that crosses the river in the city center (the bridge is shown in figure 6.1). On one day, approximately 16,000 pedestrians, 7,600 cyclists, and 5,500 cars crossed the bridge. The cars include trucks, which accounted for over half the total number of cars.[33] Thus the bicycle to passenger car ratio on the bridge was around 3:1. For the 1984 traffic plan, a traffic count was carried out in the summer of 1981. It showed 3,700 to 3,900 individual cyclists per day on the busiest bridges over the Aura River in the city center, with bicycle traffic accounting for some 10 percent of the motorized traffic there. The most popular bridge for cyclists was also the most popular one for pedestrians, whose numbers in 1983 reached 2,800–3,300 individuals per hour on the busiest sidewalks near the market square.[34]

In the thirty-three years between the traffic counts, the number of pedestrians remained roughly the same, and the number of cyclists dropped by half, but car traffic increased to seven times the 1948 volume. At the same time, the city's population increased steadily. In the 1940s, Turku already had 35,000 inhabitants, rising to 100,000 in 1950. The growth continued rapidly, as Finland transformed from a predominantly agrarian to a modern urban society. By 1975, the total population of Turku surpassed 160,000. After that, growth stagnated for two decades until a new surge in the late 1990s brought Turku's present-day population to almost 190,000.

The three decades between the traffic counts were also a period of drastic material changes in the heart of Turku. The 1952 plan for a motorized, decentralized city led to an era of frantic demolition and building activity to create broader streets in the historic grid-plan area for free-flowing motor traffic and car parking. Between the late 1950s and the early 1970s, almost two-thirds of the buildings in the city center were demolished and replaced, mostly with blocks of flats.[35] Part of the decentralization plan was building new housing areas further from the center. Although the housing development was now spread over a large area, the envisioned decentralization of the city's other services did not follow suit, leaving its residents' everyday destinations in the city separated by much greater distances than before.[36]

There are no statistics on cycling for this era, but sales of bicycles started to drop by the late 1950s in the whole country, and continued until reaching the lowest point in 1964.[37] From other European cities we know that cycling's modal share declined in many cities since the 1950s, and continued until the early 1970s, when it leveled out. Although there were some local variations in when the decline started, the general trend was the same.[38] Between the years 1952 and 1975, personal consumption doubled in Finland. Yet the government restricted automobility because of postwar import restrictions that lasted until 1962.[39] In 1955, only one-tenth of the Finnish population could have been seated in all the passenger cars in Finland, assuming a five-seater car. By 1965, after the government rescinded the import restrictions, half of the Finns could have been seated in cars, and by 1974, the entire population.[40] As in many European cities, the lobby and plans to transform Turku into a car-dominated city started well before widespread motorization, notably with the 1952 city plan.

Thus we can see that the cars' share increased strongly while the bicycles' share diminished; but exactly when and how quickly? Was the increase in the number of cars seven-fold, like the traffic counts in 1948 and 1981 suggest, or something else if more streets than one or two bridges are taken into account? Does the overall picture change in any way when the undeniably meager statistical data is compared with the information from visual data?

The street Aninkaistenkatu, leading to the bridge where the 1948 traffic count was carried out, is one of the busiest streets for car traffic in the photographs, during all the decades studied. In the 1950s and 1960s still a busy cycle route, it no longer shows any cyclists in the 1970s photographs. On this street, the visual data indicates in the 1950s a similar 3:1 ratio of bicycles to cars as in the 1948 count. A similar ratio is hard to find in the visual data of any other street. On almost all the other streets in the grid-plan area, bicycles outnumber cars to a remarkably high degree throughout the 1950s (see map 6.1). This illustrates how the modal split counted from one or a few points in the city can give a remarkably biased picture of the modal split in the city as a whole.

Olavi Laisaari, the architect of the 1952 city plan and organizer of the 1948 count, was a city and traffic planner who followed functionalist principles and was heavily influenced by the American car-city ideals.[41] Laisaari was obviously well acquainted with the traffic situation in Turku. For example, his knowledge of busy cycle routes matches the information I was able to extract from the visual sources.[42] He undoubtedly knew that the point he chose for the 1948 traffic count was one of the most motorized in the city. And even there, as map 6.1 and his own traffic count show, the share of motorized traffic was far too low to justify planning a car city. Instead, he used the statistic as a starting point to forecast the anticipated growth of car traffic in the coming years. This forecasting, rather than the statistics, motivated Laisaari's work on the car-city plans.[43] The data provided by visual sources questions our current overview of past mobilities and modal shifts based on statistical traffic count data. The seven-fold increase in the number of cars can be valid at one specific point in the city, but not representative of the city's mobility as a whole. The increase could have been lower or higher at other counting points.

## Visual Sources Show Changes in Mobility

How was the change in mobility actually manifested on the streets? The information provided by the visual sources differs from that of the statistical sources. For example, the street photographs show that cars still had a low presence on most streets in 1950s Turku. Despite a remarkable number of cars in the city and their growing share, they did not dominate the street space. Thus the situation on the street had not

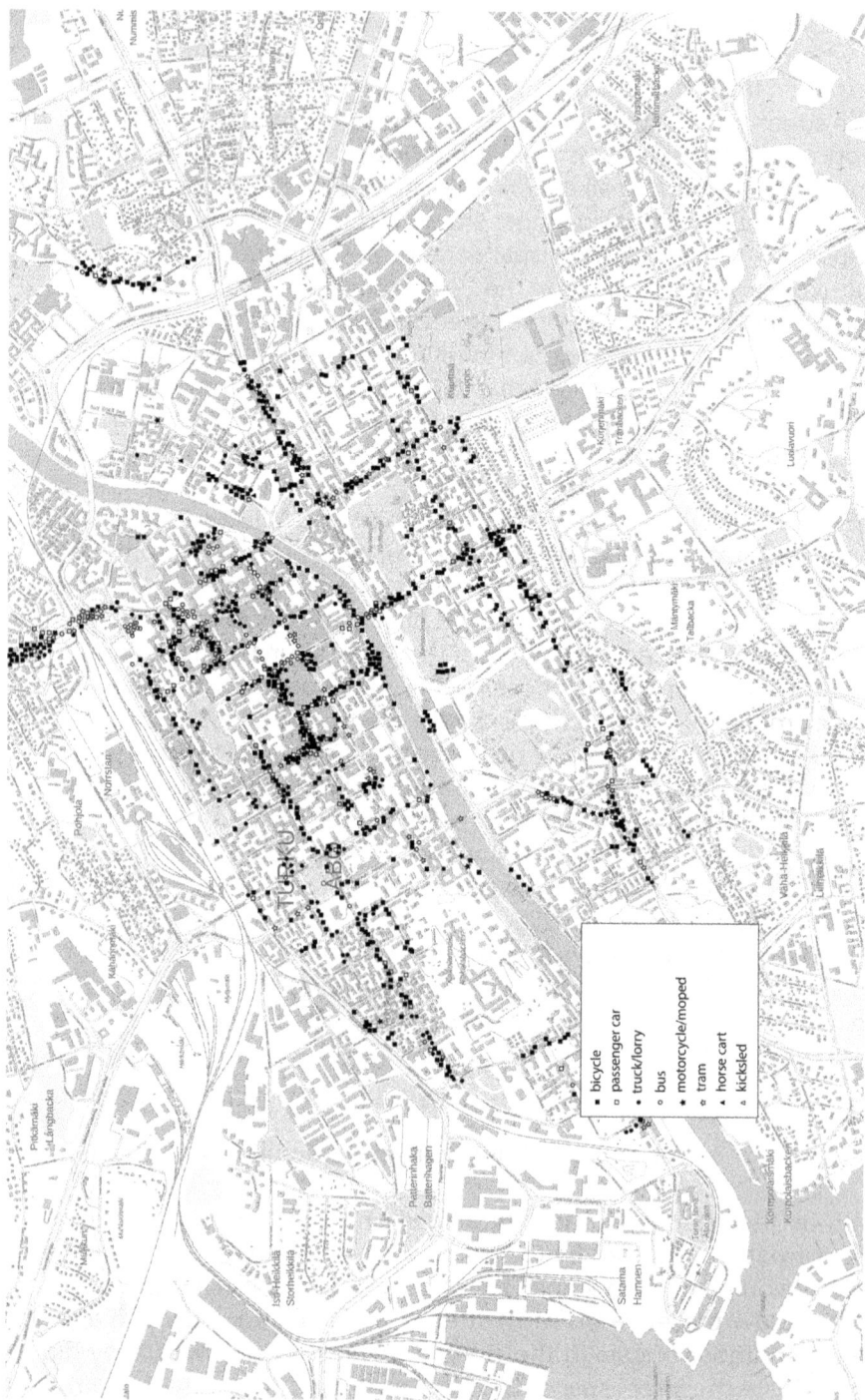

**Map 6.1.** Moving vehicles in the 1950s photographs marked on the dot map. The Tuomiokirkkosilta Bridge is the rightmost bridge with traffic, and Aninkaistenkatu is the street leading north from it. Notice how bicycles greatly outnumber motor vehicles in all but a few locations.

Map: Tiina Männistö-Funk.

**Figure 6.1.** The bridge Tuomiokirkkosilta, where the 1948 traffic count was held, shows an interesting modal split in the first half of the 1960s (precise year unknown), on the brink of large-scale motorization and decline of cycling. In this picture, the split of the moment is approximately 50 percent pedestrians, 24 percent bicycles, 20 percent cars, and 6 percent motorbikes. Cars, even as a minority in the split, already dominate the space, but cyclists still have a relatively large spatial presence.
Photo: Hans Othman, Photograph Archive of Turku Museum Centre.

dramatically changed for cyclists and pedestrians compared with the 1920s and 1930s street views. My observations are based on the geographical distribution maps I prepared, using the data from the visual sources, some of which are shown as references. The nature of the data does not enable the same kind of comparison of absolute numbers as statistical data. This is why I am looking at relative trends and changes in the relationships of the modes as well as their geographical distribution.

In the 1960s, nonmotorized modes still outnumber the motorized modes in the visual sources on every street in the city center. This changed quite abruptly in the 1970s, raising the question whether it is possible to identify a threshold after which motorization takes over and starts seriously affecting and reducing other modes through its sheer physical presence. The number of pedestrians remains relatively constant—and large—over the entire hundred-year period I studied. In street-view photographs, pedestrians form the biggest group of street-users throughout the decades. However, their possibilities and position in the streets undergo several changes. Despite their increasing or constant numbers, pedestrians are physically marginalized by other road-user groups who, although fewer in number, claim bigger parts of the street space. At the same time, pedestrians' ability to have direct communication and contact with the other groups of street-users diminishes. Stopping, lingering, and chatting become increasingly more difficult for all modes.

According to the photographic sources, the growth in number of parked cars in the city center predates any real increase in moving cars. In the early and mid-1950s, two main groups of vehicles are visible in the street photographs of Turku city center: parked cars and moving bicycles. The number of parked cars is approximately 25 percent more than the number of moving bicycles in the photographs. Both significantly outnumber all the other vehicle groups. There are nine times more moving bicycles visible than moving passenger cars, which is over 50 percent more than all the other moving vehicles combined, spread evenly over the whole grid-plan area. Parked cars visible in the photographs are heavily concentrated in the inner city, surrounding the main market square. Over the following decades, the number of parked cars grows steadily, remaining the largest group of vehicles on the street until the end of the research period in the 1980s. If we add pedestrians to the equation, from the 1950s, the two groups of street-users that dominate the visual data are pedestrians and parked cars. In the 1950s, the third largest group is cyclists; while in the 1970s, moving cars.

In the decades preceding World War II, there is no remarkable difference in the number of women and men pedestrians in the street photographs, possibly due to the fact that the available photographs from these decades concentrate on the inner city and the river banks. There are more photographs of the outer grid-plan area in the 1950s (see map 6.4) and 1960s, which show a dominance of women pedestrians. In all the outer grid-plan streets photographed more than once, women pedestrians outnumber men. On many streets, two-thirds of the pedestrians are women; on some streets, three-quarters. The numbers are more uniform in the city center, but the situation changes in the 1970s, when women pedestrians start to outnumber men there.

There are few photographs of the 1940s, probably due to photographic materials being in short supply in Finland during and after World War II. The visual data available does, however, suggest that the share of bicycles in Turku grew from the 1940s until the 1950s and only diminished after that. The number of bicycles in the whole country—one of very few statistics related to cycling available for this period—is estimated to have decreased by half during the war, but rose quite quickly again afterward. Estimated numbers of bicycles in Finland in 1944 were around 250,000 and in 1952 between 700,000 and one million bicycles in total, the national population being four million.[44]

By the late 1950s, bicycles still outnumber passenger cars in the photographs nine-fold, (see map 6.1). The photographs show an even situation in the first half of the 1960s, with the amount of moving passenger cars slightly larger than moving bicycles. In the second half of the 1960s, we see a three-fold number of moving cars compared to moving bicycles, and by the first half of the 1970s, this is already almost twenty-fold, as shown in maps 6.2 and 6.3. According to the photographic data, this modal shift transforming bicycles from the most common mode to a marginalized mode happened in less than fifteen years. During this time, the demography of cycling also changed: whereas most cyclists in the 1950s were young or middle-aged men, the cyclists in the 1970s photographs are for the most part women, children, and older men.

Although the general motorization trend is clear, visual data also demonstrates remarkable differences in modal splits of the moment and overall traffic between different streets. Until the 1960s, most car traffic was concentrated in a few streets in the city center (see maps 6.1 and 6.2). Bicycle traffic is also concentrated in specific streets and areas but more evenly spread, (see especially map 6.1). Numbers of pedestrians are highest in the inner city, but they can be seen everywhere—the mode of mobility that can be detected even if no other modes are in the picture.

Lastly, one significant change that can be detected and analyzed by using the photographic sources is the way in which streets and different modes' potential mobility routes change during the three decades of rapid motorization. When we shift the focus of analysis from mapped data to qualitative analysis of the street views, we notice that even during the first half of the 1960s, with a varied modal split and large share of cyclists, the busiest streets already show a very car-dominated street space in the frozen moments of the photographs, as in figure 6.1. In addition to moving cars, parked cars fill streets and affect the mobility

Legend:
- bicycle
- passenger car
- truck/lorry
- bus
- motorcycle/moped
- tram
- horse cart
- kicksled

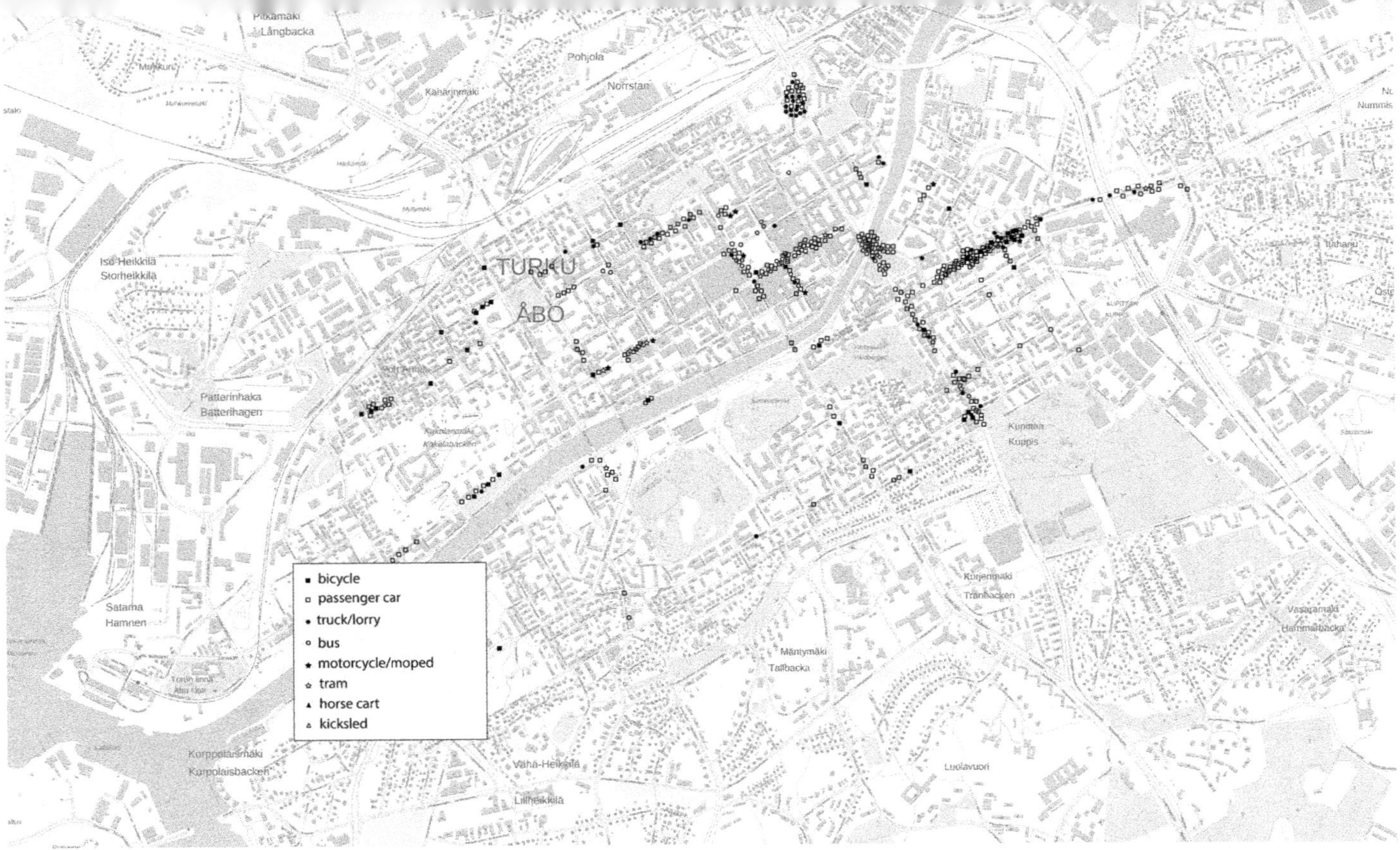

**Maps 6.2 and 6.3.** Moving vehicles in 1960s (map 6.2, *left*) and 1970s (map 6.3, *right*) photographs on dot maps. Comparing these maps, also with map 6.1, we see that the differing number and geographic locations of photographs over the decades make it impossible to draw a direct numerical comparison. However, we can analyze the shifting modal relations and the changes occurring in different locations. In the 1970s (map 6.3), we see the earlier busy bicycle node of Tuomiokirkkosilta bridge dominated by motorized modes. Hämeenkatu street (the street with a lot of traffic in map 6.3, leading out of the center on the right) still shows bicycle traffic but has also been turned into a motorized traffic corridor.

Map: Tiina Männistö-Funk.

Legend:
- bicycle
- passenger car
- truck/lorry
- bus
- motorcycle/moped
- tram
- horse cart
- kicksled

of all groups. However, until the 1970s, there is not one photograph in thousands where the amount of motorized modes on the street exceeds that of nonmotorized mobility, including pedestrians. Most streets out-side the inner city and a few other busy streets are also remarkably quiet and remain that way even in the 1970s and 1980s. What changes is that after the 1960s, policymakers had transformed the city center and most popular traffic routes into car-centered streetscapes that left little space and freedom for cyclists and pedestrians.

## The Social Patterns of (Un)Sustainability

As mobility sociologist Karel Martens pointed out, the traditional ap-proach to transportation planning, although guided by a principle of equality, has nonetheless ended up generating vastly unequal possibil-ities for mobility.[45] The visual data demonstrates this even more clearly than the traffic count–based modal share. Large-scale motorization that was supported and facilitated by the car-city planners ignored nonmo-torized modes; it directly or indirectly harmed them and reduced their possibilities by creating traffic environments that were difficult, uninvit-ing, and dangerous. The gender perspective reveals that women were the majority of pedestrians and continued to walk even after the most rapid phase of motorization and reshaping of the city. The demographic perspective of cycling shows working-age men abandoning cycling, leaving it to older people, children, and women. Based on American cases, we know that the car-city planners of this era sought to antici-pate and accommodate automobility, building decentralized cities and reshaping city centers to be more car-friendly, thereby masking class and ethnic biases in their statistics. Policymakers rarely discussed these aspects.[46] The analysis of visual sources shows that gender was equally hidden and ignored, although some contemporary commentators did try to bring these socioeconomic issues to the table.

In response, and following the international trend for new sociopolit-ical and environmental associations, the Finns set up Enemmistö ry (the Majority), a car-critical traffic policy association in 1968. It published ar-ticles blaming the car-city planners of concentrating only on the needs of the wealthy and healthy middle-aged men, ignoring all other groups. The association members argued that the majority of the population could not rely on the car for their everyday mobility, namely under-age children, elderly people, people with functional limitations, most women in one-car households, and people whose socioeconomic situ-ation did not allow car ownership. For these groups, the new decentral-ized city structure was not beneficial.[47]

In the 1980s, feminist groups of urban planners and transport researchers in northern and western Europe turned the spotlight on how city structure and transport systems, although perceived as neutral, were based on the needs and experiences of one social group: men. In their view, transport planners required more information about the needs of women in order to adapt accordingly.[48] Rather than trying to make women adopt the "male" mobility patterns of long trips by car, as the traffic plans and land use in cities urged them to do, such groups argued for the possibility of men adopting more "female" patterns. This meant shorter trips and greater use of bicycles, public transit, and walking, if the city structure was densified instead of decentralized.[49] Theorists in feminist planning have continued to argue that women's experiences are not taken seriously in planning or are handled as special interest, whereas the male perspective has a neutral and unproblematized status.[50] In recent years, the climate crisis has again made the female mobility patterns interesting as possible solutions and models in reaching climate sustainability targets.[51]

In the twentieth-first century, women worldwide are less mobile than men, make shorter trips, use fewer passenger cars on their trips, and walk more. Gender differences persist even though the proportion of men and women in the workforce has become nearly equal. Women experience more constraints and less accessibility in their mobility compared to men.[52] Susan Hanson has pointed out that from the perspective of environmental sustainability, this lesser mobility of women cannot be ignored; nor can men's mobility patterns be seen as desirable goals for personal mobility. However, she also stresses the need to address the equality of access, as not nearly enough is known about the issues where gender and mobility converge.[53] The visual data analysis demonstrates clearly how gender-related differences in mobility during the rise and breakthrough of the car-city are interlinked with socially and environmentally sustainable mobility issues. The characteristic mobility patterns of women's many short walking trips around residential areas were ignored and erased by the decentralized car-city planning, which favored long-distance motorized mobility. Women continued to walk and became the largest group of pedestrians everywhere in the grid-plan area, but they could no longer rely solely on walking. In 1960s photographs, a large number of people, especially women with their children and bags, can be seen waiting for the buses that departed from the main market square and brought people to and from the newly established suburbs. These bus stops became new congestion spots for pedestrians in the city center.[54]

Gender as social category is also closely connected to other issues of social equality. Many streets where women pedestrians dominated in the 1950s were in the areas with wooden houses, which were home to the working class and lower-middle classes. These areas also had the most cyclists. The streets leading from the old working-class suburbs just outside the grid-plan area to the center also show a high density of bicycles. These very streets were remodeled into car-traffic corridors after the 1960s.[55] The traffic planning that enabled and boosted large-scale motorization created environmental unsustainability based on socially unsustainable mobility models.

The social sustainability in mobility often seems to contradict the environmental sustainability if motorized patterns for men are seen as the gauge for socially desirable mobility. On the other hand, mobility, gender, and socioeconomic class are not rigid but co-constructed. Thus, environmentally sustainable mobility could act as a catalyst for change, also socially, and vice versa.[56] As Mimi Sheller has pointed out, a combination of social and environmental sustainability is a prerequisite for moving away from a system based on personal motorized mobility.[57] My historical analysis has highlighted how the whole motorized system of urban mobility glossed over socioeconomic and gender inequalities in its planning, and at the same time made them integral features of the system. As the two factors are co-constructed, changes in one affect the other, and this codependency should be carefully considered in planning and policy.

## Conclusions

Using historical street photographs to study pedestrian and cyclist mobility heightens our understanding of the developments that have led to present-day urban mobility situations. Maps based on visual data as well as individual photographs can be used to scrutinize groups that were not on car-city planners' radar, and to question the historical power-relations of urban mobility. Visual analysis highlights how mobility solutions based on personal motorization have been socially unequal, producing both socially and environmentally unsustainable results. It also helps us to become better aware of the environmentally most sustainable modes in the geographical and spatial locations of specific cities.

To address the issue of environmental sustainability in urban mobility, we need to consider social and gender perspectives. When studying these topics and promoting sustainability, it is important to bear in mind that systems producing unsustainable mobility at the same time produce biased information on the mobility of different groups and modes. For example, mapping cyclists and pedestrians according to their gen-

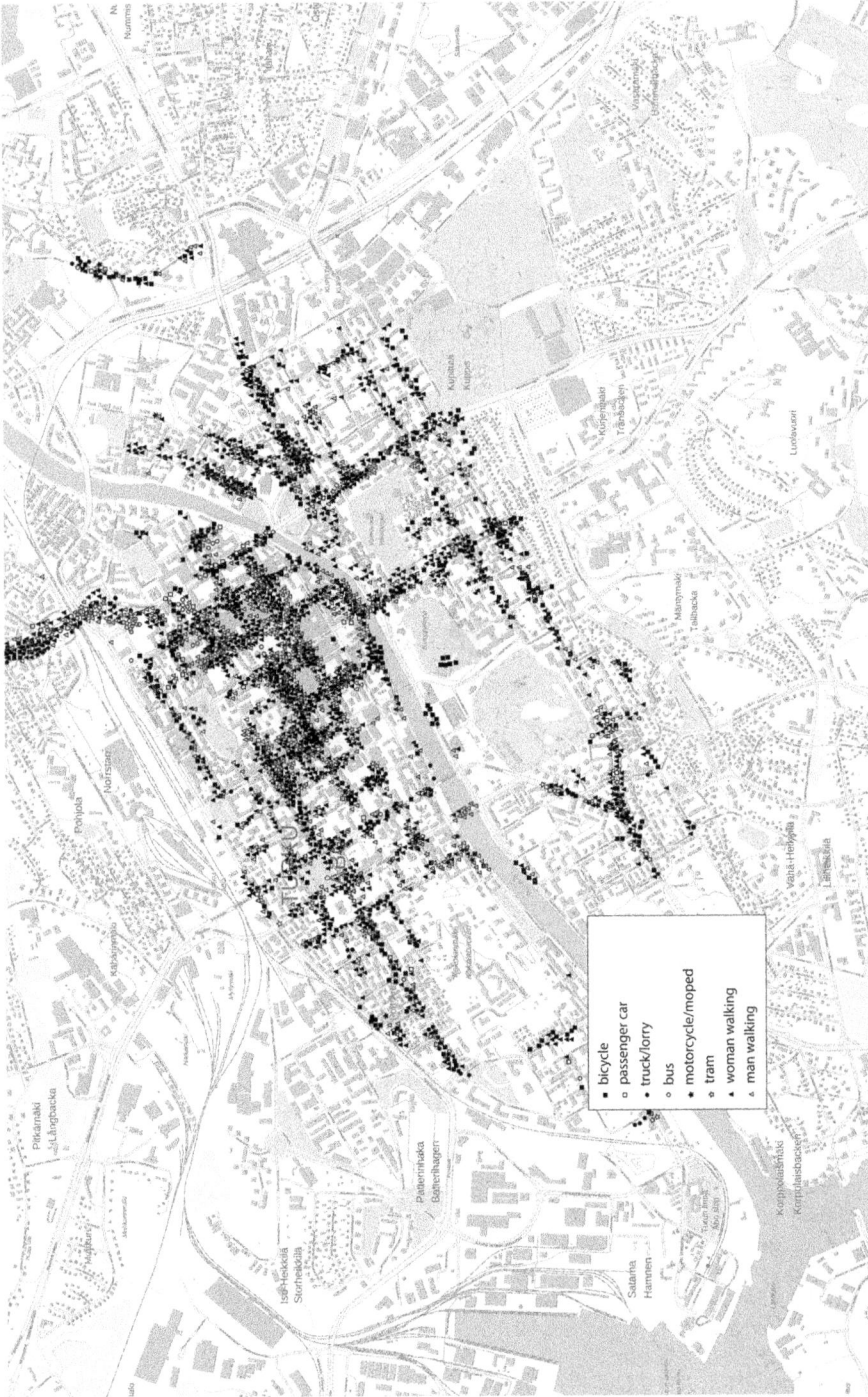

**Map 6.4.** Pedestrians and moving vehicles from the 1950s photographs on a dot map. Notice, for example, the Hämeenkatu street, leading out of the grid-plan area on the right, dominated by female pedestrians and bicycles. Map: Tiina Männistö-Funk.

der might help to plan infrastructures that promote accessibility to all groups and thereby encourage the most sustainable patterns, rather than ignore and erase them.

**Tiina Männistö-Funk**, Ph.D., researcher at Chalmers University of Technology, Sweden, is an adjunct professor at University of Turku, Finland. She is a historian of technology and specializes in user practices, material culture, and gender analysis. She has published several articles on cycling history and edited the book *Invisible Bicycle: Parallel Histories and Different Timelines* (Brill, 2019).

## Notes

1. For cases on a global level, see Michael Redclift and Colin Sage, "Global Environmental Change and Global Inequality: North/South Perspectives," *International Sociology* 13, no. 4 (1998): 499–516. For the link between socioeconomic status and the negative effects of noise and air pollution in urban areas, see *Links between Noise and Air Pollution and Socioeconomic Status*, Science for Environment Policy, In-depth Report 13 (European Commission, DG Environment by the Science Communication Unit, UWE, Bristol, 2016), Accessed 26 September 2018, http://ec.europa.eu/science-environment-policy.
2. See, for example, Peter Cox, "'A Denial of Our Boasted Civilisation': Cyclists' Views on Conflicts over Road Use in Britain, 1926–1935," *Transfers: Interdisciplinary Journal of Mobility Studies* 2 (2012): 4–30; Peter D. Norton, *Fighting Traffic: The Dawn of the Motor Age in the American City* (Cambridge, MA: MIT Press, 2008).
3. Mimi Sheller, "The New Mobilities Paradigm for a Live Sociology," *Current Sociology Review* 62, no. 6 (2014): 789–811; Tim Cresswell and Peter Merriman, "Introduction: Geographies of Mobilities—Practices, Spaces, Subjects," in *Geographies of Mobilities: Practices, Spaces, Subjects*, ed. Tim Cresswell & Peter Merriman (Aldershot: Ashgate, 2011): 5–19; Jennie Middleton, "Walking in the City: The Geographies of Everyday Pedestrian Practices," *Geography Compass* 5, no. 2 (2011): 90–105.
4. See for example Jennie Middleton, "Stepping in time: Walking, time, and space in the city," *Environment and Planning A* 41, no. 8 (2009): 1943–1961; Justin Spinney, "Cycling the City: Non-Place and the Sensory Construction of Meaning in a Mobile Practice," in *Cycling & Society*, ed. Dave Horton, Paul Rosen, and Peter Cox (Aldershot: Ashgate, 2007), 25–46; Jo Vergunst, "Rhythms of Walking: History and Presence in a City Street," *Space and Culture* 13, no. 4 (2010): 376–88.
5. David Edgerton, *The Shock of the Old: Technology and Global History since 1900* (London: Profile Books, 2006), xi.
6. Nicholas Oddy, "Cycling's Dark Age? The Period 1900–1920 in Cycling History," in *Cycle History 15: Proceedings of the 15th International Cycling History Conference*, ed. Rob van der Plas (San Francisco: Van der Plas Publications/Cycle Publishing, 2005) 79–86. For more detailed cycling related sources, see Ellen

Garvey, "Reframing the Bicycle: Advertising-Supported Magazines and Scorching Women," *American Quarterly* 47 (1994): 66–101.

7. See Ruth Oldenziel, Martin Emanuel, Adri Albert de la Bruhèze, and Frank Veraart, eds., *Cycling Cities: The European Experience. One Hundred Years of Policy and Practice* (Eindhoven: Foundation for the History of Technology, 2016); Tiina Männistö-Funk and Timo Myllyntaus, eds., *Invisible Bicycle: Parallel Histories and Different Timelines* (Leiden: Brill, 2018).

8. Deirdre Heddon and Cathy Turner, "Walking Women: Shifting the Tales and Scales of Mobility," *Contemporary Theatre Review* 22, no. 2 (2012): 224–36. On pedestrians' complaints, see Norton, *Fighting Traffic*.

9. A small part of the argumentation and results in this paper regarding women and walking has been published in Finnish; see Tiina Männistö-Funk, "Kävelevien naisten kaupunki: Sata vuotta sukupuolta Turun kadulla," in *Kaupungin varjoissa, arkistojen valossa*, ed. Topi Artukka, Jarkko Keskinen, and Taina Saarenpää (Turku: Sigillum, 2018), 77–94.

10. Turku is Finland's oldest city and was the capital until the early nineteenth century. The grid plan was introduced when the city was rebuilt after a great fire almost totally destroyed it in 1827.

11. See, for example, John E. Carter, "The Trained Eye: Photographs and Historical Context," *Public Historian* 15 (1993): 55–66; John Tagg, *The Burden of Representation: Essays on Photographies and Histories* (Minneapolis: University of Minnesota Press, 1988).

12. Ludmilla Jordanova, *The Look of the Past. Visual and Material Evidence in Historical Practice* (Cambridge: Cambridge University Press, 2012), 130.

13. Philippe Dubois, "Trace-Image to Fiction-Image: The Unfolding of Theories of Photography from the '80s to the Present," *October Magazine* 158 (2016): 155–66.

14. Jens Jäger, *Bilder der Neuzeit: Einführung in die historische Bildforschung* (Tübingen: Edition Diskord, 2000), 11–13.

15. Derrick Price and Liz Wells, "Thinking about Photography: Debates, Historically and Now," in *Photography: A Critical Introduction*, ed. Liz Wells (London: Routledge, 1997), 9–63.

16. Hans-Jürgen Pandel, "Bildinterpretation: Zum Stand der geschichtsdidaktischen Bildinterpretation," in *Visualität und Geschichte*, ed. Saskia Handro and Bernd Schönemann (Berlin: LIT, 2011), 76.

17. Jens Jäger, *Fotografie und Geschichte* (Frankfurt am Main: Campus, 2009), 87.

18. Timm Starl, *Knipser: Die Bildgeschichte der privaten Fotografie in Deutschland und Österreich von 1880 bis 1980* (Munich: Koehler & Amelang, 1995), 144–147.

19. Walter Benjamin, "The Work of Art at the Age of Its Technical Reproducibility (Second Version)," in *The Work of Art at the Age of its Mechanical Reproducibility and Other Writings on Media*, ed. Michael W. Jennings et al. (Cambridge, MA: Harvard University Press, 2008), 37.

20. Franck Cochoy, Johan Hagberg, and Roland Canu, "The Forgotten Role of Pedestrian Transportation in Urban Life: Insights from a Visual Comparative Archaeology (Gothenburg and Toulouse, 1875–2011)," *Urban Studies* 52, no. 12 (2015): 2267–86.

21. Michel de Certeau, *The Practice of Everyday Life* (Berkeley: University of California Press, 1984), 91–110.

22. On the use of statistics and traffic counts in traffic planning, see Paul Barrett and Mark H. Rose, "Street Smarts: The Politics of Transportation Statistics in the

American City, 1900–1990," *Journal of Urban History* 25 (1999): 425; Johanna Kallioinen, *Pyöräilyn institutionaalinen asema liikennesuunnittelussa* (Helsinki: Valtion taloudellinen tutkimuskeskus, 2002), 64–66. On cycling as a dying mode, see Martin Emanuel, *Trafikslag på undantag: Cykeltrafiken i Stockholm 1930–1980* (Stockholm: Stockholmia förlag, 2012); Thomas Fläschner, "Stahlroß auf dem Aussterbe-Etat: Zur Geschichte des Fahrrades und seiner Verdrängung in den 50er Jahren," *Eckstein: Journal für Geschichte* no. 9 (2000): 4–22; Ruth Oldenziel and Mikael Hård, *Consumers, Tinkerers, Rebels: The People Who Shaped Europe* (Hampshire: Palgrave Macmillan, 2013), 152–61.

23. Kallioinen, *Pyöräilyn institutionaalinen*, 70.
24. Per Lundin, *Bilsamhället: Ideologi, expertis och regelskapande i efterkrigstidens Sverige* (Stockholm: Stockholmia förlag, 2008).
25. James C. Scot, *Seeing Like a State: How Certain Schemes to Improve the Human Condition Have Failed* (New Haven: Yale University Press, 1998), 103–11.
26. Johanna Hankonen, *Lähiöt ja tehokkuuden yhteiskunta: Suunnittelujärjestelmän läpimurto suomalaisten asuntoalueiden rakentumisessa 1960-luvulla* (Tampere: Otatieto Oy, Gaudeamus, 1994), 386.
27. See Oldenziel et al. in this volume.
28. Kimmo Antila and Marko Nenonen, "Relief Works, the World Bank and Private Business: Building Highways in Finland," *Scandinavian Economic History Review* 48, no. 2 (2000): 47–71, 50.
29. Johanna Kallioinen, *Pyöräilyn institutionaalinen*, 64–65.
30. Hankonen, *Lähiöt ja tehokkuuden yhteiskunta*.
31. Mauno Hänninen, "Tieverkkosuunnittelun alku," in *Pikeä, hikeä, autoja: Tiet, liikenne ja yhteiskunta 1945–2005*, ed. Jaakko Masonen and Mauno Hänninen (Helsinki: Tielaitos, 1995), 212–21.
32. Marjatta Rahikainen, *Helsingin keskusta Suomen taloudellisen kehityksen valossa* (Helsinki: Helsingin kaupungin kaupunkisuunnitteluvirasto, 1985), 80.
33. Olavi Laisaari, *Turun yleiskaava ja kaupungin kehittämisohjelma* (Turku: Turun kaupunki, 1952), 61–66.
34. Turun kaupunki, *Keskustan liikenteen vaihekaava* (Turku: Turun Viatek, 1984), 16–17.
35. Rauno Lahtinen, *Turun puretut talot*, 5th printing, 1st added edition (Turku: Sammakko, 2013).
36. Markus Kivistö, "Kasvava katu. Autoliikenne ja modernisaatio Turussa," in *Sata lasissa*, ed. Ismo Vähäkangas (Turku: Turun Historiallinen Yhdistys, 2000), 91–103.
37. Heikki Kuva, *Kaksipyöräisten vuosisata: Polkupyörä ja mopediteollisuuden ja -kaupan vaiheet Suomessa* (Jyväskylä: Suomen Polkupyörä- ja Mopediteollisuusyhdistys ry, 1988), 196–97, 255; Tapani Mauranen, *Hopeasiipi: Sata vuotta Helkamaa* (Helsinki: Otava, 2005), 224–26, 244.
38. Oldenziel et al, *Cycling Cities*, 13.
39. Pasi Mäenpää, "Kansalaisesta kuluttajaksi," in *Suomen kulttuurihistoria 4: Koti, kylä, kaupunki* (Helsinki: Kustannusosakeyhtiö Tammi, 2004), 288.
40. Tapani Mauranen, "Autolla arkeen," in *Suomalaisen arjen historia 4: Hyvinvoinnin Suomi*. (Porvoo: Weilin & Göös 2008), 193–95.
41. See Riitta Niskanen, *Ja Jumala loi kaupungin: Kaavoittaja Olavi Laisaari ja modernismin opit* (Helsinki: Museovirasto, 2010). Laisaari became more and more devoted to the car-city ideal in the 1950s and and developed his approach in his book *Tehokas kaupunki* (The smooth-running town) (Turku: Jakelu Turun kansallinen kirjakauppa, 1962) and other 1960s works.

42. Laisaari, *Turun yleiskaava*, 65. Laisaari's proposed plan for a network of cycle paths on the busiest cycling routes in the grid-plan area was not carried out.
43. See Laisaari, *Turun yleiskaava*, 66–68. This was the case in many European cities; see Oldenziel et al, *Cycling Cities*.
44. Tapani Mauranen, "Ajatte tuulenkeveydellä!" in *Velomania: Pyörällä halki aikojen* (Tampere: Tampereen museot, 2007), 155.
45. Karel Martens, *Transport Justice: Designing Fair Transportation Systems* (New York: Routledge, 2017), 32.
46. Barrett and Rose, "Street Smarts," 427.
47. Leif Sundström, "Liikenne ja tasa-arvo," in *Alas auton pakkovalta*, ed. Leena Maunula (Helsinki: Tammi, 1969), 69–100.
48. Meike Schalk, Ulrika Gunnarsson-Östling, and Karin Bradley, "Feminist Futures and 'Other Worlds': Ecologies of Critical Spatial Practice," in *Routledge Handbook of Gender and Environment*, ed. Sherilyn MacGregor (New York: Routledge, 2017), 447–463.
49. Peter Næss, "Gender Differences in the Influences of Urban Structure on Daily Travel," in *Gendered Mobilities*, ed. Tim Cresswell and Tanu Priya Uteng (New York: Ashgate Publishing, 2008), 173–92.
50. See Susan Fainstein and Lisa G. Servon, eds., "Introduction: The Intersection of Gender and Planning," in *Gender and Planning: A Reader* (New Brunswick: Rutgers University Press, 2005), 1–14.
51. See, for example, Annica Kronsell, Lena Smidfelt Rosqvist, and Lena Winslott Hiselius, "Achieving Climate Objectives in Transport Policy by Including Women and Challenging Gender Norms: The Swedish Case," *International Journal of Sustainable Transportation*, 10, no. 8 (2016): 703–11; Christina Lindkvist Scholten and Tanja Joelsson, eds., *Integrating Gender into Transport Planning* (Cham: Palgrave Macmillan, 2019), 69–87.
52. Randi Hjorthol, "Daily Mobility of Men and Women: A Barometer of Gender Equality?" in Cresswell and Uteng *Gendered Mobilities*, 193–210.
53. Susan Hanson, "Gender and Mobility: New Approaches for Informing Sustainability," *Gender, Place & Culture* 17, no. 1 (2010): 5–23.
54. See Turun kaupunki, *Turun ydinkeskustan kehittäminen* (Turku 1997), 4–5.
55. A good example is Hämeentie, one of the streets dominated both by women and bicycles in the 1950s photographs. All the houses along this street were demolished and replaced in the 1960s and 1970s, while the street was widened to create a multilane traffic corridor. Narrow cycle paths were added to the sidewalks in the late 1970s.
56. Hanson, "Gender and Mobility," 15.
57. Mimi Sheller, "Sustainable Mobility and Mobility Justice: Towards a Twin Transition," in *Mobilities: New Perspectives on Transport and Society*, ed. Margaret Grieco and John Urry (Farnham: Ashgate, 2012), 289–304.

# Bibliography

Antila, Kimmo, and Marko Nenonen. "Relief Works, the World Bank and Private Business: Building Highways in Finland." *Scandinavian Economic History Review* 48, no. 2 (2000): 47–71.
Barrett, Paul, and Mark H. Rose. "Street Smarts: The Politics of Transportation Statistics in the American City, 1900–1990." *Journal of Urban History* 25 (1999): 405–33.

Benjamin, Walter. "The Work of Art at the Age of Its Technical Reproducibility (Second Version)." In *The Work of Art at the Age of its Mechanical Reproducibility and Other Writings on Media*, edited by Michael W. Jennings et al. Cambridge, MA: Harvard University Press, 2008.

Carter, John E. "The Trained Eye: Photographs and Historical Context." *Public Historian* 15 (1993): 55–66.

Certeau, Michel de. *The Practice of Everyday Life*. Berkeley: University of California Press, 1984.

Cochoy, Franck, Johan Hagberg, and Roland Canu. "The Forgotten Role of Pedestrian Transportation in Urban Life: Insights from a Visual Comparative Archaeology (Gothenburg and Toulouse, 1875–2011)." *Urban Studies* 52, no. 12 (2015): 2267–86.

Cox, Peter. "'A Denial of Our Boasted Civilisation': Cyclists' Views on Conflicts over Road Use in Britain, 1926–1935." *Transfers: Interdisciplinary Journal of Mobility Studies* 2 (2012): 4–30.

Cresswell, Tim, and Peter Merriman. "Introduction: Geographies of Mobilities—Practices, Spaces, Subjects." In *Geographies of Mobilities: Practices, Spaces, Subjects*, edited by Tim Cresswell and Peter Merriman, 5–19. Farnham: Ashgate, 2011.

Dubois, Philippe. "Trace-Image to Fiction-Image: The Unfolding of Theories of Photography from the '80s to the Present." *October Magazine* 158 (2016): 155–66.

Edgerton, David. *The Shock of the Old: Technology and Global History since 1900*. London: Profile Books, 2006.

Emanuel, Martin. *Trafikslag på undantag: Cykeltrafiken i Stockholm 1930–1980*. Stockholm: Stockholmia förlag, 2012.

Fainstein, Susan, and Lisa G. Servon. "Introduction: The Intersection of Gender and Planning." in *Gender and planning: A Reader*, edited by Susan Fainstein and Lisa G. Servon, 1–14. New Brunswick: Rutgers University Press, 2005.

Fläschner, Thomas. "Stahlroß auf dem Aussterbe-Etat: Zur Geschichte des Fahrrades und seiner Verdrängung in den 50er Jahren." *Eckstein: Journal für Geschichte*, no. 9 (2000): 4–22.

Garvey, Ellen. "Reframing the Bicycle: Advertising-Supported Magazines and Scorching Women." *American Quarterly* 47 (1994): 66–101.

Hankonen, Johanna. *Lähiöt ja tehokkuuden yhteiskunta: Suunnittelujärjestelmän läpimurto suomalaisten asuntoalueiden rakentumisessa 1960-luvulla*. Tampere: Otatieto Oy, Gaudeamus, 1994.

Hänninen, Mauno. "Tieverkkosuunnittelun alku." In *Pikeä, hikeä, autoja: Tiet, liikenne ja yhteiskunta 1945–2005*, edited by Jaakko Masonen and Mauno Hänninen, 212–21. Helsinki: Tielaitos, 1995.

Hanson, Susan. "Gender and Mobility: New Approaches for Informing Sustainability." *Gender, Place & Culture* 17, no. 1 (2010): 5–23.

Heddon, Deirdre, and Cathy Turner. "Walking Women: Shifting the Tales and Scales of Mobility." *Contemporary Theatre Review* 22, no. 2 (2012): 224–36.

Hjorthol, Randi. "Daily Mobility of Men and Women: A Barometer of Gender Equality?" In *Gendered Mobilities*, edited by Tim Cresswell and Tanu Priya Uteng, 193–210. Aldershot: Ashgate Publishing, 2008.

Jordanova, Ludmilla. *The Look of the Past: Visual and Material Evidence in Historical Practice*. Cambridge: Cambridge University Press, 2012.

Jäger, Jens. *Bilder der Neuzeit: Einführung in die historische Bildforschung*. Tübingen: Edition Diskord, 2000.

Jäger, Jens. *Fotografie und Geschichte*. Frankfurt am Main: Campus, 2009.

Kallioinen, Johanna. *Pyöräilyn institutionaalinen asema liikennesuunnittelussa*. VATT-keskustelualoitteita 267. Helsinki: Valtion taloudellinen tutkimuskeskus, 2002.

Kivistö, Markus. "Kasvava katu. Autoliikenne ja modernisaatio Turussa." In *Sata lasissa*, edited by Ismo Vähäkangas, 91–103. Turku: Turun Historiallinen Yhdistys, 2000.

Kronsell, Annica, Lena Smidfelt Rosqvist, and Lena Winslott Hiselius. "Achieving Climate Objectives in Transport Policy by Including Women and Challenging Gender Norms: The Swedish Case." *International Journal of Sustainable Transportation* 10, no 8 (2016): 703–11.

Kuva, Heikki. *Kaksipyöräisten vuosisata: Polkupyörä ja mopediteollisuuden ja -kaupan vaiheet Suomessa*. Jyväskylä: Suomen Polkupyörä- ja Mopediteollisuusyhdistys ry, 1988.

Lahtinen, Rauno. *Turun puretut talot*. 5th printing, 1st added edition. Turku: Sammakko, 2013.

Laisaari, Olavi. *Tehokas kaupunki* (The smooth-running town). Turku: Jakelu Turun kansallinen kirjakauppa, 1962.

———. *Turun yleiskaava ja kaupungin kehittämisohjelma*. Turku: Turun kaupunki, 1952.

Lindkvist Scholten, Christina, and Tanja Joelsson, eds. *Integrating Gender into Transport Planning*. Cham: Palgrave Macmillan, 2019.

*Links between Noise and Air Pollution and Socioeconomic Status*. Science for Environment Policy. In-depth Report 13. European Commission, DG Environment by the Science Communication Unit, UWE, Bristol, 2016. http://ec.europa.eu/science-environment-policy.

Lundin, Per. *Bilsamhället: Ideologi, expertis och regelskapande i efterkrigstidens Sverige*. Stockholm: Stockholmia förlag, 2008.

Martens, Karel. *Transport Justice: Designing Fair Transportation Systems*. New York: Routledge, 2017.

Mauranen, Tapani. "Ajatte tuulenkeveydellä!" In *Velomania: Pyörällä halki aikojen*, 95–171. Tampereen museoiden julkaisuja 98. Tampere: Tampereen museot, 2007.

———. "Autolla arkeen." In *Suomalaisen arjen historia 4: Hyvinvoinnin Suomi*, 184–197. Porvoo: Weilin & Göös, 2008.

———. *Hopeasiipi: Sata vuotta Helkamaa*. Helsinki: Otava, 2005.

Middleton, Jennie. "Stepping in Time: Walking, Time, and Space in the City" *Environment and Planning A* 41, no. 8 (2009): 1943–61.

———. "Walking in the City: The Geographies of Everyday Pedestrian Practices." *Geography Compass* 5, no. 2 (2011): 90–105.

Mäenpää, Pasi. "Kansalaisesta kuluttajaksi." In *Suomen kulttuurihistoria 4: Koti, kylä, kaupunki*, 286–315. Helsinki: Kustannusosakeyhtiö Tammi, 2004.

Männistö-Funk, Tiina. "Kävelevien naisten kaupunki: Sata vuotta sukupuolta Turun kaduilla." In *Kaupungin varjoissa, arkistojen valossa*, edited by Topi Artukka, Jarkko Keskinen, and Taina Saarenpää, 77–94. Turku: Sigillum, 2018.

Männistö-Funk, Tiina, and Timo Myllyntaus, eds. *Invisible Bicycle: Parallel Histories and Different Timelines*. Leiden: Brill, 2019.

Niskanen, Riitta. *Ja Jumala loi kaupungin: Kaavoittaja Olavi Laisaari ja modernismin opit*. Museoviraston rakennushistorian osaston aikakauskirja. Helsinki: Museovirasto, 2010.

Norton, Peter D. *Fighting Traffic: The Dawn of the Motor Age in the American City*. Cambridge, MA: MIT Press, 2008.

Næss, Peter. "Gender Differences in the Influences of Urban Structure on Daily Travel." In *Gendered Mobilities*, edited by Tim Cresswell and Tanu Priya Uteng, 173–92. New York: Ashgate Publishing, 2008.

Oddy, Nicholas. "Cycling's Dark Age? The Period 1900–1920 in Cycling History." In *Cycle History 15: Proceedings of the 15th International Cycling History Conference*, edited by Rob van der Plas, 79–86. San Francisco: Van der Plas Publications/Cycle Publishing, 2005.

Oldenziel, Ruth, and Mikael Hård. *Consumers, Tinkerers, Rebels: The People Who Shaped Europe*. Hampshire: Palgrave Macmillan, 2013.

Oldenziel, Ruth, Martin Emanuel, Adri A. Albert de la Bruhèze, and Frank Veraart, eds. *Cycling Cities: The European Experience; One Hundred Years of Policy and Practice*. Eindhoven: Foundation for the History of Technology, 2016.

Pandel, Hans-Jürgen. "Bildinterpretation: Zum Stand der geschichtsdidaktischen Bildinterpretation." In *Visualität und Geschichte*, edited by Saskia Handro and Bernd Schönemann, 69–88. Berlin: LIT, 2011.

Price, Derrick, and Liz Wells. "Thinking about Photography: Debates, Historically and Now." In *Photography: A Critical Introduction*, edited by Liz Wells, 9–64. London: Routledge, 1997.

Rahikainen, Marjatta. *Helsingin keskusta Suomen taloudellisen kehityksen valossa*. Helsinki: Helsingin kaupungin kaupunkisuunnitteluvirasto, 1985.

Redclift, Michael, and Colin Sage. "Global Environmental Change and Global Inequality: North/South Perspectives." *International Sociology* 13, no. 4 (1998): 499–516.

Schalk, Meike, Ulrika Gunnarsson-Östling, and Karin Bradley. "Feminist Futures and 'Other Worlds': Ecologies of Critical Spatial Practice." In *Routledge Handbook of Gender and Environment*, edited by Sherilyn MacGregor, 447–63. New York: Routledge, 2017.

Scot, James C. *Seeing Like a State: How Certain Schemes to Improve the Human Condition Have Failed*. New Have: Yale University Press, 1998.

Sheller, Mimi. "The New Mobilities Paradigm for a Live Sociology." *Current Sociology Review* 62, no. 6 (2014): 789–811.

——. "Sustainable Mobility and Mobility Justice: Towards a Twin Transition." In *Mobilities: New Perspectives on Transport and Society*, edited by Margaret Grieco and John Urry, 289–304. Farnham: Ashgate, 2012.

Spinney, Justin. "Cycling the City: Non-Place and the Sensory Construction of Meaning in a Mobile Practice." In *Cycling & Society*, edited by Dave Horton, Paul Rosen, and Peter Cox, 25–46. Aldershot: Ashgate, 2007.

Starl, Timm. *Knipser: Die Bildgeschichte der privaten Fotografie in Deutschland und Österreich von 1880 bis 1980*. Munich: Koehler & Amelang, 1995.

Sundström, Leif. "Liikenne ja tasa-arvo." In *Alas auton pakkovalta*, edited by Leena Maunula, 69–100. Helsinki: Tammi, 1969.

Tagg, John. *The Burden of Representation: Essays on Photographies and Histories*. Minneapolis: University of Minnesota Press, 1988.

Turun kaupunki. *Keskustan liikenteen vaihekaava*. Turku: Turun Viatek, 1984.

——. *Turun ydinkeskustan kehittäminen*, Turku, 1997.

Vergunst, Jo. "Rhythms of Walking: History and Presence in a City Street." *Space and Culture* 13, no. 4 (2010): 376–88.

# SECTION III

∽

# Persistence and Sustainable Urban Mobilities

Today we have firm ideas about which mobility modes are more sustainable: walking, cycling, and public transit. These sustainable ways to get around a city are often held back by car-oriented planning and cultures developed over the past seven decades or so. In this section, "Persistence and Sustainable Urban Mobilities," the three chapters explore whether the inertia and path dependency of these car-governed systems can be both contested and utilized.

Martin Emanuel's biography of a street in Sweden's capital Stockholm argues that steps to create livable streets nowadays are sometimes fully dependent on unsustainable decisions in the past: streets for cars only, or cars relegated to underground tunnels. He contends that before any "unbuilding" of urban infrastructures to support cars can happen, the unsustainable parallels first need to be uncovered. The other two chapters ask, can the legacies of public transit and active modes associated with urban green spaces be resurrected for a more sustainable future? Alexandra Bekasova, Julia Kulikova, and Martin Emanuel look at the communist past of Russian cities like St. Petersburg to see whether their long histories of investing in public transit can help the transition to a more sustainable future. Finally, Frank Schipper speculates how urban parks with their reservoirs of more sustainable mobilities like walking and cycling can help other parts of the city. If assembled into park networks, he suggests, these could support more sustainable mobility throughout the city.

In short, this section proposes ways to break with undesirable path dependencies. It also shows how to nurture or create paths toward a more sustainable future.

# CHAPTER 7

# State Socialism and Sustainable Urban Mobility

## Alternative Paths in St. Petersburg since the 1880s

### Alexandra Bekasova, Julia Kulikova, and Martin Emanuel

## Introduction

Was the Soviet Union's public transport the best in the world? A provocative question—since the collapse of the Soviet Union, it has become commonplace to consider the state socialist system as backward, overly rigid, and far from the world's best. To present-day proponents of automobility, eager to see Russia catch up with the West, the Soviet fascination with collective forms of mobility is only part of the country's stalled past. After 1991, many of St. Petersburg's political and business elite quickly embraced the ambition to transform their city into a modern, world-class urban center by joining the capitalist West. As part of this ambition, the mayor, Anatoly Sobchak, envisioned turning industrial areas into modern apartment blocks and Obvodnyi Canal into an "Autobahn" in 1996. To him, St. Petersburg was "still waiting for its Haussmann or new Leblanc, who would be able not just to 'touch up' old districts of the city center, but essentially to give them a completely new identity."[1]

Many Russian transport scholars think that cars will inevitably dominate the cities of the future. The authors of a recent comprehensive volume on Russian urban transport agree on the destructive effects of post-Soviet policies, but strongly question the Soviet period's "best in the world" propaganda.[2] The Soviet regime's oft-repeated claim of having outstanding public transport invites critical investigation. Evidence suggests major flaws in efficiency and comfort, particularly in the late Soviet period. But this should not blind us to state socialist urban mobility possibly being a more sustainable, public transit-oriented alternative to "Western," car-oriented regimes. The Soviet Union's strong focus on public transport ought to have produced better results from an ecological sustainability and transport justice (if not economic) perspective. Notwithstanding the new middle-class apparent desire for cars, from a sustainability point of view, the transition to automobility in Russian cities since the 1990s may be considered a step backward rather than forward. Freed from their public transport–dependent past, Russian urbanites can now, a generation later, experience the negative effects of intensive urban automobility: congestion, air pollution, and inequality of access.[3] The question is, do Russian cities benefit from their past when it comes to sustainable urban mobility?

Public transport is not inherently just, in the same way that automobility is not inherently unjust. Anthropologist Elitza Stanoeva points out that while street cars in Sofia in the early twentieth century reduced physical distances, they increased social distances: limited access "reproduced and enhanced social inequalities."[4] Still, in most contexts, public transport is more widely available and affordable than driving a car—and also consumes fewer resources and space per traveler. The economic viability of automobility and public transport is, however, subject to diametrically different interpretations, and is perhaps at the heart of "socialist" and "capitalist" models of urban mobility. In Western societies, the car is often considered the engine of economic growth and "modernity," and the "quintessential manufactured object" of the twentieth century, without which—if we are to believe the car lobbies— national economies would crumble. The car industries—and the cars they produce—are also seen by many as crucial to flexible and dynamic (urban and regional) economies. This perceived potency of cars has made them a mainstay of Western societies, although some see "cracks" appearing in the global "system" of automobility.[5] The post-2008 crisis spotlighted the fragility of the car industry, reflected in today's dire forecasts.

State socialist mobility regimes offer an interesting counterpoint: for decades, they "artificially capped"—as critics phrased it—automobility and instead bet on public transport.[6] Its collective nature matched planned economy demands and, as we will see, brought much-needed revenues to the state coffers. Given their communist pedigree and belief in collective ownership, Soviet authorities felt uneasy with the idea of individualized mobility.[7] This is not to say people in socialist countries were immobile, or that their governments lacked the means and will to produce "modern" forms of mobility as perceived by capitalist countries at the time of the Cold War.[8]

Scholars have drawn different conclusions about the particularities of Leningrad's urban mobility and Soviet cities in general. Planning scholar Peter Hall assessed the Soviet focus on public transport positively in 1966. In his 1984 third edition of *The World Cities*, he noted, "Soviet thinking is still the generous investment in a cheap and efficient public transport system." He found Moscow's investment in its subway "prodigious" compared to most Western cities, and the electric subur-ban railways, with their impressively frequent departures, "serious con-tenders for the title of the world's best commuter service."[9] In contrast, Holland Hunter, American professor of economics, in his 1968 survey of the "soviet transport experience" and its implications for developing countries, presented the Soviet policy of suppressing people's "natural" desire to drive cars as problematic: "The plain fact is that cars *are* very convenient!"[10] Without concealing his disbelief in socialist alternatives to Western models, Hunter mocked Khrushchev's attempts to encour-age a more "rational" use of automobiles by setting up car rental ser-vices. If post-Khrushchevian leadership stopped suppressing individual car ownership, the demand for cars would inevitably multiply: "Western experience demonstrates conclusively the enormous strength of the urge to own a car, if this urge is given free rein."[11] In effect, Hunter gave the "love affair" with the car—a narrative produced by U.S. "motordom" to reject any opposition to an automotive future—universal claim.[12] Hunter appreciated the problems and hoped Soviet planners would be able to develop a "compromise solution" to the complex problem of cars in cities.[13]

Others adopted a more balanced approach. Ten years after Hunter, and amid countercultural movements against automobility in the Global North, U.K. geographer Denis Shaw turned for inspiration to Leningrad and other Soviet cities. Focusing on the positive effects of systematic city planning, he found that Leningrad had "escaped many of the haz-ards and misfortunes of the 'Western' City." The Soviet Union had no declining urban centers, ghettos, massive slums, or horrible traffic jams. However, cities were struggling to provide adequate public transport services to meet the growing demand.[14]

This chapter seeks to reinterpret past Soviet urban mobility through the lens of today's sustainability debates. We do not claim completeness but consider our chapter a starting point for further fruitful investiga-tion. Drawing on primary research from the late imperial period and the interwar period, and on secondary sources for the postwar period, we outline the history of mobility in St. Petersburg-Petrograd-Leningrad over one hundred years (1880–1980). This period saw a transition from a city where most people walked, into one shaped first by tramways and later the subway—though always in combination with other forms of mobility.[15] The selection of St. Petersburg as case study requires some explanation. As Russia's second largest city, with a highly dense popula-tion, public transport was an economically viable alternative to driving cars. St. Petersburg did not succeed in attracting "prodigious" state funding like the capital Moscow. We discuss issues of continuity and change between the late imperial and state socialist periods, highlighting how the buildup of a strong public transport system began already before the Bolshevik takeover. Our narrative ends around 1980, when public transport had become unprofitable and no longer provided cheap and easy access to the city. This decline played into the hands of those wanting to see St. Petersburg rapidly equal Western cities in the presence of cars. Even so, we argue that the state socialist heritage with its focus on public transport may help cities to improve their environmental and social sustainability.

## Curbing Rail-Based Suburbanization in the Walking City

Founded as a new imperial city in the early eighteenth century, St. Petersburg was designed according to European ideas and ideals. Early urban planners were hired from abroad, such as the French Jean-Baptiste Alexander Le Blond and Swiss-Italian Domenico Trezzini. In the nineteenth century, many Italian and French architects came to work in the Imperial capital, while Russian architects often studied in Europe. As the city rapidly became a bureaucratic, political, commercial, and trade center, its geographical location around the waterfront shaped its spatial arrangement, population distribution, and mobility patterns.[16] Bridges, embankments, roadbuilding, and urban services required enormous investments, while city authorities had to balance the interests of transport companies and many individual carriers.

Around 1900, the city was facing what contemporaries regarded as a serious mobility crisis. As in other big cities, St. Petersburg residents experienced a glaring gap between their need for rapid and regular mobility and transport provision. Closely related to the industrialization process, the urban population grew rapidly in the 1880s. The city's many new factories provided thousands of migrants with employment. St. Petersburg's population doubled from half a million in the mid-nineteenth century to one million around 1900, and again to over two million before World War I. St. Petersburg became Europe's fifth largest city, surpassed only by London, Paris, Vienna, and Berlin. The principal thoroughfares, such as the Nevskii Prospect, were thronging with pedestrians and a variety of vehicles—sundry conveyances for personal hire, electrical and horse-drawn street cars competing for space and passengers—all mixing with crowds of pedestrians (see figure 7.1). Expanded economic and commercial activities and more residents in the city center increased traffic and congestion, forcing the authorities to find ways and means of facilitating traffic circulation. Thus, urban mo-

**Figure 7.1.** The Nevskii Prospect, the main St. Petersburg/Petrograd thoroughfare in the early twentieth century; traffic modes ranged from the recently launched electrical tramways to horse-drawn carriages. Pedestrians were abundant and not strictly separated from the roadway. Photo by Karl Bulla taken after 1907 and reproduced on postcards.

Source: Postcard from the collections of the Department of Engravings and of Other Visual Materials, Russian National Library in St. Petersburg.

bility and transportation were among the major issues in bureaucratic, engineering, and public debates.

Around Europe and North America, suburban commuter trains were being accepted as a solution to cities' housing problems and labor supply for new industries. In the new dormitory suburbs, workers benefitted from cheaper and better living conditions. Despite numerous debates in St. Petersburg's city council in the 1890s, nothing happened.[17] The national government was concerned that the city's transportation facilities was failing to meet the needs of the growing population. At a top bureaucratic level meeting in 1901, state department ministers found the situation unworthy of the imperial capital. Officials found it embarrassing that several other cities of the Russian Empire—unlike St. Petersburg—had already electrified their trams. They urged the city to accelerate traffic and achieve efficient transport between the center and the outskirts.[18]

Over subsequent years, the city initiated multiple projects outlining the future of mobility in St. Petersburg. Innovative solutions were proposed by civil engineers, such as Petr Balinskii, who designed various projects between 1898 and 1903. Forming intellectual coalitions with Russian and foreign engineers and architects, Balinskii's proposals included constructing a circular urban railroad and a series of new bridges, paving the canal embankments, and raising the low-lying part of Vasilyevsky Island to facilitate new train stations. Initially planned for goods and passengers, the railroad later exclusively focused on passenger traffic to ensure comfortable mass transit in a high-speed urban network.[19] Ultimately, the project failed to get off the ground. The ministries refused to invest public funds in such a large-scale project without clear profitability, and potential foreign investors backed out.[20]

The discussions revealed other tensions. The ministries and the church, along with the wealthiest and most influential property owners, resisted radical change. More surprisingly, city government representatives actively opposed the project. Fearing the high costs (seventeen million rubles), they protected traditional taxpayers—real-estate owners plus individuals and companies engaged in passenger and goods transport—who would suffer from a high-speed transport network. Furthermore, some members of the city council associated the project with soaring prices for goods and housing; additionally, the political drama of the departure of the Tsar and wealthy citizens in exchange for an increasing number of the proletariat would tarnish the capital's glorious image.[21] Bureaucrats were opposed to the engineers' and private companies' proposals that would have created urban sprawl.

The failure of the loftier plans forced the city's engineers to provide alternative swift transportation of people and goods to the business center. Meanwhile, urbanites kept on using traditional options. Although the horse-drawn tramway network expanded along with new suburban train routes, the links with the suburbs remained weak.[22] Around 1900, the city acquired a large number of privately operated horse tramway lines, which were consolidated in the Urban Railway Office in 1907.[23] Still rejecting the radical modernization proposals for transport infrastructure, the city continued to bet on the tramway and extended the network after late electrification in 1907. Initially using the lines already developed by owners of horse-drawn streetcars, by 1913 the network had established new lines and stretched further out to the northeastern and southwestern parts of the city and to the port.[24]

By contrast, individual means of transport, such as horse-drawn carriages and sledges, bicycles, and later automobiles, were expensive fads that few could afford—as suggested by their taxation as luxury goods.[25] Up until 1914, about fourteen thousand horse-drawn carriages were still available for personal hire.[26] The year before, St. Petersburg had 2,585 registered automobiles, including 328 operating as taxis.[27] Although more people traveled by public transport—at first horse-drawn cars and later especially electrical trams—not all residents could afford to use these rather expensive services regularly. Moreover, the electrified tram didn't begin operating until 8:00AM—too late for workers who started much earlier.[28] Horse-drawn trams persisted before being replaced by electrified and, primarily in the suburbs, steam engine–driven streetcars.[29] Around the same time, the municipal administration promoted and issued permits for privately operated regular bus services.[30] In 1914, electric cars handled 90 percent of the tram services in St. Petersburg and provided a fairly effective service.[31]

Most urbanites walked. As historian James H. Bater convincingly argues, the transient character of St. Petersburg's population, combined with long working hours, limited disposable income, and costly public transport fares, forced residents to live near their places of work. To avoid the daily travel costs, middle-class migrants also settled close to the city center and their workplaces, mostly within a half-hour's walking distance.[32]

We know little about the extent of walking because the thorough surveys of mobility patterns all lacked information about pedestrian traffic. However, photos of daily life in St. Petersburg feature walking as the dominant practice (see figure 7.1).[33] A comparison with public transport use in other cities suggests a low level in St. Petersburg, yet another indication of the high proportion of pedestrians. In 1893, the sixty trips made on average per person annually in St. Petersburg were slightly higher than Moscow's fifty, but marginal compared to 290 in New York, and considerably lower than European metropolises such as London (145), Berlin (140), and Paris (100), and also lower than Budapest (87) and Vienna (70).[34] St. Petersburg's eighty-eight trips per person in 1900, only half of Berlin's 185, increased to 150 in 1912. As Bater stressed, "On the basis of any set of criteria, fewer people used public transport than in most European cities, and major American ones."[35]

The new century also saw traffic plans to increase and relieve the capacity of central thoroughfares like the Nevskii Prospect. Experts took note of the people's dominant practice of walking. Engineers devised new technical regulations for street designs in the 1910s, with sidewalks as a crucial element. In 1916, Nikolai Danilevskii, an experienced engineer, compiled a detailed report on the condition and problems with the spatial organization of the city streets and sidewalks. The report alerted the city council to the fact that the streets had to be adapted to urban traffic circulation, including pedestrian flows. In Danilevskii's view, the lack of municipal standardization, combined with the fact that property owners were responsible for street paving and cleaning beside their buildings, made the city's sidewalks true "street horrors." Drawing on regulations in Munich, Berlin, and Düsseldorf, he outlined the ideal sidewalk: smooth, nonslip, geometrically uniform, and raised above the level of the carriageway. Comfort and control were mutually dependent. He argued that until sidewalks were made user-friendly, convenient, and safe for the thousands who kept on walking regardless of the mobility technologies available, people would prefer to use both roads and sidewalks.[36]

Indeed, late imperial St. Petersburg was essentially a walking city. In spite of dreams (among engineers and planners in particular) of radical change, the city administration resisted urban railways. The late creation of an electric tramway network aside, walking dominated. People living close to their workplaces produced, by international standards, very low fossil-fueled mobility. While environmentally sustainable from our present-day perspective, this was neither the city administration's nor the landowning elite's concern. Rather, they defended property values and the city's character, fearing the imperial capital would attract too many working-class residents. Several scholars have stressed that, as James Bater put it, "the revolution [should] not be viewed as a hard and fast watershed." Town planning ideas that had developed in Tsarist Russia survived and found their way into Soviet planning.[37] Regarding the tram system, the Bolsheviks could clearly build on a favorable imperial heritage. In 1913, the Urban Railways' profits amounted to over fifteen million rubles, while maintenance expenses were limited to six million rubles.[38] The very profitable private tramway enterprise and its infrastructure were thus shaped and municipalized at the end of the imperial era. Contrary to popular Soviet narratives, the new socialist regime inherited a public transport system in satisfactory condition before exploiting and further developing it.[39]

## Controlling Mobility in the Tramway City

During the destructive period of war and revolutions (1917–1920), St. Petersburg (renamed Petrograd in 1914, then Leningrad in 1924) residents faced heavy economic crises, including food supply shortages and hunger, but also irregular public transport services and an increasing need to travel significant distances on foot. After the turmoil, the city rapidly regained its former heavy traffic.[40] At the same time, much had changed. Following the Bolshevik revolution, although the city was still a center of business activities, industry, and higher education, it lost its status as the empire's capital when the new government moved superior institutions to Moscow in 1918. More importantly for the discussion here, the abolishment of private property and nationalization of land and resources gave the Bolshevik administration the opportunity to reconfigure urban space, including streets and their traffic. Years of political and economic crisis had dramatically reduced the city's population, but the outflow was only temporary, as population growth steadily regained momentum. Soviet urban transportation policy, as in the late imperial period, focused on public transport facilities, which suited the centrally planned economy.

The 1920s was the Soviet utopian decade, when urban planners' discussions centered around two competing visions: "urbanism" and "disurbanism." While "urbanists," such as Leonard Sabsovich of the State Planning Commission for a General Plan, advocated networks of compact garden cities, "disurbanists," such as Mikhail Okhitovich, economist, city planner, and theorist of constructivist architecture, embraced the international idea of extending linear settlements served by public transport. Depending on how these units were located, transport would be developed to form a grid for easy connections.[41] Despite the different visions of the ideal city, both had a similar approach to public transport: at a time when electrification earned a high status as a symbol of modernity, they shared the idea of a country-wide electric power grid to power high-velocity transportation.[42] While Sabsovich mentioned vague "electric-powered mass public transportation," Okhitovich already envisioned not only electric trains—uncommon in the Soviet Union at the time—but also airplanes and cars.

The lack of labor and finances in the 1920s called a halt to such radical solutions. By the 1930s, after Lazar Kaganovich had called off further conceptualization and declared Soviet cities "socialist" by default, the authorities concentrated on solving the housing shortage.[43] In terms of mobility, public transport was clearly the priority. In 1931, Kaganovich distinguished "socialist" from "capitalist" public transport: "While in capitalist countries different modes of transport—tram, bus, subway—compete with one another, here, in a socialist economy, these transport modes will not compete among each other. Instead, they will complement each other and give us transportation efficiency unprecedented anywhere in the world and impossible anywhere else."[44] This was not the full truth, however; given the institutionally splintered public transport system, where the administration of various forms of public transport answered to different authorities at different levels—they were arguably caught up in what has been termed "socialist competition."[45] Though foreign observers were astounded at the rapid industrialization under the Bolshevik regime, many felt uneasy about what they saw as a one-sided focus on industrial output. They were generally not impressed with the country's standard of transportation.[46]

The visionary period was characterized by lots of contacts, exchanges, and cooperation between Soviet architects and city planners with their colleagues in Europe and the United States. The Stalinist regime effectively put a stop to such exchanges, although they were resumed in the 1950s.[47] Transnational investments in "socialist construction" were also a part of the exchange process, and the field of transportation was no exception.[48] It thus comes as no great surprise that urban planning as actually practiced in the Soviet Union in the interwar period resembled that of the European modernist tradition. Leningrad's 1929 zonal plan, for example, proposed a division of the city into "core" zones, where industry was concentrated, and the flanking "living" zones with housing.[49] Public transport would be the essential link and maintain the connection between the zones, with a separate transport subsystem designed for the industrial district.[50] Leading city engineers favored public transport thanks to its superiority from an efficiency and urban economy point of view. Sergei Lebedev, transport and construction engineer, considered transportation an integral part of the urban economy. To him, mass passenger transportation was necessary due to "the industrial character of modern life," that is, to move urbanites over longer distances.[51]

Around 1930, the "Architectural workshop" of the Leningrad Executive Committee—established to generate urban reconstruction projects—also put urban traffic center stage. Streets had to be cleared of overflowing traffic; the city needed easy access between key landmarks; and railroad stations had to be relocated, as did the public transport routes.[52] Grigorii Dubelir, expert in road construction and urban transportation, considered urban transport a tool for functional separation: to maintain the city's business life and balance housing distribution. Given his international contacts and experience, the alignment with the ideas of Ebenezer Howard and the later modernist tradition of urban planning is not surprising.[53] In terms of mobility, however, he differed. To Dubelir, the key principle for the urban passenger transportation network was to sustain maximum traffic capacity at minimal cost. Given the high costs of infrastructural projects, he proposed urban plans that minimized travel, declaring that "[t]ransport is evil, evil, and it is necessary to reduce transport to minimum."[54] Dubelir's view of transport as "evil" does not seem to have been widely shared by his Soviet contemporaries. Still, his view is rather remarkable at a time when his colleagues in the West stressed mobility and circulation as the engines of growth. The urge to restrict mobility might have been spurred by the city's overloaded public transport (see figure 7.2).

Without any "Soviet" educational institutions for training specialists in urban planning and transportation until the 1930s, the Petrograd-Leningrad administration initially relied on engineers and architects of the imperial era to help conceptualize a different socialist environment.[55] The Urban Railways Office could boast experienced staff, among them Abram Zil'bertal' and Iurii Grinval'd, who had both served as engineers in the imperial period. Zil'bertal', an electrical engineer educated in Switzerland, argued for centralization, public transport, and scientific management of traffic flows in Soviet Leningrad. The combination, he argued, would allow the city to "use in the most effective way each mode of transportation and save on expenses."[56] In his *Tramvainoe khoziaistvo* (Tramway economy), he emphasized the importance of public transport for city residents' "civilizing process": it helped urbanites to experience all human achievements. To serve such a purpose, transport had to be cheap.[57]

Iurii Grinval'd actively promoted the development of public transport facilities with the tram network as their main base. He was also a key proponent of a subway network for Leningrad. For many years (1914 until the early 1930s), he presented his own designs to guide the development of the future metropolis. To Grinval'd, overcrowding in communal apartments prompted people to leave their homes more often, resulting in much unnecessary travel. Constructing multistoried houses would therefore not promote a socialist way of life; a fast, reliable, and convenient public transport network would, by ensuring the circulation of passengers between places of residence, work, and mass recreation.[58]

At ground level, Petrograd-Leningrad was turning into a true public-transport city thanks to trams. However, the crowds of passengers and electricity failures causing massive delays did not create enjoyable commutes (see figure 7.2), though these might have spurred long-distance walking.[59] Despite the poor quality and lack of comfort, people kept on demanding transport services. While old-fashioned coaches transported a total of 62 million passengers in 1921, this number rose to a striking 1.335 billion by 1932.[60] With high demand and rather expensive tickets, Urban Railways (in spite of the name, they operated tramways) had a total income in the mid-1920s of twelve million rubles, of which only about two million were allocated to expanding and maintaining the tram network; the remainder was for the "common needs of the Provincial Executive Committee and Communal Economy Department."[61] Although the official press stated that revenues went to street cleaning and sanitation, road maintenance, and reconstruction along

**Figure 7.2.** An overcrowded two-coach tram making its way across Stroganovskii (currently Ushakovskii) Bridge over Malaia Nevka River in Leningrad, 1933. The dramatic rise in population from the late 1920s to the early 1930s visibly influenced the quality of public transport, emphasizing the need for more spacious coaches. Meanwhile, "tram surfing" was commonplace, not simply as a leisurely activity among the youth but as a means of getting somewhere on time.

Source: The Central State Archive of Film, Photo, and Sound Documents of St Petersburg, Bp 7254, Tramvai s passazhirami na mostu, 1920-e gody.

the tracks, it seems safe to say that a large portion was used for other purposes.[62] The quality of transport was gradually improving as Urban Railways introduced more spacious coaches and strived to increase average speeds.[63] But the overall impact was far from overwhelming. In 1940, the tramway network amounted to 440 kilometers, little more than double that of 1913, the main extensions being new lines to the northwest and southeast, and a connecting line to the Oranienbaum electric railway.[64]

Streetcars could not serve the entire Leningrad population. The authorities had a hard time building new tramway lines to keep up with needs of the growing population settling in the suburbs. Beginning in 1926, buses served the city as well, particularly as feeder modes between new districts and the rail-bound transport hubs. Many early buses were Soviet trucks revamped using foreign technology.[65] Gradually, vehicles of local origin joined the fleet. Appreciated by the public transport administrators for their maneuverability, buses earned public recognition as more spacious and comfortable alternatives to tramcars.[66] Workers would even approach the city administration to demand bus routes to their particular workplaces.[67] In 1939, buses carried 7.6 percent of the total passenger numbers in Leningrad.[68] There were thirty bus routes, including twelve suburban areas served by 330 vehicles.[69] Ten years after the introduction of buses, the trolleybus emerged on the city streets in 1936. Received with curiosity, like the buses, they were appreciated for their greater comfort, but fared worse than buses, transporting only 3 percent of the total number of passengers in 1940.[70]

If public transport was the mainstay of the urban transport system, individual means of transport were rare. In 1928, only 1,587 individual cars were registered.[71] Cars were not sold but distributed. As a means of winning loyalty of subordinates, they circulated within gift exchange networks instead of open markets.[72] The main focus in the Soviet economy was never the production of cars for personal and private use, but tractors and trucks, train and tramcars, as well as tanks and airplanes—crucial for implementing government collectivization and industrialization programs.[73] Around 1930, some workers even resisted the Avtodor Society campaigns to promote and popularize the automobile in Soviet Russia. Urbanites preferred regular bus services and cheap bicycles to buy rather than mostly inaccessible cars for getting to work on time.[74] First reappearing in 1929, there were five hundred taxis in the city by 1940.[75] Few could afford frequent, rather expensive, rides, so residents relied on public transport—or walked.

The city's 1922 traffic regulations were modeled on a template for Soviet cities. Seeking to regulate just about all mobile subjects, the leitmotif was to set a clear border between the sidewalk and the roadway.[76] To the militia, the rules ensured the concentration of road users and lowered the risks, but they also carried a subtle political message of common needs prevailing over personal ones: "Pedestrian movement rules are necessary. Everyone needs the street. Interests of hundreds of thousands of people are meeting within it. Unitary guidance, a unitary solid system is required, or else every pedestrian will disturb the others."[77] In cities around the globe, pedestrians were being regulated to benefit motorists; in the Soviet Union, pedestrians were supposed to stay out of the way of public transport.[78]

In the interwar and postwar periods, electric trams became the backbone of Leningrad's transport system, with buses and trolley-buses as marginal complements. The authorities preferred the tram as a cheap and efficient way to transport workers to and from their workplace. Some workers were housed close to employment sites—which was only possible through the tools available in a socialist state. Although walking remained a significant element of mobility, the tram increasingly defined the city and its traffic. Significantly, however, the tramways never managed to keep up with demand, and the network was not considerably extended. Thus, while bicycles and tramways helped cities all over Europe to suburbanize in the interwar period, Leningrad remained relatively contained.[79] From a social wellbeing point of view, the compact city resulted in enormous overcrowding: in 1951, every apartment in Leningrad housed an average of 3.3 families.[80] Leningrad's public transport system was not only accessible to all; it was also extremely profitable, although it seems like the profits were channeled to other sectors of society rather than to improvements of public transport. Unlike Western cities at the time, some of Leningrad's planners aimed to reduce commuting to a minimum. This could only be achieved by restricting people's freedom to live where they wanted, but the effects correspond with present-day utopian discussions about low mobility in the compact and walkable, cyclable, and public-transport city. As we will see, these ambitions were shattered in post–World War II Leningrad.

## "Socialist" Mobility Crisis in the Subway City

As World War II was ending, Andrei Zhdanov, the city's party leader since 1934, was already drawing up plans for a Leningrad Renaissance. Zhdanov's death in 1948 and the subsequent "Leningrad Affair," when many higher (as well as lower) officials were removed from office or killed, curbed the city's influence in the highest Soviet decision-making circles. The State Defense Committee in Moscow abandoned its inter-war reconstruction efforts to shift the city core to the south, and instead reasserted the primacy of Leningrad's historic heart, investing in housing in the city center.[81]

The only part of Zhdanov's wartime vision that survived into the 1950s was the grandiose underground subway stations.[82] The initial subway construction projects date back to the nineteenth century.[83] After the success of the Moscow subway, which had begun operating in 1935, Soviet planners wanted the same in Leningrad, but their plans were stalled by the war.[84] Opened in 1955, the Leningrad subway—supported by buses—would help to change the city's spatial structure at its core.

Since the early decades of the Soviet period, the issue of overcrowding prompted the city authorities to develop suburban areas. The developments outlined in the interbellum period could not continue until a decade after the war. Under Stalin in particular, planners' aspirations and objectives were always subordinate to the needs of industry and the wishes of industrial ministries. Thus, although Leningrad was the only city besides Moscow to have a city plan before the war, little attempt was made to implement either the original 1935 plan, meant to shift the city's core to the south, or its postwar modified versions.[85] And like city planning in general, traffic planning under Stalin was guided by monumentality rather than "rationalist" approaches.[86]

After the mid-1950s, Leningrad construction trusts, in accordance with Khrushchev's housing program, began expanding the city's housing stock at an ever-accelerating rate. Families, if given the choice, increasingly opted for relatively spacious and modern apartments instead of cramped conditions in the city center. In the 1970s, the city experienced a rapid increase of residents and further development within a 50 to 75 km radius of the city, including weekend destinations such as Pushkin, Petrodvorets, Gatchina, and Lomonosov.[87] The massive housing construction efforts not only improved living conditions, but also created an urban sprawl. The prerevolutionary city of a hundred square kilometers swelled to an area fourteen times larger in 1980. Whereas half the city's population lived in the city center in the late 1950s, three-quarters lived in the suburbs by 1980. Aware of the mounting pressure on public transport, planners tried in the late 1970s to create more independent satellite centers. Their attempts largely failed, since most major jobs and services remained in the city center. By the early 1980s, half of the suburban population commuted to work downtown.[88]

The similarities between urban planning practice and development in the Soviet Union and Western Europe are striking—namely, the use of industrial building techniques and ever larger planning units.[89] Postwar suburbanization in Western cities, however, relied as much on cars and highways as public transport. In Leningrad, on the other hand, all suburbanites used public transport to move around the city's vast areas. This put immense pressure on the system. As the number of passengers using public transport doubled from 1950 to the early 1970s, there was a parallel increase in trip length and number of trips per person.[90] The intensity of street traffic increased by 4.5 percent every year. Between 1965 and 1980, the average number of rides per person and year on public transport increased from 575 to 711.[91]

Urban planners were aware of inconsistencies in the public transport network and proposed changes that would, in their opinion, rationalize the current framework through greater expansion of the subways. Like the 1966 city plan, a new transport plan issued the year after put the subway at the center of the city's development. Existing tramway tracks in the city center would be phased out in favor of new high-speed tracks. Buses would primarily deliver passengers to the subway stations, and existing subway lines had to be connected in a coherent system. Suburban transport would also be linked with the subway lines, then proceed along the shores of the Gulf of Finland. The officially estimated time to implement the new complex transport scheme was 110 (!) years.[92] Investments in the 1970s were an attempt to address the problems, and in 1975, a fifteen-year program was presented to develop public transport as part of the municipal and regional socio-economic development plan.[93] The early 1980s saw a new scheme to improve public transport by reducing commuting times and increasing the frequency of services.[94] Judging by the complaints and assessments of the deteriorating quality of public transport, the measures were insufficient.

That said, the public transport network did expand substantially. A second subway line (Moscow district to Petrograd side) followed in 1961; a third (the Nevskii Prospect to Vasil'evskii Island) emerged in 1967; and a fourth (Kirovskii to Vyborgskii district) was opened in 1975.[95] Although the subway helped to shape the city and had a major effect on travel patterns in the whole Leningrad region, other modes remained indispensable. In fact, the rapid expansion of bus routes and traffic made it more appropriate to speak of Leningrad as a metro and bus city. The bus route network expanded rapidly from 375 km in 1939 to an estimated 2,600 km in 1966. In the 1980s there were 149 urban and 293 suburban routes covering a total length of 27,000 km. Meanwhile, by the late 1970s, the tram network began a long-term retraction, surviving routes tending to serve proletarian districts. The use of streetcars slowly declined. The turning point came around 1965, when bus users outnumbered tram passengers (see figure 7.3).[96]

Numbers of Passengers Caried by Leningrad Urban Transport

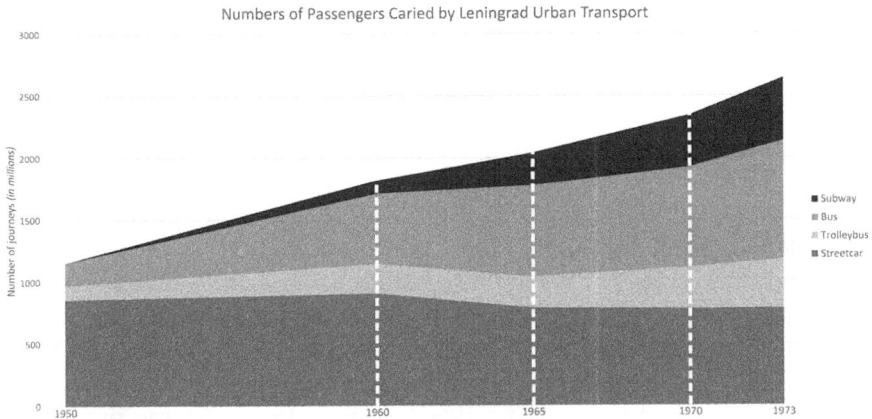

**Figure 7.3.** The millions of passengers per year in Leningrad from 1950–1973 divided over various means of public transport demonstrates the transition from trams to buses and the subway. By 2016, 42 percent of all journeys (including car trips) are by subway.
Source: Denis J. B. Shaw, "Planning Leningrad," *Geographical Review* 68, no. 2 (1978): 192.

The public transport system failed to keep pace with the increasing numbers of riders, and overcrowding was a constant factor. In a 1978 survey, Leningrad residents' complaints about public transport came in third place after housing and ecology; a similar survey in 1984 found transport at the top of the list of twelve issues.[97] In 1979, historian Martin Crouch identified the public transport shortcomings in Soviet cities: besides overcrowding, frequent breakdowns and poor coordination between the bodies in charge of the various subsystems—at a time when public transport companies in Western economies were increasingly being coordinated at the city or even regional level. Public transport suffered from the combination of rapid urbanization and lack of investment, as only a small proportion of its revenue was channeled back to the local transport sector. Adding to the problem, toward 1970, public transport in Soviet cities was running at a loss. While costs rose due to the rapid extension of the networks (80 percent for trams and 50 percent for trolleybuses from 1963 to 1972), the number of reduced fare categories increased, as did the fare-dodgers—and raising the flat fares, which had been frozen since the 1950s, was deemed politically unacceptable.[98] We do not have the exact numbers for Leningrad, but generally speaking, as a form of consumption, mobility had low priority in the production-oriented planned economy.

Where do cars come into the picture? The short answer is, they barely do: in 1975, when cars were first included in the surveys (alongside public transit), they made up a marginal 2 percent of traffic. In 1963, there were 27,304 private cars in Leningrad. Even though this was a 150 percent increase from 1959, it was a very small number compared to the city's population.[99] For a long time, cars remained tokens of prestige, available mostly to higher party officials and the *nomenclatura*.[100] Automobility did not take off until the 1970s, although still moderately so. As domestic car production rocketed, two-thirds of the cars produced were sold to the public in 1975. In 1970, 2 percent of Soviet Union households had a car; fifteen years later, 15 percent had one. By international standards, this was a very small number—and cars remained unevenly distributed among the population. Despite the prestige of car ownership, it was also a bit conspicuous in Soviet society.[101]

In spite of very low motoring levels, Soviet cities started preparing for a car-oriented future.[102] The 1966 city plan for Leningrad expanded the subway, but also private car use, while projecting a decline in other travel modes. It recommended extensive subway and highway construction programs, as well as improved services for the burgeoning car owners—although these facilities did not keep pace.[103] The 1970s saw plans to extend public transport, but also the road networks, including the completion of a semicircular highway bypassing the city center, and the designation of "fast" routes.[104]

As in many European and North American cities, Soviet city authorities were keen to separate pedestrians from vehicular traffic. Several innovations emerged in the 1960s, allegedly to ensure pedestrian safety: "safety isles," where pedestrians could stop halfway when crossing the street; "pedestrian centers," where vehicles were entirely prohibited; as well as design principles for districts (*mikroraiony*) based on walking distances between housing complexes and key facilities such as stores and primary schools.[105] In some respects, Soviet engineers were forerunners. At the 1971 PIARC congress in Prague, where international traffic engineers and road planners exchanged best practices, the Soviet delegates projected an increase in car traffic and detailed their measures to ensure traffic safety like their Western counterparts. One measure stood out: underground pedestrian passages that would "ensure complete safety to pedestrians and unobstructed traffic flow." Mandatory on expressways, such passages were to be constructed under main urban roads where traffic exceeded five hundred automobiles per lane and more than three thousand pedestrians crossing the street per hour.[106] Leningrad's first underground pedestrian crossings appeared after 1963, and by 2015 there were more than forty.[107] Linked to public transport, these underpasses effectively gave way to automobility. Although the segregation of pedestrians was promoted primarily as a safety measure, some observers viewed motorists as the real winners already in the 1960s.[108]

Between 1975 and 1990, the car's share of all trips in Leningrad increased from 2 to 8 percent. The real contestation of cars and cities, however, came in post-Soviet times, with the unfortunate combination of transport deregulation and retraction of public funding for subway expansion. By the year 2000, the car modal split reached 17 percent, and in 2016 almost every third journey was made by car.[109] As funding was allocated only to road infrastructure, public transport sank into a declining vicious circle of poorer quality and fewer users, for municipal as well as new private bus operators.[110]

Writing in 1990, American planning scholar Blair Ruble described the effects of postwar planning on Leningrad: "Unlike much of the urban sprawl in the West, local planners [in Leningrad] have relied extensively on subway-based mass transportation, rather than on the private automobile." Ruble argued that this growth strategy "inhibited the emergence of an efficient and flexible region wide service, commercial, and cultural infrastructure." Leningrad was among the few cities of its size (the others were Moscow and a few large Chinese cities) to see "such immense territorial expansion without reliance on the private automobile."[111] Ruble seemed to pity Leningraders. A carless city lacked economic dynamism, which to him equaled economic unsustainability. As we mentioned earlier, others looked to state socialist cities for alternatives to the failures, as they saw them, of Western cities with sprawl, congestion, and slums. After 1970, however, the limitations of state socialist urban mobility were becoming evident. Public transport was no longer the once profitable system it had been, and as the state did not step in—either by allowing higher fares or with more investments—it was struggling to deliver a functioning service. Consequently, in the late Soviet period, Leningraders were suffering from a mobility crisis, not of congestion but rather through lack of services—this on top of many other shortages. Interestingly, public transport's decline in Soviet cities coincided with a rediscovery, in some cases even a renaissance, of the same in other parts of the world.[112] Some thirty years later, while St. Petersburg's public transport is back on its feet, cars and their drivers are taking over a city that was not built for them. City dwellers of St. Petersburg are still suffering, not so much from lack of services, as from the congestion, the noise, and the exhaust fumes.

## Conclusion

Over the years, the city of St. Petersburg—for long periods under different names—has expanded its public transport network, seen as the backbone of urban mobility especially during the Soviet period. Although the imperial authorities pushed for well-functioning tramways during their last decade in power, St. Petersburg remained a walking city—partly due to the failure to establish an urban railway that would have considerably spread the city. While the tramway and the city developed in tandem in the interwar period, a decade into the postwar period the subway helped the city expand considerably. Buses complemented the tramways, especially in the suburbs.

Walking never stopped, but changed. While many people formerly walked to work, by the second half of the twentieth century, walking became part of multimodal journeys. This deserves further investigation, but our preliminary conclusion is that the subway-shaped city undermined walking as a viable mode, thus making cars an easy choice for those who could afford them when public transport declined. Of course, the lure of "Western" consumer goods and some people's longing to exhibit individualist lifestyles, even before the 1990s, also helped.

In the 1960s, the public transport system began to collapse under its own weight and the particularities of state socialist ideology and organization. As Kathy Burrell and Kathrin Hörschelmann argue, "one of the main failures of the socialist system was its inability to sustain the investment and labor required to 'moor' its mobility systems—to maintain and not just establish its physical infrastructure."[113] While public transport entered a vicious circle of poorer quality, fewer users, and less revenue, automobility increased, although modestly before the 1990s. In the longer term, Shaw had correctly predicted that planners would eventually shift toward a "radical stance on the question of highway construction in Leningrad."[114] But this only happened in post-Soviet times. Similarly, we never found out if Hunter was right to hope that Soviet authorities, with their stronger planning instruments, would successfully fit cars on a greater scale in the urban fabric.[115] Indeed, people blame the laissez-faire policies of post-Soviet policymakers for today's mobility problems in Russian cities.

Only a decade after the collapse of the Soviet system, the streets of St. Petersburg and other cities were populated by cars, and suffered the ensuing serious urban environmental problems. Contemporary Russian cities also suffer from injustices in terms of availability to mobility. On the one hand, Hunter was apparently right about the inevitable rise in urban automobility once the regulations preventing car ownership were lifted. On the other hand, it is important to note that the problems with public transport began long before its deregulation and the political transformation in 1991. Poor services probably drove Russian urbanites into cars more rapidly.

In recent years, the quality of public transport has improved substantially. But given middle-class urbanites' strong preference for cars, it is hard to imagine this improvement would affect motorists. Policies to counter urban automobility—albeit difficult to sell politically—appear to be the way forward. There is at least some comfort in the fact that it might not be too late. Unlike in Western cities, automobility has not yet completely altered Russians' settlement patterns. Soviet cities only sprawled when the subways came along, and so far cars have not made their imprint on the overall urban structure. The current population density of built-up areas in Russian cities equals that of many Asian cities. The share of urban space dedicated to streets and roads, however, is extremely low. Car owners do not get behind the wheel because the car has shaped the city, but because of the combination of inconvenient public transport and the status of car ownership.[116]

Nowadays Russian transport scholars argue that the state socialist past has rendered cities unprepared for intense automobility. Conversely, we could also say that the same past has resulted in Russian cities where public transport can be encouraged again, but from a better starting point than in Western cities seeking transit-oriented development (TOD). Public transport still accounts for some 70 percent of traffic in St. Petersburg (not counting walking and cycling). The subways alone serve 42 percent of all traffic. Policymakers in St. Petersburg, as in other Russian cities, still seem to be in a better position to choose alternatives. Whether they will seize the opportunity remains to be seen, but there are positive indications. A recent strategy for regional transport, outlining developments until 2030, foregrounds improvements of public transport to maintain a 30 percent car modal split.[117] Unsurprisingly coming from the head of City Electrical Transport Enterprise's prospective development department, Andrei Ulanov offered some hope in a recent interview: "We have to unload the city: to reduce the transit movement of cars and free parking places in the center, by giving the priority to public transport."[118]

Whereas our top-down approach to sustainability in this chapter suggests a positive legacy of state socialism from an environmental point of view, a bottom-up approach would likely yield dissatisfactory social effects. The improvements to transport systems under state socialist regimes from the 1930s were substantial and enjoyed by many, but over time, the disparity between political leaders' optimistic claims and the realities on the ground caused growing frustration.[119] In spite of flat and frozen fares and relatively equal accessibility of public transport, the poor quality of the service meant major everyday hardships. The contradictions surrounding the social sustainability of urban mobility under state socialism would be an interesting topic for historians to explore.

**Alexandra Bekasova** is a research fellow at the Laboratory for Environmental and Technological History and associate professor at National Research University Higher School of Economics, St. Petersburg campus, Russia. Her research and publications are on the history of technology, the environment, mobility, and transport.

**Julia Kulikova**, an M.A. student at the National Research University Higher School of Economics, Saint Petersburg, focuses in her thesis on the creation of urban public transit in Petrograd—Leningrad during the 1920s and 1930s from the perspective of late Imperial transport engineers. She obtained a Bachelor's degree in archival science and records management at Petrozavodsk State University, where she participated in research projects systematizing and cataloguing museum exhibits and the transliteration of texts. Her research interests include history of public transit, archival science, and electronic records preservation.

**Martin Emanuel**, historian of technology and researcher at the Department of Urban Planning and Environment, KTH Royal Institute of Technology, Stockholm, works at the intersection of mobility, urban, and environmental history, including tourism history. His research is on wide-ranging historical dimensions of cycling culture, urban planning, and traffic management. He has published several articles on the history of cycling and sustainable mobility, as well as the 2012 monograph *Trafikslag på undantag: Cykeltrafiken i Stockholm 1930–1980* (Excluded through planning: Bicycle traffic in Stockholm 1930–1980). He coedited and authored *Cycling Cities: The European Experience* (SHT, 2016).

## Notes

1. Quote from Catriona Kelly, *St. Petersburg: Shadows of the Past* (New Haven: Yale University Press, 2014), 16.
2. See Mikhail Blinkin and Elena Koncheva, eds., *Transport Systems of Russian Cities: Ongoing Transformations* (Cham: Springer, 2016).
3. Robert Argenbright, "Avtomobilshchina: Driven to the Brink in Moscow," *Urban Geography* 29, no. 7 (2008); Blinkin and Koncheva, *Transport Systems of Russian Cities*; Leonid Limonov, "Peculiarities and Factors of St. Petersburg Metropolitan Area Spatial Development in Post-Soviet Period," in *Sustaining Regional Futures* (Beijing: Annual Global Conference of the Regional Studies Association, 2012).
4. Elitza Stanoeva, "Socio-cultural Dimensions of Urban Mass Transportation: The Introduction of Trams in Sofia (1901–1916)," in *Social and Spiritual Aspects of Material Culture*, ed. Aneta Svetieva and Ana Ashtalkovska (Skopje: Institute of Ethnology and Anthropology, 2009).
5. See John Urry, "The 'System' of Automobility," *Theory, Culture & Society* 21, no. 4–5 (2004). In our view, Urry underestimated the large differences that exist,

for many different reasons, between various countries and parts of the world. On "cracks" in the system, see Frank W. Geels et al., eds., *Automobility in Transition? A Socio-technical Analysis of Sustainable Transport* (New York: Routledge, 2012).

6. Mikhail Blinkin, "Introduction," in Blinkin and Koncheva, *Transport Systems of Russian Cities*, xi.

7. Tracy Nichols Busch, "'Comrades, Start Your Engines!': Mobility, Legitimacy, and Roads to Socialism in the Soviet Interwar Period," *Canadian-American Slavic Studies* 47, no. 2 (2013).

8. See the introduction in Kathy Burrell and Kathrin Hörschelmann, *Mobilities in Socialist and Post-socialist States: Societies on the Move* (Houndmills: Palgrave Macmillan, 2014).

9. Peter Hall, *The World Cities* (London: Weidenfeld & Nicolson, 1984), 128–29.

10. Holland Hunter, *Soviet Transport Experience: Its Lessons for Other Countries* (Washinton, DC: The Brookings Institution, 1968), 115.

11. Ibid., 117. On the inevitability of a car future for Russian cities, see R. Antony French, *Plans, Pragmatism and People: The Legacy of Soviet Planning for Today's Cities* (Pittsburgh, PA: University of Pittsburgh Press, 1995), chapter 7.

12. For the U.S. "love affair" with the car, see Norton in this volume.

13. Hunter, *Soviet Transport Experience*, 122.

14. Denis J. B. Shaw, "Planning Leningrad," *Geographical Review* 68, no. 2 (1978): 199.These problems are elaborated in Martin Crouch, "Problems of Soviet Urban Transport," *Soviet Studies* 31, no. 2(1979): 231–56.

15. For the imperial and interwar period, the chapter builds on Alexei Manuilov's thesis and Julia Kulikova's ongoing research. We note a certain imbalance in the sources used. The imperial period builds on published and archival sources, the interwar period on published primary sources, while the postwar period uses secondary sources.

16. On the opportunities and challenges posed by St. Petersburg's geographical space, see Denis J. B. Shaw, "St. Petersburg and Geographies of Modernity," in *St. Petersburg, 1703–1825*, ed. Anthony Cross (Basingstoke: Palgrave Macmillan, 2003), 6–29. The Neva River provided services and promoted circulation of goods and passengers in the city; see Randall Dills, "The River Neva and the Imperial Façade: Culture and Environment in Nineteenth Century St. Petersburg Russia," Ph.D. thesis, Department of History, University of Illinois at Urbana-Champaign, accessed 15 August 2018, https://www.ideals.illinois.edu/handle/2142/18391; Alexei Kraikovskii, Julia Lajus, "The Neva as a Metropolitan River of Russia: Environment, Economy and Culture," in *A History of Water*, vol. 2, ed. Terje Tvedt and Richard Coopey (London: I. B. Tauris, 2010), 339–64.

17. James H. Bater, *St. Petersburg: Industrialization and Change* (London: Edward Arnold, 1976), 330.

18. *Spravka k voprosu ob uluchshenii sposobov peredvizheniia naseleniia S.-Peterburga* (St. Petersburg: Tipografiia Ministerstva vnutrennikh del, 1901), 3–4.

19. Alexei Manuilov, "Proekty sooruzheniia metropolitena v Sankt-Peterburge i Moskve: otrazrabotke k obsuzhdeniiu. Konets XIX—nachalo XX vv." Bachelor's thesis, National Research University "Higher School of Economics," St. Petersburg, 2018, 25–26.

20. Manuilov, "Proekty sooruzheniia metropolitena," 35.

21. Ibid., 34.

22. Bater, *St. Petersburg: Industrialization and Change*, 330–31.

23. James H. Bater, "The Development of Public Transportation in St. Petersburg, 1860–1914," *Journal of Transport History*, New Series 2, no. 2 (1973): 92.

24. *Peterburgskaia Gorodskaia Duma*, 239, 242; *Piatdesiat let Leningradskogo tramvaia* (Moscow: Izdatel'stvo ministerstva kommunal'nogo khoziaistva, 1957), 14. In 1914, after 193 km of tram track were electrified, the network transported over 300 million passengers that year. James H. Bater, "The Journey to Work in St. Petersburg: 1860–1914." *Journal of Transport History*, New Series 2, no. 4 (1974): 221.

25. *Peterburgskaia Gorodskaia Duma*, 206–7.

26. Bater, "The Development of Public Transportation in St. Petersburg," 97; N. N. Petrov, "Gorodskoye Upravleniye i Gorodskoye Khoziaystvo Peterburga," in *Ocherki istorii Leningrada*, vol. 3 (Moscow–Leningrad: Izdatel'stvo Akademii Nauk SSSR, 1957), 910.

27. *Ocherki istorii Leningrada*, vol. 3. (Moscow–Leningrad: Izdatel'stvo Akademii Nauk SSSR, 1956), 910.

28. James H. Bater, "Some Dimensions of Urbanization and the Response of Municipal Government: Moscow and St. Petersburg," *Russian History* 5, no. 1 (1978): 58; Bater, *St. Petersburg: Industrialization and Change*, 330–32.

29. *Piatdesiat let Leningradskogo tramvaia*, 7. As the number of electric trams grew from 525 in 1910 to 609 in 1913, the number of horse-drawn trams dropped from 545 in 1898 to 381 in 1910, and 261 in 1913. In 1908, electric trams carried 83 million of the 148 million public transport passengers in the city. The following year, the electric trams alone carried 162 million passengers—indicating their quick takeover in the late imperial period. Bater, *St. Petersburg: Industrialization and Change*, 270.

30. *Ocherki istorii Leningrada*, vol. 3, 910.

31. Crouch, "Problems of Soviet Urban Transport," 234.

32. See James. H. Bater's work: "The Journey to Work"; "The Development of Public Transportation in St. Petersburg, 1860–1914"; "Transience, Residential Persistence, and Mobility in Moscow and St. Petersburg, 1900–1914," *Slavic Review* 39, no. 2 (1980): 239–54; and *St. Petersburg: Industrialization and Change*.

33. See city council photographer Karl Bulla's photographs taken from the 1890s to 1917. Valentin Elbek et al., eds., *Pervyi fotoreporter Rossii Karl Bulla: fotomonografiia* (St. Petersburg: Fond istoricheskoi fotografii imeni Karla Bully, 2015). See Cochoy et al. and Männistö-Funk's chapters in this volume regarding the use of photographs to uncover otherwise-hidden mobilities. Pooley's chapter in this volume discusses the evolution of walking in the United Kingdom.

34. Mikhail Blinkin and Egor Muleev, "Russian Cities Mobility Culture: International Comparison," in Blinkin and Koncheva, *Transport Systems of Russian Cities*, 260.

35. Bater, *St. Petersburg: Industrialization and Change*, 275–77.

36. Nikolai Danilevskii, *Dodgdetsia li Petrograd blagoustroennykh mostovykh i trotuarov* (Petrograd: Tipografiia peterburgskogo gradonachal'nika, 1916). Danilevskii did this work for thirteen years and gained rich experience from study trips abroad.

37. James H. Bater, *The Soviet City: Ideal and Reality* (London: Edward Arnold, 1980), 6. See also French, *Plans, Pragmatism and People*, chapter 1.

38. *Peterburgskaia gorodskaia duma*, 210, 217.

39. Soviet tramway histories emphasize that most of the engineer cadre left, spare parts were scarce, and the tramways' newly established collective management "had to start everything from scratch." *Piatdesiat let Leningradskogo*, 19; Boris

Rzhonsnitskii, *Tramvai—russkoe izobretenie* (Moscow: Izdatel'stvo Ministerstva kommunal'nogo khoziaistva, 1952), 4.

40. See, e.g., Elena Alekseevna Ignatova, *Zapiski o Peterburge: Zhizneopisanie goroda so vremeni ego osnvaniia do 40-kh godov XX veka* (St. Petersburg: Amphora, 2005), 513.

41. Stephen V. Bittner, "Green Cities and Orderly Streets: Space and Culture in Moscow, 1928–1933," *Journal of Urban History* 25, no. 1 (1998): 25.

42. S. Frederick Starr, "Visionary Town Planning during the Cultural Revolution," in *Cultural Revolution in Russia, 1928–1931,* ed. Sheila Fitzpatrick (Bloomington: Indiana University Press, 1978), 212. See French, *Plans, Pragmatism and People,* chapter 2, in which he stresses the overlap in views and cross-relationships between the groups.

43. Blair A. Ruble, *Leningrad: Shaping a Soviet City* (Berkeley: University of California Press, 1990), 7; Starr, "Visionary Town Planning," 239.

44. Cited in Alexander Kulakov and Konstantin Trofimenko, "Transport Planning and Transport Modeling," in Blinkin and Koncheva, *Transport Systems of Russian Cities,* 8.

45. On socialist competition, see Katalin Miklóssy and Melanie Ilič, *Competition in Socialist Society* (London: Routledge, 2014). By the same token, the transport sector in the West was indeed full of capitalist regulation. See, e.g., Crouch, "Problems of Soviet Urban Transport."

46. For Swedish travelers' experiences visiting the Soviet Union in the 1930s, see Charlotte Tornbjer, "Modernity, Technology and Culture in Swedish Travel Reports during the 1930s," in *Technology in Time, Space, and Mind,* ed. K. G. Hammarlund and Tomas Nilsson (Halmstad: Högskolan i Halmstad, 2008).

47. Natallia Barykina, "Transnational Mobilities: Western European Architects and Planners in the Soviet Industrial Cities, 1928–1933," *Planning Perspectives* 32, no. 3 (2017): 333–52; Koos Bosma, "New Socialist Cities: Foreign Architects in the USSR 1920–1940," *Planning Perspectives* 29, no. 3 (2014): 301–28; Stephen V. Ward, "Soviet Communism and the British Planning Movement: Rational Learning or Utopian Imagining?" *Planning Perspectives* 27, no. 4 (2012): 499–524.

48. Ol'ga Erokhina and Galina Tolkunova, "Realizatsia kontsessionoi politiki v stroitel'noi otrasli Rossii v 20–30 gody XX veka," *Terra Economicus* 9, no. 2 (2011): 41.

49. Vaitens, "Osobennosti," 401.

50. Bater, *The Soviet City,* 29.

51. Sergei Lebedev, *Gorod v dvizhenii. Sredstva peredvizheniia v gorode* (Moscow: Izdatel'stvo "Rabotnik prosveshcheniia," 1926), 5–6.

52. Andrei Vaitens, "Osobennosti gradoregulirovaniia v Petrograde—Leningrade: formirovanie vnutrigorodskoi sistemy upravleniia," in *Sovetskoe gradostroitel'stvo,* vol. 1, ed. Iulia Kosenkova (Moscow: Progress-Traditsia, 2018), 390.

53. Howard's thinking was popular in Russia in the early twentieth century, and his *Garden Cities of Tomorrow* was translated into Russian. See the contributions on St. Petersburg in Lars Nilsson et al., *The European City and Green Space: London, Stockholm, Helsinki and St. Petersburg, 1850–2000,* Historical Urban Studies (Aldershot: Ashgate, 2006).

54. Grigorii Dubelir, *Planirovka gorodov. Lektsii* (n.p., 1930), 34, 40.

55. Recent studies of early Soviet urban reconstruction and regulation policies stress the continuity between the two eras: ideas generated by imperial engineers, scientists, architects and city administrators helped shape the unique regulations in interwar Petrograd—Leningrad. Vaitens, "Osobennosti," 387, 417.

56. Abram Zil'bertal', *Problemy gorodskogo obshchestvennogo transporta* (Moscow–Leningrad: Gosudarstvennoe transportnoe izdatel'stvo, 1930), 234.

57. Abram Zil'bertal', *Tramvainoe khoziaistvo* (Moscow–Leningrad: OGIZ, 1932), 18.

58. Iurii Grinval'd, *Razvitie gorodskogo i prigorodnogo passazhirskogo soobshcheniia v Leningrade* (Leningrad: Leningradskoe oblastnoe otdelenie vsesoyuznogo energeticheskogo komiteta, 1931), 5–6.

59. Aleksandr Chistikov and Liudmila Protsai, *Petrograd–Leningrad 1920–1930 gody v fotografiiakh i dokumentakh* (St. Petersburg: Liki Rossii, 2010), 200.

60. Abram Zil'bertal', "Dostizheniia Leningradskogo tramvaia," *Voprosy kommunal'nogo khoziaistva* 11 (1927): 106; Chistikov and Protsai, *Petrograd–Leningrad*, 156.

61. Iurii Grinval'd, "Ekonomika i perspektivy Leningradskogo tramvaia," *Voprosy kommunal'nogo khoziaistva* 8 (1927): 46.

62. Ibid. According to Crouch, using the example of Moscow, public transport produced high profits due to "gross overcrowding . . . and an 'efficient' use of stock." Crouch, "Problems of Soviet Urban Transport," 235.

63. "Khronika," *Voprosy kommunal'nogo khoziaistva* 3 (1926): 221.

64. *Piatdesiat let Leningradskogo tramvaia*, 22.

65. "Khronika," no. 3 (1926): 220; no. 5 (1928): 117.

66. Grinval'd, *Razvitie*, 10.

67. See "Soedinit' okrainu s gorodom," *Leningradskaia pravda* (Leningrad), 4 January 1929; P. Evdokimov, "Peshkom za 15 kilometrov," *Leningradskaia pravda* (Leningrad), 26 March 1936.

68. *Ocherki istorii Leningrada*, vol. 4, 506.

69. Then the track length of the bus network was 375 km. *Vosem'desiat let avtobusnomu dvizheniiu v Sankt-Peterburge* (Saint Petersburg: GMI SPb, 2006), 25.

70. Chistikov and Protsai, *Petrograd–Leningrad*, 156. *Ocherki istorii Leningrada*, vol. 4, 506.

71. Lev Gulevich, "Okhrana bezopasnosti dvizheniia v Leningrade," *Voprosy kommunal'nogo khoziaistva* 3 (1928): 28.

72. Valery Lazarev and Paul Gregory, "Commissars and Cars: A Case Study in the Political Economy of Dictatorship," *Journal of Comparative Economics* 31, no. 1, (2003): 19.

73. Yves Cohen, "Circulatory Localities: The Example of Stalinism in the 1930s," *Kritika: Explorations in Russian and Eurasian History* 11, no. 1 (2010): 11–45. See also Yves Cohen, "The Soviet Fordson: Between the Politics of Stalin and the Philosophy of Ford, 1924–1932," in *Ford, 1903–2003*, ed. Hubert Bonin, Yannick Lung, and Steven Tolliday (Paris: Plage, 2003), 531–58; Boris M. Shpotov, "Ford in Russia from 1909 to World War II," in Bonin, Lung, and Tolliday, *Ford, 1903–2003*, 505–29; idem, "Russia and the Americanisation Process (1900–1930s)," in *L'américanisation en Europe au XXe siècle*, ed. Dominique Barjot, Isabelle Lescent-Giles, and Marc de Ferrières Le Vayer (Lille: Université Charles-de-Gaulle, 2002), 303–14; Dana G. Dalrymple, "The American Tractor Comes to Soviet Agriculture: The Transfer of a Technology," *Technology and Culture* 5, no. 2 (1964): 191–214.

74. Tracy Nichols Busch, "Women and Children First? Avtodor's Campaigns and the Limits of Soviet Automobility from 1927 to 1935," *Russian Review* 70, no. 3 (2011): 399.

75. *Ocherki istorii Leningrada*, vol. 4, 506.

76. *Tipovye pravila dvizheniia po ulitsam i dorogam Soyuza SSSR* (Voroshilovgrad: ti-popgraphiia izdatel'stva "Voroshilovgradskaia pravda," 1940). *Ocherki istorii Leningrada,* vol. 4, 911.

77. *Spravochnik po pravilam gorodskogo peshekhodnogo dvizheniia* (Leningrad: Otdel regulirovaniia gorodskogo dvizheniia Leningradskogo oblastnogo upravleniia raboche-krest'ianskoi militsii, 1931), 7.

78. On the reinterpretation of city streets as sites for car traffic, see Peter D. Norton, "Street Rivals: Jaywalking and the Invention of the Motor Age Street," *Technology and Culture* 48, no. 2 (2007).

79. Ruth Oldenziel et al., eds., *Cycling Cities: The European Experience: Hundred Years of Policy and Practice* (Eindhoven: Foundation of the History of Technology, 2016).

80. Ruble, *Leningrad,* 64.

81. Ibid., 50.

82. W. Bruce Lincoln, *Sunlight at Midnight: St. Petersburg and the Rise of Modern Russia* (Oxford: Perseus Press, 2001), 317.

83. V. A. Gariugin et al., eds., *Metropoliten severnoi stolitsy, 1955–1995* (St. Petersburg: Liki Rossii, 1995), 8; *Ocherki istorii Leningrada,* vol. 3, 910. Upravlenie Petrogradskikh gorodskikh zheleznykh dorog, *po voprosu o sooruzhenii metropolitena i razvitii seti gorodskikh zheleznykh dorog v' gorode Petrograde* (Petrograd: 1917), 19, 48, 175

84. Gariugin et al., *Metropoliten severnoi,* 40–46. Shaw, "Planning Leningrad," 186–87.

85. Anthony R. French, *Plans, Pragmatism and People,* 66–68. On Stalinist city planning, see Heather D. DeHaan, *Stalinist City Planning: Professionals, Performance, and Power* (Toronto: University of Toronto Press, 2013).

86. Hall, *The World Cities,* 126–28. Present-day transport scholars are critical of how wide urban roads were built with adjacent buildings, contrary to foreign practice. Blinkin and Koncheva, *Transport Systems of Russian Cities.*

87. Shaw, "Planning Leningrad," 186–88, 98; Ruble, *Leningrad,* 50–65; Lincoln, *Sunlight at Midnight,* 315.

88. Ruble, *Leningrad,* 69–79; Lincoln, *Sunlight at Midnight,* 315.

89. On Anglo-Soviet exchanges regarding urban planning, see Ian R. Cook, Stephen V. Ward, and Kevin Ward, "A Springtime Journey to the Soviet Union: Postwar Planning and Policy Mobilities through the Iron Curtain," *International Journal of Urban and Regional Research* 38, no. 3 (2014); Stephen V. Ward, "Soviet Communism and the British Planning Movement: Rational Learning or Utopian Imagining?," *Planning Perspectives* 27, no. 4 (2012); "Urban Planning Visits and Anglo-Soviet Communication in the 1930s and 1950s," *Russian Journal of Communication* 8, no. 3 (2016).

90. Shaw, "Planning Leningrad," 192; Ruble, *Leningrad,* 78.

91. Shaw, "Planning Leningrad," 187.

92. *Sbornik materialov, posviashchennykh 10-letiiu ekspluatatsii Leningradskogo metropolitena imeni V. I. Lenina* (Leningrad: Tekhnicheskii otdel i RaiNTO Leningradskogo metropolitena imeni V. I. Lenina, 1967), 31–33.

93. Shaw, "Planning Leningrad," 183.

94. *Vosem'desiat let avtobusnomu dvizheniiu v Sankt-Peterburge,* 33, 39.

95. By 1965, there were 24.5 km of tracks, and the number of stations increased to eighteen. *Ocherki istorii Leningrada,* vol. 6 (Leningrad: Izdatel'stvo Akademii Nauk SSSR, 1970), 262.

96. Kelly, *St. Petersburg: Shadows,* 44–47.

97. French, *Plans, Pragmatism and People*, 162.
98. Crouch, "Problems of Soviet Urban Transport." Regarding the institutional split, see also Pavel Zyuzin and Alexander Ryzhkov, "Urban Public Transport Development: Trends and Reforms," in Blinkin and Koncheva, *Transport Systems of Russian Cities: Ongoing Transformations.*
99. Kelly, *St. Petersburg: Shadows*, 54.
100. Lewis H. Siegelbaum, *Cars for Comrades: The Life of the Soviet Automobile* (Ithaca: Cornell University Press, 2008), 188–218; Hunter, *Soviet Transport Experience*, 104–5.
101. Siegelbaum, *Cars for Comrades*, 6–7, 84–85, 223–51; Hunter, *Soviet Transport Experience*, 105–11.
102. Hall, *The World Cities*, 128.
103. Ruble, *Leningrad*, 78.
104. Shaw, "Planning Leningrad," 192.
105. Karl Aleksander, Boris Dobrer, and Oleg Kudriavtsev, *Peshekhodnye estakady i tonneli v gorodakh* (Moscow: Gosudarstvennoe izdatel'stvo literatury po stroitel'stvu, arkhitekture i stroitel'nym materialam, 1963), 13, 14, 18; Aleksander Andreev, "Peshekhodnye tonnel'nye perekhody na Nevskom prospekte," *Stroitel'stvo i arkhitektura Leningrada*, no. 4 (1961); Georgii Golubev, "Sovremennye priemy razdeleniia putei dvizheniia peshekhodov i transporta," *Izvestiia Akademii stroitel'stva i arkhitektury SSSR*, no. 3 (1962); Oleg Kudriavtsev, "Vorprosy organizatsii peshekhodnogo dvizheniia pri planirovke gorodov" in *Transport i planirovka gorodov* (Moscow: MKKH RSFSR, 1962).
106. *Proceedings of the XIVth World Road Congress, Prague 1971* (London: World road congress/PIARC, 1973), 21–22.
107. Antonina Ushakova, "Development of Underground Space as Transportation Problem Solution in St. Petersburg," *Procedia Engineering* 165 (2016): 168.
108. For the case of Moscow, see Hunter, *Soviet Transport Experience*, 120–21.
109. The modal split data is from Limonov, "Peculiarities and Factors of St. Petersburg Metropolitan Area Spatial Development in Post-Soviet Period," 7. The 2016 figures are in Direkstiia po razvitiiu transportnoi sistemy Sankt-Peterburga i Leningradskoi oblasti (hereafter Direkstiia), *Programma razvitiia transportnoi sistemy Sankt-Peterburga i Leningradskoi oblasti na period do 2020 goda. Tom 7. Podprogramma "Metropoliten i drugie vidy vneulichnogo skorostnogo passazhirskogo transporta"* (St. Petersburg, 2016).
110. Kulakov and Trofimenko, "Russian Cities Mobility Culture." On the "tyranny of the car," see French, *Plans, Pragmatism and People*, chapter 7.
111. Ruble, *Leningrad*, 66.
112. Massimo Moraglio, "Light Rail Renaissance in European Cities: Urban Mobility Agenda and City Renewals," in *The City and the Railway in the World. 19th to 21st Centuries*, ed. Ralf Roth and Paul van Heesvelde (Surrey: Ashgate, forthcoming 2021).
113. Burrell and Hörschelmann, *Mobilities in Socialist and Post-socialist States*, 6–7.
114. Shaw, "Planning Leningrad," 192–93.
115. Hunter, *Soviet Transport Experience*.
116. Zyuzin and Ryzhkov, "Urban Public Transport Development," 70–71; Elena Koncheva and Nikolay Zalesskiy, "Urban Spatial Structure as a Factor of Travel Behavior" in Blinkin and Koncheva, *Transport Systems of Russian Cities: Ongoing Transformations.*
117. Direkstiia, *Programma razvitiia transportnoi sistemy*.

118. Inessa Iushkovskaia "Novyi povorot. Peterburgskie tramvai zhdiot pereza-gruzka," *Sankt-Peterburgskie vedomosti*, accessed 28 October 2018, https://spbvedomosti.ru/news/gorod/kuda_povernet_tramvay/.
119. Burrell and Hörschelmann, *Mobilities in Socialist and Post-socialist States*, 3.

# Bibliography

Aleksander, Karl, Boris Dobrer, and Oleg Kudriavtsev. *Peshekhodnye estakady i tonneli v gorodakh*. Moscow: Gosudarstvennoe izdatel'stvo literatury po stroitel'stvu, arkhitekture i stroitel'nym materialam, 1963.

Andreev, Aleksander. "Peshekhodnye tonnel'nye perekhody na Nevskom prospekte." *Stroitel'stvo i arkhitektura Leningrada*, no. 4 (1961).

Argenbright, Robert. "Avtomobilshchina: Driven to the Brink in Moscow." *Urban Geography* 29, no. 7 (2008): 683–704.

Barykina, Natallia. "Transnational Mobilities: Western European Architects and Planners in the Soviet Industrial Cities, 1928–1933." *Planning Perspectives* 32, no. 3 (2017): 333–52.

Bater, James H. "The Development of Public Transportation in St. Petersburg, 1860–1914." *Journal of Transport History*, New Series 2, no. 2 (1973): 85–102.

———. "The Journey to Work in St. Petersburg, 1860–1914." *Journal of Transport History*, New Series 2, no. 4 (1974): 214–33.

———. "Some Dimensions of Urbanization and the Response of Municipal Government: Moscow and St. Petersburg." *Russian History* 5, no. 1 (1978): 46–63.

———. *The Soviet City: Ideal and Reality*. London: Edward Arnold, 1980.

———. *St. Petersburg: Industrialization and Change*. London: Edward Arnold, 1976.

———. "Transience, Residential Persistence, and Mobility in Moscow and St. Petersburg, 1900–1914." *Slavic Review* 39, no. 2 (1980): 239–54.

Bittner, Stephen V. "Green Cities and Orderly Streets: Space and Culture in Moscow, 1928–1933." *Journal of Urban History* 25, no. 1 (1998): 22–56.

Blinkin, Mikhail. "Introduction." In *Transport Systems of Russian Cities: Ongoing Transformations*, edited by Mikhail Blinkin and Elena Koncheva, 259–72. Cham: Springer, 2016.

Blinkin, Mikhail, and Egor Muleev. "Russian Cities Mobility Culture: International Comparison." In Blinkin and Elena Koncheva, *Transport Systems of Russian Cities: Ongoing Transformations*, 259–72.

Blinkin, Mikhail, and Elena Koncheva, eds. *Transport Systems of Russian Cities: Ongoing Transformations*. Cham: Springer, 2016.

Bosma, Koos. "New Socialist Cities: Foreign Architects in the USSR 1920–1940." *Planning Perspectives* 29, no. 3 (2014): 301–28.

Burrell, Kathy, and Kathrin Hörschelmann. *Mobilities in Socialist and Post-socialist States: Societies on the Move*. Houndmills: Palgrave Macmillan, 2014.

Busch, Tracy Nichols. "'Comrades, Start Your Engines!': Mobility, Legitimacy, and Roads to Socialism in the Soviet Interwar Period." *Canadian-American Slavic Studies* 47, no. 2 (2013): 221–46.

Chistikov, Aleksandr, and Liudmila Protsai. *Petrograd—Leningrad. 1920–1930 gody v fotografiiakh i dokumentakh*. St. Petersburg: Liki Rossii, 2010.

Cohen, Yves. "Circulatory Localities: The Example of Stalinism in the 1930s." *Kritika: Explorations in Russian and Eurasian History* 11, no. 1 (2010): 11–45.

——. "The Soviet Fordson: Between the Politics of Stalin and the Philosophy of Ford, 1924–1932." In *Ford, 1903–2003*, edited by Hubert Bonin, Yannick Lung, and Steven Tolliday, 531–58. Paris: Plage, 2003.

Cook, Ian R., Stephen V. Ward, and Kevin Ward. "A Springtime Journey to the Soviet Union: Postwar Planning and Policy Mobilities through the Iron Curtain." *International Journal of Urban and Regional Research* 38, no. 3 (2014): 805–22.

Crouch, Martin. "Problems of Soviet Urban Transport." *Soviet Studies* 31, no. 2 (1979): 231–56.

Dalrymple, Dana G. "The American Tractor Comes to Soviet Agriculture: The Transfer of a Technology." *Technology and Culture* 5, no. 2 (1964): 191–214.

Danilevskii, Nikolai. *Dodgdetsia li Petrograd blagoustroennykh mostovykh i trotuarov.* Petrograd: Tipografiia peterburgskogo gradonachal'nika, 1916.

DeHaan, Heather D. *Stalinist City Planning: Professionals, Performance, and Power.* Toronto: University of Toronto Press, 2013.

Dills, Randall. "The River Neva and the Imperial Façade: Culture and Environment in Nineteenth Century St. Petersburg Russia," Ph.D. thesis, Department of History, University of Illinois at Urbana-Champaign. Accessed 15 August 2018, https://www.ideals.illinois.edu/handle/2142/18391.

Direkstiia po razvitiiu transportnoi sistemy Sankt-Peterburga i Leningradskoi oblasti. *Programma razvitiia transportnoi sistemy Sankt-Peterburga i Leningradskoi oblasti na period do 2020 goda. Tom 7. Podprogramma "Metropoliten i drugie vidy vneulichnogo skorostnogo passazhirskogo transporta."* St. Petersburg, 2016.

Dubelir, Grigorii. *Planirovka gorodov. Lektsii.* (n.p., 1930).

Dubentsov, B. B., and V. A. Nardova, eds. *Peterburgskaia Gorodskaia Duma, 1846–1918.* St. Petersburg: Liki Rossii, 2005.

Elbek, Valentin, et al., eds. *Pervyi fotoreporter Rossii Karl Bulla: fotomonografiia.* St. Petersburg: Fond istoricheskoi fotografii imeni Karla Bully, 2015.

Erokhina, Ol'ga, and Galina Tolkunova. "Realizatsia kontsessionoi politiki v stroitel'noi otrasli Rossii v 20–30 gody XX veka." In *Terra Economicus* 9, no. 2 (2011): 39–45.

French, R. Antony. *Plans, Pragmatism and People: The Legacy of Soviet Planning for Today's Cities.* Pittsburgh, PA: University of Pittsburgh Press, 1995.

Gariugin, V. A., et al., eds. *Metropoliten severnoi stolitsy, 1955–1995.* St. Petersburg: Liki Rossii, 1995.

Geels, Frank W., René Kemp, Geoff Dudley, and Glenn Lyons, eds. *Automobility in Transition? A Socio-technical Analysis of Sustainable Transport.* New York: Routledge, 2012.

Golubev, Georgii. "Sovremennye priemy razdeleniia putei dvizheniia peshekhodov i transporta." *Izvestiia Akademii stroitel'stva i arkhitektury SSSR* 3 (1962).

Grinval'd, Iurii. "Ekonomika i perspektivy Leningradskogo tramvaia." *Voprosy kommunal'nogo khoziaistva* 8 (1927): 42–8.

——. *Razvitie gorodskogo i prigorodnogo passazhirskogo soobshcheniia v Leningrade.* Leningrad: Leningradskoe oblastnoe otdelenie vsesoiuznogo energeticheskogo komiteta, 1931.

Gulevich, Lev. "Okhrana bezopasnosti dvizheniia v Leningrade." *Voprosy kommunal'nogo khoziaistva* 3 (1928): 22–30.

Hall, Peter. *The World Cities.* London: Weidenfeld & Nicolson, 1984.

Hunter, Holland. *Soviet Transport Experience: Its Lessons for Other Countries.* Washington, DC: The Brookings Institution, 1968.

Ignatova, Elena. *Zapiski o Peterburge: Zhizneopisanie goroda so vremeni ego osnvaniia do 40-kh godov XX veka.* St. Petersburg: Amphora, 2005.

Kelly, Catriona. *St. Petersburg: Shadows of the Past*. New Haven: Yale University Press, 2014.

"Khronika." *Voprosy kommunal'nogo khoziaistva* 3 (1926): 220–21; and 5 (1928): 117–18.

Koncheva, Elena, and Nikolay Zalesskiy. "Urban Spatial Structure as a Factor of Travel Behavior," in *Transport Systems of Russian Cities: Ongoing Transformations*, 39–65.

Kraikovskii, Alexei, and Lajus, Julia. "The Neva as a Metropolitan River of Russia: Environment, Economy and Culture." In *A History of Water*, vol. 2, edited by Terje Tvedt and Richard Coopey, 339–64. London: I. B. Tauris, 2010.

Kudriavtsev, Oleg. "Vorprosy organizatsii peshekhodnogo dvizheniia pri planirovke gorodov." In *Transport i planirovka gorodov*. Moscow: MKKH RSFSR, 1962.

Kulakov, Alexander, and Konstantin Trofimenko. "Transport Planning and Transport Modeling." In *Transport Systems of Russian Cities: Ongoing Transformations*, 1–39.

Lazarev, Valery, and Paul Gregory. "Commissars and Cars: A Case Study in the Political Economy of Dictatorship." *Journal of Comparative Economics* 31, no. 1, (2003): 1–19.

Lebedev, Sergei. *Gorod v dvizhenii. Sredstva peredvizheniia v gorode*, Moscow: Izdatel'stvo "Rabotnik prosveshcheniia," 1926.

Limonov, Leonid. "Peculiarities and Factors of St. Petersburg Metropolitan Area Spatial Development in Post-Soviet Period." In *Sustaining Regional Futures*. Beijing: Annual Global Conference of the Regional Studies Association, 2012.

Lincoln, W. Bruce. *Sunlight at Midnight: St. Petersburg and the Rise of Modern Russia*. Oxford: Perseus Press, 2001.

Manuilov, Alexei. "Proekty sooruzheniia metropolitena v Sankt-Peterburge i Moskve: otrazrabotke k obsuzhdeniiu. Konets XIX–nachalo XX vv." Bachelor's thesis, National Research University Higher School of Economics, St. Petersburg, 2018.

Miklóssy, Katalin, and Melanie Ilič. *Competition in Socialist Society*. London: Routledge, 2014.

Moraglio, Massimo. "Light Rail Renaissance in European Cities: Urban Mobility Agenda and City Renewals." In *The City and the Railway in the World: 19th to 21st Centuries*, edited by Ralf Roth and Paul van Heesvelde. Surrey: Ashgate, forthcoming 2021.

Nilsson, Lars, Catharina Nolin, Mats Deland, and Peter Clark. *The European City and Green Space: London, Stockholm, Helsinki and St. Petersburg, 1850–2000*. Historical Urban Studies. Aldershot: Ashgate, 2006.

Norton, Peter D. "Street Rivals: Jaywalking and the Invention of the Motor Age Street." *Technology and Culture* 48, no. 2 (2007): 331–59.

*Ocherki istorii Leningrada*. Vols. 2–4, 6–7. Moscow–Leningrad: Izdatel'stvo Akademii nauk SSSR, 1956–1989.

Oldenziel, Ruth, Martin Emanuel, Adri Albert de la Bruhèze, and Frank Veraart, eds. *Cycling Cities: The European Experience: Hundred Years of Policy and Practice*. Eindhoven: Foundation of the History of Technology, 2016.

Petrov, N. N. "Gorodskoye Upravleniye i Gorodskoye Khoziaystvo Peterburga." In *Ocherki istorii Leningrada*, vol. 3, 910. Moscow–Leningrad: Izdatel'stvo Akademii Nauk SSSR, 1957.

*Piatdesiat let Leningradskogo tramvaia*. Moscow: Izdatel'stvo ministerstva kommunal'nogo khoziaistva, 1957.

*Proceedings XIVth World Road Congress, Prague 1971*. London: PIARC, 1973.

Ruble, Blair A. *Leningrad: Shaping a Soviet City*. Berkeley: University of California Press, 1990.

Rzhonsnitskii, Boris. *Tramvai—russkoe izobretenie*. Moscow: Izdatel'stvo Ministerstva kommunal'nogo khoziaistva, 1952.

*Sbornik materialov, posviashchennykh 10-letiiu ekspluatatsii Leningradskogo metro-politena imeni V. I. Lenina*. Leningrad: Tekhnicheskii otdel i RaiNTO Leningrad-skogo metropolitena imeni V. I. Lenina, 1967.

Shaw, Denis J. B. "St. Petersburg and Geographies of Modernity." In *St. Petersburg, 1703–1825*, edited by Anthony Cross, 6–29. Basingstoke: Palgrave Macmillan, 2003.

Shaw, Denis J.B. "Planning Leningrad." *Geographical Review* 68, no. 2 (1978): 183–200.

Shpotov, Boris M. "Ford in Russia from 1909 to World War II." In *Ford, 1903–2003*, edited by Hubert Bonin, Yannick Lung, and Steven Tolliday 505–29. Paris: Plage, 2003.

———. "Russia and the Americanisation Process (1900–1930s)." In *L'américanisation en Europe au XXe siècle*, edited by Dominique Barjot, Isabelle Lescent-Giles, and Marc de Ferrières Le Vayer, 303–14. Lille: Université Charles-de-Gaulle, 2002.

Siegelbaum, Lewis H. *Cars for Comrades: The Life of the Soviet Automobile*. Ithaca: Cornell University Press, 2008.

*Spravka k voprosu ob uluchshenii sposobov peredvizheniia naseleniia St. Peterburga*. St. Petersburg: Tipografiia Ministerstva vnutrennikh del, 1901.

*Spravochnik po pravilam gorodskogo peshekhodnogo dvizheniia*. Leningrad: Otdel regulirovaniia gorodskogo dvizheniia Leningradskogo oblastnogo upravleniia raboche-krest'ianskoi militsii, 1931.

Stanoeva, Elitza. "Socio-cultural Dimensions of Urban Mass Transportation: The Introduction of Trams in Sofia (1901–1916)." In *Social and Spiritual Aspects of Material Culture*, edited by Aneta Svetieva and Ana Ashtalkovska, 498–511. Skopje: Institute of Ethnology and Anthropology, 2009.

Starr, S. Frederick. "Visionary Town Planning during the Cultural Revolution." In *Cultural Revolution in Russia, 1928–1931*, edited by Sheila Fitzpatrick. Bloomington: Indiana University Press, 1978.

*Tipovye pravila dvizheniia po ulitsam i dorogam Soiuza SSSR*. Voroshilovgrad: tipo-graphiia izdatel'stva "Voroshilovgradskaia pravda," 1940.

Tornbjer, Charlotte. "Modernity, Technology and Culture in Swedish Travel Reports during the 1930s." In *Technology in Time, Space, and Mind*, edited by K. G. Hammarlund and Tomas Nilsson, 97–127. Halmstad: Högskolan i Halmstad, 2008.

*Upravlenie Petrogradskikh gorodskikh zheleznykh dorog. Po voprosu o sooruzhenii metropolitena i razvitii seti gorodskikh zheleznykh dorog v' gorode Petrograde*. Petrograd: 1917.

Urry, John. "The 'System' of Automobility." *Theory, Culture & Society* 21, no. 4–5 (2004): 25–39.

Ushakova, Antonina. "Development of Underground Space as Transportation Problem Solution in St. Petersburg." *Procedia Engineering* 165 (2016): 166–74.

*Vosem'desiat let avtobusnomu dvizheniiu v Sankt-Peterburge*. St. Petersburg: GMI SPb, 2006.

Ward, Stephen V. "Soviet Communism and the British Planning Movement: Rational Learning or Utopian Imagining?" *Planning Perspectives* 27, no. 4 (2012): 499–524.

———. "Urban Planning Visits and Anglo-Soviet Communication in the 1930s and 1950s." *Russian Journal of Communication* 8, no. 3 (2016): 288–301.

Zil'bertal', Abram. "Dostizheniia Leningradskogo tramvaia." *Voprosy kommunal'nogo khoziaistva* 11 (1927): 102–8.

———. *Problemy gorodskogo obshchestvennogo transporta.* Moscow–Leningrad: Gosudarstvennoe transportnoe izdatel'stvo, 1930.

———. *Tramvainoe khoziaistvo.* Moscow–Leningrad: OGIZ, 1932

Zyuzin, Pavel, and Alexander Ryzhkov. "Urban Public Transport Development: Trends and Reforms." In *Transport Systems of Russian Cities: Ongoing Transformations,* edited by Mikhail Blinkin and Elena Koncheva, 67–99. Cham: Springer, 2016.

# CHAPTER 8

# Livable Streets and Hidden Unsustainability

## The Biography of a Street in Stockholm

Martin Emanuel

## Introduction

On 9 October 1984, Stockholm politicians opened the final links of an urban highway running through Sweden's capital: the Söderleden road tunnel, taking motorized traffic below the surface of Södermalm (one of the islands that make up Stockholm, lying south of the city's central business district), and its southbound extension, the bridge Johanneshovsbron. The result was—and still is—hailed as a success from an urban livability point of view: from one day to the next, traffic on the parallel, above-ground street Götgatan more than halved (from fifty thousand to twenty thousand vehicles a day). After three decades of debates on the best way to benefit from this traffic relief, in recent years the city has been redistributing space away from cars to pedestrians and cyclists. Indeed, without the construction of the tunnel and the bridge Johanneshovsbron, the redesign of Götgatan would probably not have happened. What is even more concealed today is the tough resistance shown by Stockholm's urban environmental movement to the new infrastructures. At the time, activists were protesting against what would later become common knowledge among traffic researchers: building these infrastructures would encourage urban automobility. Whatever the impact on the traffic situation above ground, the opponents argued that Söderleden and Johanneshovsbron would increase car accessibility, get more people into cars, and more cars into the city—and ultimately jeopardize Stockholm's urban livability.

In this chapter, I explore the sustainability arguments put forward by activists in the 1970s and early 1980s. In doing so, I will uncover the unsustainable history of transforming Götgatan. This is not to disregard the recent positive steps to redesign the street. Nor is it to refute the accomplishments of present-day policymakers, who appear to be moving, although belatedly, in the right direction from an environmental sustainability and livability point of view—at least in the city center. Rather, the historical perspective helps us to better understand how change (finally) came about. It also provides a more robust assessment of these recent developments by showing how present-day steps toward livability and sustainability are in fact intertwined with, and even dependent on, earlier unsustainable developments. In historicizing Götgatan, I expose the long-term coevolution of urban infrastructure and mobility that shaped the possibility for redesign in the first place. I also offer a historical narration to show the (mostly unseen) risks of masking unsustainable trends as sustainable and livable ones.

This chapter thus traces the development of Götgatan, a street in Stockholm, together with its traffic, to situate it within larger urban planning developments. In spite of its title, the chapter does not aim to present a complete cultural biography of Götgatan—in the sense of capturing the full plethora of the street's functions and character.[1] Nor do I fully place the street as a mobility-related infrastructure in the context of other technological systems (water supply, sewerage, electricity, and street lighting) developed in the nineteenth and twentieth centuries.[2] The chapter focuses on mobility-related matters. Indeed, "mobility-biography" may be a better term for my approach to sustainability in urban mobility historically.

Why look at one particular street? As I argue, the detailed study of a street provides an opportunity to trace the (very) long-term development of mobility as coproduced by policy actors and road users, as well as place-specific circumstances. Even so, selecting a particular street raises questions of how representative the site is. As one of the two main streets of an urban district between downtown Stockholm and its southern suburbs, Götgatan resembles main streets in Stockholm and other European cities: it carries much commuter traffic but also hosts many shops and cafés; it is both a thoroughfare and a place for shopping. What distinguishes Götgatan is the parallel underground highway, Söderleden (see map 8.1). Originally planned as a local complementary street to Götgatan, by the time Söderleden was completed in 1985, for various reasons—which we will discuss later—it had metamorphosed into a depressed and roofed through-route. The case presented here is thus an example of undertunneling and its effects on the surrounding city. Whereas ideas of vertical segregation of traffic flows stretch back far in time—think, for example, of Eugène Hénard's *The Cities of the Future* (1911)—for a long while only underground urban railways were realized, often to facilitate car traffic flow at ground level.[3] Highways running right through inner cities are not as common in Europe as in the United States. European urban highways tend to encircle the inner city. Although cities such as Birmingham, Cologne, and Paris have inner-city highways, many schemes elsewhere have been canceled due to broad-based resistance to grandiose postwar traffic plans in the 1970s.[4] Götgatan-Söderleden presents a rather special case: an early example of car traffic undertunneling, where environmentally unsustainable patterns are concealed underground, which, however, does not make them more sustainable.

Such undertunneling is an example of a broader phenomenon, in which sustainability (or livability) and unsustainability are interlinked, the former hiding the latter. In contemporary cities, for example, the undisturbed green spaces of urban parks may be built on the rooftop of tunnels for motorized traffic, or come with ample car parking underground.[5] Casting the net wider, whereas there are good reasons to applaud European urbanites who leave their cars and opt for bicycles as their means of daily transportation, the sustainability gains go to waste if they happen to be simultaneously the most frequent flyers. And despite the advantages of cleaner fuels and more efficient engines, such innovations support rather than challenge the dominant unsustainable car regime, since they lend motorists a feeling of being able to carry on driving cars—business as usual. These examples, like the Götgatan-Söderleden case, seem promising at first glance, but we must not lose track of related problematic unsustainable patterns elsewhere.

Only a carefully crafted case study is able to capture the parallel stories of sustainable and unsustainable patterns. This chapter is therefore set up as a case study of Götgatan and Söderleden in Stockholm. It is structured around three episodes, which are in chronological order but also overlap. The first episode takes a long-term perspective to identify two instances of larger urban planning undertakings that gave Götgatan its present-day form. The second episode uncovers the "hidden unsustainability" of Götgatan by tracing the almost century-long process of constructing the parallel underground thoroughfare; it shows how the current measures for making Götgatan a more pleasant street, accessible to pedestrians and cyclists, are intertwined with and shaped by an environmentally unsustainable underground highway. The third episode captures Götgatan's dual identity as both a commuter thoroughfare and a local business street, and how each of these is linked with different conflicting policy aims. In conclusion, I discuss the connections or layeredness of these episodes, highlighting how past decisions continue to shape options for the future. I also comment on the strengths and weaknesses of mobility biographies of streets.

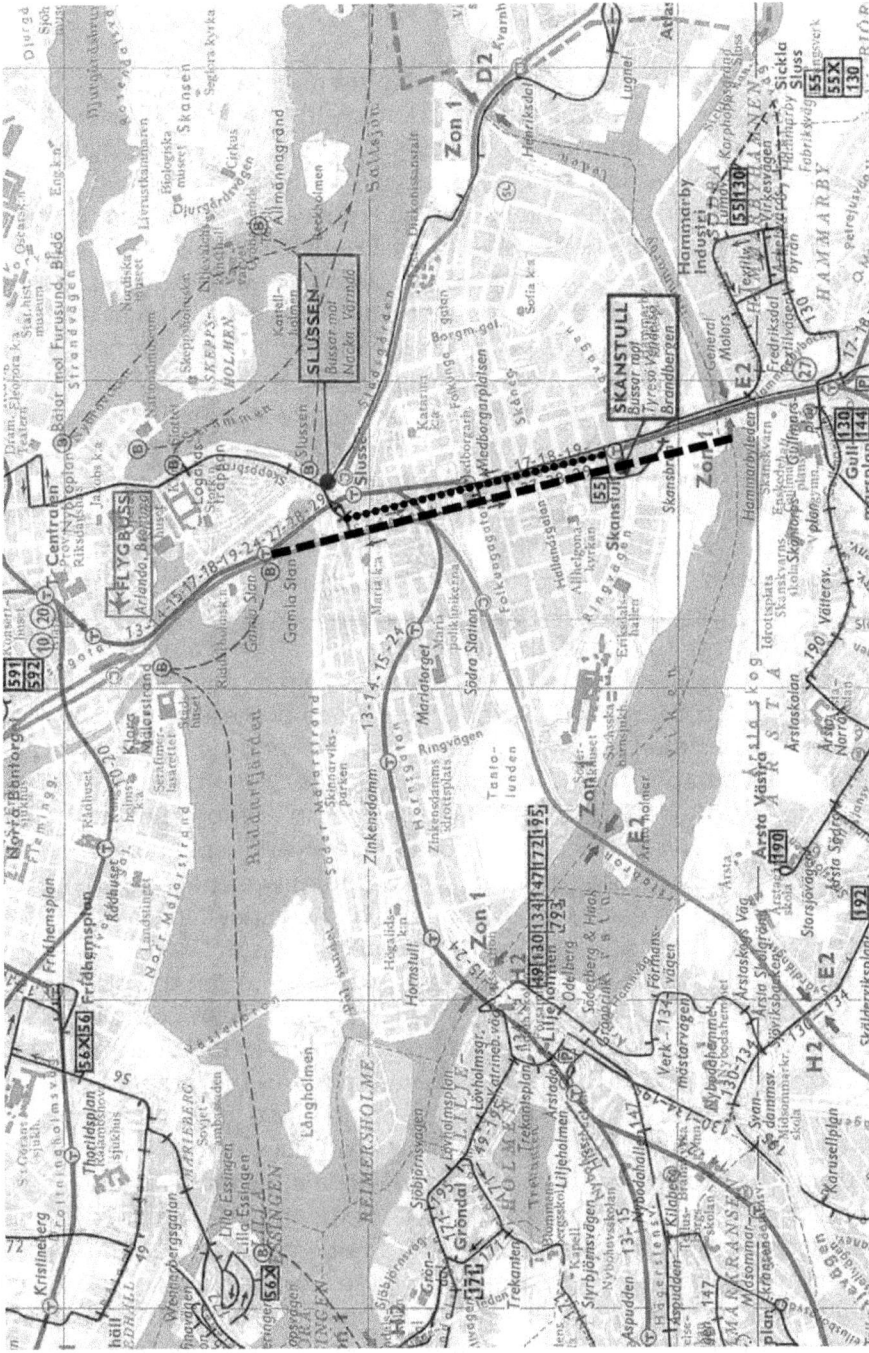

**Map 8.1.** Section of a map issued by Stockholm's public transport administration in 1976. Södermalm is the bigger island in the center; the smaller island further north is where the Old Town is located, and further north is Stockholm's central business district. Götgatan is marked by the dotted line, and Södergatan/Söderleden by the dashed line (the connection over the water to the south had not yet been built).

Source: *Stockholmskartan 1975–76*, Storstockholms lokaltrafik.

## Götgatan Regulated and Widened

Götgatan's contemporary delineation dates from the seventeenth century. At the time, Södermalm was outside (south of) the city limits. It was home to many activities considered too dirty to be located within the city: food cultivation, pasture, tar distilleries, shipyards, and rope making.[6] Götgatan, or rather its forerunners with different names, meandered into rugged terrain. It was, however, a crucial transport link with the road *Göta landsväg*, until the 1660s the only route between Stockholm and the south of Sweden.[7] In the 1640s, Götgatan, like Södermalm and indeed the entire city, was subject to plans for large-scale transformations that would do justice to Stockholm as capital of the great new European empire of Sweden. As in the rest of the city, the organically formed winding street pattern would give way to a Cartesian system: straight streets and regular blocks in Renaissance style.[8] Street regulations made the north-south Götgatan and the east-west Hornsgatan the directional streets on Södermalm. Houses that stood in the way when the streets were straightened—mostly simple wooden ones—were torn down or moved.[9] Closest to the intersection of the two streets, at the most northern part of Götgatan, the urban elite had a few stately seventeenth-century palaces built, some of which remain to this day. The further south you go, the simpler the buildings: none of these remains; many made way for street widening in the twentieth century.

It would take another two hundred years before Södermalm and Götgatan underwent changes of a similar caliber as in the seventeenth century, this time as a result of initial industrialization and rapid urbanization. If the first urban transformation of Stockholm was a display of royal power, the second illustrates the coming of industrial capitalism. By this time, Södermalm had become a low-income district, where a few bourgeois residents lived. Many residents were workers in the district's new factories (sugar mills, tobacco factories, and textile companies) and lived either in small houses with garden plots in the heart of the district or in slum-like dwellings in the outer parts. In the late nineteenth century, when construction boomed, garden plots gave way to dense urban neighborhoods with small plots and dwellings—the majority built by private property owners—to accommodate the city's rapidly growing working-class population.[10] The social demography, combined with the existence of many taverns along the southern parts of Götgatan, affected the reputation of this area among the well-to-do.

Roughly speaking, the population of Stockholm and Södermalm trebled between 1850 and 1900. Policymakers worried about the rapid growth, and, like elsewhere, the bourgeois leadership initiated a thorough modernization of the city: within a few decades, the city had new infrastructures for water supply, drainage, waste management, and street lighting. This process strengthened the character of streets as public spaces.[11] Streets were leveled out to facilitate vehicular traffic, and increasingly provided with sidewalks, gutters, and smoother surfaces for pedestrians and horse-drawn traffic.[12]

Inspired by Haussmann's regulation of Paris and the Hobrecht Plan for Berlin, a commission led by Albert Lindhagen presented a plan in 1866 that focused on traffic and urban greenery, two elements that were combined in the plan's wide and tree-lined boulevards. It would also serve the purpose of uniting the precapitalist city's many small universes into one economic unit.[13] Although one new boulevard (Ringvägen) was proposed for Södermalm, the so-called Lindhagen Plan anticipated that Götgatan and Hornsgatan would remain Södermalm's main streets. To fulfill their function, however, they had to be further straightened and have their considerably different elevation leveled out.[14] The plan proposed to double the width of Götgatan from twelve to twenty-four meters. For the southern part of the street, south of Södra Bantorget (the square adjacent to the city's southern train station, today's Medborgarplatsen), such street widenings were done successively over the following decades. North of the square, however, the plans to widen met opposition. Not only did the hilly terrain complicate things, the buildings lining the street were more valuable than further south, and belonged to the more influential urban elite. With a narrow majority, the city council voted down the city government's proposal to widen this part of Götgatan in 1880. The issue remained contested. Although goods transport from the Södra station (located halfway along Götgatan) into the city center decreased after the opening of a new, more central, train station, according to people at the time, the traffic remained intense. In the late nineteenth century, policymakers weighed up widening Götgatan against building a tunnel underneath. Soon enough, a third idea was added to the mix: supplement Götgatan by widening Repslagargatan, a parallel street west of Götgatan that had "comparatively insignificant houses." A version of this third proposed route would be realized, but only in 1945. Until then, Götgatan remained the main route for north-south traffic on Södermalm.[15]

Having sketched Götgatan's long-term development from a broader urban planning perspective, I now turn to the changes at street level. Stockholm's streets in the mid-1800s typically had a surface of large cobblestones and no sidewalk. When street surfaces became a municipal responsibility in the 1840s, a transition began of replacing the cobbles with paving stones, and adding sidewalks to the main streets.[16] Photographs from around 1900 show Götgatan with sidewalks, although not all pedestrians used them. The process of getting pedestrians to stay on the sidewalks, thus only crossing the street under controlled forms, was gradual, as seen in detailed studies of street photography. Around the globe, these measures led to fierce battles between motorists, pedestrians, and their respective protagonists.[17] For Stockholm, this part of urban history awaits a historian.

Traffic-count data together with photographs help us reconstruct the type of traffic in Götgatan. Street use was mixed: hand-pulled or horse-drawn carts and carriages shared the streets with tramcars and cyclists in the 1890s, and motorized cars and trucks soon thereafter. A short stretch of northern Götgatan was served by a horse-drawn tramline from 1887, and electrified in 1901. After 1905, another tramline served the southern part of the street, and by 1909 it was extended to a few new suburbs in the south. Passenger statistics from the public transport company indicate suburban traffic on this line doubled between 1910 and 1920.[18]

Starting around 1900, the city authorities carried out yearly traffic counts from 7:00AM to 8:00PM on a day in October or November. These counts hardly ever included pedestrians—or for that matter, until 1921, cyclists, who by that time accounted for a quarter of all vehicles in the streets of Stockholm.[19] Furthermore, in counting vehicles rather than people, the traffic data is misleading regarding the use of public transit. Even so, the traffic counts provide important clues about mobility at the time. Traffic was more intense in the north of the street closer to the city center than in the still more rural southern parts: the northern section Götgatsbacken had three times more traffic than Skanstull at the southern end. More surprisingly, the total volume of traffic was relatively stable in the first two decades of the twentieth century. Apparently, the concept of ever-increasing traffic did not apply to this period—at least not in terms of more vehicles. It is possible that the vehicles for transporting people changed in order to accommodate more passengers.

Between 1900 and 1920, the number of cars and buses surpassed the number of private, horse-drawn vehicles, while hand-pulled and horse-drawn carts and carriages still outnumbered trucks; motorization of personal mobility thus superseded that of goods transport. Goods traffic was many times greater than passenger traffic, although the gap between them shrank during the period. The ratio between "working vehicles" and "personal vehicles" also grew further south along the street. In 1905, for example, there were five times more vehicles for goods than for personal transport at mid-street level (Södra Bantorget), compared to almost twenty times more in the far south (Skanstull). This does not necessarily mean that goods surpassed people traveling the streets of Stockholm. Distances between home and work, or to run errands, were still modest, and most people with limited economic resources walked—although the engineers who commissioned the counts did not acknowledge this.

To summarize, walking and human- or horse-drawn transport dominated mobility along Götgatan for hundreds of years. The regulation that leveled and straightened Götgatan and many other streets was not, however, for the benefit of pedestrians, but for urban aesthetics, efficient transportation of goods, and, subsequently, expectations about (rather than actual) increased commuting to and from the new suburbs. When Götgatan underwent industrial reordering in the late nineteenth century, elite residences in the northern end, closer to the city center, stood in the way of widening and leveling that part of the street. In contrast, the working class's dwellings made way for redevelopment in the south—where the volume of traffic was substantially lower. This class-related differentiation of the street would later force alternative solutions to an anticipated traffic crisis.

## Parallel Streets, Parallel Stories

We cannot fully appreciate the Götgatan situation without looking at the parallel history of its modern sibling: Söderleden, today a road tunnel through Södermalm, connected to the north and south via bridges. Söderleden was constructed as a result of perceived congestion and fears, or even hopes, about traffic in the future. This example underlines the limitations of basing a strict mobility biography on a single street: it fails to recognize how broader urban-planning processes shape a street's development and its mobility.

In Stockholm, automobility really took off in the 1920s. While motorized vehicles equaled horse-drawn ones on the city streets in 1914, little more than ten years later, motorized vehicles made up 66 percent of all traffic, horse-drawn only 5 percent, and bicycles' share for the entire city was 23 percent. Not only did the number of motor vehicles grow, they also made a strong impression on many people in the 1920s. One observer described motorized traffic as becoming "the new momentum" in urban traffic.[20] An engineer in the city's Traffic Department wrote in 1929 that motorized traffic "gave the urban scene its contemporary character," and that its rapid growth, severely complicating urban traffic, called for action. Many detailed regulations were thus introduced in the 1920s to facilitate traffic and improve traffic safety in Stockholm.[21] During the

1930s depression, the number of cars in Götgatan stabilized, whereas the number of bicycles tripled, making them the most frequently spotted form of transport in this and other streets of Stockholm.[22] Even so, the anticipated increase in cars largely dictated traffic policy.

Götgatsbacken, the northern hilly part of Götgatan, still posed a challenge for Stockholm's planners. The particular topography and narrow width were difficult to reconcile with its multiple functions: an important route from Södermalm to the north of the city, and a distinctive shopping street with many pedestrians. Two tramway lines previously serving Götgatsbacken were rerouted and replaced by bus lines in 1926 to improve the flow of traffic—in spite of local businesses' fear of losing customers.[23] The city's mandate to build new suburbs south of Södermalm obviously increased the commuter traffic into the city center. Traffic in Götgatsbacken doubled between 1925 and 1935. The underground tramway built below Götgatan in 1933—later modernized as the first subway stretch in the city—aimed to ease the pressure on this street. Moreover, a high-capacity parallel street west of Götgatan remained a high priority for policymakers. In 1936, the city council finally decided to build Södergatan as a shafted street for through traffic, with local commercial streets on both sides. A competing proposal envisioned a stricter functional differentiation: a tunnel solution that would free local residents and workers from through-traffic and the accompanying noise and pollution, while strengthening Götgatsbacken's character as the district's pedestrian commercial street.[24] The shafted street won the city councilors' vote, but half a century later, as we will see, the final result looked more like a tunnel.

As construction began in 1937, three rows of housing blocks, home to the poorer working-class population, were demolished to make way for the 28-meter-wide street in a shaft ten meters below the former street level. Construction work came to a halt during World War II, and the street was opened to traffic in stages over a ten-year period after the war. In 1954, it reached Åsö Torg, where it reconnected to Götgatan. Södergatan was supposed to provide Södermalm with an equivalent to the monumental city center street Kungsgatan, which had also been constructed as a shafted street in the early twentieth century. Newspaper coverage from the opening of the first stretch in 1945 praised the new street, noting how the "motorists and cyclists swished by on the smooth and wide street with blessed smiles on their faces." But for decades, in fact, most observers reckoned it an unfinished project, a polluted and desolate ditch.[25]

Södergatan was originally meant to complement Götgatan. As well as grade-level passages under several streets, it also had several connec-

**Figure 8.1.** Bird's-eye view of Götgatan and Södergatan, Stockholm. Looking south over Södermalm's parallel streets, Götgatan runs one block to the left of Södergatan, partly concealed by buildings. Södergatan was originally meant to relieve traffic congestion in Götgatsbacken at the northern end of Götgatan (*front of the picture*). Over time, Södergatan was extended southwards and became a through-traffic route for cars only. In 1985, a few years after this photograph was taken, the Söderleden highway was connected to bridges at both ends and roofed, and the redevelopment of the area on top of it began.
Photo: © Lars Ternblad.

tions to Södermalm's local street network (figure 8.1). Fears and dreams of an automotive future, however, made Stockholm's urban planners re-envision the street as an uninterrupted thoroughfare for motorized traffic, with few connections; Södergatan would lead traffic past, not to or from, Södermalm. Although earlier plans had considered building a bridge for the continuation north of Södergatan, the new modernistic cloverleaf traffic interchange that opened in 1935 at Slussen (connecting the island of Södermalm with the old city) brought a change of plan: now traffic on Södergatan would connect to Slussen before being channeled across the water.[26] Soon enough, however, a new bridge re-emerged on the planners' design boards as part of the scheme for future traffic routes. In 1959, Södergatan had its northbound continuation, the Centralbron bridge over Norrström stream, and further north to the new traffic junction at Tegelbacken in 1967. Whereas the bridge proposed in 1947 included cycle lanes, these were scrapped in 1950. According to the engineers, cycling would decline anyhow, and the remaining few cyclists would want to access the local street network. Furthermore, the engineers argued, cycle lanes would complicate the construction of safe ramps at the endpoints of the bridge. All in all, omitting the cycle lanes meant the road could become a through-route for motor traffic. Banned from Centralbron, cyclists were advised to take an alternative route, which was a major detour.[27]

In the south, Södermalm was connected to the mainland via an openable bridge, Skansbron, built in 1923–25 to enable a new water-way. By the 1930s, Skanstull had become one of the busiest access points to Stockholm. Consequently, the city authorities pushed for a complementary bridge to cope with the expected growth in the sub-urban population and related increase in commuting.[28] Inaugurated in 1949, the new high bridge, Skanstullsbron, was built to cater to road traf-fic and the new southbound subway. Like the previous bridge, it was an extension of Götgatan. The urban planners at the time took for granted that the southern part of Götgatan, thirty-three meters wide, would be able to process all the traffic traveling north and south. Their intention at this point was thus to reconnect Södergatan to Götgatan before leading traffic to and from the bridge. The unexpected rising numbers of cars in the early 1950s, however, severely disrupted traffic in the southern part of Götgatan and in particular its junction with Ringvägen at Skanstull.[29]

The 1950s saw multiple design proposals to extend Södergatan un-derground further southward (past Ringvägen) before leading it under or above ground to Skanstullsbron. This was still the case when the city approved the 1960 *Trafikledsplan för Stockholm*, a great urban motor-way scheme with a ring road, and east-west and north-south through-routes—Söderleden being part of the latter. (Note the name change from Södergatan, a street, to Söderleden, a route.) The host of proposals had one thing in common: they were deemed technically complicated and unsatisfactory. Thus, in the early 1960s, there was yet another change of plans: now Söderleden would stretch even further south underground, then cross over the water (Årstaviken) on its own new high bridge.[30]

This high bridge in the south was briefly reconsidered in the 1970s. Like elsewhere, new traffic policies were being introduced that ques-tioned large-scale car-traffic infrastructure and modernist urban rede-velopment generally. The traffic committee commissioned to create new policies for Stockholm in 1974 presented a redesigned Söderleden, with fewer lanes, fewer local connections on Södermalm, and no new high bridge; thus another solution connecting Söderleden to the ex-isting bridges was on the table. This latest solution matched not only the new policies but also the new economic reality. The city council approved Söderleden—scaled down—in 1976, but not the proposed continuation across the water: in spite of the city's traffic policy reorien-tation, the leading political parties agreed to a new high bridge after all.

Thus Söderleden was not the issue. Most of the parties involved agreed that a tunnel for through-traffic made sense. Although many thought a new traffic route would facilitate car flow and was thus hardly in line with the new direction on policy, these same actors felt it would improve the livability of Götgatan. The vision of wide and leafy sidewalks entered the debate. The Social Services department claimed that Götgatan's transformation into a traffic route had totally spoiled its former character as a pedestrian trail and retail street, while the noise and exhaust fumes had made it "inappropriate for housing." The department noted, "The tunnel under Södermalm is a first and important step to reconcile the Söder split," and recommended "begin[ning] the adjustment of the environment within the area to other needs than those of automobility." Even the financial department stressed that "pure traffic capacity reasons" did not justify Söderleden, but rather improvements in traffic safety and the local environment.

The problem was the new high bridge. As it would facilitate flow substantially and improve travel speeds for motorists, critics argued, it would attract even more motorists. When the major political parties agreed to support the new bridge in 1976, they met huge protests. These were times of strong resistance to car-centered reconstruction and overall urban planning. Inspired by events in Copenhagen, activists painted white crosses at accident-prone junctions. Bicycle demonstrations were frequent; debates on traffic-related issues in the city council were infiltrated.[31] In this situation, the new bridge—a child of the 1960s—became a primary target for many people's environmental concerns. In 1978 alone, more than ten demonstrations took place along Götgatan. Several targeted the new bridge specifically. Urban environmental groups were joined by representatives from the smaller political parties with a "greener" profile: the Left and the Center Party.[32]

The final decision to build the new high bridge was made in 1978—against the recommendation of the city's own planning experts, who found it problematic, not least from an aesthetic point of view. Despite fierce protests from environmentalists, fearing that the bridge would attract even more car traffic into the city, the three major political parties (representing social democrats, conservatives, and liberals) voted in favor of the new bridge.[33] In spite of the shift in the 1970s toward policies curbing urban automobility, these politicians remained relatively pro-car. They were also anxious not to lose the 85 percent state funding for the entire project. For the National Road Administration, the realization of the new bridge created a link in a national road network facilitating through-traffic. The interpretations can vary: many speakers in the city council debate argued that the road administration was in effect "blackmailing" the city. While the party leaders favoring the bridge resisted such language, one speaker suggested that the proponents of the new bridge within the city were merely using the administration as an excuse to push for the decision they favored in any case.[34] The fact remains that the National Road Administration proposed similar conditions for other links in the national road network before and after this point. The situation thus highlights the importance of national policy-making at city level, even in relatively strong capital cities.[35]

The new high bridge, Johanneshovsbron, was completed in 1984. The protests and general skepticism against major road projects in the 1970s had significant effects: the city authorities slimmed down Söderleden from eight to four lanes and concealed additional sections underground. Shortly after, a decision was made to cover the parts of the route in the open shaft (completed in 1991). When the new Söderleden opened in 1985, traffic on Götgatan decreased overnight from fifty thousand to twenty thousand vehicles per day. The older high bridge, Skanstullsbron, now took on the role of local connection between Södermalm and the south.[36] The combined car traffic on the bridges increased from an average 65 thousand to 114 thousand a day between 1970 and 1992.[37]

We see that, in the twentieth century, what was initially considered a complementary street that would save the northern end of Götgatan from demolition gradually transformed into a high-capacity, underground car thoroughfare. Neither the critics of demolishing working-class dwellings nor the urban environmentalists, worrying that the route would attract more cars, were able to influence the design more than marginally. Despite their criticism, and contrary to their own official policies, local and national policymakers pushed for the implementation of a thoroughfare that would be a prerequisite for the transformation of Götgatan in the coming decades.

How does Söderleden compare to other urban highways? A comparison with the much more famous Boston Central Artery/Tunnel project (CA/T, or the "Big Dig") demonstrates similarities as well as differences. Both were built in a tunnel or depressed and roofed, mainly due to concerns about the environmental and social impact of urban highways in the 1960s and 1970s. Unlike Söderleden, however, CA/T has been conceived as a "project." Thomas P. Hughes portrays Frederick Salvucci, Boston secretary of transportation, as a system builder and project manager who cleverly navigated national funding structures, contractors, and popular discontent with an earlier elevated highway.[38] Although the final realization of Söderleden shares some of these features, it is difficult to pin down its mastermind—or for that matter frame it as a project. On the contrary, its creation has a longer, winding history, always on the planning board, but also malleable to align with concerns and policies regarding sustainability issues that prevailed in various eras: a savior of valuable houses to be demolished around 1900; part of the postwar ambition to facilitate free flow of cars; and a way to combat local environmental problems since the 1970s.

## Götgatan: Main Street, Dual Identity

Meanwhile, the island of Södermalm was subject to major renewal plans, like the rest of central Stockholm. Postwar Södermalm had a reputation as a dense working-class district with many small, outdated apartments. Many residents, particularly families, moved to the new, modern suburbs.[39] From its peak in 1942, the population gradually dropped from about a hundred thousand in the late 1960s (similar to the number today) to its lowest point of just over seventy thousand in 1981. The plan for the district presented in 1963, *Söder 67*, envisioned comprehensive redevelopment. Demolition and redevelopment provided an opportunity to also adapt the housing stock to automobility, with generous underground parking.[40]

Protests and lack of construction workers (due to the realization of a massive housing construction program in Sweden) held up the clearances, but Södermalm was still the district subjected to most demolition after the city center. The refurbishment of the city district continued throughout the 1970s; however, the turning point came in 1978, when four nineteenth-century dwellings in the housing block *Mullvaden* were demolished. The police violently evicted the squatters who were trying to prevent the demolition, but in the process the squatters gained a lot of media attention and public support, which eventually forced the city to adopt a new large-scale renovation approach instead of demolition.[41]

In addition to housing redevelopment, *Söder 67* proposed an extensive package of traffic routes and large junctions, as well as a strict differentiation of through and local traffic—similar to how new residential areas were being built in the suburbs at the time. Such schemes would have had a major impact on the cityscape. Again, protests put an end to the plans, and in the 1970s, one part of Södermalm, Katarina, underwent the first traffic zoning program (*trafiksanering*) in Stockholm. Instead of large-scale interventions, these programs introduced one-way streets and street closures, and one street (Katarina Bangata) became a pedestrian barrier, separating the area into two zones. While these measures improved the district's environment, they also transferred some through-traffic from the local street network to already congested main streets, Götgatan in particular. According to the traffic count in 1976, of the 55 thousand cars in Götgatan every day, 45 thousand had far-away destinations, and so they were through-traffic. This was a strong argument in favor of the underground highway Söderleden and the bridge Johanneshovsbron.[42]

Thus, in Götgatan, traffic zoning did little to ease nonmotorists' situation, which had deteriorated as car traffic increased. Not only had cycling declined, but also other modes of transport were phased out. When the subway was extended over Skanstullsbron and opened to traffic in 1950, tram traffic on the bridge stopped. The trolleybuses running in Södergatan and Götgatan in the 1950s stopped operating in 1964—the same year that a second subway line opened to the southwestern suburbs (the "red" line). When the last tramline closed in 1967, diesel buses were the only form of public transit operating in Götgatan. It also became increasingly difficult to operate busses due to the increasing levels of car traffic causing major congestion. In 1978, the Skanstull terminal for southbound suburban buses was moved further south, to Gullmarsplan on the other side of the bridges, and redeveloped as a new shopping mall.[43]

Above-ground traffic thus became more and more homogenous as time passed. Still, Götgatan never lost its dual character: it was, and still is, both a place for people to travel through and where they spend their leisure time (see figure 8.2). As the main street of Södermalm, Götgatan hosted many different kinds of activities. In the 1940s and 1950s, it was home to many of the city's cinemas and theaters; in 1947, there were seven cinemas, and three more in the direct vicinity. Götgatan was also a favorite venue for the youth of Södermalm, and a popular shopping street. Like today, Götgatsbacken in the north had a more distinctive pedestrian character than the leveled-out southern part. The few traffic counts that did include pedestrians—for example, one conducted in 1949—reveal that they easily outnumbered motorists and cyclists combined.[44]

Increasing car traffic raised concerns about the situation for pedestrians. Responding to a petition in 1963 to cater better to pedestrians at the Götgatan and Ringvägen intersection, the city's Traffic Department identified it as one of "the most troublesome and unsafe places in Stockholm's street network," in particular for pedestrians. With some sixty thousand cars and one hundred thousand pedestrians passing through every day, this intersection had the worst traffic in Stockholm, and thus surely in Sweden, and almost every third accident at the intersection involved a pedestrian. Long waiting times frustrated some pedestrians, the department argued, making them take great risks in crossing when

**Figure 8.2.** Götgatan close to Medborgarplatsen subway station, Stockholm, 1957. Despite its intense traffic, Götgatan never lost its character as a street for leisure and pleasure.
Photo: Unknown. Stockholm Transport Museum, SM 2017-A13560.

the traffic lights were red. Besides adjusting traffic signal timings and allocating more time for pedestrians to cross, engineers were developing plans for underground pedestrian passages. As a third measure to secure better conditions for pedestrians, the city authorities put forward the realization of Söderleden.[45]

The *Söder 67* plan addressed the separation of pedestrians and vehicular traffic with a dedicated "pedestrian system" of up to thirty grade-separated over- or underpasses. The vision for south Götgatan was wide sidewalks with trees alongside. Once the proposed traffic system had been realized, the Götgatsbacken section could be made fully car-free, and the rest of Götgatan designed as a shopping street with a considerably higher standard of pedestrian facilities. These changes would take decades. What is more, at this point, the Chamber of Commerce doubted that *Söder 67* would achieve a more pedestrian-friendly Götgatan. Even if the Söderleden highway was completed, the traffic in Götgatan would still be intense, and the width of the street would make it difficult to cross. The solution to provide safe underpasses for people was also refuted, since experience showed that these were not popular with pedestrians.[46] In the north, the buildings along Götgatsbacken were threatened with demolition in the 1960s. Around 1970, there were advanced plans to transform Götgatsbacken into a pedestrian street similar to modernist Sergelgatan in the city center, however, these were also rebutted due to strong public resistance.[47]

During the 1980s, Södermalm's population growth resumed, as it did in the inner city of Stockholm generally. When people move into inner cities, and a revaluation takes place of the old, dense city structure and its high level of services, we can speak of an urban renaissance, which is really just a less charged description of the term "gentrification" of urban areas: high-income earners moving into former working-class districts, the consequent upgrading of housing stock, rent increases that push locals out—all combine to ultimately change the character and "soul" of a district. Södermalm has undergone extensive gentrification in recent decades: a young, culturally oriented middle class has moved there.[48]

The opening of Söderleden in 1984 reduced car traffic pressure in Götgatan substantially. Several parties saw this as an opportunity to achieve a more livable ("pleasant" was the word used at the time) street.[49] For years, little happened, except the piecemeal extension of cycle lanes. The rapid growth of car traffic in the late 1980s led many analysts to predict a traffic infarct in downtown Stockholm. Politicians and planners started talking about how to recreate street environments that were in keeping with human needs, and how to restore greenery in the city. These measures would make the city attractive for residents, visitors, and investment companies. The so-called Dennis Agreement, a major infrastructure package concluded in 1991–92, called for sizeable investments in urban bypasses and rail infrastructure, as well as congestion charging. The aim was to reduce inner-city traffic by 30 percent, thus creating the space needed for transforming the streets. Moreover, some of the revenue from congestion charges would be earmarked for "street environment improvement measures."[50]

In the 1990s, city officials and stakeholders discussed how to utilize the new opportunities. In 1994, the urban planning department published a document with various "street visions" for the inner city. It described the character of Götgatan as "vague" due to the combination of it being a popular pedestrian route and its relatively large amount of motorized traffic for a thirty-meter-wide street in "the most densely populated area of Sweden." The document's two different proposals for south Götgatan contained broadened sidewalks, generous tree planting, and a reduced number of lanes in order to strengthen the street's retail and entertainment functions. There were also ideas for leading car traffic along alternative routes to create a smaller car-free precinct.[51] By 1996, the Liberal Party proposed to take action and turn Götgatan into a "living boulevard" with wider sidewalks, trees, street-side cafés, speed reductions, and safer conditions for cyclists. The Conservative Party thought it was necessary to wait until the traffic was reduced in the inner city as anticipated under the Dennis Agreement; others called for immediate action.[52]

Although these and similar ideas did not materialize at the time, they have resurfaced more recently under the label of "livable" streets and cities. The City of Stockholm has recently started to reconceptualize urban automobility—at least in the city center. The 2012 Accessibility Strategy (*Framkomlighetsstategin*) gave for the first time clear priority to walking, cycling, and public transit over automobility as energy- and space-efficient modes of transport.[53] Planning policies in Stockholm have supported reurbanization for two decades. The compact city, supposedly the result of this planning strategy, is expected to provide shorter (walkable, bikeable) distances and a better basis for public transit to compete with the car.[54] This notion should not, however, obscure the fact that Stockholm's large-scale and often regionally conceptualized infrastructural plans continue to cater to automobility.[55]

Most, but not all, stakeholders today accept a traffic policy that encourages walking and cycling in the city center—at the expense of the car if necessary. Since the 1980s, south Götgatan was gradually equipped with cycle paths and lanes. They were completed in piecemeal fashion, because the Traffic Department still considered some sections too congested with cars to allow for cycle paths. In 1993, Left Party representatives frustratingly exclaimed, "Is it bicycle haters who have planned the bicycle lanes in Götgatan?" Contrary to the department and leading politicians, they were not prepared to wait until new ring roads would reduce inner-city traffic levels.[56] Pushed by the Green Party, the Left Party, and the local urban environmental Stockholm Party, bicycle policy gradually progressed during the 1990s and was a major issue in the 1998 local elections. After the elections, the Stockholm Party managed to persuade the right-wing coalition to finally support cycle lanes in several main streets, including Götgatan.[57] By the early twenty-first century, the full stretch of south Götgatan had cycle lanes or paths.

As the northern part, Götgatsbacken, still troubled policymakers and road users, the city banned through-traffic there in 1989. A new proposal in 1993 to make it a pedestrian street was turned down, however, in favor of widening the sidewalk.[58] Götgatsbacken was finally pedestrianized in 2004, although cycling was still allowed under the rules for pedestrians.

Ironically, the parallel encouragement of these two modes has become increasingly conflict-laden, with the friction between cyclists and pedestrians taking center stage. In the redesign of south Götgatan, trialed in 2014 and made permanent in 2016, the traffic planners appeared to be more concerned with the peaceful coexistence between cyclists and pedestrians than about discontented motorists, who lost one traffic lane in each direction. In Götgatsbacken, the city's attempts before and after pedestrianization to persuade cyclists to detour via a parallel street have fallen short—and the conflicts between strolling pedestrians and speedy cyclists appear regularly in the press.

Götgatan has a long history as a street with dual functions: a through-route for commuting, and a place to visit for leisure and commerce. As bicycle commuting in the street increases at the expense of car commuting, there is tension between two versions of the livable city. On the one hand, Götgatan is a major commuter street for mostly middle-class cyclists living in the southern suburbs—they are the ones leading the upsurge in cycling and pushing for more cycle-friendly policies.[59] On the other hand, Götgatan is still a popular shopping street and the heart of Södermalm's "hipster" community. Put simply, strolling pedestrians, desired as consumers, are clashing with time-optimizing commuter cyclists, desired because their cleaner commute takes cars off the street. For the future "post-car" city center, this tension could become serious.

## Conclusion

From a present-day point of view, Götgatan's recent redesign, with two lanes appropriated for walking and cycling, appears to be a progressive step toward sustainable mobility and a livable city. If we take a more historical approach, however, the success story soon fades. In fact, what made it possible to transfer space in the first place was the half-century-long realization of a thoroughfare for motorized traffic parallel to Götgatan but below ground. Behind the seemingly successful restructuring of Götgatan lies a deeply unsustainable parallel story of the underground highway Söderleden. Burying such car infrastructures may be beneficial from a local environmental perspective and make (parts of our) cities more pleasant to be in, but this only covers up the highly problematic mobility patterns that still dominate Stockholm.

Three episodes in Götgatan's mobility biography reveal the layered-ness of its infrastructure-related history. Paths taken in the past shape present rationalities. Whereas Söderleden came about thanks to the urban elite's resistance to redeveloping the northern end of Götgatan, this same thoroughfare created a window to rethink the street many decades later. Despite the reduction in car traffic, the dual character of Götgatan remains—only now the dualism prevails as much between pedestrians and cyclists. As these two user groups epitomize the livable city (pedestrians) and the environmentally sustainable city (cyclists), their clashes in Götgatan can be framed as one between two currently highly held and conflicting urban policy aims.

Methodologically, this chapter has assessed whether the mobility bi-ography of a street is useful for analyzing urban mobility. The relevance of examining a particular street might not be self-evident. The strength lies in that it allows an analysis that goes beyond policy aims and comes closer to the reciprocal relationship between planning measures, infra-structures, and on-the-ground struggles for space. Compared to city-wide case studies, however, the detailed street-level analysis risks losing sight of the power relations involved. I would therefore argue for the broader approach in this chapter—positioning the street in wider urban planning processes—as opposed to a narrower biography.

The case of Götgatan-in-context has helped to uncover a concealed form of unsustainability, based on past decisions but still very much alive today. It belongs to a "genre" that we can call the "hidden structures of unsustainability." Although public and policy ambitions shift, infra-structures created in the past continue to embody former priorities and influence user practices, and are not easy to unbuild. Some are immedi-ately visible to the human eye, such as above-ground urban highways. They are what I have elsewhere referred to as "monuments of unsus-tainability."[60] Others, however, remain concealed underground and for-gotten—although they have the same effect from an environmental sustainability point of view. Whereas the "monuments" are constantly debated topics, the hidden structures of unsustainability will need to be "unhidden" before they can even start to be questioned. This is one kind of usable past: historical inquiry is a strong tool for uncovering what is hidden in the past, and can thus play a part in opening up the debate on sustainable futures.

**Martin Emanuel**, historian of technology and researcher at the Department of Urban Planning and Environment, KTH Royal Institute of Technology, Stockholm, works at the intersection of mobility, urban, and environmental history, including tourism history. His research is on wide-ranging historical dimensions of cycling culture, urban planning, and traffic management. He has published several articles on the history of cycling and sustainable mobility, as well as the 2012 monograph *Trafikslag på undantag: Cykeltrafiken i Stockholm 1930–1980* (Excluded through planning: Bicycle traffic in Stockholm 1930–1980). He coedited and authored *Cycling Cities: The European Experience* (SHT, 2016).

## Notes

This chapter draws on work undertaken within the project "Pilotplats Cykel," an interdisciplinary research project funded by Sweden's innovation agency VINNOVA and the City of Stockholm to evaluate infrastructure measures in order to improve the conditions for cycling along and around Götgatan. I would like to thank Daniel Normark and Pelle Envall for useful exchanges throughout the project.

1. For a popular history of Götgatan, see Maj Sandin, *Götgatan: Förr i tiden—nu för tiden* (Saltsjöbaden: Trafik-nostalgiska förlaget, 2015). An example of a cultural biography of a street is W. M. H. Hupperetz, "The Cultural Biography of a Street: Memory, Cultural Heritage and Historical Notion of the Visserstraat in Breda, the Netherlands (1200–2000)," in *Landscape Biographies: Geographical, Historical and Archaeological Perspectives on the Production and Transmission of Landscapes*, ed. Jan Kolen et al. (Amsterdam: Amsterdam University Press, 2015).

2. A commendable example of this approach is by Hans Buiter, "Constructing Dutch Streets: A Melting Pot of European Technologies," in *Urban Machinery: Inside Modern European Cities*, ed. Mikael Hård and Thomas J. Misa (Cambridge, MA: MIT Press, 2008); Hans Buiter, *Riool, rails en asfalt: 80 jaar straatrumoer in vier Nederlandse steden* (Zutphen: Walburg Pers, 2005).

3. See Oldenziel et al. in this volume.

4. On U.S. freeways, see Joseph F. DiMento and Cliff Ellis, *Changing Lanes: Visions and Histories of Urban Freeways* (Cambridge, MA: MIT Press, 2013). For traffic infrastructures in postwar European cities, see, e.g., Mathieu Flonneau, "City Infrastructures and City Dwellers: Accommodating the Automobile in Twentieth-Century Paris," *Journal of Transport History* 27 (2006): 93–114; Simon Gunn, "The Buchanan Report, Environment and the Problem of Traffic in 1960s Britain," *Twentieth Century British History* 22 (2011): 521–42; Jeffrey M. Diefendorf, "Artery: 'Urban Reconstruction and Traffic Planning in Postwar Germany,'" *Journal of Urban History* 15 (1989), 131–58.

5. See Schipper in this volume.

6. Staffan Högberg, *Stockholms historia. 1, Den medeltida köpstaden. Hans Nådes stad. Stormaktens huvudstad. Borgarnas stad* (Stockholm: Bonnier fakta, 1981), 147–48.

7. Sandin, *Götgatan*, 5; *Söderleden* (Stockholm: Stockholms gatunämnd och gatukontor, 1984), 9–10.

8. Linnea Forsberg, *Stormaktstidens Stockholm tar gestalt: Gaturegleringen i Stockholm 1625–1650* (Stockholm: Stockholmia, 2001).

9. *Södermalm: Södra Maria, del av Högalid: Byggnadshistorisk inventering 1974–75* (Stockholm: Stadsmuseet, 1978), 11.

10. Arne Munthe, *Västra Södermalm från mitten av 1800-talet: Stadsdelen och församlingslivet* (Stockholm: Sancta Maria Magdalena och Högalids församlingar, 1965), 10–12, 41–44; Mats Franzén, *Den folkliga staden: Söderkvarter i Stockholm mellan krigen* (Lund: Arkiv, 1992), 73–83.

11. Anders Gullberg, "Nätmakt och maktnät: Den nya kommunaltekniken i Stockholm 1850–1920," in *Den konstruerade världen*, ed. Arne Kaijser and Pär Blomkvist (Eslöv: Symposion, 1998); Buiter, "Constructing Dutch Streets."

12. Margareta Cramér, "Gatubeläggning i Stockholm," in *Sankt Eriks årsbok* (Stockholm: Samfundet S:t Erik, 1983), 77–106.

13. Gösta Selling, *Esplanadsystemet och Albert Lindhagen: Stadsplanering i Stockholm åren 1857–1887* (Stockholm: Stockholms stadsarkiv, 1970), 46–47; Franzén, *Den folkliga staden*, 107; Françoise Choay, *The Modern City: Planning in the 19th Century* (London: Studio Vista, 1969), 15ff.

14. Munthe, *Västra Södermalm*, 35–37.

15. Arne Dufwa, *Stockholms tekniska historia: Trafik, broar, tunnelbanor, gator* (Stockholm: Kommittén för Stockholmsforskning, 1985), 178. Insignificant houses, Stockholms stads/kommunfullmäktiges handlingar (Records of Stockholm City/Municipal Council, hereafter SF), Report (*Utlåtande*) 1890: 174. Multiple proposals, see SF Report 1880: 20, Appendix (*Bihang*) 1885: 133, Appendix 1888: 14, Report 1890: 174, Appendix 1902: 3.

16. Cramér, "Gatubeläggning i Stockholm."

17. Street photography, see Franck Cochoy et al., "The Forgotten Role of Pedestrian Transportation in Urban Life: Insights from a Visual Comparative Archaeology (Gothenburg and Toulouse, 1875–2011)," *Urban Studies* 52, no. 12 (2014): 1–20. Battles, see Peter Norton, "Street Rivals: Jaywalking and the Invention of the Motor Age Street," *Technology and Culture* 48 (2007): 331–59; Tomás Errázuriz, "When Walking Became Serious: Reshaping the Role of Pedestrians in Santiago, 1900–1931," *Journal of Transport History* 32 (2011): 39–45.

18. *Statistisk årsbok för Stockholm* (*Statistical yearbook for Stockholm*; hereafter SÅS), various years.

19. Dufwa, *Stockholms tekniska historia*, 74–75.

20. Gotthard Johansson, *Trettiotalets Stockholm* (Stockholm: Rekolid, 2004 [1942]), 26; Dufwa, *Stockholms tekniska historia*, 76–77; Martin Emanuel, "Constructing the Cyclist: Ideology and Representations in Urban Traffic Planning in Stockholm, 1930–70," *Journal of Transport History* 33 (2011): 67–91.

21. C. G. Bergman, *Trafiken och gatorna i Stockholm* (Stockholm: Nordisk bokhandel, 1929), 7, 10; Dufwa, *Stockholms tekniska historia*, 82–108.

22. As measured in the northern part of Götgatan, at the intersection with Hornsgatan, the number of cars per day increased from 1,700 in 1912 to 3,800 in 1929, but remained stable in the 1930s. In the same period, the number of cyclists rose from about 2,000 to 6,500 per day. *SÅS*, various years.

23. SF Report 1926: 150; Statements (*Yttranden*) 1926 (7): 203–22.

24. SF Report 1936: 235; Report 1936: 400; Protocol (*Protokoll*) 1936 (9): 192.

25. Dufwa, *Stockholms tekniska historia*, 179; *Söderleden*, 7; Britta Petersson, "Pressklipp i Faktarummmet," *Stadsvandringar* 13 (1990): 92–102.

26. Albert Lilienberg, *1928 års förslag till generalplan för Stockholms tätare bebyggda delar* (Stockholm, 1929). SF Report 1936: 235.

27. Martin Emanuel, "Monuments of Unsustainability: Planning, Path Dependence and Cycling in Stockholm," in *Cycling and Recycling: Histories of Sustainable Practices*, ed. Ruth Oldenziel and Helmuth Trischler (New York: Berghahn Books, 2015).

28. *Skansbroleden: Högbron vid Skanstull jämte tillfarter: Redogörelse på uppdrag av Stockholms stads gatunämnd* (Stockholm: K. L. Beckman, 1947), 5–8; Martin Nauclér and Nils Östergren, *Johanneshovsbron: Reportage om ett brobygge* (Stockholm: Byggförlaget, 1984), 24–26.

29. *Söderleden*, 14–15. Although we do not have traffic counts on this junction, the data on the intersection Götgatan–Hornsgatan in the north and the bridges at Skanstull give an indication. Whereas bicycle traffic at Hornsgatan outnumbered cars by a factor of ten during World War I, things changed rapidly: shortly after 1950, the number of cars equaled the number of bicycles (4,000 per day), and five years later, this had risen to 4,700 cars compared to 1,500 bicycles. In 1950, the two bridges Skansbron and Skanstullsbron carried 3,500 and 8,500 cyclists per day; in 1988, the numbers were 620 and 660 respectively. Car traffic on Skansbron, however, increased almost ten-fold, from slightly more than 2,000 in 1950 to nearly 20,000 in 1970, whereas this increased by five-fold on Skanstullsbron from almost 9,000 to 45,000 in the same period. *SÅS*, various years.

30. Dufwa, *Stockholms tekniska historia*, 180; *Söderleden*, 16; *Trafikledsplan för Stockholm 1960* (Stockholm: Generalplaneberedningen, Stockholms stad, 1960).

31. Martin Emanuel, *Trafikslag på undantag: Cykeltrafiken i Stockholm 1930–1980* (Stockholm: Stockholmia, 2012).

32. Nauclér and Östergren, *Johanneshovsbron*, 46–47. Olle Bengtzon, "Stoppa bron som ingen vill ha," *Expressen*, 11 January 1978; Lars Rydberg, "Fullmäktige-ja till ny Skanstullsbro," *Svenska Dagbladet*, 25 January 1978; Olle Bengtzon, "Myglet kring högbron," *Expressen*, 3 July 1978. For the focus on environmental concerns by local political parties, see Sven Lilja, "'Miljö' som makt i stockholmpolitiken 1961–1980," in *Stockholm blir välfärdsstad: Kommunalpolitik i huvudstaden efter 1945*, ed. Thorbjörn Nilsson (Stockholm: Stockholmia, 2011).

33. *Söderleden*, 16–18. SF Report 1978: 7, Report 1978: 203.

34. SF Report 1976: 42; Statements 1976 (3): 235–46, Report 1978: 7; Report 1978: 203, Statements 1978 (1): 25–59.

35. Emanuel, *Trafikslag på undantag*; Emanuel, "Monuments of Unsustainability."

36. *Söderleden*, 18–19.

37. The 1970s, however, had seen a slight drop in car traffic on the bridges due to the recession, gasoline prices, and measures restricting car traffic in the inner city. After 1988, traffic on the bridges increased dramatically, with 10,000 and 15,000 additional motor vehicles per day on Skanstullsbron and Johanneshovsbron over a five-year period, only to stabilize and drop to late 1980s' levels, mostly due to the congestion charge introduced in Stockholm in 2006.

38. Thomas P. Hughes, *Rescuing Prometheus* (New York: Pantheon Books, 1998), 197–254.

39. Franzén, *Den folkliga staden*, 386–87; U. Sax, *Den vita staden: Hammarbyhöjden under femtio år* (Stockholm: Komm. för Stockholmsforskning, 1989).

40. *Söder 67: Översiktligt planprogram för Södermalm* (Stockholm: Stockholms stad, Generalplaneberedningen, Expertutskottet, 1968).

41. Mats Franzén, "New Social Movements and Gentrification in Hamburg and Stockholm: a Comparative Study," *Journal of Housing and the Built Environment* 20 (2005): 51–77; Torbjörn Tenfält, "Den långa ockpationen av Mullvaden," in *Från almstrid till trängselskatt: De stora slagen om Stockholm*, ed. Börje Karlsson and Torbjörn Tenfält (Stockholm: Kommittén för Stockholmsforskning/Stockholmia, 2011).

42. Sten Holmstedt, *Ett halvsekel i Stockholmstrafiken: Politik, planing och utbyggnader* (Stockholm: Stockholmia, 2012), 182–83; *Söderleden*, 14; SF Report 1963: 235; Report 1973: 164.

43. Johan Eriksson and Per Lindroos, *Söder-tur 1: Följ med till det försvunna Söder öster om Götgatan: 1954–1974* (Saltsjöbaden: Trafik-nostalgiska förlaget, 2011), 165– 67; Dufwa, *Stockholms tekniska historia*, 229–31.

44. On two occasions, once in 1938 and again in 1949, the Traffic Department conducted pedestrian counts as part of the yearly October counts. The 1938 counts showed that 27,000 pedestrians visited the area around Södra Bantorget, 21,000 came to Mariagränd in upper Götgatsbacken, and 17,000 to a spot in south Götgatan. In 1949, nearby places showed slightly lower numbers for the first two first locations, but significantly more, 29,500 pedestrians, in the most southern spot, close to Ringvägen. *SÅS*, various years.

45. SF Report 1963: 235.

46. SF Report 1968: 267.

47. Eriksson and Lindroos, *Söder-tur 1*, 165.

48. Franzén, *Den folkliga staden*, 387; Franzén, "New Social Movements"; Sharon Zukin, "Gentrification: Culture and Capital in the Urban Core," *Annual Review of Sociology* 13 (1987): 129–47.

49. See, e.g., Trafikkontorets arkiv (hereafter TA), Gatukontorets arkiv (hereafter GA), Änr 2275/84, Clas Ifvarsson till Gatunämnden 30 Nov 1984, "Program för förbättringar för Götgatan."

50. Holmstedt, *Ett halvsekel i Stockholmstrafiken*; Anders Gullberg and Karolina Isaksson, eds., *Congestion Taxes in City Traffic: Lessons Learnt from the Stockholm Trial* (Lund: Nordic Academic Press, 2009).

51. Per Kallstenius et al., eds., *Gatuvisioner: Idéer för en grön och levande innerstad* (Stockholm: Stockholms stadsbyggnadskontor, 1994).

52. SF Report 1996: 79 Statements 1996-09-09, 128–35, Protocol 1996: 14, 23–24.

53. Daniel Firth, "Framkomlighetsstrategin," (Stockholm: Stockholms stad, Trafikkontoret, 2012), 5, 17–18, 27.

54. *Regional utvecklingsplan för Stockholmsregionen: RUFS 2010* (Stockholm: Regionplanenämnden, Stockholms läns landsting, 2010); *Promenadstaden: Översiktsplan för Stockholm* (Stockholm: Stadsbyggnadskontoret, 2010).

55. Martin Emanuel, "Waves of Cycling: Policies of Cycling, Mobility, and Urban Planning in Stockholm since 1970," in *Invisible Bicycle*, ed. Tiina Männisto-Funk and Timo Myllyntaus (Leiden: Brill, 2018).

56. TK, GK, 1993-322-1541. Margareta Olofsson och Stig Dedering (v) till GFN 1993-05-25; GFK: tjänsteutlåtande 1994-03-08.

57. Emanuel, "Waves of Cycling Policy."

58. SF Report 1993: 181; Statements 1993 (12): 114–20; Protocol 1993(12): 21–22.

59. Emanuel, "Waves of Cycling Policy."

60. Emanuel, "Monuments of Unsustainability."

# Bibliography

## Archival Sources

Statistisk årsbok för Stockholm (Statistical yearbook for Stockholm)
Stockholms stads/kommunfullmäktiges handlingar (Records of Stockholm City/Municipal Council)

## Published Sources

Bergman, C. G. *Trafiken och gatorna i Stockholm*. Stockholm: Nordisk bokhandel, 1929.

Buiter, Hans. "Constructing Dutch Streets: A Melting Pot of European Technologies." In *Urban Machinery: Inside Modern European Cities*, edited by Mikael Hård and Thomas J. Misa, 141–62. Cambridge, MA: MIT Press, 2008.

———. *Riool, rails en asfalt: 80 jaar straatrumoer in vier Nederlandse steden*. Zutphen: Walburg Pers, 2005.

Choay, Françoise. *The Modern City: Planning in the 19th Century*. Planning and Cities, 99-0147047-1. London: Studio Vista, 1969.

Cochoy, Franck, Johan Hagberg, and Roland Canu. "The Forgotten Role of Pedestrian Transportation in Urban Life: Insights from a Visual Comparative Archaeology (Gothenburg and Toulouse, 1875–2011)." *Urban Studies* 52, no. 12 (2014): 1–20.

Cramér, Margareta. "Gatubeläggning i Stockholm." In *Sankt Eriks årsbok*, 77–106. Stockholm: Samfundet S:t Erik, 1983.

Diefendorf, Jeffry M. "Artery: 'Urban Reconstruction and Traffic Planning in Postwar Germany.'" *Journal of Urban History* 15, no. 2 (1989): 131–58.

DiMento, Joseph F., and Cliff Ellis. *Changing Lanes: Visions and Histories of Urban Freeways*. Cambridge, MA: MIT Press, 2013.

Dufwa, Arne. *Stockholms tekniska historia: Trafik, broar, tunnelbanor, gator*. Stockholm: Kommittén för Stockholmsforskning, 1985.

Emanuel, Martin. "Constructing the Cyclist: Ideology and Representations in Urban Traffic Planning in Stockholm, 1930–70." *Journal of Transport History* 33, no. 1 (2011): 67–91.

———. "Monuments of Unsustainability: Planning, Path Dependence and Cycling in Stockholm." In *Cycling and Recycling: Histories of Sustainable Practices*, edited by Ruth Oldenziel and Helmuth Trischler. New York: Berghahn Books, 2015.

———. *Trafikslag på undantag: Cykeltrafiken i Stockholm 1930–1980*. Stockholm: Stockholmia, 2012.

———. "Waves of Cycling Policy: Cycling, Mobility, and Urban Planning in Stockholm since 1970." In *Invisible Bicycle: Parallel Histories and Different Timelines*, edited by. Tiina Männisto-Funk and Timo Myllyntaus. Leiden: Brill, 2018.

Eriksson, Johan, and Per Lindroos. *Söder-tur 1: Följ med till det försvunna Söder öster om Götgatan: 1954–1974*. Saltsjöbaden: Trafik-nostalgiska förlaget, 2011.

Errázuriz, Tomás. "When Walking Became Serious: Reshaping the Role of Pedestrians in Santiago, 1900– 1931." *Journal of Transport History* 32, no. 1 (2011): 39–45.

Firth, Daniel. "Framkomlighetsstrategin." Stockholm: Stockholms stad, Trafikkontoret, 2012.

Flonneau, Mathieu. "City Infrastructures and City Dwellers: Accommodating the Automobile in Twentieth-Century Paris." *Journal of Transport History* 27, no. 1 (2006): 93–114.

Forsberg, Linnea. *Stormaktstidens Stockholm tar gestalt: Gaturegleringen i Stockholm 1625–1650*. Stockholm: Stockholmia, 2001.

Franzén, Mats. *Den folkliga staden: Söderkvarter i Stockholm mellan krigen*. Lund: Arkiv, 1992.

———. "New Social Movements and Gentrification in Hamburg and Stockholm: a Comparative Study." *Journal of Housing and the Built Environment* 20, no. 1 (2005): 51–77.

———. "New social Movements and Gentrification in Hamburg and Stockholm: a Comparative Study." *Journal of Housing and the Built Environment* 20 (2005): 51–77.

Gullberg, Anders. "Nätmakt och maktnät: Den nya kommunaltekniken i Stockholm 1850– 1920." In *Den konstruerade världen*, edited by Arne Kaijser and Pär Blomkvist. Eslöv: Symposion, 1998.

Gullberg, Anders, and Karolina Isaksson, eds. *Congestion Taxes in City Traffic: Lessons Learnt from the Stockholm Trial*. Lund: Nordic Academic Press, 2009.

Gunn, Simon. "The Buchanan Report, Environment and the Problem of Traffic in 1960s Britain." *Twentieth Century British History* 22, no. 4 (2011): 521–42.

Holmstedt, Stig. *Ett halvsekel i Stockholmstrafiken: Politik, planing och utbyggnader*. Stockholm: Stockholmia, 2012.

Hughes, Thomas Parke. *Rescuing Prometheus*. New York: Pantheon Books, 1998.

Hupperetz, W. M. H. "The Cultural Biography of a Street: Memory, Cultural Heritage and Historical Notion of the Visserstraat in Breda, the Netherlands (1200–2000)." In *Landscape Biographies: Geographical, Historical and Archaeological Perspectives on the Production and Transmission of Landscapes*, edited by Jan Kolen, J. Renes, and Rita Hermans, 309–25. Amsterdam: Amsterdam University Press, 2015.

Högberg, Staffan. *Stockholms historia. 1, Den medeltida köpstaden. Hans Nådes stad. Stormaktens huvudstad. Borgarnas stad*. Stockholm: Bonnier fakta, 1981.

Johansson, Gotthard. *Trettiotalets Stockholm*. Stockholm: Rekolid, 2004 (1942).

Kallstenius, Per, Peter Lundevall, and Mats Fager, eds. *Gatuvisioner: Idéer för en grön och levande innerstad*. Stockholm: Stockholms stadsbyggnadskontor, 1994.

Lilienberg, Albert. *1928 års förslag till generalplan för Stockholms tätare bebyggda delar*. Stockholm: 1929.

Lilja, Sven. "'Miljö' som makt i stockholmpolitiken 1961–1980." In *Stockholm blir välfärdsstad: Kommunalpolitik i huvudstaden efter 1945*, edited by Thorbjörn Nilsson, 295–331. Stockholm: Stockholmia, 2011.

Munthe, Arne. *Västra Södermalm från mitten av 1800-talet: Stadsdelen och församlingslivet*. Stockholm: Sancta Maria Magdalena och Högalids församlingar, 1965.

Nauclér, Martin, and Nils Östergren. *Johanneshovsbron: Reportage om ett brobygge*. Stockholm: Byggförlaget, 1984.

Norton, Peter D. "Street Rivals: Jaywalking and the Invention of the Motor Age Street." *Technology and Culture* 48, no. 2 (2007): 331–59.

Petersson, Britta. "Pressklipp i Faktarummmet." *Stadsvandringar* 13 (1990): 92–102.

*Promenadstaden: Översiktsplan för Stockholm*. Stockholm: Stadsbyggnadskontoret, 2010.

*Regional utvecklingsplan för Stockholmsregionen: RUFS 2010*. Stockholm: Regionplanenämnden, Stockholms läns landsting, 2010.

Sandin, Maj. *Götgatan: Förr i tiden—nu för tiden*. Saltsjöbaden: Trafik-nostalgiska förlaget, 2015.

Sax, Ulrika. *Den vita staden: Hammarbyhöjden under femtio år.* Stockholm: Komm. för Stockholmsforskning, 1989.

Selling, Gösta. *Esplanadsystemet och Albert Lindhagen: Stadsplanering i Stockholm åren 1857–1887.* Stockholm: Stockholms stadsarkiv, 1970.

*Skansbroleden: Högbron vid Skanstull jämte tillfarter: Redogörelse på uppdrag av Stockholms stads gatunämnd.* Stadskollegiets utlåtanden och memorial. Bihang 1947:14. Stockholm: K. L. Beckman, 1947.

*Söder 67: Översiktligt planprogram för Södermalm.* Stockholm: Stockholms stad, Generalplaneberedningen, Expertutskottet, 1968.

*Söderleden.* Stockholm: Stockholms gatunämnd och gatukontor, 1984.

*Södermalm: Södra Maria, del av Högalid: Byggnadshistorisk inventering 1974–75.* Stockholm: Stadsmuseet, 1978.

Tenfält, Torbjörn. "Den långa ockpationen av Mullvaden." In *Från almstrid till trängselskatt: De stora slagen om Stockholm,* edited by Börje Karlsson and Torbjörn Tenfält, 57–68. Stockholm: Kommittén för Stockholmsforskning/Stockholmia, 2011.

*Trafikledsplan för Stockholm 1960.* Stockholm: Generalplaneberedningen, Stockholms stad, 1960.

Zukin, Sharon. "Gentrification: Culture and Capital in the Urban Core." *Annual Review of Sociology* 13, no. 1 (1987): 129–47.

# CHAPTER 9

# Green Urban Spaces and Sustainable Mobility

## Parks as Pockets of Persistence since the 1830s

Frank Schipper

## Introduction

For the first time since the automobile entered Prospect Park, Brooklyn, in the late nineteenth century, New Yorkers experienced a car-free summer there from 17 July to 10 September 2017. This was in response to a request by local residents and commissioners to close the park's West Drive to motorized traffic in 2015. Back in 1867, when the park opened to the public, the automobile was still a thing of the future. The park was designed by Frederick Law Olmsted and Calvert Vaux, the famous landscape architects of Central Park. New York City Council's Parks Committee welcomed the closure, stating, "For countless New Yorkers, our city's green spaces are a refuge. New Yorkers shouldn't have to worry about looking over their shoulder for on-coming traffic if they are out on a bike ride, going for a run, or taking a walk with their kids in a city park."[1] Since the trial closure did not create problems on nearby roads, the car ban became permanent from January 2018. Central Park followed suit on 27 June 2018.[2]

Closing off a historic urban park to a particular mode of transportation suggests a shift in convictions about the proper ways to be mobile in that space. Such shifts typically take time and often meet resistance. As early as 1966, the New York Parks Department had run a pilot banning motorized vehicles from Prospect Park during summer weekends.[3] Other motorized vehicle closures followed: during "exercise hours" (3:00–7:00PM in Central Park), on weekends, and during national holidays. Transportation Alternatives, a nonprofit organization promoting sustainable urban mobility in New York City, set up a Car-Free Central Park Committee in 1995. These actors were thus preparing the ground for limiting automobility in the city's large parks.

The happenings in the summer of 2017 and their roots in history's longer trajectory highlight urban green spaces as interesting sites to research sustainable urban mobility. The recent changes were possible in a context of a long-term slow decline in the use of cars in cities across the mass-motorized world, a phenomenon sometimes identified as "peak car."[4] More importantly for my argument, what we now call more sustainable forms of mobility continued to thrive in urban green spaces, yet declined in other parts of the city, primarily due to car-centered planning. Urban walking has been falling off for a long while, even at short distances.[5] Yet walking has always been the main—and, in the opinion of many, the most appropriate—form of mobility in urban parks. Phrased differently, we see evidence that the modal split within green spaces in most cities worldwide is skewed toward more sustainable mobilities compared to the modal split for the city as a whole. Even though cars were allowed to enter, urban green spaces seem to have been less susceptible to car-centered urban planning than elsewhere in cities.[6]

How does this characteristic of urban green spaces help us face the challenge of sustaining mobility equitably for future generations on a planet of finite resources? Elizabeth Shove has hypothesized that the remnants of more sustainable past mobility systems can give us a head start for making mobility more sustainable today.[7] Such "pockets of persistence"—material structures, practices, or institutions, where former sustainable urban mobility systems coexisted alongside upcoming alternatives that replaced them elsewhere—can also be reactivated and incorporated in new configurations covering today's city. Could the urban park, as a repository of alternative, more sustainable mobilities, be the "pocket of persistence" to aid their revival and reintroduction?

If so, the study of urban mobility in green spaces is a concrete example of a usable past as described in the introduction to this book. It provides a convenient recipe for transforming urban mobility in many different places, since every city has green spaces. My argument is that mobility in urban green spaces holds promise to improve the overall sustainability of urban mobility today. An exploration of secondary literature demonstrates that it is worthwhile investigating mobility in urban green spaces for sustainability transitions. Notably, the available historiography on urban green spaces rarely puts mobility at the core of its investigations, while mobility scholarship has focused more on extra-urban nature than urban green spaces.

This chapter proposes a cross-fertilization of the two themes, focusing almost exclusively on human mobility. Although urban green spaces are an equally excellent site to research the history of *nonhuman* mobilities, they remain beyond the scope of this chapter.[8] Time-wise, I concentrate on the period in the nineteenth century when urban green spaces became more important to the industrializing city and hence more widespread. I end with very recent developments in Singapore and Washington, D.C., Geographically, the chapter deliberately explores different corners of the world, moving beyond the best-known examples, such as Central Park, without any pretense of being fully comprehensive.

My argument is made in three main steps. I begin by highlighting mobility as an inherent characteristic of the urban green spaces that emerged since the 1830s. After all, the essence of the park is to allow urbanites to move through, to, and from it. The subsequent section sketches some of the continuities and changes in mobility in urban green spaces since the civic urban park appeared in the mid-nineteenth century. Comparison with the average mobility in the city suggests that parks became, in Shove's terminology, a pocket of persistence of past, more sustainable urban mobility systems. The final section discusses how these more sustainable mobilities could move beyond the park and be part of today's transition in urban mobility.

## Mobility in Green Spaces Keeps the City Alive

Urban green spaces were essential in organic conceptualizations of the city. Haussmann and many others referred to them as the "lungs" of the city.[9] Lewis Mumford interpreted the city as a living organism in the natural environment where it was located. The circulation between the green corridors connecting green spaces to the rural world beyond the city limits helped to keep the city "alive."

When dedicated urban green spaces appeared in the nineteenth century, the aim was to open up privately owned land to a wider public, and create purpose-built green spaces. Initially, these emerged on leftover land in the urban fabric. As city walls became obsolete for defense purposes, municipalities were given permission to knock them down. These areas became popular spots for walking. Many cities developed plans for landscaped parks with public walks in an attempt to formalize and enhance the former fringes of their inner city for the growing population. In the Dutch city of Delft, Jan David Zocher Jr. designed a romantic pleasure ground full of winding tree-lined paths from where walkers would see amazing vistas. The plan never left the drawing board due to insufficient financial means. However, the authorities did create simpler paths near the former city walls allowing walkers to look out over the meadows beyond the city, and created the post of special supervisor for urban parks and walks.[10]

In contrast, Lucas Pieters Roodbaard successfully redeveloped the ramparts of the Dutch city of Leeuwarden in six successive municipal assignments between 1830 and 1842. The parks he created were not only appealing green spaces; being at the edge of the city, with artificial hilliness thanks to former fortifications, they also provided good views over the landscape surrounding the city. Hills and trees helped to hide the city from view, creating a green idyll visually devoid of urban influences. With the last of the six projects linking the redeveloped fortifications, Roodbaard aimed to make the walk around Leeuwarden both appealing and seamless.[11]

These examples were part of a nation-wide phenomenon in the Netherlands.[12] Such initiatives befitted the romantic ideal of walking in nature, but actually took place in urban settings rather than in some remote wilderness. They also reveal the close connection between the development of urban green spaces and particular types of mobility—in this case walking as an appropriate form to appreciate the urban greens. Going for a walk was incorporated in their design; words referring to walking featured in the titles of the initiatives, as well as in the names of newly created parks, as we will see later in this chapter. Even though this was considered a type of top-down pedestrianism by the elites and planners, walking eventually became an inherent element of urban green spaces, notwithstanding the fact that sports and outdoor pursuits also became part of the park's activities—sometimes much to the dismay of the said elites and planners.

One such actor illustrating the intimate connection between walking and urban green spaces is the Select Committee on Public Walks in the United Kingdom, which complained in 1833 that many cities were devoid of open public spaces. Rapid urbanization had increased the need for "exercise or amusement" for the lower and middle classes, for whom the fresh air of the open countryside was not easy to access.[13] As part of the urban environmentalism emerging in the nineteenth century, parks addressed one of the challenges facing industrializing cities. The Royal Parks in London, originally recreational hunting grounds for the British monarchy, constitute the largest green spaces in central London. The parks were gradually opened up to the public in the nineteenth century, starting with Regent's Park in 1845. The Crown Lands Act of 1851 turned all of them into public parks.

Purpose-built urban parks emerged in addition to the repurposing of leftover land and opening of previously closed-off greens. An early example was in Birkenhead, a town opposite the city of Liverpool, where Joseph Paxton designed Birkenhead Park, opened in April 1847. Olmsted's visits to this park would later influence his design for Central Park, New

York.[14] While inspired by European examples, American cities sought creative ways to make "nature" an inherent part of the city, not least to distinguish themselves as wilder than their tame European counter-parts.[15] Park practices and planning ideals circulated between cities and across the Atlantic. Cities took pride in their parks and advertised them widely, sharing their considerations and designs. In Paris, the opening of the Parc des Buttes-Chaumont coincided with the official opening of the 1867 world's fair in the French capital. The timing ensured massive attention abroad. Cities creating parks of their own actively sought examples to copy.

This did not mean urban parks and how locals used them became one and the same everywhere. Local authorities appropriated the widely circulating ideas and visions, perhaps most prominently in the Atlantic world.[16] Europeans were inspired by the rational systematism of America's municipal park systems, which served as a tool to steer overall spatial and social urban development. American park planners equally appreciated and appropriated artistic elements of the European urban park tradition.[17] During the rapid expansion of Latin America's capital cities in the nineteenth century, their urban authorities looked abroad for inspiration and advice. Buenos Aires attracted French landscape architects to enhance the vibrant capital of thriving Argentina with greens similar to those in global metropolises at the time. Jules Charles Thays arrived there in 1889 and was Director of Gardens and Public Walks from 1891 to 1913. Landscape architect Jean Claude Nicolas Forestier, creator of the first cycle path in the Parisian Bois de Vincennes in 1890, came to Buenos Aires in the 1920s.

Dedicated urban parks fulfilled many more functions than the ribbon landscapes built on demolished city walls: Haussmann's reconstruction of Paris included parks as part of a broader set of measures to improve public hygiene.[18] They helped combat foul smells and brought in fresh air.[19] In addition, urbanites used parks for exercise and sports. However, team sports, archery, or horse riding did not combine well with the peace and quiet other visitors expected to find in the park. A stroll or a ride in the park offered urbanites a pleasurable diversion. The careful selection of plants and artistic embellishments certainly captured the visitors' attention. Those with a more scientific approach to the parks hoped these elements would transfer to visitors, particularly the working classes, a kind of awe for the wonders of the scientific world.[20]

Mobility was crucial for all activities in the park, and for getting to and from the park. When the citizens of Amsterdam took the initiative in 1864 to create a park commensurate with its status as the Dutch capital, the group overseeing the endeavor was called the Association for the

Creation of a Driving and Walking Park.[21] Writers in the United States often referred to "driving parks." Two-thirds of the visitors to Central Park in 1863 arrived by horse-drawn carriage.[22] A more systematic analysis of such naming of actors and parks may well reveal that as the nineteenth century progressed, there was a greater variety of mobility beyond walking in urban green spaces.

In any case, mobility had clearly become an inherent feature of urban parks, judging by the park designs and regulations. Park planners designed urban parks for visitors on the move. The best way to appreciate specific spaces within the parks was by using the mobility incorporated in their design. Parks were often tailored to a range of mobilities: pedestrians strolling along the paths, equestrians riding their horses, or the bourgeoisie gazing from the windows of their carriages or cars. The urban park displayed the characteristics of an incipient traffic separation system early on.[23] Mobility also became an inherent feature of urban greens because of the way park planners sought to control how people moved through the park. This started with the entry to the parks: some remained open day and night; others closed in the evening. Park regulations touched on many topics, but most concerned mobility: to encourage proper mobile behavior, prevent misconduct, safeguard the safety of all visitors, and mitigate the potential for conflict between different users of the park. Think of the considerable amount of energy that went into keeping visitors off the grass and preventing them from trampling on precious plants.[24]

By the late nineteenth century, urbanites were developing an ever deeper passion for "nature." Buying second homes in the countryside and traveling to nature became part of their routine.[25] At the same time, as this section has shown, urban parks became a prominent way to counteract the disappearance of green from the city; cities implemented the greening of abandoned structures like city walls; and dedicated spaces, such as royal gardens, were opened up to the public. Mobility was the key in all these.

## Parks as Pockets of Persistence

Should we interpret mobilities in urban green spaces as pockets of persistence to help us achieve more general sustainable urban mobility today? This question led me to explore mobilities over time, and to argue that they were probably more sustainable in urban green spaces than in the city overall. It also prompted another question: what would make the pocket of persistence move out of its territorial niche to affect mobility in the city at large?

An important caveat is that landscape planners' designs and ideals should not be taken at face value. Practices in the park could differ considerably, and it is therefore important to complement official accounts of park history with a user perspective.[26] When contemplating the string of parks known as the Emerald Necklace in Boston, for example, it is important to know that Olmsted had specific ideas of what constituted responsible forms of recreation in parks. The interconnected parks system, created in the 1880s–1890s, was supposed to instill peace and tranquility in visitors; his vision did not include activities other than a leisurely stroll along the park's paths.[27]

User agency became visible in relation to mobility when urbanites, particularly the upper class, brought new mobilities to the park in the form of their recently acquired vehicles. They turned the mobility infrastructures within urban green spaces into, essentially, a shared space. Park roads are a good example of the conversion to a kind of "commons" to be shared by visitors using different modalities.[28] When bicycles became more popular in New York, they simply entered the roadways in Central Park, mingling with other traffic, such as horse-drawn carriages. Indeed, parks turned into hotspots for the burgeoning cycling culture in the late nineteenth century, as happened in Bois de la Cambre in Brussels. The Avenue Louise connecting this forest park with central Brussels had a steady stream of cyclists.[29]

New mobilities in the park did meet opposition from existing users and the authorities, who forbade cycling on pedestrian paths in several parks, and banned it altogether from Englisher Garten, Munich's preeminent urban green space, and Kungsparken in Malmö, Sweden.[30] Something similar happened in Central Park, where the park commissioners prohibited high-wheel bicycles in 1879. Cyclists challenged this in court, with financial support from bike manufacturer Albert Pope. When the New York Supreme Court judges ruled that the commissioners were entitled to decide whether bikes should be allowed in parks, the challenge was taken to the state capital Albany, where the 1887 Liberty Bill granted cyclists access to park highways open to other "pleasure carriages."[31] Lawyer Isaac B. Potter, prime mover on a national level for the bicyclists' organization the League of American Wheelmen, celebrated the fruit of two years expensive campaigning as the "wheelman's Magna Carta."[32]

How people got to and from the park has not been systematically researched, but we can assume that many of those who lived close by used the same mobilities as in the park. Here we need to distinguish between neighborhood parks for those living nearby, and "central parks" where the catchment area was the entire city.[33] Initially, many planners wanted urban civic parks ideally to be within walking distance for large numbers of urbanites. Amsterdam's Vondelpark was deliberately located close to the city center and the most populous neighborhoods.[34] By definition, neighborhood parks were within walking distance.

But central parks were not necessarily within easy reach, as some were suburban. When the Dutch municipality of Heemstede, a posh suburb of the larger city Haarlem, acquired the Bosbeek-Groenendaal estate in 1913, it opened it up to the public, renaming it a "walking wood." The name epitomized how the municipality envisioned its citizens would enjoy the space.[35] In the case of these parks further away, walking *in* the park did not necessarily correspond with walking *to* and *from* the park. Both a bus and motorboat service were set up to transport the residents of Haarlem and Heemstede to and from the park.[36]

Depending on the ebb and flow of mobilities, new dedicated infrastructures sometimes emerged within the park.[37] In response to the rising popularity of cycling, New York's Central Park opened its first dedicated cycle path on 15 June 1894. As motorization increased on the park roads, the use of bikes was gradually restricted to these dedicated paths.[38] Some urban park roads transformed into motorized traffic corridors. Parkways provided a purpose-built infrastructure for motorists, befitting the masculine conquest of nature, even though not within a true wilderness but in its urban park replacement in the city environment.[39]

Walking paths were typically the densest infrastructure in the parks, suggesting that walking counted as the overall main activity.[40] Park designers created paths to suit their ideals, sometimes alternating straight lines and serpentine twists. They formed visual connections with the surroundings beyond the park gates, as well as separations that created different atmospheres within the park. Park designers who considered themselves stylists liked to surprise visitors with twists and turns on a woodland path that would suddenly burst into an open vista or an unexpected sculpture or monument. Curvilinear designs had additional advantages. They gave visitors the illusion of spaciousness.[41] This was certainly an asset in smaller parks and helped to moderate speed, ensuring visitors were exposed long enough to the vistas they were supposed to appreciate.[42]

There were never-ending attempts to control where and how people walked in the park. The park's structures were a permanent reminder of planners' ideals for mobility. Control over visitor mobility ensured they would see what they ought to see. Open areas accommodated a variety of sporting activities, winding paths in the woods closed off the view for making adventurous explorations, while wide terraces to let visitors enjoy the scenery simultaneously enabled social control or policing. Actual practices in the park, however, did not always correspond with these scripts. Grassy fields in the park are a case in point. They were excellent areas for walking, but too large crowds would harm the quality and cover of the grass. Landscape planners therefore typically instructed users to keep off the grass. In fall 1860, the posters listing rules for visitors to Central Park began with a warning not to walk on the grass except for the Commons. Yet these placards and signs did not manage to keep people's behavior in line.[43]

The coexistence of modalities in the park also applied to all the city streets, on which cars had become a dominant presence in the course of the twentieth century.[44] The same might have happened in the park, but it did not. Whereas cars were able to implant themselves in the urban fabric, the city's green spaces remained relatively immune to this dynamic. Active, more sustainable forms of mobility continued to thrive in the park, even though, as we have seen, this did not necessarily apply to how people actually came to the park. In New York City, sizeable parking areas were added to the parks, viewed by Robert Moses as recreation facilities.[45] The idea of the parking lot was that people would continue into the park on foot. In the German city of Hannover, during car-centered practices in the heyday of technocratic urban planning from the 1950s until the mid-1970s, engineers kept cycle lanes available in the green parts of the city, such as Eilenriede Forest and along the River Leine. In these areas, cycling continued as a recreational activity.[46]

Mobility in the urban green spaces, these examples show, has remained more sustainable than the city average. In line with this book's theme, the park's more sustainable plans and practices could help mobility in the city overall become more sustainable. This aligns well with the renewed appreciation in innovation studies for enduring technologies—how defunct arrangements persist and reappear. When such remnants of the past happen to be more sustainable than current alternatives, there is a strong case to revive them. According to sociologist Elizabeth Shove, the "practicalities of revival and reinvention depend, to some degree, on the extent to which fragments of failed regimes persist."[47] She calls them "pockets of persistence."

Historians specialize in investigating these pockets and can thus guide us in resurrecting older technologies for a new purpose.[48] In the case of sustainable urban mobility, such pockets can be user routines where a sustainable form of mobility has survived, or materialities that have supported their persistence. Mobility in urban green spaces provides clear examples of both. But moving more sustainable mobilities from the park to the rest of the city is an impossible task if the park is a mere museum of old mobilities, reminiscent of the "car-free islands with concentrated activity, surrounded by motorways and parking facilities" that Stig Nordqvist, a leading Swedish traffic planner, claimed were part of the "natural organization of the car society."[49] He mentioned housing areas, shopping centers, office complexes, and schools as concrete examples, but he could easily have added urban green spaces to the list.

At least two elements need to be addressed in order to successfully move these sustainable mobilities. The first, as Shove argues for cycling, is to break the recreational connotation of park-based mobilities so they can also apply to utilitarian mobility. According to Sousa, Van Wesemael, and Oldenziel (this volume), a logistical logic should be superimposed on the recreational green infrastructures, parks, and parkways mobility concept as developed by Olmsted and others. The second—a *sine qua non* to make the first even remotely possible—concerns the spatial expansion of sustainable mobility networks in the park beyond its gates. The next section discusses the infrastructural ramifications.

## Park Systems Shaping Mobility in the Entire City

Parks are a spatial resource for new infrastructure at a wider city level, and benefit from a systematic approach to urban green space. We could say that the creation of the Emerald Necklace in Boston as a park system was more important than founding Central Park in 1858 as the first landscaped park in the United States. Park systems made it possible for green infrastructures to become a shaping device for an entire city. Buffalo, New York, was probably the first city where Olmsted tested this comprehensive park system–based planning, with a citywide system of interconnected parks and parkways.[50]

The garden city movement went a step further by promoting a type of place that would blur the distinction between the city and countryside altogether. The garden city would have its own sizeable central park. Combining the principle of preserving a greenbelt around cities ensured that the green spaces would be within a few minutes' walk or ride. The Greater London Regional Planning Committee sanctioned a Metropolitan Green Belt in 1935.[51] We can see elements of these ideals in the City Beautiful Movement some decades earlier (1890s–1910s) in the United States. The inclusion of municipal and metropolitan park systems structured, ordered, and confined cities—and connected them to their rural environments. In Forestier's mind, all urban green space formed part of a citywide hierarchy that included neighborhood parks and children's playgrounds.[52] These lines of thought extended into the ideals of functionalist urban planning, which assigned a great deal of space to green purposes—despite the modernist aversion to chaos that removed the natural look of urban parks and green spaces. Even in Le Corbusier's Ville Contemporaine, only 15 percent of the urban terrain was reserved for buildings and infrastructure.[53] The rest was green.

The Garden City Movement and functionalist restructuring of cities have generally not affected full cityscapes. The cities where the systematic approach to parks has affected large parts stand the best chance of moving park-based mobilities to these areas. Olmsted's interconnected park systems in Boston and Buffalo are good examples. The garden cities' greenbelts were semicircular, not unlike the earlier walking paths along derelict city fortifications. An equally popular alternative with early twentieth-century urban planners was using the organizing principle of wedges to get the green into the heart and outskirts of the city, thus maximizing the urban population's access to green open spaces.[54]

In the quest for sustainable urban mobility, it is worthwhile exploring whether the networked approach to nature can help to move a pocket of persistence from its restricted space to larger parts of the city. There are numerous potential benefits. First, the green spaces are spatial assets that provide sufficient scope for dedicated cycling and walking infrastructures. Second, this spatial quality can in fact reduce potential conflict. Repurposing a street will meet more opposition than providing facilities that resonate well with the public image of appropriate mobilities in the park, although grumbling environmental quarters might claim an unwarranted sacrifice of green space. In this way, the mobile past in urban green spaces may become usable for present-day purposes. Finally, cycling in the green, away from the exhaust fumes, can add to the bicycle's appeal and potentially crank up the low cycling figures in many cities' modal split.

Some places already have sustainable urban mobilities incorporated in the design of their green structures—for example, the greenways in Japan's "new towns" built in the late 1950s.[55] As corridors amid trees, bushes, and lawns, they enable people to walk comfortably, separated from roadways. They have different manifestations. In Tsukuba Science City, the forty-eight kilometers of greenways are connected via a spinal greenway running the length of the city. Kohoku New Town has a green matrix system, with several trunk greenways along conserved natural valleys. Intended to support both recreation and commuting, the greenways in Japan's new towns are therefore not good examples of sustainable urban mobility moving out of a pocket of persistence;

they exemplify networks where recreation and logistics coincided right from the start.

Washington, D.C., is a better example of a city with a system of interconnected parks serving sustainable urban mobility purposes today. As the city's centenary was approaching, the District of Columbia's Senate Park Improvement Commission initiated a process to beautify the nation's capital. The resulting McMillan Plan, named after Senator James McMillan, not only proposed a redevelopment of the National Mall, but complemented it with a system of parks covering the entire district. Rock Creek National Park, the largest and also one of the oldest in the United States, created in 1890, sits right in the heart of downtown Washington, D.C. At its southern tip, Rock Creek Park connects to the National Mall, the national capital's monumental axis lining up Capitol Hill, memorials, ministries, and museums. These spatial assets have provided plenty of space for cycling infrastructure since the 1970s.[56] John A. Volpe, secretary of transportation under Nixon, considered cycling valuable in urban mobility, for example to achieve cleaner air. He backed a National Park Service plan to close a lane on the Rock Creek Park Road to provide space for cyclists.

This heralded a return to history: the nine-mile "pleasure drive" was originally built for cyclists and horse-drawn carriages. In the 1920s, motorists had started using a part of it, Beach Drive, as a handy shortcut not only to reduce their commute but also to make it more appealing, since the scenery was stunningly beautiful. The pilot to close off the lane went ahead, but created considerable conflict. When Wayne Aspinall, congressman and chair of the House Interior and Insular Affairs Committee from 1959 to 1973, got stuck in traffic at the closed-off lane, he told Russ Dickinson, then National Capital Park's director, to end the pilot. As a compromise, they agreed to pave a bridle path that would accommodate cyclists. This turned out to be the first step toward providing more serious cycling infrastructure throughout the park.[57] New cycle paths in the capital's green spaces have supported the local increase in cycling. Yet the number of commuters on bikes for the 2008–2012 period remained a modest 3.2 percent, and the use of most trails primarily recreational: for the scenic Mount Vernon Trail recreational use was estimated at 75 percent.[58]

Washington, D.C., thus exemplifies an existing system of city parks allowing cycling to shift from its recreational pocket of persistence to utilitarian commuting, even if only modestly. This can only happen in cities endowed with a park system that includes effective green interconnections. Singapore is an example of how a city devoid of such connections can move sustainable mobility from its pocket of persistence. The urban authorities in Singapore have recently embarked on a program to connect green spaces. The city has many of these, because soon after independence, Singapore sought to create a Garden City image. This entailed substantially greening the city through the systematic planting of trees and shrubs. The authorities also embarked on a "Keep Singapore Clean" campaign in October 1968. Both endeavors aimed to turn Singapore into a clean and green oasis, different from its neighboring states.

Safeguarding minimum green space in Singapore became the task of the Parks and Recreation Division, created in 1974. It came under the Public Works Department within the Ministry of National Development. Two years later, this division became a department in its own right, with a team of about forty people.[59] The Garden City ideals reached a new phase in the late 1980s, when a greenway movement pleaded for a network of green corridors covering the entire city-state. The plans cleverly planned pilot corridors along underutilized land, encouraging the actors involved to back the idea.[60] These areas represent the category of "informal space" that can complement more formal, landscaped city parks. Such informal urban green spaces, often with lush vegetation, include vacant plots or leftover strips of land alongside roads or rail tracks.[61]

The first generation of corridors consisted of tree-lined trails with benches and bins. The trees were essential for a metropolis in the tropics, where shade and forms of protection against torrential rains are the key requirements for feasible active mobility. The Garden City Action Committee expanded the greenway initiative by adopting a complementary Park Connector Network proposal in 1991. The network consisted of seven regional loops, each twenty to forty kilometers long. According to the committee, its aim was to allow Singaporeans to "hop on a bicycle, put on a pair of rollerblades or simply jog along the park connectors and appreciate the myriad of sensory delights and adventures on offer."[62] The loops covered a large part of, but not the entire, city-state. To resolve this, in 2011 the National Parks Board proposed the Round Island Route, a 150 km park connector that could be considered the apex of the Singaporean authorities "City in a Garden" vision. Construction on the first section, the Coastal Adventure Corridor, began in late 2016. The route would be six meters wide instead of the usual four meters for park connectors, and would have amenities such as shelters, seating areas, lookouts, toilets, and bike repairs.[63]

Given the rise of ecological concerns, a Nature Ways network such as Singapore's complements the urban park system with the biomobilities of nature itself.[64] Trees form the basis of the Nature Ways network, creating continuous routes on four levels, from the understory and the creatures that dwell there, all the way up to the towering giants of the forest

canopy. Thus the Nature Ways create optimal conditions for biomobilities, as well as for human visitors to appreciate nature in its full diversity.
Increasing numbers of people are making use of the greenways. From
modest beginnings, a recent survey indicated that by 2011, approximately a quarter of Singaporeans had used the network, primarily to
exercise.[65] But here too, we see signs of the more sustainable mobilities
in urban green spaces moving from their pocket of persistence: people
living close to the network indicated that they are using the connectors
for their daily commute. Depending on their former commuting routine,
this could translate into real sustainability gains in urban mobility. With
regard to the social aspects of sustainability, it is a hopeful sign that users
already greatly appreciate the network. In the words of one Singaporean,
"Park connectors really give us cyclists a route that is meant for us. This
way we can see and feel the beautiful surroundings in safe conditions."[66]

## Conclusion

This chapter explores the links between green spaces in the city and
sustainable urban mobility. We see that mobility in the park has taken
a significantly different course than the average urban modal split by
being typically more sustainable.[67] Indeed, park planners felt that active
mobility—above all walking—should be supported in and by the urban
park. Much more research is needed to examine the variety of mobilities
in urban green spaces, and how the park planners' aims were translated
in practice. This chapter clearly demonstrates that urban green spaces
were not exclusively for walkers: all mobilities entered the park. A careful comparison of modal splits could highlight the differences between
the park and the rest of the city.

More importantly, to make a convincing claim for urban parks as
"pockets of persistence," research needs to investigate how mobilities
in the park impacted the world beyond its gates and vice versa. For a
pocket of persistence to become a usable past supporting urban transitions entails breaking loose from the constraints of the park. Giving certain mobilities a more prominent place in specific parts of the city, with
a very particular recreational function thrown in, may have nurtured an
old-fashioned or place-specific image, thus making the park's mobilities
more vulnerable in the city at large; it may have led to a too-strict separation of functional and recreational urban mobilities.[68]

The dynamics in Washington, D.C., and Singapore suggest a different
scenario. There, urban parks have not remained mere "pedestrian islands in the car society."[69] Particularly since the renewed urban environ-

mentalism of the 1970s, urban parks have become a valuable resource for planning citywide sustainable mobility. A systematic approach to urban parks in the past has provided the space for dedicated new infrastructures today, a form of a usable material past. Active modes now make up a greater part of the city's overall modal split where there are urban parks. As the Greenways in Singapore show, clever connections with other infrastructures can forge new greenway networks. Earlier examples from Japan highlight that greenways require continuous maintenance to ensure people keep on using them.

There seems to be sufficient evidence to test whether urban green spaces have an overall positive effect on the level of sustainable mobility in a city. A more formal and quantitative approach could investigate correlations between the density of green areas in a city and its sustainable modes. A further step could be to develop location-based measures indicating where people work and live, and whether urban green spaces are advantageously located between the two. These measures could increase the potential to align recreational and commuter routes; location is everything.

Four final considerations for further research: first, as the examples in this chapter do not come from the poorest parts of the planet, do they only or primarily apply to cities in wealthier parts of the world? Such wealth may also be vital to conduct the necessary maintenance of greens and infrastructures. The use of the Japanese greenways has been declining due to an ageing population experiencing them as too dark and nontransparent. This is sending the message that the greens must be continually maintained for park-based mobilities to thrive within and beyond the urban green space. Second, a similar question concerns the city level: are wealthier neighborhoods better placed, literally and figuratively, to shift sustainable mobility from its pocket of persistence? There are important social equality and racial issues to bear in mind.[70] Third, researchers should keep a close eye on potentially hidden structures of unsustainability relating to the park. For example, in Boston, Madrid, and Seoul, motorized road tunnels lurk beneath the lush greens of the parks. Finally, the examples in this chapter describe infrastructures of sustainable urban mobility entering the park and connecting it to the city. Yet other kinds of infrastructures can transform and become parks. The Promenade Plantée or Coulée Verte René-Dumont in Paris (opened in 1993), and the High Line in New York City (opened in 2009) are both examples of obsolete infrastructures, such as railroads, that have been transformed into elevated lined parks exclusively accessible to active modes—literally bringing the relation between urban green spaces and sustainable urban mobility to the next level.

**Frank Schipper**, an independent scholar specializing in mobility and infrastructure studies, has researched the history of roads, telegraphy, and tourism. Currently he is working on pedestrians and cyclists in cities and nature. He is author of *Driving Europe: Building Europe on Roads in the Twentieth Century* (Amsterdam University Press, 2008), co-author of *The History of the European Travel Commission* (European Travel Commission, 2018) and *Cycling Cities: The Rotterdam Experience* (SHT, 2019), and has edited special issues on infrastructure-related topics for the journals *Comparativ*, *History and Technology*, and *Métropoles*.

## Notes

1. NYC Office of the Mayor, "Mayor de Blasio Announces Prospect Park Will Go Entirely Car-Free for First Time This Summer," NYC: Official Website of the City of New York, 10 July 2017, accessed 25 November 2019, https://www1.nyc.gov/office-of-the-mayor/news/466-17/mayor-de-blasio-prospect-park-will-go-entirely-car-free-first-time-this-summer.
2. NYC Office of the Mayor, "Mayor de Blasio Announces Central Park, World's Most Iconic Greenspace, Will Become Permanently Car-Free," NYC: Official Website of the City of New York, 20 April 2018, accessed 25 November 2019, https://www1.nyc.gov/office-of-the-mayor/news/206-18/mayor-de-blasio-central-park-world-s-most-iconic-greenspace-will-become-permanently/#/0.
3. NYC Department of Parks & Recreation, "History of Bicycling: A Revolution in Parks," NYC Parks, accessed 25 November 2019, https://www.nycgovparks.org/about/history/bicycling.
4. Phil Goodwin, "Peak Travel, Peak Car and the Future of Mobility: Evidence, Unresolved Issues, Policy Implications, and a Research Agenda" (Paris: International Transport Forum, 2012).
5. Pooley, "Pedestrian Stories: Recovering Sustainable Urban Mobility," this volume.
6. On urban car-centeredness in Europe in general, see Ruth Oldenziel and Mikael Hård, *Consumers, Tinkerers, Rebels: The People Who Shaped Europe* (Houndmills: Palgrave Macmillan, 2013), ch. 4.
7. Elizabeth Shove, "The Shadowy Side of Innovation: Unmaking and Sustainability," *Technology Analysis & Strategic Management* 24, no. 4 (2012): 363–75
8. On the latter, see Sandra Swart, "Animating Animals: Historiography and Biomobilities," in *Mobility in History*, ed. Peter Norton et al., *T2M Yearbook* 4, no. 1 (2013): 50–61.
9. Dorothee Brantz and Sonja Dümpelmann, "Introduction," in *Greening the City: Urban Landscapes in the Twentieth Century* (Charlottesville: University of Virginia Press, 2011), 1–13; Friedrich Lenger, "Defining the Modern Metropolis: Universal Expositions from the Mid-Nineteenth to the Mid-Twentieth Century," *Bulletin of the German Historical Institute* 58, no. 1 (2016): 33–46.
10. Ingrid van der Vlis, *Vooruit met veel verleden: Geschiedenis van Delft vanaf 1795* (Zwolle: WBOOKS, 2016), 70–71, 84.
11. Els van der Laan-Meijer and Willemieke Ottens, *Roodbaards rijkdom: Landschapsparken Noord-Nederland 1800–1850 Friesland, Groningen en Drenthe* (Rotterdam: BONAS, 2012).

12. Elisabeth Cremers, Fred Kaaij, and C. M. Steenbergen, *Bolwerken als stadsparken: Nederlandse stadswandelingen in de 19e en 20e eeuw* (Delft: Delftse Universitaire Pers, 1981); Auke van der Woud, *Het lege land: De ruimtelijke orde van Nederland 1798–1848* (Amsterdam: Olympus, 2017).

13. Michael A. Reed, *The Landscape of Britain: From the Beginnings to 1914* (Lanham, MD: Rowman & Littlefield, 1990), 297.

14. Witold Rybczynski, *A Clearing in The Distance: Frederick Law Olmsted and America in the 19th Century* (New York: Simon and Schuster, 2013).

15. Andrew Jamison, "Greening the City: Urban Environmentalism from Mumford to Malmö," in *Urban Machinery: Inside Modern European Cities*, ed. Mikael Hård and Thomas J. Misa (Cambridge, MA: MIT Press, 2008), 285–88.

16. For a more elaborate discussion of the transnational circulation of mobility models and ideas, see Oldenziel, Sousa, and Van Wesemael, "Designing (Un)Sustainable Urban Mobility from Transnational Settings, 1850–Present," this volume.

17. Sonja Dümpelmann, "Creating Order with Nature: Transatlantic Transfer of Ideas in Park System Planning in Twentieth-century Washington D.C., Chicago, Berlin and Rome," *Planning Perspectives* 24, no. 2 (2009): 143–73.

18. Lenger, "Defining the Modern Metropolis," 36–37.

19. Indeed, today the World Health Organization promotes urban green spaces as a way to support public health in relation to Sustainable Development Goals, WHO, "Urban Green Spaces," World Health Organization, accessed 25 November 2019, http://www.who.int/sustainable-development/cities/health-risks/urban-green-space/en/.

20. Hilary A. Taylor, "Urban Public Parks, 1840–1900: Design and Meaning," *Garden History* 23, no. 2 (1995): 201–21.

21. Jan Feith, *Ons Gouden Vondelpark* (Amsterdam: N.p., 1914).

22. Timothy Davis, *National Park Roads: A Legacy in the American Landscape* (Charlottesville, VA: University of Virginia Press, 2016).

23. Ibid.

24. Roy Rosenzweig and Elizabeth Blackmar, *The Park and the People: A History of Central Park* (Ithaca, NY: Cornell University Press, 1992).

25. Auke van der Woud, *Een nieuwe wereld: Het ontstaan van het moderne Nederland* (Amsterdam: Bert Bakker, 2006), ch. 10.

26. Bart Tritsmans, "Versatile Green: An Alternative Perspective on Urban Green Space in Late Nineteenth-Century Antwerp," *Urban History* 42, no. 1 (2015): 89–112; Stephen Hardy, "'Parks for the People': Reforming the Boston Park System, 1870–1915," *Journal of Sport History* 7, no. 3 (1980): 5–24.

27. Hardy, "Parks for the People."

28. This interpretation is inspired by Longhurst's interpretation of urban streets as "commons"; see James Longhurst, *Bike Battles: A History of Sharing the American Road* (Seattle: University of Washington Press, 2015).

29. Stijn Knuts and Pascal Delheye, "Cycling in the City? Belgian Cyclists Conquering Urban Spaces, 1860–1900," *The International Journal of the History of Sport* 29, no. 14 (2012): 1942–62.

30. Knuts and Delheye, "Cycling in the City?"; Adri A. Albert de la Bruhèze and Ruth Oldenziel, *Cycling Cities: The Munich Experience* (Eindhoven: Foundation for the History of Technology, 2018), 9–11; Martin Emanuel, *Cykelstad Malmö 1870–2000* (Malmö: Malmö stad, 2014), 22–25.

31. Longhurst, *Bike Battles*, 44.

32. Carlton Reid, *Roads Were Not Built for Cars: How Cyclists Were the First to Push for Good Roads & Became the Pioneers of Motoring* (Washington, DC: Island Press, 2015), 73.

33. Richard Sennett, *Building and Dwelling: Ethics for the City* (New York: Allen Lane, 2018).

34. Feith, *Ons gouden Vondelpark*.

35. Historische Vereniging Heemstede-Bennebroek, "Heemstede, Groenendaal (complex)," accessed 25 November 2019, https://hv-hb.nl/topic-heemstede_groenendaal_complex/.

36. Dienstregeling (Timetable) van de N.V. Autobusdienst "Groenendaal-Heemstede-Haarlem en terug" te Heemstede, 1914, 3000–18422, Noord-Hollands Archief.

37. Such infrastructures could also occasionally shift modality. Roads that have fallen in disuse for motorized traffic have been repurposed for cycling and/or walking.

38. NYC Department of Parks & Recreation, "History of Bicycling: A Revolution in Parks," NYC Parks, accessed 25 November 2019, https://www.nycgovparks.org/about/history/bicycling.

39. Gijs Mom, *Atlantic Automobilism: Emergence and Persistence of the Car, 1895–1940* (New York: Berghahn Books, 2014).

40. For London, see Matti O. Hannikainen, *The Greening of London, 1920–2000* (London: Routledge, 2017).

41. Taylor, "Urban Public Parks, 1840–1900," 214–17.

42. Rosenzweig and Blackmar, *The Park and the People*.

43. Rosenzweig and Blackmar, ch. 9.

44. For one of the most detailed studies of this process, see Peter D. Norton, *Fighting Traffic: The Dawn of the Motor Age in the American City* (Cambridge, MA: MIT Press, 2011).

45. Galen Cranz and Michael Boland, "Defining the Sustainable Park: A Fifth Model for Urban Parks," *Landscape Journal* 23, no. 2 (2004): 102–20,

46. Adri A. Albert de la Bruhèze and Martin Emanuel, "Hannover: Sidelining the Bicyclist," in *Cycling Cities, the European Experience: Hundred Years of Policy and Practice*, ed. Ruth Oldenziel et al. (Eindhoven: Foundation for the History of Technology, 2016), 112–23.

47. Shove, "The Shadowy Side of Innovation," 369.

48. Ruth Oldenziel and Helmuth Trischler, "How Old Technologies Became Sustainable: An Introduction," in *Cycling and Recycling: Histories of Sustainable Practices*, ed. Ruth Oldenziel and Helmuth Trischler (New York: Berghahn Books, 2015), 1–12.

49. Cited in Per Lundin, "Mediators of Modernity: Planning Experts and the Making of the 'Car-Friendly' City in Europe," in *Urban Machinery: Inside Modern European Cities*, ed. Mikael Hård and Thomas J. Misa (Cambridge, MA: MIT Press, 2008), 274.

50. Theodore S. Eisenman, "Frederick Law Olmsted, Green Infrastructure, and the Evolving City," *Journal of Planning History* 12, no. 4 (2013): 287–311.

51. In the 1950s, Londoners started to leapfrog the greenbelt and live in villages and towns beyond it; see Gavin Weightman and Steve Humphries, *The Making of Modern London* (London: Ebury Press, 2008).

52. Jean-Claude-Nicolas Forestier, *Grandes Villes et Systèmes de Parcs* (Paris: Hachette, 1908).

53. Brantz and Dümpelmann, "Introduction."

54. Fabiano Lemes de Oliveira, *Green Wedge Urbanism: History, Theory and Contemporary Practice* (New York: Bloomsbury Academic, 2017).
55. Makoto Yokohari, Mamoru Amemiya, and Marco Amati, "The History and Future Directions of Greenways in Japanese New Towns," in *Greenway Planning around the World*, special issue of *Landscape and Urban Planning* 76, no. 1 (2006): 210–22.
56. This example is based on Carlton Reid, *Bike Boom: The Unexpected Resurgence of Cycling* (Washington, DC: Island Press, 2017).
57. National Park Service, Rock Creek Park, *Bicycle Trails* (Washington, DC: NPS, 2010).
58. Ralph Buehler and John Stowe, "Bicycling in Washington, DC Region: Trends in Ridership and Policy since 1990," in *Capital Dilemma: Growth and Inequality in Washington, D.C.*, ed. Derek Hyra and Sabiyha Prince (New York: Routledge, 2016), 180–206.
59. Timothy Auger, *Living in a Garden: The Greening of Singapore* (Singapore: Editions Didier Millet, 2013), 24.
60. The connectors would typically exploit linear spaces too narrow for other uses, e.g., along waterways. Kiat W. Tan, "A Greenway Network for Singapore," in *Greenway Planning around the World*, special issue of *Landscape and Urban Planning* 76, no. 1 (2006): 45–66.
61. Christoph D. D. Rupprecht and Jason A. Byrne, "Informal Urban Green-Space: Comparison of Quantity and Characteristics in Brisbane, Australia and Sapporo, Japan," *PLoS ONE* 9, no. 6 (2014): e99784.
62. National Parks Board, "Park Connector Network," National Parks, accessed 25 November 2019, https://www.nparks.gov.sg/gardens-parks-and-nature/park-connector-network.
63. National Parks Board, "Park Connector Network."
64. National Parks Board, "Nature Ways," National Parks, accessed 25 November 2019, https://www.nparks.gov.sg/gardens-parks-and-nature/nature-ways.
65. Poon Hong Yuen, "Park Connectors: Living Large in Small Spaces," *Urban Solutions* 2 (2013): 36.
66. Auger, *Living in a Garden*, 104.
67. The beneficial sustainability effects of urban green spaces are not restricted to mobility: their vegetation improves air quality; they cool urban heat islands; some even include their aesthetic qualities as an improvement of sustainability in urban settings. See Shah Md Atiqul Haq, "Urban Green Spaces and an Integrative Approach to Sustainable Environment," *Journal of Environmental Protection* 2, no. 5 (2011): 601.
68. Oldenziel, Sousa, and Van Wesemael, "Designing (Un)Sustainable Urban Mobility," this volume.
69. Nordqvist, quoted in Lundin, "Mediators of Modernity," 258.
70. Mimi Sheller, "Mobility Justice and the Velomobile Commons in Urban America," this volume.

# Bibliography

Albert de la Bruhèze, Adri A., and Martin Emanuel. "Hannover: Sidelining the Bicyclist." In *Cycling Cities, the European Experience: Hundred Years of Policy and Practice*, edited by Ruth Oldenziel, Martin Emanuel, Adri A. Albert de la Bruhèze, and Frank Veraart, 112–23. Eindhoven: Foundation for the History of Technology, 2016.

Albert de la Bruhèze, Adri A., and Ruth Oldenziel. *Cycling Cities: The Munich Experience*. Eindhoven: Foundation for the History of Technology, 2018.

Auger, Timothy. *Living in a Garden: The Greening of Singapore*. Singapore: Editions Didier Millet, 2013.

Brantz, Dorothee, and Sonja Dümpelmann. "Introduction." In *Greening the City: Urban Landscapes in the Twentieth Century*, 1–13. Charlottesville: University of Virginia Press, 2011.

Buehler, Ralph, and John Stowe. "Bicycling in Washington, DC Region: Trends in Ridership and Policy since 1990." In *Capital Dilemma: Growth and Inequality in Washington, D.C.*, edited by Derek Hyra and Sabiyha Prince, 180–206. New York: Routledge, 2016.

Cranz, Galen, and Michael Boland. "Defining the Sustainable Park: A Fifth Model for Urban Parks." *Landscape Journal* 23, no. 2 (2004): 102–20.

Cremers, Elisabeth, Fred Kaaij, and C. M Steenbergen. *Bolwerken als stadsparken: Nederlandse stadswandelingen in de 19e en 20e eeuw*. Delft: Delftse Universitaire Pers, 1981.

Davis, Timothy. *National Park Roads: A Legacy in the American Landscape*. Charlottesville: University of Virginia Press, 2016.

Dümpelmann, Sonja. "Creating Order with Nature: Transatlantic Transfer of Ideas in Park System Planning in Twentieth-century Washington D.C., Chicago, Berlin and Rome." *Planning Perspectives* 24, no. 2 (2009): 143–73.

Eisenman, Theodore S. "Frederick Law Olmsted, Green Infrastructure, and the Evolving City." *Journal of Planning History* 12, no. 4 (2013): 287–311.

Emanuel, Martin. *Cykelstad Malmö 1870–2000*. Malmö: Malmö stad, 2014.

Feith, Jan. *Ons gouden Vondelpark*. Amsterdam: N.p., 1914.

Forestier, Jean-Claude-Nicolas. *Grandes Villes et Systèmes de Parcs*. Paris: Hachette, 1908.

Goodwin, Phil. "Peak Travel, Peak Car and the Future of Mobility: Evidence, Unresolved Issues, Policy Implications, and a Research Agenda." Paris: International Transport Forum, 2012.

Hannikainen, Matti O. *The Greening of London, 1920–2000*. London: Routledge, 2017.

Haq, Shah Md Atiqul. "Urban Green Spaces and an Integrative Approach to Sustainable Environment." *Journal of Environmental Protection* 2, no. 5 (2011): 601.

Hardy, Stephen. "'Parks for the People': Reforming the Boston Park System, 1870–1915." *Journal of Sport History* 7, no. 3 (1980): 5–24.

Jamison, Andrew. "Greening the City: Urban Environmentalism from Mumford to Malmö." In *Urban Machinery: Inside Modern European Cities*, edited by Mikael Hård and Thomas J. Misa, 281–98. Cambridge, MA: MIT Press, 2008.

Knuts, Stijn, and Pascal Delheye. "Cycling in the City? Belgian Cyclists Conquering Urban Spaces, 1860–1900." *International Journal of the History of Sport* 29, no. 14 (2012): 1942–62.

Laan-Meijer, Els van der, and Willemieke Ottens. *Roodbaards rijkdom: Landschapsparken Noord-Nederland 1800–1850 Friesland, Groningen en Drenthe*. Rotterdam: BONAS, 2012.

Lenger, Friedrich. "Defining the Modern Metropolis: Universal Expositions from the Mid-Nineteenth to the Mid-Twentieth Century." *Bulletin of the German Historical Institute* 58, no. 1 (2016): 33–46.

Longhurst, James. *Bike Battles: A History of Sharing the American Road*. Seattle: University of Washington Press, 2015.

Lundin, Per. "Mediators of Modernity: Planning Experts and the Making of the 'Car-Friendly' City in Europe." In *Urban Machinery: Inside Modern European Cities*, edited by Mikael Hård and Thomas J. Misa, 257–79. Cambridge, MA: MIT Press, 2008.

Mom, Gijs. *Atlantic Automobilism: Emergence and Persistence of the Car, 1895–1940*. New York: Berghahn Books, 2014.

National Park Service, Rock Creek Park, *Bicycle Trails* (Washington, DC: NPS, 2010).

Norton, Peter D. *Fighting Traffic: The Dawn of the Motor Age in the American City*. Cambridge, MA: MIT Press, 2011.

Oldenziel, Ruth, and Mikael Hård. *Consumers, Tinkerers, Rebels: The People Who Shaped Europe*. Houndmills: Palgrave Macmillan, 2013.

Oldenziel, Ruth, and Helmuth Trischler. "How Old Technologies Became Sustainable: An Introduction." In *Cycling and Recycling: Histories of Sustainable Practices*, edited by Ruth Oldenziel and Helmuth Trischler, 1–12. New York: Berghahn Books, 2015.

Oliveira, Fabiano Lemes de. *Green Wedge Urbanism: History, Theory and Contemporary Practice*. New York: Bloomsbury Academic, 2017.

Reed, Michael A. *The Landscape of Britain: From the Beginnings to 1914*. Lanham, MD: Rowman & Littlefield, 1990.

Reid, Carlton. *Bike Boom: The Unexpected Resurgence of Cycling*. Washington, DC: Island Press, 2017.

———. *Roads Were Not Built for Cars: How Cyclists Were the First to Push for Good Roads & Became the Pioneers of Motoring*. Washington, DC: Island Press, 2015.

Rosenzweig, Roy, and Elizabeth Blackmar. *The Park and the People: A History of Central Park*. Ithaca, NY: Cornell University Press, 1992.

Rupprecht, Christoph D. D., and Jason A. Byrne. "Informal Urban Green-Space: Comparison of Quantity and Characteristics in Brisbane, Australia and Sapporo, Japan." *PLoS ONE* 9, no. 6 (2014): e99784.

Rybczynski, Witold. *A Clearing in the Distance: Frederick Law Olmsted and America in the 19th Century*. New York: Simon and Schuster, 2013.

Sennett, Richard. *Building and Dwelling: Ethics for the City*. New York: Allen Lane, 2018.

Shove, Elizabeth. "The Shadowy Side of Innovation: Unmaking and Sustainability." *Technology Analysis & Strategic Management* 24, no. 4 (2012): 363–75.

Swart, Sandra. "Animating Animals: Historiography and Biomobilities." In *Mobility in History*, edited by Peter Norton, Gijs Mom, Liz Millward, Tomás Errázuriz, and Mathieu Flonneau. *T2M Yearbook* 4, no. 1(2013): 50–61.

Tan, Kiat W. "A Greenway Network for Singapore." in *Greenway Planning around the World*, special issue of *Landscape and Urban Planning* 76, no. 1 (2006): 45–66.

Taylor, Hilary A. "Urban Public Parks, 1840–1900: Design and Meaning." *Garden History* 23, no. 2 (1995): 201–21.

Tritsmans, Bart. "Versatile Green: An Alternative Perspective on Urban Green Space in Late Nineteenth-Century Antwerp." *Urban History* 42, no. 1 (2015): 89–112.

Vlis, Ingrid van der. *Vooruit met veel verleden: Geschiedenis van Delft vanaf 1795*. Zwolle: WBOOKS, 2016.

Weightman, Gavin, and Steve Humphries. *The Making of Modern London*. 1st edition. London: Ebury Press, 2008.

Woud, Auke van der. *Een nieuwe wereld: Het ontstaan van het moderne Nederland.* Amsterdam: Bert Bakker, 2006.

——. *Het lege land: De ruimtelijke orde van Nederland 1798–1848.* Amsterdam: Olympus, 2017.

Yokohari, Makoto, Mamoru Amemiya, and Marco Amati. "The History and Future Directions of Greenways in Japanese New Towns." In *Greenway Planning around the World,* special issue of *Landscape and Urban Planning* 76, no. 1 (2006): 210–22.

Yuen, Poon Hong. "Park Connectors: Living Large in Small Spaces." *Urban Solutions* 2 (2013): 32–37.

# SECTION IV

# Research Agendas for the Future

Urban mobility is responsible for a great part of our global carbon dioxide emissions. Currently, it also tends to segregate rather than integrate social groups, and strengthen rather than reduce their inequalities. Developing more sustainable mobility is a major challenge for our cities today. What can historical understanding contribute, if at all?

This final section, "Research Agendas for the Future," first asks how we can better understand sustainable mobility today. Mimi Sheller warns that ecological and social sustainability do not always go hand in hand when pushing for urban cycling. We should take a much broader look at mobile commons to avoid focusing on only one aspect of sustainability at the cost of another. Second, how can we measure urban mobility? Jan-Pieter Smits and Frank Veraart suggest that historians also consider quantitative data and offer the UN sustainability indicators as a worthwhile tool. Finally, what do policymakers find useful for understanding historical work? Two policymakers, Hans Jeekel and Bert Toussaint, divulge what they find the most promising insights in this book.

In short, this section presents how we can use history for current policymaking and future research.

# CHAPTER 10

# Mobility Justice and the Velomobile Commons in Urban America

Mimi Sheller

## Introduction

North American cities are currently facing the urgent question of how to make the transition to more sustainable mobilities. Generally, this involves a combination of policies to promote active transport and improve public transport. Cities with older colonial cores, such as Philadelphia, New York, Montreal, or Toronto, have a very compact walkable street grid and transit-friendly physical layout. They are therefore amenable to promoting a gradual transition toward more sustainable modes of active transport using tools such as complete street designs, changes in zoning codes, building bicycling infrastructure, introducing bike share systems, restricting automobile use in the city center, and investing in public transit. The transition is more difficult in sprawling cities such as Los Angeles or Atlanta. Yet many North American cities' policies promoting active transport have become associated with the gentrification and displacement of African American, Latinx, and immigrant enclaves, and historically "white ethnic" working-class neighborhoods from more central areas, especially because these policies have not been framed in terms of inclusive mobility justice. This has fostered political mobilization in some cities *against* sustainable transport policies (by both the middle-class automobile-dependent suburbanites and the working-class urban majority who are at risk of displacement from "green gentrification" in city centers).

While active transport policy ideas mirror those found in European cities, in this chapter I want to suggest that the "sustainable mobility transition" in North America needs to be understood within a specific historical context that was built on distinctive spatial and racial formations: white colonial settler societies and "racial capitalism."[1] By locating sustainable mobility transitions within their deeper historical context, we can better understand why seemingly common-sense policies such as constructing protected bike lanes or more walkable pedestrian zones, limiting automobility and promoting transit-oriented development, have generated such intense political conflict in the United States. On the one hand, there are strong *advocates for* automobility who resist any efforts to constrain or reduce the use of cars. These suburban and rural political constituencies have used state-level electoral politics to keep gasoline taxes extremely low and investment in roads and highways very high. On the other hand, urban minority communities who distrust cycling advocacy have used city-level and neighborhood (city council) electoral politics to challenge or undermine bike infrastructure because this is often associated with processes of gentrification and displacement.

I argue that American cities will not achieve a reduction in car use and transition toward more sustainable urban mobility unless we recognize (and directly address) the racial and class histories of uneven mobilities that have formed our racially segregated cities and automobile-dependent suburbs. This chapter draws on my larger book *Mobility Justice: The Politics of Movement in an Age of Extremes* (Verso, 2018), which lays out a more detailed conceptualization of "mobility justice" and a theory of kinopolitics. Here I highlight the historical dimensions of kinopolitical struggles for mobility justice in North American white settler societies founded on slavery, racial capitalism, theft of indigenous lands, displacement of Native Americans and Mexicans, and labor exploitation of Latino/a and Asian migrants.[2] Whether dealing with the freedom to move or the right to stay in place—which are closely intertwined—race and class have been crucial to the uneven distribution of "mobility power" in the United States. By "mobility power" I refer not only to the capability for mobility and its various potentials, but also the self-determination of when, where, how, and whether (or not) to be mobile.

The societal challenge consists of democratically transitioning toward both more sustainable and socially just mobility systems. The question is, how can American cities promote sustainable transport transitions while also being socially inclusive and equitable? I draw on the recent social movements that have begun to challenge the silence of mainstream bicycling advocacy groups on these issues. Emily Reid-Musson observes about these movements:

> As North American cities have started to embrace bicycling, a group of pro-bicycling advocates and researchers has argued that U.S. bicycling movements have too often ignored issues of equity and justice. . . . While

bicycling augurs more sustainable and equitable horizons, marginalized bicyclists' needs and voices need to gain more traction within bicycling movements if bicycling is to realize its potential on both social and ecological fronts.[3]

In the following sections I first briefly introduce the history of American automobile dependence, the racialization of transportation inequities, and the problem of mobility injustices. Then I describe several recent North American social movements that have taken a critical approach to bicycling advocacy and brought a strong, historically grounded racial, gender, and migrant justice approach into the conceptualization of mobility justice. I conclude with a discussion of the "mobile commons" as an alternative way of framing movements for sustainable mobility that surpasses "color-blind" transport-centered policies such as bicycling advocacy. The concept of commoning mobility brings historical depth to understanding the struggles of various groups to gain capabilities for movement. As developed by Anna Nikolaeva et al., the concept of mobility as commons embraces

> forms of thinking about and organizing mobility that draw on the logics of commoning such as communal decision-making practices, openness to new forms of perceiving the right to mobility as well as the right to immobility (the right not to be displaced), the awareness of the social production of mobility and the power relations inherent in it, as well as the commitment to creating equity and working in the interest of the public good.[4]

By uncovering the relationship between historically racialized spatial patterns and transport inequities, we can better understand the contours and fault lines of the contemporary sustainable transportation movements in the United States. By recovering the concept of the mobile commons, I argue that transport justice advocates could make a stronger case for protecting shared common goods (i.e., streets as shared public spaces) while avoiding individualistic frameworks that lead to the appropriation of the right to mobility without concern for its impact on others (including its economic, social, spatial, and environmental injustices). Insofar as such movements still involve bike advocacy, though repositioned through a critique of racial capitalism, we can refer to this as the making of a "velomobile commons."

The concept of velomobility "relates to mobilities research around cycling. The term velomobility (also often spelled 'vélomobility') tends to be used as a phrase to capture mobility that happens by bicycle. The term is often used in parallel, or in opposition to the term automobility."[5]

Like automobility, then, it refers not just to a vehicle, but to an entire set of practices around the 'physical movement of cyclists,' 'the power relations in urban traffic spaces,' the 'representation of bicycling,' and 'experience of the movement.'"[6] Thus the concept of velomobility takes us beyond the bike or the bike lane, as generic technologies, to instead consider the wider social relations and power structures in which cycling is spatialized, racialized, and gendered.

## Automobile Dependence and Mobility Justice

In the twentieth century, processes of suburbanization and automobile dependence dominated the spatial structuration of North American metropolitan regions, especially in the United States. Many injustices were built into these mobility systems. There is a long and well-known history in the United States of racial and class discrimination in mobility rights and freedoms, from slavery to post-emancipation "Jim Crow" systems, which carried over into the age of automobility. The post–World War II building of the federal highway system, the "red-lining" of African-American neighborhoods (preventing access to mortgages and depressing real estate prices), and the urban redevelopment projects that razed many communities—these together created entrenched spatial, racial, and mobility injustices for poor, racial minority, and new immigrant neighborhoods over long periods of time.[7] Within the field of "transportation justice," the existing literature has highlighted the inequitable distribution of transport access, including race and class barriers to mobility, creating what Tim Cresswell calls the "mobility poor."[8] We can think of this as creating the uneven distribution of mobility capabilities, and hence leaving behind patterns of uneven mobility power.

Such transport inequity accompanies and fundamentally supports the ecologically unsustainable system of automobility in the United States. Forms of racialized labor, racial embodiment, and state racial projects are closely tied to economic structures that rely on cheap energy and produce racially segregated urbanism, suburbanization, and a heavy carbon footprint linked to long commutes by car, large energy-hungry suburban houses, and status competition to drive ever larger or more powerful cars. As historian Zack Furness argues, "The postwar redevelopment of the United States was problematic not only because it helped transform the metropolis into an autopolis but also because simultaneously it facilitated both mass suburbanization at home and the geopolitical policies necessary to ensure steady supplies of oil from abroad."[9] Living in the midst of what sociologist John Urry called the "dominant system of automobility" makes it difficult to see how we will move beyond it. Nevertheless, the past teaches us that even mobility systems that have been around a long time will eventually be replaced.

Mobility systems persist and combine into local, national, and even transnational cultural assemblages of mobility that remain very durable over long periods of time.[10] Some urban planners refer to a shift already occurring toward a "new mobility paradigm" based on sharing, connectivity, and accessibility. However, I suggest that the introduction of cleaner vehicles, alternative fuels, active transport, bicycling infrastructure, and improved public transport systems such as bus rapid transit will promote sustainability only in a very limited sense if they are not coupled with reconfigurations of wider mobility power relations and kinopolitical practices.

While much attention has been given to sustainable transportation in response to climate change, future mobility transition must encompass wider mobility justice concerns. Pedestrian and cyclist traffic fatalities, for example, have been one of the most politically galvanizing forces to trigger transport reform movements in the United States, where around thirty-seven thousand people die in car crashes every year. Despite modest reductions in overall traffic fatalities, the number of pedestrians struck and killed by cars between 2009 and 2016 increased by nearly 50 percent nationally, from around four thousand to nearly six thousand.[11] Many poorer communities have the highest rates of crash "hot spots" leading to disproportionate fatalities. In Los Angeles, for example, following protests and vigils over the hit-and-run killing of cyclist Frederick Frazier, age twenty-two, by a woman driving a Porsche SUV (who was eventually located and who pleaded guilty), reports state that

> in poor areas of the city, where people are more likely to depend on walking and cycling as the sole means of transportation, residents complain of a disregard for their well-being by drivers who treat their neighborhood streets like highways. City data shows that the dangers to pedestrians and cyclists are particularly acute in South Los Angeles—where Mr. Frazier was killed—which lags the rest of the city in safety infrastructure.... In year-to-date comparisons between 2017 and 2018, bicycle-involved collisions in the Southeast division of South Los Angeles have increased 70 percent.[12]

Frazier was a member of a cycling group known as Chief Lunes, which loosely organized weekly or biweekly night rides where cyclists "ride en masse," a phenomenon now found in many American cities. Now protestors are demanding the installation of protected bike lanes in South L.A., a city where 489 pedestrians and cyclists were killed by cars between 2013 and 2017.

I now turn to social movements that have mobilized for mobility justice and challenged existing paradigms of transport planning and mainstream (white) bicycling advocacy. These are international movements historically, but have recently taken off in new ways in the United States, offering a fascinating shift in how sustainable mobility is envisioned, and how opposition to automobility is being mobilized—through a mobility justice lens with deep historical sensitivity to racial injustice and uneven spatial formations. These movements alert us to the delicate interplay between economic justice, racial justice, spatial justice, and environmental justice issues, which are combined in various ways through social movement building efforts around sustainable transport that can now be grouped under the rubric of "People for Mobility Justice," one of the newly emerging organizations.

## Mobilizing for Mobility Justice

Political conflicts over cyclists and automobiles sharing road space have a long history in the United States, which I cannot fully recount here, but which has been addressed, for example, by Zack Furness and James Longhurst.[13] Here I focus on more recent efforts by young Black, Indigenous, and People of Color (BIPOC), to broaden the framing of cycling advocacy toward wider mobility justice concerns. As described in a recent event on mobility justice at the University of California Davis:

> Mobility justice and racial justice offer powerful frameworks that account for how complex systems of history, power, and oppression affect people's movement and ability to live, work, and play. Mobility justice emerged simultaneously from the field of critical mobilities studies and from a collective of Black, Indigenous, and People of Color (BIPOC) working in bicycling and sustainable transportation. Mobility justice examines how the racialized histories of cities and transportation systems limit the mobilities of certain communities in uneven ways. Racial justice scholarship seeks to account for how histories of colonialism and ongoing structures of white supremacy have produced systems of inequality for communities of color. It also examines alternative models that undo harmful practices and foster healing.[14]

We can trace the emergence of this mobility justice approach through specific grassroots organizations that challenged mainstream cycling advocacy and policy frameworks.

Cycling is one way for those who have been marginalized to make a claim on public space. This kind of embodied politics is a far cry from more top-down efforts to influence urban cycling through expert-led policy, and illustrates how alternative visions of mobility justice might be embodied, literally, through bringing different bodies out on the streets, on bikes. Through such corporeal mobilities, participants begin to generate alternative mobility futures on larger scales. By moving deliberately toward more inclusive and open streets, these movements potentially draw in more people and connect not only with urban-planning processes, but also with neighborhood concerns such as health, safety, and preventing violence—a key aim of recent BIPOC-led mobility justice movements. Such movements would constitute a kind of velomobile commons through practicing new ways of "commoning mobility."

The tradition of Open Streets initiatives was embraced in many cities around the world to implement a kind of utopian experiment offering the experience of people-centered streets by closing them to car traffic. This began with the famous Ciclovía in Bogotá, Colombia, in 1974 and grew to include over one million people using the streets on every Sunday and holiday throughout the year. Open Streets initiatives now include events such as CicloRecreoVia on Sundays in Santiago, Chile; and events in New York City; Nairobi, Kenya; and Pune, India; also CicLAvia in Los Angeles, which ties into the city's Mobility Plan 2035 by using streets targeted for improved biking and walking infrastructure. These were also an inspiration to community cycling events such as Slow Roll Detroit and Slow Roll Chicago, which I discuss below. The Institute for Transportation and Development Policy (ITDP) argues that despite the limitations, "above all, open streets events let people live briefly in an alternate reality where their city prioritizes streets for people. This alternate reality challenges what people experience in their daily life, and argues that streets where people come first are not only possible but better than the current reality."[15]

Such events, however, lack the political edge of earlier movements, such as Reclaim the Streets (RTS), that began in the United Kingdom in the 1990s, which more aggressively aimed to stop car traffic (and corporate globalization) by reclaiming community ownership of public spaces. RTS grew out of the squatting movement, which also reclaimed property as a commons. It was closely allied with the anti-roadbuilding direct actions in England around the same time, when people sought to stop bulldozers by burrowing in their path or chaining themselves high up in trees. RTS also parallels the emergence of Critical Mass bike rides, which started in San Francisco and the Bay Area in the 1980s and early 1990s, as direct-action anarchic collective rides to reclaim roads for cyclists. Critical Mass rides seek to "assert a positive vision of how things should be in order to expose the current injustice of car-dominated public space."[16] These disruptive subversions of the utilitarian efficiency of horizontal automobile traffic sought to enact a new kind of kinopolitics through direct bodily mobilizations in automobility spaces. Unfortunately, those bodies were predominantly white, male, and middle class, generating critiques for excluding those whose bodies held less dominant mobility power (including women, people of color, and disabled people).

Furness describes how Critical Mass participants experienced the rides as "radically transforming people's collective engagement with, and experience of, urban space (and mobility, for that matter)," and thus they became "a gesture rooted in the positive refusal of constraints, the reconceptualization of urban space and the exploration of desires outside of, or apart from, the framework of consumption and utilitarian mobility."[17] Here we can learn from social movements that are developing a critique of the typical forms of predominantly white, middle-class, able-bodied, and male-dominated bicycle advocacy and transport planning. Critics see this kind of aggressive "refusal of constraints" as perpetuating racial inequalities and spatial injustices through their appropriation of streets and prime central urban space for a particular gendered and racialized group. The issues that BIPOC-led social movements raise can critically extend projects of velomobility that have the potential to encompass wider constituencies in many cities around the world. A more inclusive understanding of commoning mobility would combine movements for social, environmental, and economic sustainability with a critique of racial capitalism and spatial exclusion.

For example, in an area of Los Angeles (a.k.a. the ancestral territories of the Tongva, Tataviam, and Chumash Indigenous communities, now known by the colonial name of Los Angeles County), a phenomenon has emerged of all-women cycling brigades doing monthly "Luna Rides," annual "Clitoral Mass" rides, and "Black Mass" rides, organized by a group known as O.V.A.S. (Overthrowing Vendidxs, Authority & the State). They describe themselves as supporting "young woman of color leadership through a credo that believes in feminist ideals with *indigena* understanding and an urban/hood mentality."[18] In some U.S. cities, there have also been spontaneous "invasions" of public urban highways, especially during Black Lives Matter protests, but also just in random flash mobs (which have sometimes turned violent). These events are less about transport justice than they are about claiming a right to urban space, and to be in the streets, which could be framed in terms of racial justice but also constitutes a claim for "mobility justice" in gentrifying city centers that have increasingly excluded young people of color from public spaces.

It is crucial to recognize the community-based organizing that is already happening in the United States, which makes sense within the historical contextual development of racially segregated North American cities. The Slow Roll Chicago Bicycle Movement, cofounded by Jamal Julien and Olatunji Oboi Reed in 2014, builds on community bicycling events to advocate "racial equity, increased mobility and racial justice to make lives better for Black, Brown and Indigenous people of color across the United States."[19] They claim to mobilize bicycling not just as transportation, but as a tool to build community health, cohesion, and jobs, which in turn will help build trust and counter urban violence. Slow Roll Chicago makes a point of bringing together otherwise fragmented communities around casual, slow, cycling events that purposely deemphasize cycling as transportation.

As cofounder Reed explains, the aim is to bring communities together in a ritual of social cohesion, where they can move together in public spaces, share stories, and in doing so improve individual health, as well as rebuild community trust in neighborhoods shattered by violence. Once people build trust and cohesion, they are more likely to come out and support local businesses, thereby creating local jobs and helping to suppress violence on their streets. As their motto says, "We ride bikes to make our neighborhoods better."[20] This communal self-mobilization serves as a model for the mobile commons. Reed's new organization Equiticity was also recently formed to promote wider mobility justice issues.

The path to "sustainable" mobilities will undoubtedly depend on embodied kinopolitical struggles that directly challenge the dominant system of automobility, in which Reclaim the Streets and Critical Mass explicitly participated, but without the racial justice lens that movements such as Equiticity continue to expand upon today. Rather than simply being bicycling advocacy groups, we could frame these actions as kinopolitical movements for mobility justice. Rather than the mainstream narrative of an incremental change in daily transportation "choices" supported by emerging "disruptive" technologies leading to "sustainable transportation transitions," we can begin to imagine a broader mobility justice movement that would articulate goals around which diverse groups could coalesce and mobilize a new velomobile commons.[21] I next turn to one of the most active groups of this kind in the United States, known as the Untokening, and its offshoot, People for Mobility Justice.

## The Untokening and People for Mobility Justice

The Untokening is a U.S.-based "multiracial collective that centers the experiences of marginalized communities to address mobility justice and equity."[22] It built on earlier efforts by several cycling advocates

such as Allison Mannos and Adonia Lugo who had "noticed that, at a
time when more public resources than ever before were going toward
"sustainable" or "active" transportation infrastructure projects, these investments weren't being guided by the many people of color out there
using bicycles as a mobility solution." Their initial organization City of
Lights/Ciudad de Luces (CoL) formed in 2008 and eventually developed
into Multicultural Communities for Mobility (MCM) in 2012, which "focused on documenting and addressing the transportation needs voiced
by L.A.'s communities of color, who have been disproportionately impacted by deaths and injuries caused by motor vehicles. They are also
at risk for law enforcement harassment while walking or biking in their
neighborhoods."[23] The group has recently been renamed People for
Mobility Justice, whose mission statement reads as follows:

> People for Mobility Justice operates with loving accountability, joy, and
> solidarity centered on black and brown communities in order to transcend
> systems of oppression and violence. We uplift each other to actively resist
> displacement, the police state, transphobia, homophobia, sexism, racism,
> classism, ageism, ableism, anti-Blackness, xenophobia, Islamophobia, Eu-
> rocentric indoctrination, tokenization, exploitation, oppression, and colo-
> nization. We embrace growth and the challenges that come with it.

Several of the founders of these groups were involved in holding a
series of "convenings" known as the Untokening. The Untokening held
their first "convening" in Atlanta in 2016, in conjunction with the Facing
Race conference. Next, Untokening California was held in Los Angeles
on 4 November 2017, Untokening Detroit took place on 11 November
2018, and Untokening Durham, in October 2019. In Detroit, for example,
they described their focus as "Our Collective Mobility Future":

> To co-create a rust-free future, we're bringing The Untokening to the
> Motor City! Untokening Detroit will showcase struggles and successes in
> mobility advocacy, implementation, and engagement we're seeing as we
> shift from Rust Belt to Legacy Cities. Holding space for people with dis-
> abilities and seniors while addressing transportation-related development
> in the local context of Detroit and the Rust Belt region, our day-long event
> will create a space to focus on the personal and interpersonal work it
> takes to be Black, Indigenous, People of Color (BIPOC) in mobility advo-
> cacy, planning, and policy spaces.[24]

Organizers of the Untokening first began using the term "mobility justice" due to dissatisfaction with existing terminology such as "transportation equity" or "bicycle justice," which seemed too restrictive.[25] Mobility
justice, for them, is not simply about equitable access to transportation within cities, though that is an important part, but also about the

smaller micro-mobilities at the bodily scale that are inflected by racial and classed processes, gendered practices, and the social shaping of differential age, abilities, and sexualities. It also concerns larger macro-level questions of justice, relating to colonialism, racism, and capitalism. They seek to center these issues rather than "add in" people of color simply as representatives of "diversity" within mainstream (white) bicycle advocacy organizations. As Lugo put it during the Untokening Durham event, "We need to think about mobility justice as a concept that addresses gender-based harassment on the streets, the fear immigrants may face existing in the world, the criminalization black and brown people may face walking, etc."[26]

The Untokening developed their own "Principles of Mobility Justice" through a community-based discussion process, which was compiled and edited by Adonia Lugo, Sarah Mccullough and Do Lee. They suggest that we first need a deeper historical approach to uneven mobilities:

> Historical disenfranchisement, disinvestment, disproportionate exposure to pollution, and repressive policing in communities of color continue to negatively impact our collective health, wealth, mobility, and security. . . . Mobility Justice demands that we fully excavate, recognize, and reconcile the historical and current injustices experienced by communities—with impacted communities given space and resources to envision and implement planning models and political advocacy on streets and mobility that actively work to address historical and current injustices experienced by communities.[27]

Mobility justice furthermore includes the rights of women and queer people to not be subjected to sexual harassment and bodily assault in the workplace, and the rights of transgender people to move free of violence, find public bathrooms, dress as they choose to, and carry forms of nonbinary identification. As the Untokening notes,

> When people live at the intersection of multiple vectors of oppression, unfettered access to mobility and public space are not guaranteed. Racism, sexism, classism, ableism, xenophobia, homophobia, and constraints imposed upon gender-non-conforming folks can make the public space hostile to many. Bodies encounter different risks and have different needs. Yet this has seldom been the starting point for envisioning more sustainable transportation. It should be. When cities plan for active transportation, low-carbon transitions, or smart mobility, these voices need to be heard.[28]

Combining social justice, racial justice, sexual justice, migrant justice and climate justice lenses, movements like this are beginning to connect neighborhood-level racial inequities (such as biased policing,

transport access, and health access), to national-level migrant justice issues (such as exclusions of noncitizens from legal entitlements to freedom of mobility), to global level climate justice and human rights issues
(such as land grabs for mining and oil drilling that are contributing to
climate change and driving people from their homes). The Untokening also challenges expert knowledge that often dominates transport
planning and even bicycling advocacy groups, by calling for inclusion
of local knowledge and everyday experience. This can be referred to as
*epistemic justice*, which involves recognizing and creating new forms of
knowledge, new facts, and new ways of reconciling seemingly incom-
mensurable ways of knowing.[29]

Epistemic justice comes across very clearly in the position taken by
groups working from marginalized perspectives, such as the Untokening. In their "Principles of Mobility Justice," they call for opening information access, including the languages used in planning, and drawing
on local knowledge:

> Mobility Justice de-centers Eurocentric solutions as the default model and
> looks toward dynamic, grassroots approaches and solutions elsewhere,
> such as South and Central America, and Southeast Asia. It demands lan-
> guage justice and information access that does not exclude some be-
> cause they speak different languages or through professional, technical,
> or academic jargon. . . . Value the local knowledge of these communities
> and compensate them for sharing that wisdom.

When we rely on quantitative data to inform decision-making, or
particular ways of expressing "facts," they argue, we may be "actively
rejecting the knowledge and erasing the struggle and contributions of
community residents." Moreover, the "experiences and input of marginalized communities are often disputed or disbelieved by institutions of
power." This leads them to call for new kinds of decision-making systems in which the marginalized can have power:

> Mobility Justice recognizes that communities are often treated as if they
> are unfit to design their own futures, guide public spending, or under-
> stand the "real" issues at hand—and demands that new decision-making
> systems and structures are created by and for these communities to cen-
> ter their visions and cultivate operating principles that align with their val-
> ues and lived experiences. Communities must be able to reject oppressive
> frameworks and processes and create systems and spaces centered in our
> experiences. Decision-making processes must meet communities where
> they are, and embrace full leadership from these communities—not in
> ratifying or amending pre-ordained ideas but building new ways of inter-
> acting and sharing power.[30]

While sustainable transportation is one important focus of social movements for urban spatial justice, the mobility justice perspective can help us see that such movements are also part of a wider kinopolitics associated with global urbanization, labor migration, gendered, aged, and sexual spatialities, all of which intersect with issues of public health and social protection. People for Mobility Justice (PMJ) explains what mobility justice entails:

> Mobility justice calls our attention to the fact that individuals face different challenges in transportation because the way we are socially controlled in public spaces manifests differently. To move toward more just mobility, we must *end discrimination based on race, class, legal status, ability, gender, or age in how our travel is regulated and accommodated.* PMJ acknowledges the intersections between transportation and the other parts of people's lives and we strive toward radical safety for all through multiracial organizing, self-determination, and economic empowerment.[31]

Above all, these groups call for space and resources for people of color, women, the poor, the elderly, and others historically excluded from transport planning to envision and implement actions from their own knowledge base, and to contribute to theorizing mobility justice as well as bringing about real transformations toward more equitable and sustainable mobility and urban planning, along many intersectional axes. Understanding the history of mobility injustice, and its grounding in white supremacist racial capitalism and colonialism, is crucial to this project, which shifts the discourse of such movements far beyond that typically found in discussions of sustainable mobility transitions. The "Principles of Mobility Justice" are currently being translated into Spanish and French, which also calls for addressing differing European colonial histories.

## Toward the Mobile Commons

Ivan Illich noted that "the road has been degraded from a commons to a simple resource for the circulation of vehicles."[32] The notion of "commoning mobility" has recently been advocated by mobilities scholars working on low-carbon mobility transition policies. Anna Nikolaeva et al. argue that the "commons lens" can help us to transformatively envision more "inclusive and collaboratively governed" cities as part of a new "politics of mobility" that would allow for fairer, greener, more just mobilities. Beyond the individualized "right to move," these researchers focus on "how collective social needs are mediated through mobilities."[33] This might mean access to shared vehicles or public mobility systems, reducing energy consumption for the common good, or producing shared spaces of communal access; but it might also suggest a different kind of politics: a politics of commoning mobility.

Migration studies have begun to discuss an "ontology of moving people" in which mobile commons are an "infrastructure of connectivity" that is "generated, used, and extended . . . between people on the move," including the "shared knowledge, affective cooperation, mutual support and care between migrants" while on the move.[34] In this view, the mobile commons arises out of an ethics of care and mutual support, sharing, and cooperation, and it is affective as much as practical knowledge. Most importantly, it is self-generated by people themselves, in solidarity and autonomy.

A mobile commons does not imply maximizing mobility for all people as an individual "right to mobility," nor is it simply about access to transport or a right to the city. Instead, it implies protecting the capability for human and more-than-human shared mobilities and free spaces for movement by regulating excessive mobilities, limiting unnecessary speed, regulating corporations, pricing the externalities of transportation, and preventing its harms. The mobile commons suggests access to the cooperative social territories and shared infrastructures of movement (both material and immaterial)—the pathways, ways, and means of moving, sharing, and communicating, which have been cooperatively produced by human relation to others, both human and more-than-human, through common passage, translation, and co-usage over time.

However, in my interpretation, mobile commons also differ from "common pool resources" in the sense that they do not have to imply a resource or a particular shared space. While the concept of commons has been applied to histories of the use of streets in Germany and India, and to historical cultural practices such as "civic roads" in Sweden, which "are managed directly by the actual road users living nearby" and involve an organization of road users to build and maintain them, commoning mobility goes beyond the road infrastructure itself as a shared space.[35] Instead, it implies a kind of social infrastructure for assembling, gathering, and sharing while on the move. I think of it more as a verb or an action than as a place through which people move. In such usage, the term "commoning" is often brought to the foreground, and is suggestive of the historical forerunners that might inform contemporary practices.

In their works on *Multitude* and *Assembly*, for example, Michael Hardt and Antonio Negri also note the significance of migrants, who, they say, play a fundamental role in shaping the contemporary world since they engage in making new commons:

> [Those] who cross borders and nations, deserts and seas, who are forced to live precariously in ghettos and take the most humiliating work in order to survive, who risk the violence of police and anti-immigrant mobs, demonstrate the central connections between the processes of translation and the experience of "commoning": multitudes of strangers, in transit and staying put, invent new means of communicating with others, new modes of acting together, new sites of encounter and assembly—in short they constitute a new commons without ever losing their singularities.[36]

This sense of encounter and "commoning" as an ongoing effort at translation across difference, rather than communal homogeneity, is crucial to understanding the mobile commons as a kinopolitical project for building more sustainable mobilities. Commoning mobility lies at the heart of social movements such as Reclaim the Streets, Equiticity, the Untokening, and People for Mobility Justice, and offers a critique of uneven mobility power that goes far beyond more gradualist and nondisruptive institutional forms of mainstream political advocacy for sustainable transport.

What interests me most about these projects is the way they are pushing toward a more mobile imaginary of the commons, or commoning, as a political action—and one which the contemporary moment demands, yet is historically grounded in a critical understanding of how we got to where we are now. What if the commons is not just a territory, a space, a resource, or a product, but the mobile affordances and capabilities for practices of moving, traveling, gathering, and assembling, as well as pausing and being present? What if we conceived of mobility itself as a commons that enabled people not only to share streets more equitably, but also to collectively describe, extend, protect, and negotiate more sustainable and equitable mobility capabilities beyond the system of automobility? And what if we imagine a velomobile commons, built around the social and spatial practices of "light individual transportation" (LIT) rather than automobiles?

In conclusion, I suggest that such a mobile ontology of the commons can become the basis for creating greater mobility justice. In mobilizing the commons of people in movement together, and thereby commoning mobility itself, we might generate unexpected shared spaces of movement and a different kind of urbanism that connects across scales in more sustainable ways—socially sustainable, environmentally sustainable, and economically sustainable. Creating velomobile commons, ultimately, might be the best way to bring about alternative ontologies that have the potential to undermine the uneven spatiality and differential mobility power that are the legacy of racial capitalism, colonialism, and the freedom (of some) to move.

**Mimi Sheller**, professor of sociology and founding director of the Center for Mobilities Research and Policy at Drexel University in Philadelphia, is founding coeditor of the journal *Mobilities* and past president of the International Association for the History of Transport, Traffic and Mobility. She has helped to establish the interdisciplinary field of mobilities research. She is author or coeditor of twelve books, including most recently *Mobility Justice: The Politics of Movement in an Age of Extremes* (Verso, 2018) and *Aluminum Dreams: The Making of Light Modernity* (MIT Press, 2014), and the forthcoming *Island Futures* (Duke University Press, 2020).

## Notes

1. The concept of racial capitalism draws from Cedric Robinson, *Black Marxism: The Making of the Black Radical Tradition*, 2nd ed. (Raleigh: University of North Carolina Press, 2000).
2. For an excellent history of cycling, automobility, and racialized kinopolitics in California, see Genevieve Carpio, *Collisions at the Crossroads: How Place and Mobility Make Race* (Berkeley: University of California Press, 2019).
3. Emily Reid-Musson, "Shadow Mobilities: Regulating Migrant Bicyclists in Rural Ontario, Canada," *Mobilities* 13, no. 3 (2018): 308–24; Aaron Golub et al., eds., *Bicycle Justice and Urban Transformation* (New York: Routledge, 2016); Melody L. Hoffman, *Bike Lanes Are White Lanes: Bicycle Advocacy and Urban Planning* (Lincoln, NE: University of Nebraska Press, 2016); Adonia Lugo, "Decentering Whiteness in Organized Bicycling: Notes from Inside," in Aaron Golub et al., *Bicycle Justice*, 180–88; John Stehlin, "Regulating Inclusion: Spatial Form, Social Process, and the Normalization of Cycling Practice in the USA," *Mobilities* 9, no. 1 (2014): 21–41.
4. Anna Nikolaeva et al., "Commoning Mobility: Towards a New Politics of Mobility," *Transactions of the Institute of British Geographers* 44, no. 2 (2019): 346–60, here 353.
5. Frauke Behrendt, "Why Cycling Matters for Electric Mobility: Towards Diverse, Active and Sustainable E-Mobilities," *Mobilities* 13, no. 1 (2018): 64–80. See also Dave Horton, Paul Rosen, and Peter Cox, eds., *Cycling and Society* (Hampshire, UK: Ashgate 2007).
6. Till Koglin and Tom Rye, "The Marginalisation of Bicycling in Modernist Urban Transport Planning," *Journal of Transport & Health* 1 no. 4 (2014): 220.
7. Robert Bullard, Glenn Johnson, and Angel Torres, eds., *Just Transportation: Dismantling Race and Class Barriers to Mobility* (Gabriola Island, BC: New Society Publishers, 1997); Paul Gilroy, "Driving While Black," in *Car Cultures*, ed. Daniel

Miller (New York: Berg, 2001), 81–104; Don Mitchell, *The Right to the City: Social Justice and the Fight for Public Space* (New York: Guildford Press, 2003); Tim Cresswell, *On The Move: Mobility in the Modern Western World* (London: Routledge, 2006); Cotton Seiler, *A Republic of Drivers: A Cultural History of Automobility in America* (Chicago: University of Chicago Press, 2008); Peter Norton, *Fighting Traffic: The Dawn of the Motor Age in the American City* (Cambridge, MA: MIT Press, 2011).

8. Bullard and Johnson, *Just Transportation*; Robert Bullard, Glenn Johnson, and Angel Torres, "Dismantling Transportation Apartheid: The Quest for Equity" in *Sprawl City*, ed. Robert Bullard, Glenn Johnson and Angel Torres (Washington, DC: Island Press, 2000), 39–68; idem, *Highway Robbery: Transportation Racism and New Routes to Equity* (Cambridge, MA: South End Press, 2004); Cresswell, *On the Move*; and see Karel Martens, *Transport Justice: Designing Fair Transportation Systems* (London: Routledge, 2016).

9. Zack Furness, *One Less Car: Bicycling and the Politics of Automobility* (Philadelphia: Temple University Press, 2010), 52.

10. Gijs Mom, *Atlantic Automobilism: Emergence and Persistence of the Car, 1895–1940* (New York: Berghahn Books, 2014).

11. Association for Safe International Road Travel, asirt.org.

12. Jose A. Del Real, "Their Friend Died in a Hit-and-Run: Can They Take on Car Culture in Los Angeles," *New York Times*, 23 June 2018.

13. James Longhurst, *Bike Battles: A History of Sharing the American Road* (Seattle: University of Washington Press, 2015); Furness, *One Less Car*.

14. "Addressing Cycles of Inequality: A Workshop on Mobility Justice," 1–2 November 2019, hosted by the National Center for Sustainable Transportation, the UC Davis Institute for Transportation Studies, and the UC Davis Feminist Research Institute.

15. International Open Streets Movement, Institute for Transportation and Development Policy, 12 April 2017, available at itdp.org.

16. Furness, *One Less Car*, 78–83.

17. Furness, *One Less Car*, 92.

18. See ovarianpsycos.com; thanks to Anna Davidson, whose Ph.D. dissertation (2018) "Mobilizing Bodies: Difference, Power and Ecology in Urban Cycling Practices," in the School of Geography and the Environment at Oxford University, brought this group to my attention.

19. SlowRollChicago.org and Equiticity.org. Many thanks to Olatunji Oboi Reed for sharing his thoughts on these organizations during a visit to Philadelphia in March 2018.

20. O. O. Reed, public talk in Philadelphia, 26 March 2018.

21. For an insider account of such movements, see Adonia Lugo, *Bicycle/Race: Transportation, Culture, & Resistance* (Portland, OR: Microcosm Publishing, 2018).

22. Untokening.org, lead co-organizers Zahra Alabanza and Adonia Lugo.

23. "About Us," People for Mobility Justice website, accessed 6 November 2018, https://www.peopleformobilityjustice.org/about-us/.

24. "Untokening Detroit (2018)," Untokening Events page, accessed 6 November 2018, http://www.untokening.org/events.

25. Personal communication with Adonia Lugo, April 2018.

26. Adonia Lugo, Untokening Durham, Durham, NC, 6 October 2019.

27. The Untokening Collective, "1.0: Principles of Mobility Justice" (2017), available at untokening.org. Many thanks to Adonia E. Lugo for sharing her thoughts on the organization by email.
28. The Untokening Collective, "1.0: Principles of Mobility Justice."
29. For more extensive discussion of theories of justice in relation to mobility see Mimi Sheller, *Mobility Justice: The Politics of Movement in an Age of Extremes* (London: Verso, 2018).
30. The Untokening Collective, "1.0: Principles of Mobility Justice."
31. People for Mobility Justice, "Mission & Vision," accessed 6 November 2018, https://www.peopleformobilityjustice.org/mission.
32. Ivan Illich, "Silence Is a Commons," *The CoEvolution Quarterly* (Winter 1983): 3.
33. Nikolaeva et al., "Commoning Mobility," 346.
34. Dimitris Papadopoulos and Vassilis S. Tsianos, "After Citizenship: Autonomy of Migration, Organisational Ontology and Mobile Commons," *Citizenship Studies* 17, no. 2 (2013): 178–96, here 191–92; Nicos Trimikliniotis, Dimitris Parsanoglou, and Vassilis S. Tsianos, *Mobile Commons, Migrant Digitalities and the Right to the City* (Basingstoke: Palgrave Macmillan, 2015), 19; idem, "Mobile Commons and/in Precarious Spaces: Mapping Migrant Struggles and Social Resistance," *Critical Sociology* 42, nos. 7–8 (2016): 1035–49, here 1041; Carla Angulo-Pasel, "The Journey of Central American Women Migrants: Engendering the Mobile Commons," *Mobilities* 13, no. 6 (2018): 894–909.
35. Pär Blomkvist and Jesper Larsson, "An Analytical Framework for Common-Pool Resource–Large Technical System (CPR-LTS) Constellations," *International Journal of the Commons* 7, no. 1 (2013) 113–39, here 122; Angela Jain and Massimo Moraglio, "Struggling for the Use of Urban Streets: Preliminary (Historical) Comparison between European and Indian Cities," *International Journal of the Commons* 8, no. 2 (2014): 513–30.
36. Michael Hardt and Antonio Negri, *Assembly* (New York: Oxford University Press, 2017), 152–53.

## Bibliography

Angulo-Pasel, Carla. "The Journey of Central American Women Migrants: Engendering the Mobile Commons." *Mobilities* 13, no. 6 (2018): 894–909.
Behrendt, Frauke. "Why Cycling Matters for Electric Mobility: Towards Diverse, Active and Sustainable E-Mobilities." *Mobilities* 13, no. 1 (2018): 64–80.
Blomkvist, Pär, and Jesper Larsson. "An Analytical Framework for Common-Pool Resource–Large Technical System (CPR-LTS) Constellations." *International Journal of the Commons* 7, no. 1 (2013): 113–39.
Bullard, Robert D., and Glenn Johnson, eds. *Just Transportation: Dismantling Race and Class Barriers to Mobility*. Gabriola Island, BC: New Society Publishers, 1997.
Bullard, Robert, Glenn Johnson, and Angel Torres. "Dismantling Transportation Apartheid: The Quest for Equity." In *Sprawl City*, edited by Robert Bullard, Glenn Johnson, and Angel Torres, 39–68. Washington, DC: Island Press, 2000.
———. *Highway Robbery: Transportation Racism and New Routes to Equity*. Cambridge, MA: South End Press, 2004.
Carpio, Genevieve. *Collisions at the Crossroads: How Place and Mobility Make Race*. Berkeley: University of California Press, 2019.

Cresswell, Tim. *On the Move: Mobility in the Modern Western World*. London: Routledge, 2006.

Davidson, Anna. "Mobilizing Bodies: Difference, Power and Ecology in Urban Cycling Practices." Ph.D. dissertation, School of Geography and the Environment at Oxford University, 2018.

Furness, Zack. *One Less Car: Bicycling and the Politics of Automobility*. Philadelphia: Temple University Press, 2010.

Gilroy, Paul. "Driving While Black." In *Car Cultures*, edited by Daniel Miller, 81–104. New York: Berg, 2001.

Golub, Aaron, Melody L. Hoffmann, Adonia E. Lugo, and Gerardo F. Sandoval, eds. *Bicycle Justice and Urban Transformation*. New York: Routledge, 2016.

Hardt, Michael, and Antonio Negri. *Assembly*. New York: Oxford University Press, 2017.

Hoffman, Melody L. *Bike Lanes Are White Lanes: Bicycle Advocacy and Urban Planning*. Lincoln, NE: University of Nebraska Press, 2016.

Horton, Dave, Paul Rosen, and Peter Cox, eds. *Cycling and Society*. Hampshire, UK: Ashgate 2007.

Illich, Ivan. "Silence Is a Commons: Computers Are Doing to Communication What Fences Did to Pastures and Cars Did to Streets." *The CoEvolution Quarterly* (Winter 1983).

Jain, Angela, and Massimo Moraglio. "Struggling for the Use of Urban Streets: Preliminary (Historical) Comparison between European and Indian Cities." *International Journal of the Commons* 8, no. 2 (2014): 513–30.

Koglin, Till, and Tom Rye. "The Marginalisation of Bicycling in Modernist Urban Transport Planning." *Journal of Transport & Health* 1, no. 4 (2014): 214–222.

Longhurst, James. *Bike Battles: A History of Sharing the American Road*. Seattle: University of Washington Press, 2015.

Lugo, Adonia E. *Bicycle/Race: Transportation, Culture, & Resistance*. Portland, OR: Microcosm Publishing, 2018.

———. "Decentering Whiteness in Organized Bicycling: Notes from Inside." In *Bicycle Justice and Urban Transformation*, edited by Aaron Golub, Melody L. Hoffmann, Adonia E. Lugo, and Gerardo F. Sandoval. New York: Routledge, 2016.

Martens, Karel. *Transport Justice: Designing Fair Transportation Systems*. London: Routledge, 2016.

Mitchell, Don. *The Right to the City: Social Justice and the Fight for Public Space*. New York: Guildford Press, 2003.

Mom, Gijs. *Atlantic Automobilism: Emergence and Persistence of the Car, 1895–1940*. New York: Berghahn Books, 2014.

Nikolaeva, Anna, Peter Adey, Tim Cresswell, Jane Yeonjae Lee, Andre Nóvoa, and Christina Temenos, "Commoning Mobility: Towards a New Politics of Mobility." *Transactions of the Institute of British Geographers* 44, no. 2 (2019): 346–60.

Norton, Peter. *Fighting Traffic: The Dawn of the Motor Age in the American City*. Cambridge, MA: MIT Press, 2011.

Papadopoulos, Dimitris, and Vassilis S. Tsianos. "After Citizenship: Autonomy of Migration, Organisational Ontology and Mobile Commons." *Citizenship Studies* 17, no. 2 (2013): 178–96.

Reid-Musson, Emily. "Shadow Mobilities: Regulating Migrant Bicyclists in Rural Ontario, Canada." *Mobilities* 13, no. 3 (2018): 308–24.

Robinson, Cedric. *Black Marxism: The Making of the Black Radical Tradition*, 2nd edition. Raleigh: University of North Carolina Press, 2000.

Seiler, Cotton. *A Republic of Drivers: A Cultural History of Automobility in America*. Chicago: University of Chicago Press, 2008.

Sheller, Mimi. *Mobility Justice: The Politics of Movement in an Age of Extremes*. London: Verso, 2018.

Stehlin, John G. "Regulating Inclusion: Spatial Form, Social Process, and the Normalization of Cycling Practice in the USA." *Mobilities* 9, no. 1 (2014): 21–41.

Trimikliniotis, Nicos, Dimitris Parsanoglou, and Vassilis S. Tsianos. "Mobile Commons and/in Precarious Spaces: Mapping Migrant Struggles and Social Resistance." *Critical Sociology* 42, no. 7–8 (2016): 1035–49.

——. *Mobile Commons, Migrant Digitalities and the Right to the City*. Basingstoke: Palgrave Macmillan, 2015.

The Untokening Collective. "1.0: Principles of Mobility Justice." 2017. Accessed at untokening.org.

∽⧼⧽∾

# CHAPTER 11

# Toward a Long-Term Measurement System of Sustainable Urban Mobility

Jan-Pieter Smits and Frank Veraart

## Introduction

Given the worldwide awareness of how urgent it is that society, including the mobility sector, becomes more sustainable, what role can historians play in this transition? The search for more efficient and "greener" forms of production and consumption to ensure our wellbeing concerns not only the present generation, but also future generations. Decisions made by previous generations have shaped our current societies. As the intergenerational aspect of how we define sustainability foregrounds the issue of time, history is therefore a key discipline to provide insight and guidance in achieving sustainability.

The contributions in *A U-turn to the Future: Sustainable Urban Mobility since 1850* offer historical insights into the path dependencies of (un)sustainable urban mobility—insights from the roads not taken and the 'pockets of persistence' that could be revived for a more sustainable future. We aim to look deeper into the usable past concept by focusing on methodology in a more experimental fashion. We sketch the methods and sources historians can employ in the intergenerational search for sustainability—specifically in urban mobility.

Studies on how to transform society sustainably concentrate on energy transition. Regrettably, the transition to sustainable mobility has been undertheorized. At a time when 68 percent of EU citizens live in cities, mobility is a key aspect of their everyday lives. For businesses, too, mobility is essential. Given the importance of cities today and how much mobility-related carbon dioxide emissions are escalating compared to other sectors, we need to know whether urban mobility is currently meeting sustainability criteria. Alongside urban mobility's positive contribution to employment, and easy yet affordable transport, we should consider the negative effects, such as the emission of pollutants (greenhouse gasses, particulate matter, or noise), on people's quality of life and the economy. As shown by many contributions in this volume, throughout the past, citizens and policymakers alike have been concerned about the trade-offs and entanglements in these different forms of wellbeing.

Next to the largely qualitative approaches in this volume, we think it is worthwhile to explore the quantitative side of such trade-offs and entanglements. Applying quantitative data retrospectively to historical analysis is, we argue, fruitful for the fast-growing field of environmental humanities. Although this does not imply that only numbers tell the tale, it could be the first step in a more comprehensive mixed-method approach to understanding the sustainability of urban mobility. Notably, (urban) mobility usually does not feature in sustainable development indicator sets—even though the United Nations Sustainable Development Goals (SDGs) include cities and mobility.

We need to come to an agreement on how to measure sustainable urban mobility for three important reasons. First, sustainable development should be operationalized meaningfully; sustainability is often cited as a "container" concept with no clear definition. Second, policymakers need sustainable mobility indicators in order to monitor whether society is moving in a more sustainable direction. This explains why former UN Secretary-General Ban Ki-moon called for a data revolution to support the SDG strategy. Last, a systematic compilation of statistics on urban mobility enables a thorough analysis of significant trade-offs. Only by building datasets with time-series for several indicators can policymakers chart the long-term costs and benefits. Such an indicator set serves as historical understanding or "usable past" to study path dependency and lock-in effects.

This chapter proposes a framework of key indicators to chart sustainable urban mobility. Based on our earlier work, we distinguish the dimensions of mobility's wellbeing effects: "here and now" versus "later" and "elsewhere."[1] A first attempt at charting the history of wellbeing and sustainability using Commission of European Statisticians (CES) indicators is the study *Well-Being, Sustainability and Social Development: The Netherlands 1850–2050* by Lintsen et al. It observes the evolution of Dutch society's wellbeing, and its impact on future generations or people elsewhere,[2] while providing important new insights on long-term changes in sustainability. Drawing on that work, our chapter invites a similar historical analysis for urban mobility. To illustrate the benefit of quantitative analysis, we first review the historical narratives by international authors in this volume. The rich insights can be meaningfully translated into policy domain using indicators.

### The Challenges of Measuring Sustainable Urban Mobility

Past decisions on mobility influence the wellbeing of later generations due to developed behavior, preferences, and spatial lock-ins in the urban fabric.[3] Thus, present-day sustainability problems such as air pollution, accessibility, and traffic jams are rooted in prior generations' choices. Historical analysis reveals which developments have led to the current urban mobility problems and provides deeper insights because sustainability is essentially an intergenerational issue. That said, measuring the sustainability of mobility is quite a challenge. Numerous case studies present datasets on urban mobility for specific cities.[4] The fact that no standardized measurement system has been developed surprises many authors, given the enormous policy relevance.[5] To rectify this omission, our starting point is the *CES Recommendations on Measuring Sustainable Development*, based on the seminal Brundtland Report, *Our Common Future*.[6] Famously, the report's definition of sustainable development sought to capture human wellbeing for the present generation in a given country, and, perhaps even more ambitious, the wellbeing of later generations and people living elsewhere. The report states, "Sustainable development is a development which meets the needs of the present without compromising the ability of future generations to meet their needs." Furthermore, the report emphasizes the fairness of social developments on a global scale. In an increasingly globalized world, measurement approaches should reflect the transboundary impact of sustainability. What would a system for measuring sustainable mobility look like? The volume's essays clearly illustrate the challenges involved.

Unsurprisingly, given the narrative traditions in the field, few contributions are quantitative in nature. Yet, they demonstrate the potential to cross-fertilize quantitative and qualitative analyses, connect these with indicators, and impact policy. The historical analyses are strong in detecting hidden biases in our language and imagined futures that find their way into statistics. Norton argues that to achieve a more sustainable world, we should escape the old modernist and growth-oriented *motordom*, while Divall points out that many mobility concepts embedded in the paradigm of modernization either focus exclusively on economic efficiency, or make a broader and all-inclusive social sweep. Here statistics may help to debunk some of the myths and hidden assumptions. Divall explains that, despite claims to the contrary, environmental issues are downplayed in many policy recommendations for economic "sustainability," while Norton stresses the naive belief in technology— that we can prevent the negative environmental impact of economic growth by introducing green technologies. Such narrative-based analyses could benefit from comparing key indicators of economic growth with data on environmental pressure. They would tell us whether modernist assumptions regarding "green growth" are plausible.[7]

Historical research and source criticism covered in this volume also remind us to tread very carefully with our current data sets. Data may underrepresent systematically certain groups or mobilities, as Männistö-Funk shows for women and low-wage-earners who walk and cycle, using nonstatistical sources like photographs to "see" what was going on in the street. This oversight has led to biased statistics in which men and higher-income groups are overrepresented. To prevent such bias, statisticians should provide sufficiently distributional data regarding gender, socioeconomic status, and age. Present-day policy initiatives often focus too much on national, aggregate goals and indicators, and neglect various social groups. The UN Sustainable Development Goals initiative is a step in the right direction, as it emphasizes the "leaving no-one behind" principle.

Other contributors highlight a strong bias against walking and cycling in mobility statistics. By examining diaries, Pooley observes that walking, despite being the most sustainable form of transport, is almost invisible in (historical) statistical records. He also shows how uncomfortable people were walking down the street once cars become popular; it made them feel like second-class citizens. Cochoy et al. discover, through analyzing photographs of pedestrians carrying certain items, that it is important not only to capture the numbers, but also to identify people's behavior and experiences. These authors claim that reintroducing comfortable transport can encourage more sustainable forms of mobility, particularly a better interconnection of various travel modes like walking and cycling with motorized forms of transport. One way to incorporate such insights is by compiling statistics on how consumers perceive the quality of the mobility system. Insights from social practices may avoid falling into the trap of technocratic initiatives that fail to meet people's mobility needs.

Capturing spatial dimensions in statistical information is equally important. After all, mobility involves people using space. In his biography of one thoroughfare in Stockholm, Emanuel shows how the city redesigned a more livable and sustainable street that displaced the issue of sustainability "elsewhere." Pointing out that urban densification may achieve a more sustainable urban mobility system, Cochoy et al. recommend "relocating certain activities, such as food supply, to the city center," which "may lower the number of motorized shopping trips to large suburban commercial areas." Similarly, in his study on urban greens, Schipper underlines the importance of understanding a city's spatial dimension, showing that mobility in parks was much more sustainable than elsewhere and asks "how mobilities in the park impacted the world beyond its gates and vice versa." These spatial dimensions are indeed crucial. Transport and mobility statistics mostly focus on infrastructural issues or quantity and quality, but scarcely take into account the interrelationship with the spatial dimension of socioeconomic change. These case studies remind statisticians that they need to link urban sustainable mobility to information on the use of space, including aspects of concentration and deconstruction of socioeconomic and cultural activities.

Historical studies give us important insights on how transitions were shaped, how new paradigms formed, how alternative perspectives were pushed to the background, and how different timeframes present different insights. Norton reflects that, in hindsight, the way the urban mobility system developed may seem unavoidable; however, in the past, many different urban mobility futures were possible. It is therefore important not to get stuck in tunnel vision—insights are significant for the process of current policy formation. In their monograph on two centuries of sustainability in the Netherlands, Lintsen et al. recommend adopting different timeframes when formulating policy agendas. In the shorter term, say until 2030, the key focus should be the effective use of *existing* technologies. We should also examine radical new technologies, which are not yet available, but could change the whole outlook on sustainability. Smits shows that for the longer term, say until 2050, policy circles should promote experimentation with technologies in several niches.[8] Even though it is not yet possible to identify technological "winners," we must keep all our options open; this will avoid any lock-in effects in technological trajectories that are suboptimal from a wellbeing and sustainability perspective. We need to heed consumer preferences much more than in the past, when profitability was the guiding principle.

Compelling stories of past sustainable experiences can help to overcome a dominant perspective that overemphasizes economic aspects and marginalizes the social and ecological aspects of sustainability. Our measurement framework outlined below focuses on the economic, social, and environmental aspects of sustainability. Insights from historical case studies can ensure that major aspects are indeed taken on board.

At the same time, these studies prompt the question, how can statisticians measure sustainable mobility in a long-term perspective that captures the social practices and avoids the trappings of cultural framings that lead to lock-ins?

## Indicators for Historians

The next challenge is connecting these rich historical narratives into a joint framework and analysis. Our statistical monitoring framework to investigate and better understand sustainability development not only links the narratives, but also opens them up to quantitative-oriented engineering and policy domains. Based on the Brundtland definition, we distinguish three dimensions in our proposed indicators for sustainable mobility: the wellbeing of the present generation in one particular country (referred to as "here and now"), the wellbeing of future generations ("later"), and the wellbeing of people living in other countries ("elsewhere"). This comprehensive approach enables us to assess whether the present generation's choices can cause problems "elsewhere" or "later." The selected indicators should also redefine, using a top-down approach, the reductionist model of economics.[9] There is also a bottom-up approach common in the social sciences: using information from policy reports, often dependent on stakeholder consultations.[10] The work of the World Business Council for Sustainable Development, a CEO-led organization of over two hundred leading businesses, is valuable in this respect.[11]

Quantification forces researchers to carefully operationalize the concept they are measuring. This applies especially to the field of sustainability, where the term is often used without a clear definition. Moreover, quantitative information is relevant because policy debates are dominated by defined targets that governments must monitor in order to assess their policies' effectiveness. We should select indicators carefully, and continually ask ourselves whether we are measuring what really matters to people and the planet.[12] Insights from historical mobility research can significantly help to overcome such dilemmas and facilitate the use of indicators in policy formation. To chart the here and now, later, and elsewhere dimensions of sustainable urban mobility, table 11:1 provides an overview or "dashboard" of data sources (also see table 11:3 in the appendix for more elaboration on measurements and possibly sources). Although factors like the quantity and quality of transport remain constant, the indicators that measure them may vary over time. To explore the three dimensions, we offer a roadmap for future research.

**Table 11.1.** Dashboards of data sources for "Here and Now," "Later," and "Elsewhere."

| Dashboard "Here and Now" (HN) | | | | |
|---|---|---|---|---|
| | Category | Unit | Possible sources | Remarks |
| *Quantity of transport* | | | | |
| HN 1.1 | Passenger transport | Pass. km | National Statistics | Often used to show economic/ commercial value |
| HN 1.2 | Goods transport | Ton km | National Statistics | Often used to show economic/ commercial value Cyclists + pedestrians often not counted |
| HN 1.3 | Passenger transport intensity | | *Calculations needed* | Modal split before 1980, based on traffic counts |
| HN 1.4 | Goods transport intensity | | *Calculations needed* | Modal split before 1980, based on traffic counts |
| *Quality of transport* | | | | |
| HN 2.1 | Comfort | | | Bias toward public transit |
| HN 2.2 | Commuting travel time | Distance per 30 minutes | | |
| HN 2.3 | Congestion and delays | Minutes | | Bias toward motorized vehicles with 3 or more wheels |
| HN 2.4 | Traffic Safety | Annual fatalities | | Indicator can focus on driver and/or victim |
| HN 2.5 | Crime | Stolen vehicles | Police/insurance data | Some vehicles are easier to steal than others—does not focus on public transit |
| *Quality of mobility system* | | | | |
| HN 3.1 | Functional diversity | 1–10 functions | City maps | |
| HN 3.2 | Intermodal Connectivity | No. of transfer points | City maps | Specialized roads / networks are additions to existing streets |
| HN 3.3. | Intermodal integration | 1–10 parking facilities | Stakeholder reports | |
| *Access* | | | | |
| HN 4.1 | Physical access | | Maps / city plans | Bias toward public transit |
| HN 4.2 | Impaired groups | | Stakeholder reports | Bias toward public transit or car traffic |
| HN 4.3 | Economic Access | Costs/km | | |

*(continued)*

**Table 11.1.** *continued*

|  | Category | Unit | Possible sources | Remarks |
|---|---|---|---|---|
| *Economic significance* | | | | |
| HN5.1 | Share of city transport | | | |
| HN 5.2 | Mobility revenues | | City Council financial reports | Taxation, parking, tolls, and ticket revenues |
| *Negative effects on wellbeing* | | | | |
| HN 6.1 | Emissions | NOx per year | Reconstructed fuel mix | |
| HN 6.2 | Health emissions | Kton particles | Reconstructed fuel mix | |
| HN 6.3 | Noise | | | |
| **Dashboard "Later" (L)** | | | | |
|  | Category | Unit | Possible sources | Remarks |
| *Connection to surrounding areas* | | | | |
| L1.1 | Mobility networks | Km | National / municipal statistics | Specialized networks are merely additions to existing streets |
| L1.2 | Number of transport modes | Number | | |
| *Natural capital* | | | | |
| L2.1 | Mobility space | Km | Land use statistics, land surveys | |
| L2.2 | Energy consumption | PJ | Reconstructed fuel mix | |
| L2.3 | Energy consumption | PJ | | |
| L2.4 | Transportation costs | | See HN4.3 & HN5.2 | |
| L2.5 | Greenhouse gas (GHG) emissions | | See HN5.2 & HN6.3 | |
| **Dashboard "Elsewhere" (E)** | | | | |
|  | Category | Unit | Possible Sources* | Remarks |
| *Connection to surrounding areas* | | | | |
| E1.1 | Distance traveled in 30 minutes | Km | Average speed calculations | Bias toward public transit, because no network influence |
| E1.2 | Cost to travel 30 minutes | | See HN4.3 | |

**Table 11.1.** *continued*

|  | Category | Unit | Possible Sources* | Remarks |
|---|---|---|---|---|
| **Connection to other cities** | | | | |
| E2.1 | Travel time to other cities | Minutes | Maps + average speed and network | |
| E2.2 | Travel cost to other main cities | | See HN4.3 | |
| **Connection to other countries** | | | | |
| E3.1 | Travel time to air and seaports | Minutes | Historic maps | |
| E3.2 | Travel costs to air and seaports | | | |

\* The table in the appendix shows types of historical sources for finding appropriate indicators.

## Urban Mobility "Here and Now"

The main indicators of urban sustainable mobility "here and now" are the volumes of passenger and goods transport (expressed in passenger-kilometer and ton-kilometer). An increase in mobility can have many negative effects on wellbeing, ranging from traffic jams to air pollution. The first-order effect, however, focusing on how easily persons and goods flow within a city, is positive. On the downside, there are many trade-offs. Increasing "here and now" mobility can affect later generations, and even the current generation. Systematically compiling indicators that address these positive and negative effects enables a solid analysis of the urban mobility sector. Preferably, these indicators should not be presented at aggregate level, but distinguish various transport modes—what policymakers call the modal split. From an environmental perspective, it is important to note and compare the varying utilization of (fossil) energy sources between transport modes (pedestrians, cyclists, cars, busses, trams, and subways), to accurately assess which are ecologically sustainable.

## Urban Mobility "Later"

Potentially negative effects on wellbeing are not restricted to the present era because some types of damage only manifest themselves in the long term. We should bear in mind the risk of depleting vital natural capital stocks. When evaluating the impact of the transport sector on society's vital resources, we need to consider investments in infrastructure and modern transport equipment; otherwise, increases in mobility can be jeopardized in the longer run. The "later" dashboard gives an overview of long lasting, multi-generational elements.

### Urban Mobility "Elsewhere"

This dashboard has three different categories: first, the rural area surrounding the city. Efficient transport is important, as some goods and services are only available in cities. Thus, the time and cost of traveling from rural areas to the nearest city are important determinants for the wellbeing of people outside the city. Second, we consider the transport links between a city and other major urban centers. With economies of scale continually expanding, and cities merging into megacities, good mobility services have become fundamentally important. Third, in a globalizing world, we must consider a city's connection to other countries, including the distance and travel costs to the nearest airport, harbor, or train station.

## A Measurement Framework Enriches Historical Analysis

Statistics on the three wellbeing dimensions of urban mobility enable scholars to study the fundamental trade-offs at the heart of sustainability debates: namely, whether the wellbeing the present generation generates is at the expense of future generations, or has detrimental effects elsewhere. Chapters in this book offer promising narratives that would benefit from additional quantitative evidence.

Statistical data is a good starting point for deeper analysis. Quantitative evidence helps to identify important trends and the major issues confronting society. The "mixed method approach" combines studying quantitative and qualitative sources to understand the motives of various historical actors. The long-term analysis of sustainability for the Netherlands produced a rich historical narrative. Its distinction between ex-post and ex-ante evaluations provided key insights, enabling us to analyze the changes in sustainability. Our initial approach focused on contemporary challenges. We asked, in which time periods, in which segments of society, and using what types of technology were sustainability problems like the excessive use of raw materials and the emission of pollutants concentrated? Some might consider such an approach anachronistic because previous generations were totally unaware of present-day problems such as climate change. It does, however, help us to better understand the connection between complex processes like economic growth and environmental degradation.

The second approach analyzes "past futures"—in other words, how each generation views its own wellbeing and sustainability issues. Based on a rich variety of qualitative sources, this analysis shows us how certain sustainability issues are identified and put on the political agenda. It also explains how changes in technologies and institutional settings have helped to overcome previous sustainability issues.

The sustainability framework can be used as a "lens" to observe the complex and multidimensional phenomenon of sustainable urban mobility, inviting us to scrutinize the main trade-offs. Although indicators are not required for every single phenomenon, it is useful to chart these trade-offs based on a limited number of indicators. This approach also identifies what indicators are missing so that additional research can use other (qualitative) sources.

Over the years, data has been gathered with particular, and historically changing, reasons to either include or exclude modes of transport. Even the search for data shows people's changing views on the importance of different modes. The monitoring system can generate research questions on why preferences changed and on the impact on urban planning and mobility decisions. In 1938, the Netherlands Statistics Agency (CBS) observed various transport modes including the popular modes of the late 1930s, such as bicycles, transport bicycles, carriages, and hand or dog carts. The data could be combined with traffic counts or used to measure the economic value of goods transport.[13]

After World War II, economic value calculations did not return; nor did (transport) bicycles or carts appear in ton-kilometer statistics. Table 11.2 shows the number of vehicles in the Netherlands in later years. The indicators in table 11.2 refer to the accessibility of various modalities. The gaps are due to nonsystematic collection: the data was collected for taxation purposes, and therefore detailed cars, motorcycles, and buses; data on bicycles, however, disappeared after the bicycle tax

**Table 11.2.** Number of vehicles in the Netherlands (in thousands).

|            | 1930 | 1938 | 1950 | 1960 | 1970 | 1979  |
|------------|------|------|------|------|------|-------|
| Cars       | 68   | 94   | 139  | 522  | 2465 | 4180  |
| Buses      |      | 4    | 5    | 9    | 9    | 10    |
| Motorcycles|      | 55   | 95   | 173  | 72   | 92    |
| Mopeds     |      |      |      |      |      | 1095* |
| Bicycles   | 2700 | 3500 |      |      |      | 10317 |

*1978
Sources: Statistics Netherlands (CBS); Albert de la Bruhèze and Veraart.[14]

was rescinded in 1941.[15] Generally, policymakers' attention to cycling declined in the 1950s and 1960s as they no longer considered the number of bicycles relevant for mobility policies.[16] These numbers returned only in the wake of the renewed interest in cycling in the 1970s. Table 11.2 illustrates the perceived importance of each form of transport in various time periods. The sustainability monitor can be a starting point for further (qualitative) research and can identify major shifts in mobility systems, even with less accurate indicators.

Cochoy et al. offer an insightful example of a mixed-method approach. Their quantitative evidence gives a precise description of traffic, whereas their qualitative use of photographs captures social practices and gives a stronger sense of proportion as slower forms of transport become more visible. Similarly, Männistö-Funk shows how visual sources can complement and even question statistics. They present a different picture of how people actually used the space and experienced changes in mobility on the streets.

The main contribution of qualitative analysis is detecting hidden biases, imagined futures, and social practices. Systematic qualitative analysis of the urban mobility system and its wellbeing dimensions offers the potential of rich cross-fertilization: by providing historical insights to engineers, spatial planners, and policymakers, historians can have a more positive role in the policy domain of urban sustainable mobility than at present.

## Conclusion

Historical studies on mobility often lack statistical data. This chapter proposes a framework for measuring sustainable urban mobility, building on the *CES Recommendations on Measuring Sustainable Development*. By distinguishing the dimensions of wellbeing, this measurement tool can explain major trade-offs in sustainability debates—namely to what extent one generation's creation of wellbeing affects later generations or people elsewhere. The international contributions in this volume not only offer a roadmap for statistical analysis to enrich sustainable development narratives, but also provide qualitative insights that will strengthen a research agenda for urban sustainable measurement. A mixed-method approach using both quantitative and qualitative data, and the measurement framework as a heuristic, may lead to new perspectives on sustainable mobility. Such a dual approach will develop a usable past that may convince policymakers to take on board the many important insights from historical studies.

# Appendix
## Sources for Measuring Historical Sustainable Mobility

**Table 11.3.** Detailed dashboards for "Here and Now," "Later," and "Elsewhere."

| | Category | Type of data Numbers Qualitative Calculation | Urban level Yes/No/ Rare | Types of transport(s) | Sources | Period |
|---|---|---|---|---|---|---|
| | **Dashboard "Here and Now" (HN)** | | | | | |
| *Quantity of transport* | | | | | | |
| HN 1.1 | Passenger transit | N | Yes Rare Rare | Public transit Private motorized Private nonmotorized | Annual reports / city statistics | 1890–now 1920–now 1920–1940/ 1980–now |
| HN 1.2 | Goods transit | N | Rare Yes No | Public transit Private motorized Private nonmotorized | National statistics | 1920–now |
| HN 1.3 | Passenger transit intensity | C | Rare Yes Rare | Public transit Private motorized Private nonmotorized | Traffic counts Modal split | 1910–1990 (now) 1980–now |
| HN 1.4 | Good transport intensity | C | No Yes No | Public transit Private motorized Private nonmotorized | Traffic counts Modal split | 1910–1990 (now) 1980–now |
| *Quality of transport system* | | | | | | |
| HN 2.1 | Comfort | Q | Yes No No | Public transit Private motorized Private nonmotorized | Annual reports | 1950–now |
| HN 2.2 | Commut- ing travel time | C | Yes Yes Yes | Public transit Private motorized Private nonmotorized | May be based on estimates | 1890–now |
| HN 2.3 | Conges- tion and delays | Q | Rare Yes No | Public transit Private motorized Private nonmotorized | City & national reports | 1970–now |
| HN 2.4 | Traffic safety | N | Rare Yes Yes | Public transit Private motorized Private nonmotorized | National reports City reports | 1930–now 1950–now |
| HN 2.5 | Crime | N | No Yes Yes | Public transit Private motorized Private nonmotorized | National reports City reports | 1950–now 1950–now |

*(continued)*

**Table 11.3.** *continued*

|  | Category | Type of data Numbers Qualitative Calculation | Urban level Yes/No/ Rare | Types of transport(s) | Sources | Period |
|---|---|---|---|---|---|---|
| *Quality of mobility system* | | | | | | |
| HN 3.1 | Functional diversity | N | Yes | 1–10 functions | City maps | 1890–now |
| HN 3.2 | Intermodal Connectivity | N | Yes | Number of transfer points | City maps | 1890–now |
| HN 3.3. | Intermodal integration | N | Yes | 1–10 Parking facilities | City maps | 1920–now |
| *Access* | | | | | | |
| HN 4.1 | Physical access | C N N | Yes Yes Yes | Public transit Private motorized Private nonmotorized | Grid density, maps Vehicles/ capita Vehicles/ capita | 1890–now 1920–now 1920–now |
| HN 4.2 | Impaired groups | Q | Rare No No | Public transit Private motorized Private nonmotorized | Stakeholder reports | Unknown |
| HN 4.3 | Economic access | Q C | Yes Yes No | Public transit Private motorized Private nonmotorized | Annual reports Fuel price | 1890–now 1920–now |
| *Economic significance* | | | | | | |
| HN5.1 | Share of city transport | C C | Yes Rare No | Public transit Private motorized Private nonmotorized | Annual reports | 1890–now |
| HN 5.2 | Mobility revenues | N | Yes Rare Rare | Public transit Private motorized Private nonmotorized | City council financial reports | 1890–now |
| *Negative effects on wellbeing* | | | | | | |
| HN 6.1 | Emissions | C C | Yes Yes Yes = 0 | Public transit Private motorized Private nonmotorized | Reconstructed fuel mix | 1890–now 1920–now |

**Table 11.3.** *continued*

| | Category | Type of data Numbers Qualitative Calculation | Urban level Yes/No/ Rare | Types of transport(s) | Sources | Period |
|---|---|---|---|---|---|---|
| HN 6.2 | Health emissions | C C | Yes Yes Yes = 0 | Public transit Private motorized Private nonmotorized | Recon- structed fuel mix | 1890–now 1920–now |
| HN 6.3 | Noise | Q | | Public transit Private motorized Private nonmotorized | | Unknown |
| **Dashboard "Later" (L)** | | | | | | |
| | Category | Data Type Numbers Qualitative Calculation | Urban level Yes/No/ Rare | Types of transport | Sources | Period |
| *Economic capital* | | | | | | |
| L1.1 | Mobility networks | C | Yes Yes Rare | Public transit Private motorized Private nonmotorized | City map Grid calculations | 1890–now |
| L1.2 | Number of transport modes | Number | Rare Yes Yes | Public transport Private motorized Private nonmotorized | | |
| *Natural capital* | | | | | | |
| L2.1 | Mobility space | Km2 | | | Land use statistics Land surveys | |
| L2.2 | Energy consump- tion | PJ | Yes Yes Yes = 0 | Public transit Private motorized Private nonmotorized | Recon- structed fuel mix | |
| L2.3 | Energy consump- tion | PJ/ton km | Rare Yes Yes= 0 | Public transport Private motorized Private nonmotorized | | |
| L2.4 | Trans- portation costs | | See HN4.3 & HN 5.2 | | | |
| L2.5 | GHG emissions | | See HN6.1 & HN6.3 | | | |

*(continued)*

**Table 11.3.** *continued*

| | | Dashboard "Elsewhere" (E) | | | | |
|---|---|---|---|---|---|---|
| | Name | Type of data Numbers Qualitative Calculation | Urban level Yes/No/ Rare | Transport categories | Sources | Periods |
| *Connection to surrounding region* | | | | | | |
| E1.1 | Distance traveled in 30 minutes | N | Yes Yes Yes | Public transit Private motorized Private nonmotorized | Estimates | 1890–now 1920–now 1890–now |
| E1.2 | Cost of 30 min. travel | N/C | Yes Yes Yes | Public transit Private motorized Private nonmotorized | Annual reports Fuel price calculations Estimates | 1890–now 1920–now 1890–now |
| *Connection to other cities* | | | | | | |
| E2.1 | Distance to other cities | N | Yes | All | City/ county maps | 1890–now |
| E2.2 | Travel cost to other main cities | N/C | Yes Yes Yes | Public transit Private motorized Private nonmotorized | Annual reports Fuel price calculations Estimates | 1890–now 1920–now 1890–now |
| *Connection to other countries* | | | | | | |
| E3.1 | Distance to air and seaports | N | Yes | All | City/ county maps | 1890–now |
| E3.2 | Travel costs to air and seaports | N | Yes | All | City/ county maps | 1890–now |

Note: Travel distances (per mode) can be calculated using average speeds. The transport costs can be calculated based on fuel prices and annual public transit reports. The connections to cities and other countries could be expressed as "catchment" areas.

**Jan-Pieter Smits**, senior statistical researcher at Statistic Netherlands and project leader of the Monitor of Well-Being presented annually to the Dutch parliament, is a professor at Eindhoven University of Technology. He has been working on defining a measurement system for sustainability in a UN international taskforce, OECD, the European Commission, and the World Bank, and is an active member of the UN working group to define indicators for Sustainable Development Goals. His publications include *Well-Being, Sustainability and Social Development: The Netherlands 1850–2050* with Harry Lintsen, Frank Veraart, and John Grin (Springer, 2018).

**Frank Veraart**, assistant professor of history of technology at Eindhoven University of Technology, specializes in modern history, including mobility, environmental studies, spatial planning, and computing. He focuses on how technology and actors shape social development. His latest research examines the historical development of (social, economic, and ecological) sustainability trade-offs in transnational resource chains. His co-authored publications include *Cycling Cities: The European Experience* with Ruth Oldenziel, Martin Emanuel, and Adri A. Albert de la Bruhèze (Eindhoven, 2017), and *Well-Being, Sustainability and Social Development: The Netherlands 1850–2050* with Harry Lintsen, Jan-Pieter Smits, and John Grin (Springer, 2018).

## Notes

1. Our experimental analysis strongly relies on work by Jan-Pieter Smits and Rutger Hoekstra of the UNECE/European Commission/OECD Task Force for Measuring Sustainable Development, whose final report in 2014 has since been endorsed by sixty-five countries. CES, *Commission of European Statisticians Recommendations on Measuring Sustainable Development*, Report of the Joint UNECE/OECD/ Eurostat Taskforce for Measuring Sustainable Development (Geneva: United Nations, 2014). Jan-Pieter Smits was cochair, and Rutger Hoekstra coeditor.

2. Harry Lintsen, Frank Veraart, Jan-Pieter Smits, and John Grin, *Well-Being, Sustainability and Social Development: The Netherlands 1850–2050* (New York: Springer Verlag, 2018).

3. Also see Cornelis Disco and Frank Veraart, "A Farewell to Big Planning? 1990–2010," in *Builders and Planners: A History of Land-Use and Infrastructure Planning in the Netherlands*, ed. J. Arts et al. (The Hague: Rijkswaterstaat, 2016), 351–43; Martin Emanuel, "Monuments of Unsustainability: Planning, Path Dependence, and Cycling in Stockholm," in *Cycling and Recycling: Histories of Sustainable Practices*, ed. Ruth Oldenziel and Helmuth Trischler (New York: Berghahn Books, 2015), 101–24; and Annique Hommels, *Unbuilding Cities: Obduracy in Urban Sociotechnical Change* (Cambridge, MA: MIT Press, 2005).

4. For a literature overview, see Hossein Haghshenas and Manouchehr Vaziri, "Urban Sustainable Transport Indicators for Global Comparison" *Ecological Indicators* 15, no. 1 (2012): 115–21, and Herb Castillo and David Pitfield, "Elastic: A Methodological Framework for Identifying and Selecting Sustainable Transport Indicators," *Transport research. Part D: Transport and Environment* 15 no. 4 (2010): 179–88.

5. See Desta Mebratu, "Sustainability and Sustainable Development: Historical and Conceptual Review" *Environmental Impact Assessment Review* (1998): 493–521; Henrik Gudmundsson, "Making Concepts Matter: Sustainable Mobility and Indicator Systems in Transport Policy," *International Social Science Journal* 55 (2003): 199–217; and C. Jeon and A. Amekudzi, "Addressing Sustainability in Transportation Systems: Definitions, Indicators and Metrics," *Journal of Infrastructure Systems* 11, no. 1 (2005): 31–50.

6. Gro Harlem Brundtland, *Our Common Future*, World Commission on Environment and Development (Nairobi: United Nations Environment Programme, 1987).

7. In "Measuring What Matters: a Long-Term View of Sustainability" (Inaugural lecture, Eindhoven University of Technology, 2018), Smits shows that the relationship between economic growth and sustainability is not constant. Until

ca. 1960, economic growth was more or less unsustainable, in the sense that present-day sustainability norms were not surpassed. However, since the 1960s, economic growth has become distinctively unsustainable, showing that some paradigms with optimistic technological views such as *green growth* are simply not in line with (historical) reality.

8.  Jan-Pieter Smits, "Measuring What Matters."
9.  Mark Reed, Evan Fraser, and Andrew Doujill, "An Adaptive Learning Process for Developing and Applying Sustainability Indicators with Local Communities," *Ecological Economics* 59 (2006): 406–18.
10. PSUTA (Partnership for Sustainable Urban Transport in Asia), "Sustainable Urban Transport in Asia: Making the Vision a Reality" (2006), accessed 27 September 2018, http://pdf.wri.org/sustainable_urban_transport_asia.pdf; and M. Costa, A. N. R. Silva, and R. A. R. Ramos, "Sustainable Urban Rural Mobility: a Comparative Study and the Basis for a Management System in Brazil and Portugal," in *WIT Transactions on The Built Environment* 77 (2005): 323–32.
11. WBSCD, *Methodology and Indicator Calculation for Urban Sustainable Mobility*, Sustainable Mobility Project 2.0 (SMP 2.0) (Geneva: World Business Council for Sustainable Development, 2015).
12. Smits, "Measuring What Matters."
13. CBS, *Verkeerswaarnemingen van den Rijkswaterstaat. Bewerkt door denRijkswaterstaat, Wegen- en Verkeersstatistiek en het Centraal Bureau voor de Statistiek* (The Hague: CBS, 1938).
14. Statistics Netherlands (CBS): CBS, *Veertig jaren verkeers- en vervoersstatistiek in tijdreeksen 1938–1978*; CBS, *Zakboek verkeers- en vervoerstatistieken*, 1984; CBS, *Mobiliteit van de Nederlandse bevolking in 1978*; CBS, *Mobiliteit van de Nederlandse bevolking in 1984*; Frank Veraart and Adri A. Albert de la Bruhèze, *Fietsverkeer in praktijk en beleid in de twintigste eeuw* (The Hague: Ministerie van Verkeer en Waterstaat, 1999).
15. Adri A. Albert de la Bruhèze and Ruth Oldenziel, "Who Pays, Who Benefits? Bicycle Tax as Policy Tool, 1890–2012," in Oldenziel and Trischler, *Cycling and Recycling*, 73–100.
16. Albert de la Bruhèze and Veraart. *Fietsverkeer in praktijk en beleid in de twintigste eeuw*; Ruth Oldenziel, Martin Emanuel, Adri A. Albert de la Bruhèze, and Frank Veraart, eds., *Cycling Cities: The European Experience* (Eindhoven: Foundation for the History of Technology, 2016).

## Bibliography

Albert de la Bruhèze, Adri A., and Ruth Oldenziel. "Who Pays, Who Benefits? Bicycle Tax as Policy Tool, 1890–2012." In *Cycling and Recycling: Histories of Sustainable Practices*, edited by Ruth Oldenziel and Helmuth Trischler, 73–100. New York: Berghahn Books, 2015.

Brundtland, Gro Harlem. *Our Common Future: World Commission on Environment and Development*. Nairobi: United Nations Environment Programme, 1987.

Castillo, Herb, and David Pitfield. "Elastic: A Methodological Framework for Identifying and Selecting Sustainable Transport Indicators." *Transport Research. Part D: Transport and Environment* 15 no. 4 (2010): 179–88.

CBS (Centraal Bureau voor de Statistiek Netherlands). *Mobiliteit van de Nederlandse bevolking in 1978*.

——. *Mobiliteit van de Nederlandse bevolking in 1984*.

——. *Verkeerswaarnemingen van den Rijkswaterstaat. Bewerkt door den Rijkswaterstaat, Wegen—en Verkeersstatistiek en het Centraal Bureau voor de Statistiek*, 1938.

———. *Veertig jaren verkeers- en vervoersstatistiek in tijdreeksen 1938–1978.*

———. *Zakboek verkeers- en vervoerstatistieken,* 1984.

CES (Commission of European Statisticians). *Conference of European Statisticians Recommendations on Measuring Sustainable Development.* Report of the Joint UNECE/OECD/Eurostat Taskforce for Measuring Sustainable Development. Geneva: United Nations, 2014.

Costa, M., A. N. R. Silva, and R. A. R. Ramos. "Sustainable Urban Rural Mobility: A Comparative Study and the Basis for a Management System in Brazil and Portugal." *WIT Transactions on the Built Environment* 77 (2005): 323–32.

David, Paul A. "Path Dependence: A Foundational Concept for Historical Social Science." *Cliometrica* 1, no. 2 (2007): 91–114.

Disco, Cornelis, and Frank Veraart. "A Farewell to Big Planning? 1990–2010." In *Builders and Planners: A History of Land-Use and Infrastructure Planning in the Netherlands,* edited by Jos Arts, Ruud Filarski, Hans Jeekel, and Bert Toussaint, 351–437. The Hague: Rijkswaterstaat, 2016.

Emanuel, Martin. "Monuments of Unsustainability: Planning, Path Dependence, and Cycling in Stockholm." In Oldenziel and Trischler, *Cycling and Recycling: Histories of Sustainable Practices,* 101–24.

Gudmundsson, Henrik. "Making Concepts Matter: Sustainable Mobility and Indicator Systems in Transport Policy." *International Social Science Journal* 55 (2003): 199–217.

Haghshenas, Hossein, and Manouchehr Vaziri. "Urban Sustainable Transport Indicators for Global Comparison." *Ecological Indicators* 15, no. 1 (2012): 115–21.

Hommels, Annique. *Unbuilding Cities: Obduracy in Urban Sociotechnical Change.* Cambridge, MA: MIT Press, 2005.

Jeon, Christy M., and Adjo Amekudzi. "Addressing Sustainability in Transportation Systems: Definitions, Indicators and Metrics." *Journal of Infrastructure Systems* 11, no. 1 (2005): 31–50.

Lintsen, Harry, Frank Veraart, Jan-Pieter Smits, and John Grin. *Well-Being, Sustainability and Social Development: The Netherlands 1850–2050.* New York: Springer Verlag, 2018.

Mahoney, James. "Path Dependence in Historical Sociology." *Theory and Society* 29 (2000): 507–48.

Mebratu, Desta. "Sustainability and Sustainable Development: Historical and Conceptual Review." *Environmental Impact Assessment Review* (1998): 493–521.

Oldenziel, Ruth, Martin Emanuel, Adri A. Albert de la Bruhèze, and Frank Veraart, eds. *Cycling Cities: The European Experience.* Eindhoven: Foundation for the History of Technology, 2018.

PSUTA (Partnership for Sustainable Urban Transport in Asia). "Sustainable Urban Transport in Asia: Making the Vision a Reality." 2006. Accessed 27 September 2018, http://pdf.wri.org/sustainable_urban_transport_asia.pdf.

Reed, Mark, Evan Fraser, and Andrew Doujill. "An Adaptive Learning Process for Developing and Applying Sustainability Indicators with Local Communities." *Ecological Economics* 59 (2006): 406–18.

Smits, Jan-Pieter. "Measuring What Matters: A Long-Term View of Sustainability." Inaugural lecture, Eindhoven University of Technology, 2018.

Veraart, Frank, and Adri A. Albert de la Bruhèze. *Fietsverkeer in praktijk en beleid in de twintigste eeuw.* The Hague: Ministerie van Verkeer en Waterstaat, 1999.

WBSCD. *Methodology and Indicator Calculation for Urban Sustainable Mobility.* Sustainable Mobility Project 2.0 (SMP 2.0). Geneva: World Business Council for Sustainable Development, 2015.

# Reflections from a Policy Perspective

Hans Jeekel and Bert Toussaint

In twelve stories, *A U-Turn to the Future* addresses urban mobility prac-tice: what actually happened on the street and how people found their way around the city. Many patterns emerged from the original concepts, strategies, and insights discussed in policy circles. What takes place on city streets, squares, and roads is related to the insights of experts and decision makers who feel the need to build, demolish, and restructure their cities. Citizens either cherish or resist such realities framed by pol-iticians and experts. Despite policy visions and directives, as the book shows, "pockets of persistence" can be found throughout history. People kept on walking and cycling, and used parks as radical "other-mobility" locations. The book articulates the vision that the past is "usable."[1] The introduction applies this concept to urban mobility: in providing a long-term perspective, today's car-dominated mobility appears not to be an inevitable outcome of societal progress, but rather the result of con-tested policy choices, leading to the marginalization of cycling and walking. This approach is equally relevant to policymakers. So what can we take from all twelve narratives?

We see at least five useful insights: the reflection on how statistics are constructed; the need for an unequivocal and encompassing definition of "sustainability"; the importance of preserving "pockets of persistence"; the sensitivity to power relations; and the necessity of tracking reality and actual practice. These lessons expand on the potential the usable past can offer.

The first historical insight for current policymakers is the *importance of good statistics*. What becomes clear throughout this book is that sta-tistics on slow transport modes are lacking. It is not merely a matter of neglect, but rather a structural feature that resulted from past de-cision making. Statistics have been created for the "real stuff," albeit in the eyes of the decision makers, and this meant car-oriented mobil-ity and public transit. Consequently, certain groups and certain types of mobility have been systematically neglected in urban statistics, as Frank Veraart and Pieter-Jan Smits point out. They propose a long-term measurement framework for urban sustainable mobility that includes robust data on walking and cycling. This is important, as there is little insight in the magnitude of walking and cycling in most Western cities. Tiina Männistö-Funk explores the potential of visual sources as key to reconstructing city mobility patterns, focused on walking and cycling. Using the alternative method of photography, she demonstrates for the Finnish city of Turku the important role of women in the unaccounted practice of walking. Cochoy et al. study the evolving patterns of pedestrian practices and devices focusing on three locations in the city of Toulouse. They extract data from photos to show the importance of pedestrians carrying bags and parcels, thus recovering a forgotten dimension of load bearing in urban mobility. Their account, via photos, of the numbers of walkers and cyclists at key locations looks like a subversive strategy.

The second historical insight is the *importance of elaborate criteria for what a sustainable city should look like*. Veraart and Smits make it very clear that sustainable mobility is still a concept in need of clear definition and scope. Operationalizing what constitutes sustainable urban mobility has not yet happened. This is quite remarkable, given how often the concept is used. The lack of a clear definition also reflects the highly contested nature of the concept. Without appropriate criteria, the realization of sustainable cities remains elusive, becoming vulnerable to the aggressive power of well-established interests and future visions pointing in an unsustainable direction. Peter Norton shows how the well-established car interests in the United States—"Motordom"—worked hard to prepare ordinary Americans and decision makers for the coming of the Automobile Age and adapting the city to the needs of the car. This was done via books, such as "The New Necessity," which conveyed a "drive anywhere" future, and through the 1939 World's Fair in New York.

The third historical insight is *the key role of keeping "pockets of persistence" in cities*. During every historical period, planners created urban rebuilding and mobility strategies. Case studies demonstrate that earlier engineering decisions have had an enormous impact on the city and the region: the alignment layouts directly and indirectly influenced the regional transport system, economic vitality, and the integration of residential areas with their surroundings. Such studies indicate the ecological impact: lock-in mechanisms shape—perhaps even determine—the decision-making leeway afforded to politicians and planners. They also offer us a fuller picture of the embedded transport system features, including the financial, engineering, and social investments required to realize a transition toward sustainability.

Take the modernization discourse. Norton discusses how after World War II, decision makers in many national contexts adopted a modernization discourse aimed at creating car environments. Colin Divall unravels the mobility policy debates and practices in South East Dorset, England, from the mid-1950s until the mid-1970s. Economic modernization was pivotal in these policy arguments. Following rationalization criteria, many railway tracks were thus removed in the early sixties. Yet as Bekasova et al. show in their case study of Leningrad/St. Petersburg, modernization need not be car-based, even in the postwar period. Indeed, socialist dedication to public transit may, they argue, be a beneficial heritage from an environmental sustainability point of view.

Colin Pooley explores evolving pedestrian attitudes and risk perceptions in London and Edinburgh since the 1890s. He sees that walking declined there but was never abandoned. Importantly, Pooley discerns that attitudes to walking—unaccompanied children in particular—have recently become much more restrictive, due to more acute risk awareness in parents and children alike. Martin Emanuel depicts the infrastructural and mobility development of the Stockholm thoroughfare Götgatan. Planning decisions to facilitate motorization led to the marginalization of cycling, and the end of trolleybus and tram operations, replaced by the subway and the diesel bus. This was supplemented with the building of a parallel underground highway, creating a hidden modernization. Emanuel calls this a "hidden structure of unsustainability."

Wise decision makers should never allow full 100 percent implementation of such concepts because this often leads to path dependency and lock-ins that are hard to change. The wisdom of one period shapes the city for a long time despite shifting needs and insights. Indeed, extraordinary disinvestments are required to change path dependencies and lock-ins from an earlier period. Thus, decision makers should cherish certain elements, strategies, and practices that may not fit in with the current dominant regime; insights that lead to a more flexible planning process can facilitate the development of a greater diversity of transport modes, equally addressing the mobility needs of nonmotorists.

Walking has always been a pocket of persistence, despite car-oriented urban planning. Cochoy, Canu, and Calvignac prove that in Toulouse, walking increased in the twentieth century hand in hand with this provincial city's growth to a metropolis in southwest France. As Frank Schipper shows, however, parks—or the urban greens in general—could be considered "pockets of persistence" for an urban mobility transition toward sustainability: mobility in parks remained sustainable in the heyday of unsustainability, between 1950 and 1990. Whereas city governments tried to control walking and cycling elsewhere, in parks these slow modes were cherished or at least tolerated. Another striking example is the concept of "shared space," articulated by the Belgian minister of Public Works Auguste Delbeke in the early 1910s, and described in the chapter by Oldenziel et al. In Delbeke's view, the street belonged to all road participants, and thus an inclusive traffic concept was vital.

The fourth historical insight for current policymakers is about *not ignoring the inherent power relations in cities and in mobility planning.* There is disregard for the perspectives of women and low-income groups. In gentrification processes, where poorer urban households are replaced by richer ones, gender, race, and economic conflicts ensue in cities, as Mimi Sheller points out in Philadelphia. In the United States, bicycle advocacy should also have meant a shift toward greater mobility justice. Sustainability should never be exclusively about ecological and environmental issues but include creating a dynamic interaction between ecological, social, and economic sustainability dimensions.

Power is also created deliberately, as we see in Norton's chapter. Oldenziel et al. provide valuable insights on the role of experts, urban planners, and mobility planners in shaping the future for car domination in cities. By introducing concepts and lines of argument over two centuries, they explain the intricate power relations between experts in international urban planning (IFHP), urban policymaking (UIV), civil engineering (PIARC), and the national power elites. These experts and national elites carefully developed new planning and mobility strategies that became hegemonic in the postwar period when the mobility needs of women and low-income groups slipped under the radar. Between 1950 and 1970, these experts reached the pinnacle of their power; thereafter they were increasingly seen as ambassadors of the dominant car-oriented regime.

Put simply: transport and mobility planners tend to underestimate the mobility needs of underprivileged groups: women, immigrants, the disabled, and the elderly. Broadly speaking, they tend to forget social sustainability. Transport planning often exhibits a hidden class and gender bias. Most development scheme designs cater to middle-class citizens—often male breadwinners. Visions and schemes aiming for a sustainability shift should take this bias into account and have a more socially equitable and integrative scope. For instance, planners designing smart mobility systems should equally address the less competent digital capabilities of some disabled and elderly citizens. This volume contains many examples of gender and social marginalization processes that are a consequence of one-sided car-oriented planning decisions.

The final historical insight for policymakers is about *avoiding concepts and instead considering social practices in cities.* The modernization discourse has created path dependencies that are difficult to overcome. How people, businesses, and mobility seekers actually behave in and around their cities relates, as Pooley mentions, to cultural changes, such as in travel behavior norms, in personal circumstances, and altered perceptions of risk. In various English-speaking countries, the unwillingness to walk short distances has increased in modern times. Pooley sees that due to the change in risk perception, people now expect to be able to achieve most tasks as quickly using other forms of mobility as car drivers. Decision makers have acted on such perceptions for too long.

Several essays in this book demonstrate that mobility user practices and preferences are complex. They tend to be the result of an intricate mix of past and new behavior shaped by economic incentives, cultural norms, lifestyle trends, and public representations of transport modes. Through their case studies of specific local contexts in this book, such as Stockholm, Toulouse, and Turku, historians can untangle the traveler's often complex conduct that baffles policymakers.

Thus, on the eve of a huge sustainability transition, we offer some observations from the policymakers' point of view. The sustainability policy agenda does not seem to take disadvantaged groups sufficiently into account. Moreover, the marriage of the ecological and social dimensions of sustainability is not always a happy one. Planners underrate cultural mechanisms as major factors in the resistance to systemic change. Transport and spatial development studies need to take the long-term historical trends into account to identify the major locked-in factors that hinder change. It is obviously necessary to look at real-life mobility practices and the importance of walking as starting points for designing urban mobility policies. This book provides ample learning material on the development of cycling as a promising sustainable mode of transport. As we are currently witnessing a widespread cycling renaissance, planners can make good use of the insights offered here on evolving user preferences and practices as well as the planning repertoires that included or excluded cycling and walking as modes in their own right. This book is a plea to consider, for every period, the full story of urban mobility in people's daily lives.

**Hans Jeekel**, a senior research advisor at the Dutch Public Works Administration, is professor in the Department of Technology, Innovation, Society at Eindhoven University of Technology, and focuses on social aspects of smart mobility. His expertise includes urban and rural planning, vehicle and transport technology, and traffic and transport studies. He has been on the board of several international organizations and chaired the OECD/ITF working party on the Resilience of Surface Transport Systems (2010) as well as the board of the Association of European Transport.

**Bert Toussaint**, a corporate historian at the Dutch Public Works Administration, specializes in water management history, infrastructure history, land-use and planning history, and history learning. His coedited and authored publications include *Two Centuries of Experience in Water Resources Management*, with John Lonquest, Joe Manous Jr., and Maurits Ertsen (Institute for Water Resources, 2014); *Builders and Planners: A History of Land-Use and Infrastructure Planning in the Netherlands*, with Jos Arts, Ruud Filarski, Hans Jeekel (Eburon, 2016); and *Modern wereldwonder*, with Willem van der Ham, Eric Berkers, Paul Brusse, Hans Buiter, and Alex van Heezik (Boom, 2018).

## Note

1. For recent insights on the concept "usable past," see Colin Divall, Julian Hine, and Colin Pooley, *Transport Policy: Learning Lessons from History* (Farnham: Ashgate, 2016); Richard F. Hirsh, "Historians of Technology in the Real World: Reflections on the Pursuit of Policy-Oriented History," *Technology and Culture* 52, no. 1 (2011): 6–20; Per Lundin, "Making History Matter," *Mobility in History* 8 (2017): 7–16.

## Bibliography

Divall, Colin, Julian Hine, and Colin Pooley. *Transport Policy: Learning Lessons from History*. Farnham: Ashgate, 2016.
Hirsh, Richard F. "Historians of Technology in the Real World: Reflections on the Pursuit of Policy-Oriented History." *Technology and Culture* 52, no. 1 (2011): 6–20.
Lundin, Per. "Making History Matter." *Mobility in History* 8 (2017): 7–16.

# Index

www.ingramcontent.com/pod-product-compliance
Lightning Source LLC
Chambersburg PA
CBHW062107040426

42336CB00042B/2307